COME,
LORD
JESUS!

Dr Motyer rightly urges in his Preface the vital importance of this too-often neglected subject. He has produced a very readable, clear, vivid, non-technical response to this need. He handles Mark 13, Mark 9:1, and First and Second Thessalonians with competence and common sense. I commend this book for study.

Anthony C. Thiselton, FBA, Emeritus Professor of Christian Theology, University of Nottingham

COME, LORD JESUS!

A BIBLICAL THEOLOGY OF THE SECOND COMING OF CHRIST

STEPHEN MOTYER

APOLLOS (an imprint of Inter-Varsity Press)
36 Causton Street, London SW1P 4ST, England
Email: ivp@ivpbooks.com
Website: www.ivpbooks.com

First published 2016

British Library Cataloguing-in-Publication Data
A catalogue record for this book is available from the British Library.

ISBN: 978-1-78359-414-6
eBook ISBN: 978-1-78359-464-1

Set in Monotype Garamond 11/13pt
Typeset in Great Britain by CRB Associates, Potterhanworth, Lincolnshire
Printed and bound in Great Britain by Ashford Colour Press Ltd, Gosport, Hampshire

Inter-Varsity Press publishes Christian books that are true to the Bible and that communicate the gospel, develop discipleship and strengthen the church for its mission in the world.

IVP originated within the Inter-Varsity Fellowship, now the Universities and Colleges Christian Fellowship, a student movement connecting Christian Unions in universities and colleges throughout Great Britain, and a member movement of the International Fellowship of Evangelical Students. Website: www. uccf.org.uk. That historic association is maintained, and all senior IVP staff and committee members subscribe to the UCCF Basis of Faith.

To my father
with deep gratitude

CONTENTS

PREFACE

The second coming of Jesus Christ has frequently been a neglected topic for Christians. Many, asked when they last heard a sermon devoted to it, will reply, 'I can't remember!' Preachers tend to steer clear of it, (a) because the scriptural texts that deal with it are often very difficult to interpret, and (b) because – in spite of (a)! – opinions about it in some quarters are so strong that the preacher's orthodoxy might be questioned, if he or she doesn't quite hit the right emphasis.

The second coming has been such a controversial issue – on a spectrum from outright denial by some to precise datings and detailed end-time programmes by others – that many Christians have decided to steer clear, and to leave the arguments to those who seem to know what to do with the difficult Scriptures and issues involved. But the arguments go on, because *it is clearly an absolutely vital issue*. Is Jesus really coming again? If so, can we know when? And what will his coming mean for the world? What will it look like? Or should we step aside from a literal interpretation of the Bible's second coming texts, and read them as encouragements to allow Jesus to *come now* into our lives and worship?

That's the rub. It's all about the interpretation of biblical texts, and more particularly about how we combine biblical texts into an overall pattern or picture. All the standard schemes – premillennial, postmillennial or amillennial – are at root not different versions of end-time expectation, but different ways of reading the Bible.

This fills me with hope, not despair. What Protestant Christians usually do when they disagree (indeed, what they *ought* to do) is to turn again to the

Scriptures and listen to them afresh, with open minds, not presuming an 'answer' but wanting genuinely to let the texts suggest their own answer. That's difficult, because we can't help but bring our own assumptions and presuppositions to the party. They dance around the room, arm in arm with the texts. The trick is to let the *texts* do the steering and dictate the steps. If we push the texts across the dance floor, they will feel unappreciated and we're bound to tread heavily on their toes. That is not a recipe for a happy dance. But if we can listen carefully to the texts, and with genuine openness let all our theologies and convictions be shaped by Scripture, rather than the other way round . . . this is the hope that animates this book! It's a hope for a new dance, to a new tune – because the Scriptures can be always fresh to us.

This book started life as a contribution to the IVP *Bible Speaks Today* series, in which passages relating to a particular theme are collected and expounded. But it grew beyond the aim of that series, and has become a bigger attempt to discover a *biblical theology of the second coming of Jesus Christ*. I'm very glad and grateful to Inter-Varsity Press that they were willing to let the book grow in this way, not least because it means that this piece of 'biblical theology' stays very close to biblical texts. My aim has been to choose the absolutely key passages, in both Testaments, that enable us to develop an overall biblical understanding of the second coming, and to listen with care to their *detail*, to their *context*, and to their *relationship* with each other.

The choice of passages is mine, so my own convictions are not sitting shyly in the corner of the ballroom. They're out there, dancing around with the texts (and, I must say, enjoying themselves hugely). I've revised the list of passages many times during the course of the work, seeking to be as open as I can both to their individual voice, and to the collective voice of Scripture.

There is one passage which I regret that I have not been able to include. Zechariah 12 – 14 is a section of that prophecy often interpreted as looking forward to the second coming. I would love to have invited those chapters onto the dance floor, had not the band stopped playing and the MC told us all to get our coats (i.e., I ran out of space). In fact, however, its interpretation is so difficult that I'm not sure that I would have been able to reach any clear con- clusions about its contribution to our biblical theology of the second coming. I'm left hoping that I haven't trodden heavily on Zechariah's toes in thinking this! He has danced well with others, but not with me.

One of the particular challenges has been to keep the focus on the second coming, and not to let the book become a general study of eschatology or 'the last things'. The second coming is intimately related to many other scriptural themes and ideas under the overall heading of 'eschatology'. The passages have helped here, because I have only chosen passages which focus on the second coming, and not on general eschatology. Other themes of course pop up, but by keeping the focus *exegetical* – i.e., sticking close to the texts themselves, and trying to hear their voice above the babble of the ballroom – I've tried to make sure that we gain a clear sense of how the second coming relates vitally to the other great themes of Christology, redemption, re-creation, judgment and power. That has been the aim, anyway!

So what you hold in your hands is an attempt to 'hear' the biblical theology of the second coming of Jesus Christ, through fourteen passages that are crucially important for that; starting with three Old Testament passages to provide a biblical framework, and following with eleven New Testament passages which – in very different ways – develop the expectation. I have greatly enjoyed writing it, and I hope you enjoy reading it! But I feel humble about the outcome. The Scriptures are always greater than our attempts to understand them, so this is definitely not the last word about the last things.

The *Bible Speaks Today* volume, by the way, is 'coming soon' (but may become superfluous if someone else comes sooner!).

When quoting Old Testament passages I have used the New Revised Standard Version (NRSV), unless otherwise indicated. When quoting from the Greek version of the Old Testament (the Septuagint) or from the New Testament, I have provided my own translations. When quoting from the texts that are the focus of each chapter, I've used italics rather than quotation marks. Everywhere I'm indebted to the work and scholarship of others, but I have only burdened the pages with references to biblical or other scholarship where necessary or helpful.

I want to dedicate this book to my father Alec Motyer, because of the incalculable debt I owe to him. His influence has been huge, in every area. Still writing biblical commentary at the age of ninety-one, he models for me not only the passionate, daily love of the Scriptures and consequent life of obedience and prayer, but also the love of literary analysis as a vital exegetical tool in biblical study (for lots of examples, see below!), and the desire to let the Scriptures speak constantly with freshness, over against our human and theological traditions. Thank you, father.

Steve Motyer
Friday, 21 August 2015

ABBREVIATIONS

ASV	American Standard Version
CEV	Contemporary English Version
ESV	English Standard Version
Gk	Greek
GNT	Good News Translation (formerly Good News Bible)
Heb.	Hebrew
JB	Jerusalem Bible
KJV	King James Version
Lat.	Latin
LXX	Septuagint
NASB	New American Standard Bible
NIV	New International Version
NKJV	New King James Version
NLT	New Living Translation
NRSV	New Revised Standard Version
REB	Revised English Bible
RSV	Revised Standard Version

INTRODUCTION

The second coming of Jesus Christ is the core of the biblical world view, the climax of the biblical message, the cornerstone of biblical theology, and the centrepiece of authentic biblical faith for the twenty-first century.

These are bold claims to make – and this is the conviction that emerges through this book. At the heart of it is the claim that Jesus Christ is the 'centre' of the Scriptures, even though he only appears at the end. For the New Testament writers, Jesus Christ revolutionized their understanding of the Scriptures, gave them a whole new way of reading them, and a new centre around which to interpret the work of God in the world. And the climax of that work is the 'second coming' of that same Jesus Christ.

The New Testament writers used what we call the Old Testament (which was to them simply 'the Scriptures') to understand everything about Jesus, including his second coming. Indeed, Jesus himself used the language of the Scriptures to promise his 'coming again', the 'coming of the Son of Man'. So we need to set our study of it into a whole-biblical frame. It is worth pausing a little on the reasons for this, in order to set the scene.

The Old Testament prophets proclaimed the coming 'Day of the Lord', the day when God would appear powerfully in judgment and deliverance of his people: this expression appears eighteen times in the Old Testament prophetic books.[1] But in the New Testament the 'Day of the Lord' becomes 'the day of

---

1. For instance Amos 5:18–20 and Joel 2:31; 3:14.

the Lord *Jesus*'.[2] In 1 Corinthians 16:22 Paul records a little Aramaic prayer which must date from the very earliest years of the church, and which attests both calling Jesus 'Lord' and the longing for him to 'come': *Maranatha!*[3] *Come, Lord Jesus!*

This is an amazing shift within biblical theology. 'God has made him both Lord and Christ', proclaims Peter, 'this Jesus whom you crucified!',[4] bringing to a climax his Pentecost sermon in which he claims the fulfilment of Joel's glorious expectation of the 'Day of the Lord'.[5] Remarkably, the expectations and faith attached to Yahweh, the Lord who is the God of Israel, are transferred to Jesus Christ, his crucified, resurrected and *glorified* Son. It is Jesus who will one day bring in the Day of the Lord, and judge the nations on behalf of his Father.[6] (And therefore – even more amazingly – it is the pre-incarnate Son, the Wisdom of God himself, who at the starting of time called the universe into being and gave it life in the first place.[7])

So the whole of biblical theology is caught up into what we might call the 'ultimacy' of Jesus Christ. Yes, God is ultimate, says Paul – he is the one *from* whom, and *through* whom, and *for* whom, all things exist.[8] But there is also now one 'Lord Jesus Christ, *through* whom are all things',[9] *in* whom everything was created, and *for* whom all things have been made.[10] The same glorious, all-embracing prepositions are applied to the Lord Jesus, as to God himself. And therefore, within biblical theology and the biblical view of history, Jesus Christ has become the ultimate focus of all things; and there is no clearer signal of the 'ultimacy' of Jesus Christ within biblical faith, than his second coming in glory to judge and to save.

---

2. See this extraordinary movement in 1 Cor. 5:5; 2 Cor. 1:14. In other places, too, Old Testament references to 'the Lord' are applied to Jesus (e.g., Rom. 10:13; Phil. 2:10–11). On this, see L. J. Kreitzer, *Jesus and God in Paul's Eschatology* (Sheffield: Sheffield Academic Press, 1987), especially pp. 112–129. This suggests that elsewhere, when the expression 'the Day of the Lord' appears, here too Jesus is the Lord referred to (e.g., 1 Thess. 5:2; 2 Thess. 2:2; 2 Pet. 3:10).

3. Literally 'Our Lord, come!'

4. Acts 2:36.

5. Acts 2:20.

6. Matt. 25:31–46; John 5:27; Rom. 2:16.

7. John 1:1–5; Col. 1:16.

8. Rom. 11:36.

9. 1 Cor. 8:6.

10. Col. 1:16.

So we need the whole of Scripture to understand what the second coming means for us today. A 'biblical theology' of the second coming is a sense of the way in which the message of the whole of Scripture surrounds and shapes the way in which we think of the second coming. The fact that the whole Bible ends with the prayer which forms the title of this book – 'Come, Lord Jesus!'[11] – is deeply appropriate. The second coming is the 'end' of the biblical message, as we'll see: its 'Omega Point', its grand finale, the denouement when all the players in the drama of earth's history, both human and angelic, are gathered in the drawing room to hear the Master unpack the plot and give the verdict. Most of the passages we will look at are found in the New Testament, as a glance at the contents page will reveal. But the first section exploring the wider 'biblical frame' is absolutely vital, because it sets the scene for all that follows.

This raises a really interesting and vital question of method. The passages that feature in this book are my choice, and I weave together a whole-biblical message that emerges from them. It is a glorious message, full of hope and encouragement, but it is only right to come clean about the underlying *method* and *presuppositions* that have guided my choice of the passages, and my exposition of them. The rest of this introduction does that.

The second coming features largely in many prophetic schemes that claim to have uncovered the biblical teaching about the end-times, and often set out the events of the End in a clear timetable of events. The 'Left Behind' series of novels and films by Tim LaHaye and Jerry Jenkins (63 million copies sold to date, according to their website[12]) is the best known of these, unpacking in story form the series of events which begins with the rapture (the sudden disappearance of true believers from the earth into heaven), and continues with the appearance of the antichrist, the final tribulation, the battle of Armageddon, the coming of Jesus as judge to Jerusalem, and the unfolding events of his following thousand-year reign on earth (the 'millennium'), especially the final battle.

Such prophetic schemes all depend on a creative putting together of prophetic biblical passages, drawn especially from Daniel, Ezekiel, Zechariah, Matthew and Revelation, which are allowed to interpret one another and build up an overall narrative of the series of events that make up 'the End'. The 'Left Behind' version of this is essentially the premillenarian prophetic scheme, which was first developed in the early church but lay largely dormant in Christian

---

11. Rev. 22:20.

12. www.leftbehind.com, statistic as given in July 2015. The first novel, *Left Behind*, was published in 1995 (Wheaton: Tyndale House Publishers). The sixteenth and final title, *Kingdom Come*, was published in 2007.

expectation until the early nineteenth century, when it grew in popularity (according to Prof. Richard Bauckham) in response to the anxiety people felt over the rapid political and cultural changes in that era, especially the French Revolution and its aftermath.[13] This way of reading the prophetic passages of the Bible was particularly developed by J. N. Darby (1800–82), the highly gifted founder of the Plymouth Brethren, whose prophetic scheme came to be known as 'dispensationalism', and was popularized in the *Scofield Reference Bible* published by Oxford University Press in 1909, and still in print today.

There has been intense debate among its proponents about the details of this prophetic scheme. But there has been little disagreement about the interpretative method underlying the debate, and this is the issue of chief interest for us here. The method that produces such prophetic schemes can be summarized like this:

1. The prophetic passages of the Bible are a distinct stream within biblical literature, giving inspired prediction of the future.
2. These predictions should be interpreted 'literally', according to their plain sense, unless it is obvious that they are symbolic, and if no literal fulfilment has already taken place then the prediction must be still future.
3. Trusting the inspired word, we can carefully combine prophecies so that they fit together mutually, and produce an overall narrative of end-time events.

A good example of this method in action would be Paul's prediction of the conversion of Israel, 'and so all Israel will be saved'.[14] It has not happened yet, so it must be still to come. The plain meaning of this statement would be that, at some future date, all Jews then alive will be converted to Christ. But Paul says nothing about *when* this will occur, or how it might be timed in relation to other end-time events like the 'coming of the Son of Man',[15] or the great tribulation,[16] or the battle of Armageddon,[17] or the appearance of the 'abomination of desolation'[18]

---

13. Richard Bauckham, 'Must Christian Eschatology be Millenarian? A Response to Jürgen Moltmann', in K. E. Brower and M. W. Elliott (eds.), *'The Reader Must Understand': Eschatology in the Bible and Theology* (Leicester: Apollos, 1997), p. 271.
14. Rom. 11:26.
15. E.g. Matt. 24:27.
16. E.g. Luke 21:12–26.
17. Rev. 16:16.
18. Dan. 11:31; Matt. 24:15.

and the 'man of lawlessness',[19] or the thousand-year reign of the saints,[20] or indeed the final judgment.[21] How do these all fit together? Darby's answer was an elaborate scheme in which a period of tribulation immediately precedes the second coming of Jesus, which ushers in a thousand-year earthly reign, at the start of which all Jews are converted to their Messiah, and at the end of which the battle of Armageddon occurs immediately before the final judgment. Thus the conversion of Israel takes its place within an eschatological timetable.

Or we might focus on the rapture, which seems to happen at the same time as the second coming in 1 Thessalonians,[22] and immediately before it in Matthew.[23] But by the time it has been woven into a prophetic scheme with all the other end-time events, as in the Left Behind reconstruction, it has become separated from the second coming by several other events. Data from Daniel 9 give a timing to this separation – the rapture precedes the second coming by seven years, during which the antichrist will appear, the temple will be rebuilt in Jerusalem, and the great tribulation will occur.[24]

There are many different orderings of these end-time events. The vital points to note here are (a) that the *ordering* of these events is entirely the construct of the biblical interpreter, and (b) that it is in the *connection between* the different biblical passages that the main thrust of the scheme emerges. If we connect the 'man of lawlessness' with the 'great tribulation', then we can make the former the cause of the latter – and then both of them can be brought to an end by the coming of Jesus.[25] The fact that Paul does not mention a tribulation preceding the second coming in 2 Thessalonians 2 (nor in 1 Thess. 4:13 – 5:11) is neither here nor there, because it is supplied by Matthew 24. Similarly, the fact that the conversion of Israel is not mentioned in Revelation 20 does not matter, because the connection between Israel and the millennium is made by the combination of these biblical passages by the interpreter. And because literal fulfilment is a crucial interpretative principle in all this, we must presume that none of it has happened yet. It is all still to come.

---

19. 2 Thess. 2:8.

20. Rev. 20:4.

21. E.g. 2 Thess. 1:7–10.

22. 1 Thess. 4:17.

23. Matt. 24:37–42.

24. See for instance Dave Hunt, *When Will Jesus Come? Compelling Evidence for the Soon Return of Christ* (Eugene: Harvest House, 1993). In some schemes, the battle of Armageddon takes place at the end of this seven-year period.

25. Matt. 24:15–31; 2 Thess. 2:1–11.

Are these methods of biblical interpretation, specifically of biblical prophecy, sound and good? Rather than getting into arguments about the details of differing prophetic schemes which combine prophetic passages in different ways, it is vital to go deeper and tackle the issue of method, because methods employed often determine outcomes achieved. Have you heard of the visiting Martian who decided to find out about meat consumption in London by observing everyone with the surname 'Butcher' in the London phone book?

This discussion has been around for a long time. In 1854 the annual[26] Bampton Lectures in Oxford University were given by Samuel Waldegrave, later Bishop of Carlisle, on *New Testament Millennarianism, or the Kingdom and Coming of Christ as Taught by Himself and His Apostles,* interacting with the new pre-millenarian interpretations of biblical prophecy (though not with J. N. Darby, interestingly, whose influence grew later in the nineteenth century through the writings of his followers).[27] Waldegrave's first lecture is given over to a discussion of method: 'Before we begin our Scriptural researches,' he wrote, 'it is most important that the principles according to which they are to be conducted should be clearly defined. For there is no discussion in which fixed laws of Biblical interpretation are more needed,—there is none in which they have been less observed.'[28]

Like Waldegrave 160 years ago, I confess to feeling very uncomfortable about the method on which these premillenarian prophetic schemes rest. The best way to articulate my discomfort would be to propose and argue for a different set of interpretative principles, developing Waldegrave's ideas in the light of more recent insights into hermeneutics, the science of interpretation:

1. *Context and role:* The prophetic passages of the Bible cannot be separated out as a distinct stream, but must be interpreted within their different scriptural settings – indeed, within the setting of the whole canon of Scripture. We must seek carefully to see what the role of these prophetic passages is *within the whole message of Scripture.*
2. *Genre:* Within this setting, we must pay careful attention to their literary genre, which will mean keeping an open mind about whether their

---

26. The Bampton Lectures invite a leading scholar to choose and address a topic of significance in contemporary theology. Until 1895 they were delivered annually, thereafter biennially.
27. The lectures were published immediately and then revised and republished: London: William Hunt & Co, 1866.
28. Waldegrave, *Millennarianism,* p. 7.

language should be interpreted literally or not. A basic starting point is
that they will probably let us know how to read them.

3. *Original purpose:* God spoke his inspired word to others first, and so the
meaning Scripture seems to have had *in its original setting* and *for its original
readers* must feature largely for us in our reading today.

4. *Careful dialogue:* It is certainly right to combine different passages, and to
bring them into dialogue with each other – but principles 1 to 3 need to be
applied carefully first, before we do this! We cannot presume that they
can simply be merged like jigsaw pieces.

These principles need some expansion and justification.

1. Context and role

This point is well illustrated in the opening paragraphs above, about the way in
which Old Testament expectation of 'the Day of the Lord' is taken up in the
New Testament and becomes 'the Day of the Lord Jesus'. And as we look more
closely at this, we notice that the Old Testament notion of 'the Day of the Lord'
is applied, in fact, to three different 'comings' in the New Testament: (a) to the
initial coming of Jesus in his ministry,[29] (b) to the coming of the Holy Spirit at
Pentecost,[30] and (c), as we noticed, to the second coming of the Lord Jesus.[31] So,
if we are going to understand (c) well, we must bear in mind (a) and (b) also, and
think about how the second coming relates to all the other ways in which Jesus
makes God present to us – through his incarnation, and through his coming to
us in the Holy Spirit. As we will see, this is vital for a true biblical appreciation
of 'the last things'! We need, in fact, to bear in mind the whole sweep of biblical
thinking about salvation and how it is achieved: its basis, its scope and its goal.

We will seek to put this principle into operation throughout this book, but
it will be especially significant for Part One on *the biblical framework*.

And reflecting on the *role* of the prophetic passages, it is worth noticing one
thing about them at this stage: they seem to be not at all interested in giving us
a timetable, or a sequence, of end-time events. As we will see, only 1 Corinthians
15:20–28 might give some kind of sequence, but even then it is not at all clear,
and leaves out many of the other end-time events that feature in prophetic

---

29. See how Mal. 4:5 is used in Matt. 11:14.

30. See Peter's quotation of Joel in Acts 2:20.

31. 1 Cor. 5:5; 2 Cor. 1:14.

schemes: there is no mention of the conversion of Israel, the rapture, the great tribulation or the man of lawlessness!

So we are in the strange situation that the prophetic schemes so popular today emphasize the one thing that the Bible seems to be disinterested in supplying, namely a sequenced timetable of events. I believe that God gives us what we need, in Scripture. We can learn, of course, from other sources too, but Scripture is the *measure* and the *guide* as well as the *chief source* of the instruction that we need in order to live well in God's world. God does not seem to think that we need a timetable of end-time events. Why do we seek to construct one?

2. Genre

The *genre* of a piece of writing is about how we might classify its *type*: 'prophetic' writing is one broad genre, and within the Bible prophecy is simply about speaking God's word on his behalf, with clear present import for those addressed. 'Thus says the Lord . . . !' The word that the Lord says may be concerned in different ways with the *future*, but always in order to impact the *present*. Prophetic words are never about simply giving information about future events. The closest we get to simple 'prediction' is the long vision in Daniel 11, but even here the purpose of the vision is to prepare and encourage Daniel (and so also his readers), in the face of the perplexing and threatening events about to occur.[32]

The genre of a piece of writing is thus closely linked to its purpose. When we want to raise the mood of a group, we tell a joke. We immediately spot the difference between a piece of fiction which is meant to entertain, and a news report which is meant to inform – and we get cross when this distinction is blurred by tabloid newspapers. And within prophecy there is a more particular genre which will concern us especially, that of *apocalyptic*. This is a genre of writing that frequently uses reports of visions or of dreams, and often employs 'cosmic' language of various kinds – massive storms, great cosmic events, earthquakes, strange appearances of beasts or heavenly portents, or indeed of angels and of heaven itself. We will find ourselves encountering apocalyptic language frequently in this book, so it is vital to ask what its *purpose* is, and whether it gives us any tips about interpretation.

I will not attempt to answer these questions in advance, because I think it is vital that we look at the passages themselves and allow ourselves to be prodded forward in the directions that they themselves prompt. It is not right, I think,

---

32. See Dan. 10:18–21.

to decide in advance that apocalyptic should be interpreted literally unless there are clear indications to the contrary. That's like presuming that every bus goes to London unless it actually says 'not going to London' on the front. Disaster could result. We need to get on the bus, and ask the driver what it means when it says 'Manchester' on the front.

3. Original purpose

Here the word 'original' is the most important, and controversial, point. In hermeneutics (the science of the theory of interpretation) a long and intense discussion has taken place about the role of 'original meaning' in contemporary interpretation of texts. And generally speaking, in biblical interpretation, it has been *evangelical* scholars – because of our high view of Scripture – who have argued that we must seek to hear the text through the ears of those to whom God first addressed it. Then we can move across to today, and ask 'If God said *this* to *them then*, what would he say to *us now*?'[33]

This is a very subtle interpretative process. It is not easy. But it seems to follow necessarily from believing in the inspiration of Scripture, and recognizing that Scripture comes to us fully clothed in the garb of the time and place where it was first given. We cannot be true to the Scriptures that God has given, and indeed to the God who gave them, unless we take seriously this *fellowship* with the original receivers of his word.

So it is deeply ironic that our good evangelical brothers and sisters who are so passionately committed to premillenarian constructions like the 'Left Behind' series, should have apparently abandoned this excellent principle in favour of a view of Scripture that makes it address just our needs today. They do not appear to ask, for instance, what Jesus' words about the coming tribulation in Matthew 24:15–22 might have meant to the disciples who sat listening – and in particular they do not discuss whether these disciples were wrong to see Jesus' words fulfilled in the awful suffering associated with the Jewish War of 67–73, just a few years after he spoke.

It could well be, of course, that prophecies can have multiple fulfilments. This may be one of them! But we must surely *start* with the meaning of Jesus'

33. See for instance Gordon D. Fee and Douglas Stuart, *How to Read the Bible for All Its Worth*, 4th ed. (Grand Rapids: Zondervan, 2014); Grant R. Osborne, *The Hermeneutical Spiral: A Comprehensive Introduction to Biblical Interpretation*, 2nd ed. (Downers Grove: InterVarsity Press, 2006).

words for those disciples, before we jump across to today – and certainly before we start building prophetic schemes by combining this passage with other passages which, likewise, were first given in order to meet the spiritual needs of first-century believers.[34]

4. Careful dialogue

We will certainly bring passages into dialogue with each other as we make our way through them in this book. But this will not be by simply combining them. We will do our best to apply principles 1 to 3 first, and that very process will throw up pointers to connections between the passages. For instance, we will find that we cannot interpret Mark 13 without looking at Daniel 7, because there are close connections of language between them. Then we will find that we cannot interpret 1 Thessalonians 4 and 2 Thessalonians 2 without looking at Mark 13 – for the same reason! The passages themselves generate the links. We don't have to create them out of our own ingenuity.

It is actually this interconnectedness of texts – sometimes called their 'inter-textuality' – which will enable us to come close to achieving our goal of a *biblical theology of the second coming of Jesus Christ*, even though we are just looking at a selection of texts, and not at the whole Scripture. These key passages will themselves take us in vital wider directions, which will in turn will help us to put them into their proper context (principle 1).

In many ways the second coming has been a forgotten doctrine. So far as I can tell, Samuel Waldegrave's lectures of 1854 represent the only occasion on which the second coming and associated biblical themes have been addressed in the Bampton Lectures in the entire 235 years since they were founded in 1780!

---

34. There are many versions of premillenarianism, and some are more open than others
    to reading Scripture in the light of 'original purpose'. One such would be John
    MacArthur, *The Second Coming* (Wheaton: Crossway, 2003). MacArthur takes
    seriously the position of Jesus' disciples as the first hearers of the 'Olivet Discourse'
    in Matthew 24 – 25. But in spite of Jesus' words that 'this generation will not pass
    away until all these things have taken place' (Matt. 24:34), MacArthur reads the
    whole discourse as applicable to the events of the End that we are now
    experiencing. For many premillenialists, a big impetus towards the contemporary
    focus in the interpretation of prophecy was the re-establishment of the state of
    Israel in 1948, which is taken to be a direct fulfilment of biblical prophecy
    (especially Ezek. 36 – 37; also Luke 21:24).

There has been a sense, for many Christians, that belief in the second coming of Jesus has been stolen away by those for whom it has become an exclusive focus in their world view; and horror stories like the Jonesville massacre and the sorry end of the Waco 'Branch Davidian' cult have underlined, for many, the conviction that strong views about the second coming – even *any* views about it – are to be avoided.

However, in the last twenty years things have changed. Hymns and worship songs have begun to celebrate the theme, previously absent. The popularity of the 'Left Behind' series has grown out of a feeling that we *want* the Lord to come: with climate change, population growth, the threat of militant Islam, and the failing global supplies of vital resources, what lies ahead for planet Earth, if he does not? As John Carroll comments, introducing his recent book on it, 'With the arrival of the year 2000, fascination with apocalyptic themes has grown exponentially, in both religious and secular arenas.'[35] This vital biblical theme seems to hold special significance for us, as we seek to find *hope* for the world, and to offer it to others. Planet Earth has a Saviour, and he says he's coming soon![36]

One other comment is necessary. Our focus is on the second coming, and not on millennialism or the end times. This means that some readers may be disappointed that, for instance, there isn't a section on Daniel 9:24–27[37] in the chapter on Daniel, or any specific discussion of the thousand-year reign of Christ in the chapter on Revelation. I've tried to be disciplined in the focus on the second coming, in order to provide the fundamental biblical theology that must underlie our whole sense of God's future for his world.[38]

---

35. John T. Carroll, *The Return of Jesus in Early Christianity* (Peabody: Hendrickson, 2000), p. vii.
36. Rev. 22:7, 12, 20.
37. Daniel's 'seventy weeks' prophecy, which is absolutely crucial for premillennial schemes.
38. An excellent critical evaluation of premillenialism is provided by Sam Storms, *Kingdom Come. The Amillennial Alternative* (Fearn: Christian Focus, 2013).

PART 1:

THE BIBLICAL FRAME

1. HISTORY AND TIME (PSALMS 89 – 90)

This is a strange place to start in our search for the biblical theology of the second coming of Jesus Christ! Why here, in these two psalms? It is not even obvious that they should be read together, because Psalm 89 ends Book 3 of the Psalms (marked by the little doxology added in v. 52), and Psalm 90 begins Book 4 with a glorious and unique 'Prayer of Moses, the man of God'.

Christopher Seitz suggests that placement of texts like this can be quite deliberate, and that in this case there is a profound sense in which Psalm 90 answers Psalm 89.[1] Psalm 89 brings before us – as we will see shortly – the huge problem of the apparent non-fulfilment of God's promises: his *absence* when he promised his *presence*. Psalm 90 then responds by taking us back to a bigger vision of God, beyond the particular 'facts' of our experience, to the hugeness of God's eternity. And so, in a very profound way, these psalms together take us deep into a theology of *history* and of *time*, and of the relationship between the two. And what could be more important for us, as backdrop to our search for a biblical theology of the second coming?

---

1. Christopher R. Seitz, 'Royal Promises in the Canonical Books of Isaiah and the Psalms', in *Word Without End: The Old Testament as Abiding Theological Witness* (Grand Rapids: Eerdmans, 1998), pp. 150–167, see p. 162.

The second coming brings us face to face with these two 'biggies' by which our whole experience of being human is framed. Within history and the process of time by which it moves forward, we experience the storyline of our lives as a sequence of highs and lows. There are great moments when we seem to know who we are, and who God is, and what life is about, and where we are heading. But then it all falls apart. Each of us can fill in the details – those points in the story when God seems to have vanished, hope has deserted us, and we can't see beyond our own shrunken horizons. And, looking beyond our own experience, the same up and down process seems to be true of the history of nations, and indeed of the world. Psalm 89 arises at just such a moment in the history of Israel.

At those moments, profound existential questions and anxieties grip us. Where is God when it matters? Does he not see our pain? Are we too small? What right do we have to expect that he might be interested in the pain of one of the 7.25 billion people on earth? Are we not completely insignificant? One tiny planet near the end of one arm of one mind-bogglingly huge galaxy (100,000 light years big, home to 300 billion stars like our sun), which itself is one *tiny* galaxy in a universe of *billions* of galaxies. And alongside space we set time. The vastness of the universe and the vastness of time go together, according to modern cosmology; my little blip of a moment, my life, is the briefest pinprick in the vast process of time in the 4.5 billion years of Earth's history, let alone the 13.5 billion years which take us back to the birth of the universe.[2] *What is our life?*

What we need, when questions like these grip us – along with good friends! – is a *biblical theology of time and history*. And it is against the backdrop of this wider theology that we need to place the second coming of Jesus. So these psalms together help us to give shape to the wider biblical frame that we need, in order to understand truly what we mean when we say that 'Jesus is coming again!' Let's look at them more closely.

1. An overview of both psalms

Though so different from each other, these two psalms are clearly linked by common themes. The phrase *for ever* is a very important one in Psalm 89,

---

2. I'm aware that not all readers may accept these figures, which are the widely agreed scientific estimates of the age of Earth and of the universe. But hang on in there – a theology emerges from these psalms which speaks to all of us, both to those who believe in a 'young earth' and to those who believe in long-term evolution!

occurring seven times (vv. 1, 2, 4, 28, 36, 37, 52). In these verses the great Hebrew word *'ōlām* is used, signifying the biggest possible extent of time applicable in the given circumstances: the extent of our praise (v. 1); of God's *steadfast love* (v. 2); of the covenant promise to David (v. 4); of both of these together (v. 28); and so of David's dynasty (vv. 36–37). This term highlights the agonizing problem at the heart of the psalm – that God's 'for ever' is anything but 'for ever'. The covenant with David lies shattered, buried in the ruins of Jerusalem (vv. 39–40).

Then Psalm 90 begins with the same term, though now changed up into a new gear: *from everlasting to everlasting you are God* (v. 2) – literally 'from *'ōlām* to *'ōlām'*. God's 'everlastingness' is bigger than any individual 'for ever'. He embraces them all. It seems as though the final blessing at the end of Psalm 89, which rounds off the whole of Psalms Book 3, also profoundly introduces Psalm 90: *Blessed be the LORD for ever. Amen and Amen* (89:52). Similarly, both psalms begin with the expression *to all generations* – another time-notice expressing permanence: compare 89:1, 4 with 90:1.

We will see more of what this means shortly. But as we collect themes that unite the psalms let us also note the great term *hesed*, 'steadfast love'. This too is a key theme in Psalm 89, also occurring seven times: vv. 1, 2, 14, 24, 28, 33, 49. Throughout the Old Testament it is particularly connected with the covenant, and we see that connection explicitly here in verses 28 and 49. God's *hesed* is that quality of his which impels him to enter into 'covenant' with his people – i.e., to commit himself to be their God and to maintain the relationship with them, come what may. Hence the frequent English translation 'steadfast love'.

The issue in Psalm 89 is agonizing: following the destruction of Jerusalem, and the end of the Davidic dynasty, *Lord, where is your steadfast love of old?* (v. 49). God's *hesed* is that which particularly was meant to be 'for ever' – *I will not remove from him my steadfast love* was the promise (v. 33) – but it's gone, swept away by the conquering Babylonian armies that destroyed Jerusalem and *defiled his crown in the dust* (v. 39). Has God's *hesed* now gone 'for ever'?

This great term pops up also in Psalm 90, at the crucial turning-point in the psalm, as we will see: *Satisfy us in the morning with your steadfast love, so that we may rejoice and be glad all our days* (v. 14). But there we face the vital question: on what does faith in God's steadfast love rest, when it seems to be anything other than steadfast?

Finally there's the theme of *wrath*. Three different terms for God's wrath are used here, in Psalm 89:38, 46 and then in Psalm 90:7, 9, 11. It seems that God's wrath is what we are experiencing, when he abandons us. But his 'wrath' has a particular twist here; it is closely connected to the shortness of life and the inevitability of death: compare Psalm 89:47–48 with 90:5–6, 9–10. *For what nothingness hast thou created man!*[3] (89:47). And in relation to this 'nothingness', both psalms include the cry *How long, O LORD?* (89:46; 90:13).

As we will see below, this takes us right to the heart of the message of Psalm 90, and indeed to the heart of our biblical theology of time and history. In order to develop this, let us now take a closer look at each psalm in turn.

2. Psalm 89

We start with the vital theme of God's *faithfulness* in Psalm 89, his *'ĕmûnāh*. This word also occurs seven times in the psalm: vv. 1, 2, 5, 8, 24, 33 and 49.[4] In five of these verses, it is paired with *ḥesed*, *steadfast love*. This is the basic, awful, faith-stretching dilemma of the psalm. Though faith says that *your faithfulness is as firm as the heavens* (v. 2), and though there is no lack of public commitment on God's part, even before the heavenly court (vv. 3–8), and no lack of awesome strength to put it into effect (vv. 9–14), and no lack of past experience of his faithfulness in action (vv. 15–20), and no lack of verbal assurance that his faithfulness will never be taken away, even if David's descendants fall into sin (vv. 21–37) – all of which makes David's throne as secure as heaven itself (vv. 29, 36–37) – yet the awful truth remains: *You have spurned and rejected him; you are full of wrath against your anointed. You have renounced the covenant . . .* (vv. 38–39).

To get into the terrible feeling of this psalm, we need to know the facts behind it. Clearly it dates from the period immediately after the dreadful experiences of the Babylonian war and captivity in 587 BC, written during the period of exile that followed. The terrible story is told in 2 Kings 25: the destruction of Jerusalem and of the temple; the deportation of all but the poorest people to Babylon; the failure of a last royalist uprising; and the sad end, in exile, of Jehoiachin, the last direct descendant of David to sit on his throne. Perhaps we should imagine Ethan the Ezrahite, to whom the psalm is ascribed, among the exiles in Babylon, feeling with them the awfulness of their loss – of their home, of their king, and of their confidence in a God who had apparently not been able to save them. (See Psalm 137 for the depth of feeling among these exiles!) Psalm 89 thus sits alongside the book of Lamentations, which was also written

---

3. This is the translation offered in Francis Brown, S. R. Driver and Charles A. Briggs, *A Hebrew and English Lexicon of the Old Testament* (Oxford: Clarendon Press, 1972), p. 996, commenting on the meaning of *šāw'*, the Hebrew word used here.

4. A different Hebrew word for faithfulness is used in v. 14.

in this period, and which also wrestles theologically with this terrible experience of loss and exile.

There is one other reference to Ethan the Ezrahite in the Bible. In 1 Kings 4:31 he is included in the list of the men than whom Solomon was wiser. In other words, in order to emphasize how wise Solomon was, the author of 1 Kings casts around for the wisest men he can think of, and then says that Solomon was *even wiser* than this group of world-renowned sages. So it is important to ask, where is the *wisdom* of Ethan the Ezrahite to be seen in this powerfully-worded complaint that God has abandoned his covenant faithfulness to the house of David?

a. His focus

First, his wisdom is seen in his focus on the Lord. His complaint could not be more directly or clearly expressed, but he has not fallen into cynicism or bitterness, or unbelief. Clearly he feels that it is still worth addressing the God who seems to have abandoned his promise. His faith burns bright – in fact it is his faith in the covenant which energizes the whole psalm. Behind his agonized cry, *How long, O LORD? Will you hide yourself for ever?* (v. 46), we can see his faith still clinging to the hope that exile may not be the end of the story. It's worth complaining to this God! Ethan is still the Lord's *servant* (v. 50), and the servants of this God do not button their lips but let him have it, with both barrels if necessary.

b. His honesty and clarity

And so secondly, his wisdom appears in the sheer honesty and clarity of his complaint. There is no fudging here, no attempt to make the Lord look better, or to answer his complaint for him. He draws on God's own language in his poignant expression of the covenant promises (vv. 19–37), especially the language of the promise to David in 2 Samuel 7:8–16. By expanding it so powerfully, Ethan piles on the agony until the punchline arrives with devastating force in verse 38. We can learn so much from this for our own prayer. We rush to make excuses for God, and tell ourselves that we ought not to feel that he has let us down, because God does not break his promises. We hesitate to complain, therefore, because it seems so unspiritual and unbelieving. Nonsense, Ethan would tell us; faith is much better expressed by telling God exactly what it's like for us, on the receiving end of his *wrath* (vv. 38, 46) – even if God doesn't look too good as a result.

It is important to note the wide meaning that the word *wrath* has, both here and in Psalm 90 (vv. 7, 9, 11). Psalm 90 links it to punishment for sin (vv. 7–8), but its meaning is wider than just this. In fact, here in Psalm 89 it has to be something bigger, because – as Ethan reminds the Lord – the promise to David's house included an assurance that punishment for sin would always fall short of abandoning the covenant (vv. 30–34). God's wrath, therefore, is felt more widely in the way he leaves us in our insignificance, condemns us to the shortness of our lives, doesn't rescue us from the *nothingness* that he has created us for, and from inevitable death (vv. 47–48). Maybe (we hear Ethan hinting) if God's wrath didn't condemn us to this short 'nothingness', we might be able to see a bigger picture in which his *steadfast love* and *faithfulness* would be obvious, as in former times (v. 49). But as it is, no such vision is possible. All we can see is loss.

c. Bearing the Lord's pain

Thirdly – and most powerfully – we see Ethan's wisdom in his bearing of the Lord's pain:

> *Remember, O Lord, how your servant is taunted;*
>   *how I bear in my bosom the insults of the peoples,*
> *with which your enemies taunt, O LORD,*
>   *with which they taunted the footsteps of your anointed.*
> (vv. 50–51)

In his agony over the exile, he does not renounce who he is. He belongs to this God, who seems to have abandoned his people and their God-given king, and opened himself up therefore to the taunts of the nations that he is a weak God. This God could not protect his people from the power of the armies of Babylon. Ethan feels the pain of that charge, and bears it publicly. He is a servant of that God. He remembers the humiliation of God's anointed king, perhaps thinking especially of the way in which King Zedekiah was publicly shamed and tortured by the Babylonians.[5]

Ethan makes this pain his own – and this is true, and wonderful, wisdom. Though he complains against the Lord about the whole situation, he holds the insults against the Lord in his own heart. The greatest Son of David will one day say exactly the same thing, and go to a cross bearing the insults directed at God himself, the giver of his rejected Anointed One.[6] Ethan did not know it as he wrote those words about his own pain, but he here expresses the great principle of the cross. He bears the pain of the rejected Messiah (the Anointed One) just as do all Christians faithfully bearing persecution for the name of Christ in many

---

5. 2 Kgs 25:6–7.
6. See Rom. 15:3 (quoting Ps. 69:9).

parts of the world today, and thus associating themselves publicly with the one who, himself, 'bore all *our* pains and sorrows on the tree'.[7] Every time we bear the pain of another, we step right into the centre of the purposes of this God – even if the pain we bear is that of apparent abandonment by God.

So Psalm 89 presents us vividly with the problem of time. We're stuck in it, and torn between its shortness and its length. The *to all generations* nature of the promise (v. 1) does not match the short-time nature of my experience of it (v. 47). But that's history for you – the history of our lives, as well as of Israel. History is definitely overrated. Unless we deceive ourselves massively (and wise men like Ethan the Ezrahite don't), we have to admit the *incredibly limited nature of the perspective* available to us, from our vantage point in time. How can we tell the truth about anything? Every day the news is full of passionate voices claiming to tell the truth about everything under the sun – but there would be no 'news', were there not conflicting voices saying the opposite with equal conviction. And we can't even tell the story of our own lives with truth! The future is unknown; and the past, praise God, is *plastic*, from our viewpoint in the present. As I look back on my life, do I tell my story as a depressing one of opportunities missed, gifts undeveloped, potential unrealized, relationships broken, faith compromised by fear? Or is it more *truly* about the challenges faced, the lessons learned, the growth achieved, the relationships hard-won, and faith conquering fear? Or is the truth some delicate combination of both perspectives?

Praise God for his *judgment*. He is the one who truly tells the story of the history of planet Earth and of each of us, in all its amazing complexity, from a perspective that transcends the whole. And that brings us to Psalm 90.

3. Psalm 90

From Ethan the Ezrahite, writing one of the youngest psalms in the Psalter (sixth-century BC), we move back at least 700 years[8] to 'Moses the man of God', writing what is certainly the oldest psalm in the Psalter, if this ascription is

---

7. See Isa. 53:4; Matt. 8:17; 1 Pet. 2:24.

8. 'At least' here is meant to accommodate the different views of the date of the Exodus! There are two main contenders: 1440 BC and 1290 BC. If the older date is correct, then Psalm 90 may be nearer 900 years older than Psalm 89. For a good summary and evaluation of the evidence, see Dennis Bratcher, 'The Date of the Exodus: The Historical Study of Scripture', at www.crivoice.org/exodusdate.html (accessed July 2015).

correct. There is little reason to dispute it, and it will certainly have been accepted by the compiler of the Psalter – maybe Ethan himself! – who placed it here so tellingly after Psalm 89. 'There is nothing else like this in the entire Psalter', says Christopher Seitz, because it takes us back beyond David and Jerusalem, to the great lawgiver who first gave the promise of kingship to Israel, and who mediated the *prior* covenant on Sinai, before ever Israel had a special covenant centre.[9]

In our search – our *need* – for a biblical theology of time and history, this psalm stands supreme, especially in its dialogue with the psalm that precedes it. *History* (Ps. 89) leaves us confused and bewildered, unable to tie up the loose ends, or rather unable to untangle the ball of wool after the cat got at it. What we need, facing the mess that is history, is a view of *time* which allows God to be God, and makes *that* God our *dwelling place* (v. 1). Psalm 89 celebrated God's faithfulness, as reliable as the heavens and the earth which he has made, the great mountains which *joyously praise your name* (89:11–12). Psalm 90 takes us back *before the mountains were brought forth, or ever you had formed the earth and the world: from everlasting to everlasting you are God* (v. 2).

So Psalm 90 begins before creation, and presents us with a God who encompasses all that is within himself, and invites us to 'dwell' in him: a God before whom *a thousand years . . . are like yesterday when it is past, or like a watch in the night* (v. 4), a God whose *wrath* has made us completely insignificant in the vast sweep of time (vv. 5–9), but who can still *make us glad* (v. 15), can still *prosper for us the work of our hands* (v. 17), and supremely can *satisfy us in the morning with your steadfast love* (v. 14). This God sits above and beyond the local perspectives that trap us within our *seventy years, or perhaps eighty, if we are strong*, where we feel *only toil and trouble* (v. 10). It may be significant that 'seventy years' was the predicted length of the exile,[10] so that it was possible to live a full lifespan embedded in the awful Psalm 89 situation in which God seems to have abandoned his faithfulness. We need a bigger place to live!

But what exactly is time? We must reflect on this, as we seek to get under the skin of this psalm and formulate our biblical theology. Famously St Augustine asked himself this question, and replied, 'I know well enough what it is, provided that nobody asks me; but if I am asked what it is and try to explain, I am baffled.'[11] For Augustine it was obvious that time exists, because we measure it and can compare long times with short ones (as in these psalms). But what is it? Our experience of time, he said, divides it into three modes: future, present and past.

---

9. Seitz, 'Royal Promises', p. 162.

10. Jer. 25:11; Dan. 9:2; Zech. 7:5.

11. Augustine, *Confessions*, 11:14:17; http://www.ccel.org/ccel/augustine/confess.html.

But the future does not exist, because it is not yet; the past does not exist, because it is no more; and the present exists only as a moment of infinitesimal duration, which is passing away. So to Augustine, from a philosophical perspective, it seemed that time does not exist, even though we know that it does.

Yes, we know it. And in that *knowledge* that time exists, Augustine found the solution to his dilemma. He made time psychological. There are not three modes of time, he suggested, but three modes of *the present*: the future-as-present, the present-as-present, and the past-as-present. 'The present of past things is the memory; the present of present things is direct perception; the present of future things is expectation.'[12] Augustine resisted the view of others that time exists as a consequence of the regular movement of the heavenly bodies, because, he said, if the moon should suddenly speed up or slow down, we would be aware of this. Our *prior* sense of the passage of time would enable us to spot such a change. The same argument still applies, even to the almost exactly regular oscillations in the crystals that control atomic clocks, by which even the tiny variations in the earth's rotation and in its orbit around the sun can be measured. Time is not to be identified with its measurement.

Does time exist only in our minds, then, as Augustine suggested? He is surely basically right – with two qualifications to be made (see below). We can conceive of eternity beyond time, as Psalm 90 invites us to, because we can *imagine* – hold in our minds – that God is not bound by time (v. 4), that he created it along with everything else (v. 2), that he superintends its passage (e.g. v. 9), that he holds the final judgment of the significance of events in time (vv. 7–8, 11), and that he alone can teach us to measure time (v. 12). How foolish we are, to imagine that time is measured just by the oscillations of a crystal at the heart of an atomic clock! Sure, it measured Usain Bolt's record-breaking run at the World Athletics Championships in Berlin in August 2009, at which he set the fastest-ever time for the 100 metres, 9.58 seconds; but the point about this was not the bare measurement but the *competition*, the *achievement* and the post-race *evaluation* of it. The time measurement was just the prelude to the excited 'measurement' of the *significance* of this Lightning Bolt on the track.

The prayer in Psalm 90:12 is not that we may make no mathematical mistakes in totting up the number of days we live. It is a prayer for wisdom, that we may measure our days in a way that lines up with God's judgment of us. When I tell the story of my life, when I *evaluate* who I have been, what I have done, how I have fulfilled my roles as son, brother, husband, father, grandfather, teacher, pastor, counsellor, friend, do I 'count' my days wisely? That is to say, do I plunge

12. *Confessions*, 11:20:26.

into delusion and self-deception and tell a story wildly at odds with other people's experience of me or God's evaluation of me, or is my telling of my story more 'true' than that?

This is an issue often faced by counsellors and psychotherapists, as they meet clients who come into therapy giving self-accounts of their lives that sound wide of the mark. Often, the work of therapy is about standing with clients as they rewrite the stories of their lives more helpfully and truly: for instance, a client who suffered abuse in childhood finds the strength to tell her story as one of resilience and survival, rather than of self-blame and victimhood. But can we ever truly tell our story? What is it, truly? The wisdom that enables a wholly true account is that of God the judge, and that is the wisdom for which Psalm 90:12 prays.

This simply underlines the truth of Augustine's view of time. We hold the past within ourselves as a *present* account that has significance for us now. For instance, my wedding day is present to me now not as a twenty-four-hour period but as a kaleidoscope of impressions attached to a *feeling* that arises not just from the day itself, but from what my wife has meant to me over the many years of our marriage. The story of the day has been greatly amplified.

Actually, I am qualifying Augustine's view by filling it out with this notion of story. Augustine simply developed the idea of the threefold present. In adding 'story', I am drawing on the work of Paul Ricoeur, who in his magnificent work *Time and Narrative* compares Augustine's view of time to the way in which Aristotle developed a view of time through the notions of 'story' and 'plot' as a way of interpreting the disordered, even chaotic events of our lives. The Greek dramatists told stories which *interpreted* real life – stories which contained chaotic and disruptive events, but also supplied reasons and outcomes, and thus ultimately gave order to the chaos. By the way in which we hold the past in the present – and indeed the *future* in the present – we do exactly this, not just for our own individual lives but for our understanding of the cosmos.[13]

The exiles in Babylon had lost their home, amid terrible trauma. Moses' voice calls them back to a time before ever Jerusalem was Israel's home, when they were aliens in Egypt or wanderers in the Sinai desert, and invites them to find their *dwelling place* in the sovereign Lord who made heaven and earth, and who is *from everlasting to everlasting* (90:1–2). Will they rewrite their story within this bigger frame? Within this frame, Jerusalem and the temple fade in significance,

---

13. See Paul Ricoeur, *Time and Narrative*, 3 vols., transl. Kathleen McLaughlin and David Pellauer (Chicago: University of Chicago Press, 1984, 1985 and 1988). Ricoeur's basic case about Augustine and Aristotle is made in the first two chapters of vol. 1, pp. 5–51.

and they simply stand before God, profoundly aware of their frailty (vv. 5–6), their sins (v. 8), their insignificance (v. 9), and their impermanence (v. 10), but knowing that there, in that place of terrifying 'nothingness' (89:47), they can truly find *compassion* and *steadfast love* to sustain them (vv. 13–14).

So the psalm ends by looking ahead (vv. 13–17). Augustine's 'future-as-present' is the way in which we hold, right now, an imagination of what is yet to be. The psalm ends with seven prayers (the number may be significant): for God's *compassion* to meet our sinfulness and weakness (v. 13); for his *steadfast love* to give us a sense of home when we wake in the morning (v. 14a); for joy to match, even outweigh, the pain we have felt (vv. 14b–15); for deeper under-standing of God and his *work* (v. 16a); for real experience of his *glorious power* at work in the world (v. 16b); for his *favour* to rest on us (v. 17a); and for the satis-faction of being able to achieve something solid and good in our lives, before our little day is over (v. 17b).

Paradoxically, in this way of thinking about time, we have far more power over the past than over the future. Popular culture today puts it the other way round – we have no power to change the past, but we can work to make things better in the future. But the history of politics – at least in democratic societies where politicians seek periodic election on the basis of campaign promises – shows how illusory this claimed power to shape the future really is. Against this background, Psalm 90 says to us: you have enormous power to reshape the past, by reframing it and telling the story differently. And when you do that, the future takes a different shape, too, although you can do very little to determine what pops over the horizon to greet you.

It is fascinating that this prayer of Moses offers nothing to the exiles to assure them that it's really OK. There is no theodicy here, to explain or justify what has happened to them. There is no implicit prediction of the restoration of Jerusalem, or promise that exile will not last long. There is no comfort of that sort. There is simply an invitation to let their prayer of complaint, *O LORD! How long?* (v. 13a; cf. 89:46) rise to a *bigger* God, not one who has tied himself just to the house of David, but one who offers us a *dwelling place* just by virtue of being our Creator. The future comes to us from this Creator, by gift from him, with no strings attached. All that is appropriate, in response, is prayer expressing our heart-felt longings.

4. Onward to biblical theology!

We conclude this chapter with some reflections on where this takes us in our search for a biblical theology of history and time to form the big framework in

which to set our theology of the second coming of Jesus. It seems to have five
key elements within it, which we will meet repeatedly as we pursue the second
coming through Scripture.

a. The interaction between chronos and kairos

These are the two Greek words for time: *chronos* is time measured by a watch,
while *kairos* is time marked on a calendar. *Chronos* is time just passing by ('time
hung so heavily on our hands'), but *kairos* is time to be celebrated ('we had a
great time!'). Psalm 90 underlines for us how *chronos* is a scourge: our lives are
so short, even if we get our seventy or eighty years (v. 10). If we use just *chronos*
to measure our lives, then all we end up with is a 'chronicle' of *toil and trouble
... soon gone*. Stuck within that timeframe, we can't see beyond the Psalm 89
experience of God's apparent inconsistency, wrath and unfaithfulness. What
we need is the wisdom to discern the points of *kairos* in our lives, the moments
of real significance and depth (90:12), and to pray that there may be many more
such moments, when we get to know him and experience his power, love and
joy. The second coming of Jesus is just such a moment, a *kairos* point when we
will get to know him supremely. But it could be anticipated by many other
moments of deepening in our relationship with him.

Within this theology, it is a grave mistake to focus upon *chronos* in thinking
about the second coming. It's not a matter of timetables, of getting events in
the right order, or of predicting when it will all be. *Chronos* is just about the
substructure of the universe. It seems to be built into the physical stuff of
the universe, that matter exists in movement. Time and matter are brother and
sister in deeply mysterious ways, as Einstein discovered, and this 'timeliness' of
matter is echoed in our own bodies.[14] Their circadian rhythms tick inexorably
forward from moment to moment. Our ageing is unstoppable. I think this is
the second respect in which we need to supplement Augustine's view of time:
time is not just held in our minds, but even more in our bodies, and in the matter
of which they are composed, where *chronos* reigns supreme. Framed by this
bodily reality, we seek the *kairos* moments of our lives, which are often symbolic
moments that hold great meaning for us. We retell our stories around these
symbolic events, which can either hold great joy or great pain: the day I met
Jesus, the day I got married, the day my mother died, the day Jerusalem was
sacked, the day God stepped into my woe.

---

14. See Paul Davies, *About Time: Einstein's Unfinished Revolution* (London, etc.: Viking,
    1995) – a beautiful introduction to the ways in which time (as *chronos*) is flexible,
    relative to space and matter.

And I already hold the day of my death, and with it the day of the second coming of Jesus, as the two great for-sure *kairos* moments that frame my future life for me. They are the only secure points in my future-as-present! I don't need to know them as *chronos*, but I already embrace them as *kairos*.

b. The significance of the present moment

Whose initiative makes this moment a *kairos*-point in my life? God could step in, and do something remarkable, turning drab *chronos* into glorious *kairos*. All heaven could blaze over this minute speck. This is what grace (*hesed*, steadfast love) does. But I could take the initiative, too; and that is what these psalms invite, by presenting themselves to me so that I can pray them. Right now I can take them onto my lips and into my heart, and allow them to express for me not just my right-now anguish, but also my right-now grasp on God's greatness beyond all the immediate mess. The psalms themselves offer me the opportunity to *confess* as I turn towards God and speak words that lift me into a different *dwelling place*.

In later chapters we'll be looking at Jesus' offer of a seat at the heavenly banquet, the 'wedding feast of the Lamb',[15] and of the 'dwelling place' that he is preparing for us 'in my Father's house'.[16] But in both cases we will notice that the offer of a heavenly away-from-here dwelling place is accompanied by another offer – to come and live with us right now, in the murk and mess of our present lives.[17] In fact, as we develop our biblical theology, one of the strong themes that will emerge is the way in which the future coming of the Lord, and his *present* coming by his Spirit, are two sides of the one coin.

Right in the present moment, we can move out of Psalm 89 into Psalm 90, and not leave our suffering behind, but find it framed by our God in an entirely different way. It is fascinating to see something similar happening in secular psychology and psychotherapy. Daniel Stern's book *The Present Moment in Psychotherapy and Everyday Life*[18] has had a considerable impact on psychotherapy training in recent years. Stern researched the precise moment-by-moment inter-actions between babies and their mothers, noting the amazing ways in which 'intersubjectivity' (deep emotional connection) is regulated from moment to moment as mum and baby look into each other's eyes and gurgle at each other.

---

15. Rev. 19:9; ch. 14 below.

16. John 14:2–3; ch. 6 below.

17. John 14:23; Rev. 3:20.

18. Daniel N. Stern, *The Present Moment in Psychotherapy and Everyday Life* (New York and London: Norton, 2004).

Stern then draws implications for our contact with each 'other' in adult life, too, and in particular for the deep intersubjective contact that can develop between clients and their therapist. The present moment, he says, can hold our whole life story as we relate with each other out of the deep wells of instinct and presumption about ourselves and others. But the present moment can also begin to reframe our lives, as the old stories and patterns are challenged by new experiences of intersubjective connection.

That is exactly what Psalm 90 offers us! It is a moment of reconnection with God in a different way, seeing him as a *dwelling place* not limited to a specific time and place and set of expectations (Jerusalem, sixth century BC, the covenant with the house of David), but altogether bigger – more terrifying, but also more secure.

The vital significance of the present moment is the hot tip in secular spirituality right now. Eckhart Tolle's *The Power of Now* has sold millions of copies worldwide, promoting a kind of present-moment 'mindfulness' in which we let go of our guilt-ridden and regretful thoughts about the past, and our anxious thoughts about the future, and allow ourselves simply to 'be', in our bodily reality, right now.[19] This can be extremely helpful. But from a Christian perspective the present moment is one of *relationship*; we do not simply dip into the inner life of our own soul, as we sit in quiet mindfulness of our bodies and feelings right now. That inner place is precisely where we meet the Lord – where *he* becomes a *dwelling place* for us. And *he* calls us, not to forget our past or dismiss our future (the Tolle prescription), but to embrace both with his *grace*, so as to let his *steadfast love* lift us out of wrath and insignificance into joy and confidence.[20]

c. Mystery

These two psalms certainly underline this for us. Psalm 90 does not solve the mystery of the broken Davidic covenant and the exile – it simply invites us to hold such things within the bigger mystery which is God himself, whose wrath condemns us to insignificance while his steadfast love raises us to meaning. Can we understand that? We can certainly say more about the second coming than this, but it will – and should – never lose this element of 'mystery'. It is wrapped in the inscrutability of God himself, 'whose judgments are unsearchable and

---

19. Eckhart Tolle, *The Power of Now: A Guide to Spiritual Enlightenment* (Vancouver: Namaste Publishing, 1997).

20. On Christian mindfulness, see Shaun Lambert, *A Book of Sparks: A Study in Christian Mind*full*ness* (Watford: Instant Apostle, 2014).

... ways past finding out'.[21] And part of the mystery may well involve the kind of inconsistency and unexpected disruption with which these psalms wrestle – the non-fulfilment of promises, the disappointment of hopes, the absence of God when we expected his presence.

As we will see, it looks as though some, at least, in the early church expected Jesus to return very soon, and then had to come to terms with his non-appearance. We will wrestle with the very mysterious way in which Jesus' words in Mark 13 were fulfilled but also *not* fulfilled in AD 70. And we'll meet another element of mystery in the extraordinary differences between the pictures of the second coming that we will encounter in the various passages we'll examine: some huge and awe-inspiring, some comforting and domestic, some dark and dreadful emphasizing judgment and destruction. Our biblical theology will need to 'hold' all these differences faithfully.

d. Judgment

The penultimate prayer in Psalm 90 is *Let the favour of the Lord our God be upon us* (v. 17a). *Favour* is the Hebrew word *nō'am*, an interesting word which usually means 'delightfulness', 'pleasantness' or 'loveliness', as in the phrase 'the beauty of the Lord'.[22] Some translations use 'beauty' here, most notably the King James and New King James versions: 'Let the beauty of the Lord our God be upon us.' Probably 'favour' is the right translation, however, because this word is often used of loveliness *expressed* in words or deeds. This is a prayer that the Lord's beauty, rather than his wrath, may be expressed towards us. The Aaronic blessing gives an idea of what this means: 'The LORD bless you and keep you; *the LORD make his face to shine upon you*, and be gracious to you . . .'[23] His face shines towards us, expressing grace and blessing and 'favour' so that the same beauty rests on us, too.

So God's wrath leaves us helpless in our fleetingness and frailty (Ps. 90:5–10), but his 'loveliness' upon us will mean that *the work of our hands* is 'established', 'made firm' – i.e., will *last*. This is not a prayer that our work will prosper or be successful (against some translations here, e.g. CEV and NRSV), but that it will have solidity, permanence – that it won't pass away *like a sigh* (v. 9), but stand firm before the Lord.

This last verse of Psalm 90 makes explicit what has been implicit throughout, that everything and everyone is ultimately subject to God's judgment. He is the

---

21. Rom. 11:33. We will look at this passage in ch. 8 below.

22. Ps. 27:4.

23. Num. 6:24–26.

Judge who, when he expresses his 'loveliness' towards us, will deliver us from the terrible frailty and impermanence which is our lot under his 'wrath'. This is the presupposition that underlies the agony in Psalm 89, too. If the Lord were not responsible for what had happened to 'David', there would be no problem. But it's down to the Lord: you *have broken through all his walls;* you *have laid his strongholds in ruins . . .* you *have exalted the right hand of his foes . . .* you *have not supported him in battle . . .* you *have covered him with shame* (89:40–45). The Judge has acted in *wrath* (v. 46) towards his anointed king, condemning him and his people to the 'nothingness' which is our fate (v. 47), unless he should *turn* (90:13) and let his beauty rest upon us instead.

As we will see, judgment is a constant theme connected to the second coming of Jesus. When Jesus comes, will it be wrath or beauty which rests upon us?

e. Steadfast love and faithfulness

In our search for a theology of time and history it is worth pausing on this phrase which appears in Psalm 89:14. A different word for 'faithfulness' is used here (Heb. *'ĕmet*), because the whole phrase *steadfast love and faithfulness – ḥesed wĕ'ĕmet* – has a life of its own in the Old Testament. It appears fifteen times, usually celebrating the solid foundation of the covenant in these absolutely reliable qualities of the Lord. Most notably, the phrase appears in Exodus 34:6, where the Lord proclaims his own name and character before Moses hiding in the rock: 'The Lord, the Lord, a God merciful and gracious, slow to anger, and abounding in steadfast love and faithfulness . . .'

Walter Brueggemann, the noted Old Testament scholar, makes Exodus 34:6–7 the centrepiece of his presentation of Old Testament theology, because of the teasing way in which God's 'steadfast love and faithfulness', expressed in his readiness to 'forgive iniquity and transgression and sin', is balanced by his determination – in the same passage! – 'by no means to clear the guilty' and to 'visit the iniquity of the parents upon the children and the children's children, to the third and the fourth generation'.[24] Throughout the Old Testament, suggests Brueggemann, we see these two sides of God in tension. He writes, 'I can find no evident way in which the two parts of this formulation can be readily and fully harmonized. The faithful God who forgives iniquity is the same God who visits offenders for their iniquity.'[25] So, on the one hand, David is forgiven for his sin with Bathsheba; but on the other, Saul is rejected for

---

24. Exod. 34:7.

25. W. Brueggemann, *The Theology of the Old Testament: Testimony, Dispute, Advocacy* (Minneapolis: Augsburg Fortress, 1997), p. 270.

hot-headedly offering the sacrifice without Samuel, and for not completely destroying the Amalekites.[26] God is ready to make the promise in Psalm 89:30–34 to the house of David, but not to the house of Saul.

Brueggemann maintains that the Old Testament never delivers us from this tension. We never know whether we are going to meet the Lord 'abounding in steadfast love and faithfulness' or 'by no means clearing the guilty'. And that tension is exactly what we meet in Psalms 89 and 90, and indeed within Psalm 90. Will God leave us under his 'wrath', or meet us with his 'steadfast love'?

This tension may not be resolved in the Old Testament, but it certainly is in the New! The same phrase, but now in Greek, appears in John 1:14: 'We beheld his glory, glory as of the only Son of the Father, *full of grace and truth.*' And then again, very tellingly, in John 1:17: 'The law was given through Moses; *grace and truth* have come into being through Jesus Christ.'[27] Moses gives us law, and with it the uncertainty whether our transgressions of it will be met with wrath or with forgiveness. But Jesus Christ puts our relationship with God on a wholly different footing. The 'grace and truth' which was proclaimed to Moses has now fully 'come into being' through Jesus.[28] So it is no surprise to hear, later in John's Gospel, that 'I came not to judge the world, but to save it'.[29] Judgment is now reserved for the End: '*On the last day* the word that I have spoken will serve as judge.'[30] Until that day – 'the day of wrath and revelation of the righteous judgment of God' – it is God's 'kindness and forbearance and patience' through which he relates to his world.[31]

This is truly a *turn* (Ps. 90:13) within the history of God's relationship to the world. And it is the capstone to our biblical theology of time and history. History hinges around Jesus Christ, who becomes the focus of God's dealings with us:

---

26. 1 Sam. 13:8–14 and 15:17–31 (Saul); 2 Sam. 11 – 12 (David).

27. It was A. T. Hanson who first made the connection between this phrase in John 1:14 and 17, and Exod. 34:6: A. T. Hanson, 'John 1:14–18 and Exodus 34', *The New Testament Interpretation of Scripture* (London: SPCK, 1980), pp. 97–109. Hanson points out that 'no one has ever seen God' in John 1:18 alludes to the way in which Moses was prevented from seeing God directly in that revelation (Exod. 33:21–23). But things are different now – 'we have beheld his glory'! (John 1:14).

28. 'Come into being': the verb in John 1:17 is the same as in John 1:2, 'all things came into being (Gk *egeneto*) through him'. There is new creation in the air, as Jesus brings into being the era of the gospel.

29. John 12:47.

30. John 12:48.

31. See Rom. 2:4–5.

at his first coming, expressing God's 'steadfast love and faithfulness'; and then at his second, God's 'wrath and . . . righteous judgment'. As we will see, God's judgment is that wholly true telling of the story which reveals the secrets of all hearts and of all history: a past-as-present moment, a *kairos* when all is truly revealed, and in particular Jesus Christ is revealed as the one in whom, and through whom, and for whom, all things are.

2. PRESENCE IN POWER (PSALM 18)

1. Introduction

Psalm 18 adds a further element to our understanding of the wider biblical frame that surrounds our theology of the second coming of Jesus Christ. It is not, of course, about the second coming, but it is crucially about the *coming of the Lord*. It is one of those vital passages at the heart of the whole biblical understanding of salvation – about how the Lord *comes*, or more specifically *comes down*, in response to the prayers and need of his people. *He bowed the heavens, and came down* (v. 9), is David's testimony here, using the verb *yārad*, to 'come down', which is used on at least twenty further occasions in the Old Testament to express this 'coming down' of the Lord to visit or rescue his people.[1] The equivalent Greek verb, *katabainō*, is used at least fourteen times in the New Testament, to express the 'coming down' of the Holy Spirit,[2] of Jesus in incarnation[3] and at his second coming,[4] and indeed the 'coming down' of the heavenly Jerusalem.[5]

---

1. See for instance Exod. 3:8; 19:11, 18, 20; 33:9; 34:5; Ps. 144:5; Is. 64:1, 3. Sometimes the 'coming down' is in judgment (e.g. Gen. 11:7) or just to see (Gen 11:5; 18:21), or to meet with his people (Num. 11:25; 12:5).
2. E.g. Matt. 3:16; John 1:32.
3. E.g. John 6:41, 50; Eph. 4:9–10.
4. 1 Thess. 4:16.
5. Rev. 3:12; 21:2.

This psalm also uses some remarkable apocalyptic language to describe this 'coming' of the Lord, which will help us begin to develop a perspective on this language used also of the second coming.

Psalm 18 stands out among the psalms of David,[6] because of its testimony significance. The little historical introduction at the head of the psalm (v. 1 in the Hebrew) is also found in 2 Samuel 22:1, where in fact the whole psalm is then repeated, with small variations. It stands there, in 2 Samuel, as a final word of testimony looking back over David's life, witness to the wonderful way in which the Lord had *delivered him from the hand of all his enemies, and from the hand of Saul* – all those *kairos* moments when the Lord had met and saved him. It expresses, therefore, the theology which causes such agony in Psalm 89, where God seems to have rejected David's house:

> *Great triumphs* [lit. acts of salvation] *he gives to his king,*
> *and shows steadfast love to his anointed,*
> *to David and his descendants for ever.*
> (v. 50)

Though placed at the end of David's career in 2 Samuel, it looks as though this psalm was in fact written earlier – maybe around the time when, after much war and conflict, David at last began his thirty-three-year reign as king of all Israel in Jerusalem.[7] The psalm has a young man's feel to it, because of his confidence in his own rightness, and his readiness to see his final victory as a reward for his righteousness (vv. 20–24). It is all too clear that the David who wrote Psalm 51 – broken and repentant after his sin with Bathsheba and his murder of Uriah – is a very different man. How fascinating, therefore, that the author of 2 Samuel, the chronicler who put together the story of David's life and reign, has chosen to use this psalm as a whole-life summary testimony. It is not that suddenly the awful events of 2 Samuel 11 – 12 (the story of Bathsheba and Uriah) are being forgotten. It is probably the same chronicler who, a little later in the story, comments that 'David did what was right in the sight of the LORD, and did not turn aside from anything that he commanded him all the

---

6. I'm assuming the truth of the ascription to David at the head of this psalm (v. 1 in Heb.). Some scholars dispute the reliability of the psalm ascriptions, but in this case particularly, because of the link with 2 Sam. 22, it seems safe to connect the psalm with David's life.

7. See 2 Sam. 5:1–12. The reference to the Lord's promise to his *descendants* (v. 50) perhaps puts the psalm after 2 Sam. 7.

days of his life, *except in the matter of Uriah the Hittite*.[8] How could something as dreadful as that cold-blooded adultery, deception and murder – that 'high-handed' sin for which there is no atonement under the law[9] – be simply forgotten?

I imagine that, for the author of 2 Samuel, the promise of the Lord never to remove his covenant love from the house of David – the promise reiterated in this psalm, and evidenced in all David's victories – still stands, irrespective of David's dreadful collapse. It was not a fall *from grace*. So David's super-confidence in his own righteousness might have been dented, but not his super-confidence in God's power to save.

The language of this psalm is not infrequently echoed in the New Testament – most notably in Mary's and Zechariah's songs in Luke 1, and in the quotation of verse 49 in Romans 15:9, to which we will return in due course.

2. Structure and language

The psalm has a really interesting structure, which works out like this:

A. Introduction (vv. 1–3)

This neatly balances the conclusion in vv. 46–50, with themes in common, as we will see. In between introduction and conclusion, the psalm falls into two broad sections:

B. The headline testimony, or the outer story (vv. 4–19)

 a) The need (vv. 4–5)
 b) The call to the Lord (v. 6)
 c) The Lord's response (vv. 7–15)
 d) The deliverance (vv. 16–19)

This section thus has a narrative quality – it tells the story of David's experience, not relating to one particular occasion but to his whole-life experience of the Lord's 'coming down'.

C. The testimony unpacked, or the inner story (vv. 20–45)

 a) David's deserving: the recompense principle (vv. 20–27)

---

8. 1 Kgs 15:5.
9. See Num. 15:27–31.

  b) God's agency: the synergy principle (vv. 28–45)

       i)   Strength (vv. 26–33)
      ii)   Know-how (vv. 34–38)
     iii)   Back-up (vv. 39–42)
      iv)   Success (vv. 43–45)

  We go behind the scenes of David's testimony, and watch him unpacking the
  principles operative within it.

  D. Conclusions – praise and confidence (vv. 46–50)

This psalm is absolutely beautiful poetry. We may imagine David at about the
age of thirty-seven,[10] sitting in his temporary palace in Jerusalem, newly established as king of all Israel, looking back over about fifteen years of constant
warfare, first as Saul's armour-bearer but then as an outlawed warlord, pursued
by his former master, constantly struggling to support his robber band and to
keep his life – and to maintain his trust in the Lord through it all. It could be
that the imagery of the *rock* and the *fortress*, occurs to him because of the *refuge*
he found in the cave of Adullam and in other lonely mountain *strongholds*.[11]
Those places of refuge symbolized the Lord for him. Now, with all that insecur-
ity behind him, David, 'the anointed of the God of Jacob, the sweet psalmist
of Israel',[12] took his lyre and started to compose.
     We will take each section in turn, seeking to hear it in its own terms, but also
to draw out its significance for our biblical theology of the second coming.

3. The introduction and conclusion (vv. 1–3, 46–50)

These two balancing sections develop the four interlinked themes of (a) God
as *rock*, (b) deliverance from *enemies*, (c) *praise*, and (d) confidence for the future
– in this order, in both cases. These are the themes that frame the whole psalm.
The fundamental point is that the relationship which David has with the Lord
now will extend into the future. It will never be broken. Hence the praise,
and the sense of security even in the face of a dangerous and threatening
world.

----

10. 2 Sam. 5:4–5.

11. 1 Sam. 22:1; cf. 1 Sam. 22:5; 23:19, 29.

12. 2 Sam. 23:1, RSV. This translation has been abandoned by NRSV, where David is no
      longer a 'sweet psalmist'!

Paul says the same thing about our relationship with the Lord (i.e., the Lord *Jesus*):

> None of us lives to himself, and none of us dies to himself. If we live, we live to the Lord; and if we die, we die to the Lord. Whether we live or whether we die, we are the Lord's. For Christ died and lived for this purpose, that he might be the Lord of both the dead and the living.[13]

This is radical belonging. We are his, and therefore secure. David does not lift his eyes beyond his earthly enemies in this psalm – he does not think of life beyond death, although his thoughts drift in that direction elsewhere.[14] But for Paul, of course, death is the 'last enemy' from which finally we will be saved by Christ,[15] and the *second* coming of the Lord is the crucial point of deliverance from that last enemy.

Psalm 18:1 does not appear in the parallel in 2 Samuel 22:2: *I love you, O LORD, my strength*. It is interesting to wonder why this should be. This is the only place in the Old Testament where this particular verb, *rāḥam*, is used of love for God. It is not the word used in the great commandment to 'love the LORD your God with all your heart, and with all your soul, and with all your might'.[16] That verb, *'āhab*, is especially connected with loving *obedience*. The verb David uses here – and which may have been just a bit too much for the chronicler in 2 Samuel – is a word of deep feeling, often translated 'have compassion', and used some thirty-four times of the Lord's compassion for his people. It is linked to the word for womb, and thus has a beautiful maternal quality.

So David is not saying 'I'm good at obeying the commandment to love you, O Lord my strength – I do it!' Much more he is saying, 'Lord, I am *passionate* about you, passionate with all the strength you give me! I am *com*passionate towards you, feeling what you feel, and strongly delighting in you.' *Strength* here is also an unusual word, different from the 'might' with which we are commanded to love the Lord in Deuteronomy 6:5. The word used there means 'muchness, force, abundance';[17] we might paraphrase it, 'Love the Lord your God as hard as you can!' But *strength* here means 'strength of body and of mind, capacity,

---

13. Rom. 14:7–9.
14. See especially Ps. 16:9–11.
15. 1 Cor. 15:26.
16. Deut. 6:5.
17. This is the definition in Francis Brown, S. R. Driver and Charles A. Briggs, *A Hebrew and English Lexicon of the Old Testament* (Oxford: Clarendon Press, 1972), p. 547.

firmness, hardness'.[18] The Lord gives David this strength, and David loves the Lord back with all the tender passion and feeling that this strength enables.

This is very important as background to the section later where David expounds the recompense principle underlying his story (vv. 20–27). He does *not* claim a strict 'I scratch your back, you scratch mine' relationship with the Lord, with the Lord's deliverance a payment for services rendered. David's relationship with God begins with this passionate attachment based on the strength that God himself provides, because of his prior commitment to David and his house.

4. The headline testimony: The outer story (vv. 4–19)

David tells his story. Starting with the awful need in which he found himself, facing death at any moment as he fled from Saul (vv. 4–5), he very simply outlines his *cry for help* (v. 6a) and the Lord's first response, which is simply to *hear* (v. 6b). *Temple* almost certainly means his *heavenly temple*, because there was no earthly temple at this time.

But verse 6b simply serves as an introduction to the beautiful, elaborate description of the Lord's 'coming' in verses 7–15. There is little to match this poetry in all of Scripture. The coming of the Lord calls forth our best, most evocative, most powerful language, not because it defies description, but because of the wonder, the awesomeness, the magic of it. That he should *bow the heavens, and come down* to deliver us! David could simply have reported what the Lord actually did to deliver him on numerous occasions. Similarly, we could simply report the bare fact of the Lord's coming again – or the facts (plural), trying to get all the related events into the right order as the various premillenarian schemes do. But that is not the approach David commends here. There is a time to use the most exalted, symbolic language, because that alone matches the grandeur and the grace of God's action.

We will meet language like this repeatedly in the passages ahead of us, because the second coming of Jesus Christ is just such an event. So it is important to pause and notice this language, and how it works. Artur Weiser points out that the original 'theophany' (appearance of God) at Sinai probably influences David's words here.[19] There, too, we meet earthquake (v. 7), smoke and fire (v. 8),

---

18. This is my summary of Brown, Driver and Briggs' article on this word (ibid., pp. 304–305).

19. Artur Weiser, *The Psalms: A Commentary* (London: SCM Press, 1962), p. 189.

cloud (v. 11), thunder and lightning (vv. 13–14), and of course the 'coming down' of the Lord.[20] Weiser thinks that David is describing a theophany here, too, but of course this is not true. David is using the *language of* theophany to give substance to the awesomeness of the grace of God in meeting him, in so many detailed ways, in the long history of his life of need and prayer. It *amounts to* a sharing of that amazing experience of Israel before Sinai, when God came down and spoke directly to them. David shares the grace of that, in the stories he has to tell.

Others have used the expression 'storm symbolism' to describe language like this. We meet it all over Scripture: for instance, in the language describing Deborah and Barak's victory over Sisera and the Canaanites;[21] in several of Isaiah's descriptions of the Lord's powerful interventions to save his people, both past and future;[22] in Habakkuk's glorious prayer of trust;[23] and of course in many other psalms[24], as well as in numerous New Testament passages, as we will have ample opportunity to see. Storm symbolism is frequent in the book of Revelation, appearing especially in the 'opening of heaven' passages that mark the transition from one series of seven to the next.[25] In particular, clouds stand out as special within the spectrum of these storm symbols, marking the presence and the power of God.

This language clearly needs to be handled carefully in interpretation. The symbolism would not have power, if it did not rest in the conviction that the Lord appeared literally in fire and cloud on Mount Sinai, and that the mountain really did quake with the power of his presence and his voice.[26] Surely David believed this. It may indeed have literally rained on Sisera's army, creating panic.[27] Some of the plagues of Egypt incorporate storm symbols. The cloud of God's presence did indeed descend on the tabernacle, and later on Solomon's temple.[28] His cloud and fire truly went before Israel in the wilderness.[29] But these literal

---

20. See Exod. 19:10–20.

21. Judg. 5:4–5, 20–21.

22. E.g. Isa. 19:1; 24:23; 29:5–6; 30:25–28; 42:15–16; 64:1–4.

23. Hab. 3:3–15.

24. E.g. Pss 50:3; 68:7–10; 97:1–5; 104:1–4; 144:5–8.

25. See Rev. 8:3–5; 11:19; 15:8; 16:18–21; not to mention the various ways in which storm symbolism appears in the main visions, the seals and the bowls in particular.

26. Cf. Heb. 12:18–24.

27. Judg. 5:21; cf. 4:15.

28. Exod. 40:34–38; 1 Kgs 8:10–13.

29. Exod. 13:21–22.

events generate a way of speaking about God and his intervention in the world, so that David can use this marvellously evocative language in Psalm 18 – language which here of course we must not take literally, because the whole point is its poetic power to evoke God's creative, gracious, overwhelming intervention in his life on numerous occasions. And clearly the prophets take up this tradition, as they write about the Lord's *future* interventions, as opposed to the past, as here.

There is more to it even than this. This is *cosmic*, and not just *storm*, symbolism. Here in Psalm 18 the earthquakes are gigantic – *the earth reeled and rocked* (v. 7), *the channels of the sea were seen, and the foundations of the world were laid bare* (v. 15). This is no 'ordinary' earthquake, because this is *God coming*. The earth truly moves when he turns up! How could it not? He is its creator, and so when he arrives, his whole creation responds by bowing before his power.[30] Again and again, we find the prophets using this kind of cosmic language to express the power of God's presence, whether to judge or to deliver – sometimes involving dramatic things happening to heavenly bodies.[31] We notice that this symbolism moves over naturally into predicting the wonderful transformation that the Lord will bring to the whole cosmos, for the sake of his people. If he is *that* mighty, able to push the heavenly bodies around at will, then nothing will stop him from bringing the deliverance he promises.

So, in describing the literal victories that God gave him over his enemies, David uses language that has an enormous biblical pedigree and onward history, as we will see in later chapters. We will face, of course, the challenge of interpretation in each case: do we read this language literally, or symbolically? For instance, when Haggai speaks the Lord's word, 'Once again, in a little while, I will shake the heavens and the earth and the sea and the dry land',[32] does he expect a literal earthquake? Even more importantly, when Jesus predicts that 'there will be great earthquakes, and here and there famines and pestilences, and there will be fearful portents and great signs from heaven',[33] should we

---

30. In the reference to the exposure of 'the channels of the sea' in v. 15, we should probably see an allusion to the parting of the waters at the Red Sea (Exod. 14:21; cf. 15:8). David feels that he has been saved, like Israel from Pharaoh.

31. See for instance Job 9:1–12; Isa. 13:4–13; 35:1–10; 43:1–2; 65:17–25; Joel 2:28–32; Ezek. 32:7–10; Hag. 2:6–7; and of course Matt. 24:29–31; Acts 2:16–21 (quoting Joel); Heb. 12:26–29 (quoting Haggai), and many passages in Revelation that employ this kind of cosmic symbolism.

32. Hag. 2:6.

33. Luke 21:11.

interpret this literally? Or is this – as here in Psalm 18 – the language of cosmic disruption used to describe the dramatic, overwhelming intrusion of God into his world?

We need to look at each passage carefully within its own terms. In the case of the example from Haggai, it becomes clear that the shaking of earth and heaven is a vivid and dramatic way of underlining the Lord's glorious intention to rebuild the temple in Jerusalem. But when Hebrews reuses Haggai's symbols, they have a bigger, more literal meaning, contrasting the solidity and permanence of the kingdom of God with the impermanence and fragility of the physical universe.[34] We will look closely at Jesus' language in due course.

Behind such language lies the reality and power of God the Creator and Redeemer. He intervenes in our lives now in dramatic and wonderful ways, and he will do so again. One day he will transform this old earth, sweep it up into the redemption that Christ brings,[35] and create 'new heavens and a new earth'[36] – truly, and literally. But whenever he shows up in power, *the earth moves.* The wonderful thing about this language, so beautifully illustrated here in Psalm 18, is that it takes chaos and disaster – not just awe-inspiring but *destructive* cosmic events, lightning, earthquake, volcanic eruption – and uses these as symbols of deliverance and rescue. Embedded in the language itself there lies the experience that David uses it to describe: the wonderful way in which God turns disaster into new life, and brings order out of chaos.

One further footnote to David's 'headline testimony' here. The symbolism is angry, as indeed the Lord is.

> *The earth reeled and rocked . . .*
> *because he was angry.*
> *Smoke went up from his nostrils,*
> *and devouring fire from his mouth;*
> *glowing coals flamed forth from him.*
> (vv. 7–8)

The word for anger here (*ḥārâ*) is yet another word, different from the three we met in Psalms 89 and 90. This word connotes the burning heat of anger – fiery rage – and thus gives a powerful sense that the Lord is equally passionate about David (see v. 1). We tend to put these words the other way round: we get *angry*

---

34. Heb. 12:26–29.

35. Rom. 8:19–21.

36. Isa. 65:17–25; Rev. 21:1–4.

about the injustices and pains we experience, and then call on the Lord to be *compassionate* towards us. But here David feels *compassionate* towards the Lord – not because he pities him in any sense, but because he delights so deeply in who the Lord is – and the Lord feels *angry* about David's *distress* (v. 6); the hot, burning rage of indignation and passion to save.

This is another dimension of the biblical view of the wrath of God. This is not his wrath that hates our sin,[37] nor his wrath before which we fade in insignificance,[38] but his wrath that hates our enemies, and motivates him to deliver us. In fact, finally, this is probably the most profound sense of the wrath of God in the Bible. His wrath is always directed towards salvation, towards cleansing and delivering his world, and us. To that, he is passionately committed, with hot, burning anger against all that enslaves and crushes us (vv. 17–19). His wrath, therefore, is an aspect of his love. As Tony Lane puts it, *'God's love itself implies his wrath. Without his wrath God is simply not loving in the sense that the Bible portrays his love.'*[39]

5. The testimony unpacked: The inner story (vv. 20–45)

This longer section of the psalm is a fascinating supplement to the 'headline' story. David digs underneath it, and unpacks *two vital principles* which he discerns in his own story, both concerned with his inner relationship with the Lord. Essentially, he uncovers the dynamics of that relationship, and gives us insight into *God and David, home alone together.*

a. The recompense principle: David's deserving (vv. 20–27)
I debated long and hard whether 'deserving' was the right word to use in this heading. It is using a noun where David uses a preposition, *according to*, which appears four times in these verses:

> The LORD *rewarded me according to my righteousness;*
> *according to the cleanness of my hands he recompensed me . . .*

---

37. Ps. 90:7–8.

38. Ps. 90:9–11.

39. A. N. S. Lane, 'The Love of God as an Aspect of the Wrath of God', in Kevin J. Vanhoozer (ed.), *Nothing Greater, Nothing Better: Theological Essays on the Love of God* (Eerdmans: Grand Rapids, 2001), pp. 138–167. A truly excellent article also available at www.theologynetwork.org (July 2015). Italics original.

> *Therefore the Lord has recompensed me according to my righteousness,*
> *according to the cleanness of my hands in his sight* (vv. 20, 24).

Between these two very similar summary statements, David records his faithfulness to the *ways* (v. 21), the *ordinances* and the *statutes* (v. 22) of the Lord, which meant that he was *blameless*, free from *guilt* before him (v. 23). Then in verses 25–27 he claims that the Lord acts towards us as we act towards him. It is hard not to use the word 'deserve' to summarize this. But is David really claiming that he 'deserved' to be rescued – that God's glorious intervention was a *reward* (v. 20) for his faithful obedience?

This is a problem, for it seems to be the starting-point of the gospel that we are all sinners, not righteous. 'There is none righteous, not even one', writes Paul,[40] for 'all have sinned, and fall short of the glory of God.'[41] But gloriously, at the judgment we do *not* receive what we deserve. Instead we are received with grace rather than wrath, not because of our own righteousness but because of Jesus, who 'rescues us from the coming wrath', as Paul puts it.[42] Which of us could really claim to be *blameless* (v. 23) like David here? And was he not deceiving himself, anyway? While on the road with his outlaw band, he was not above a spot of extortion,[43] and was extremely violent and merciless towards the villages he raided.[44] Indeed, later in his life David certainly discovered how vital it is that the grace of God covers even our most awful sins and *lack* of deserving. 'The Lord has put away your sin', was the prophet Nathan's simple assurance to the repentant David, after his adultery with Bathsheba and murder of Uriah were exposed.[45] David experienced the sheer, unmerited (and officially impossible, under the law) forgiveness of the Lord.[46]

So maybe we just meet the youthful, over-confident David here, who does not understand the deep possibility of wickedness in his own heart? If he

---

40. Rom. 3:10, quoting a combination of Ps. 14:3 (//Ps. 53:3) and Eccl. 7:20.

41. Rom. 3:23.

42. 1 Thess. 1:10.

43. 1 Sam. 25:2–8.

44. 1 Sam. 27:8–9.

45. 2 Sam. 12:13.

46. See Ps. 51:14–19: for a sin of this sort, a 'high-handed', rebellious sin, atoning sacrifice could not be offered. God would 'have no delight in sacrifice'. But if God will 'deliver me from bloodshed', then David will again be able to 'sing aloud of your deliverance', and offer 'right sacrifices' in which God will again 'delight'.

himself would not have written this ten years later, perhaps we should discount this confidence. But that seems hardly to take seriously the way in which the psalm functions in 2 Samuel 22.

So maybe – alternatively – we come face to face here with the chief respect in which the old covenant is transcended by the new. The old covenant prized, and asked for, the doing of the law. But we no longer seek 'the righteousness that comes from the law', says Paul; we rest on 'the righteousness that comes from faith', which simply looks to Jesus, confessing him as Lord and trusting him for salvation.[47] So, from the perspective of a whole-biblical theology, we could supplement David's claim here, in effect saying to him, 'Sure: the Lord recompensed you according to your righteousness – but remember that he *gave* you that righteousness in the first place, and that we only ever stand before him clothed in his righteousness, and not our own.'

That would be fine, except that it is precisely *not* what David says here. He claims that the Lord rewarded him for *his* righteousness, not someone else's! How can we solve this dilemma?

We need to go back to Paul, and to note that Paul, too, believed in judgment by works. 'We must all appear before the judgment seat of Christ', he writes, 'so that each may receive recompense according to what he has done in the body, whether good or bad.'[48] This is surprising, in view of his emphasis on not claiming our own righteousness before God. Even more strikingly, in 1 Corinthians 3 he pictures the work of the leading apostles, including himself, as buildings erected on the foundation of Jesus Christ, which will be tested by fire on 'the Day': If the buildings are of straw, 'the builder will suffer loss; the builder will be saved, but only as through fire'.[49] The quality of the building – that is, the quality of the whole life of service offered to God through Jesus Christ – will determine the 'recompense' at the day of judgment.

Paul clearly felt no tension between believing in righteousness as a gift, because of universal sinfulness, and in the importance of our own righteous achievement before God. But how do they fit together? I believe that both for Paul, and for David in Psalm 18, the resolution lies in *the quality of our relationship* with the Lord. The point about David's obedience in verses 21–23 is not that

---

47. This is a summary of Rom. 10:5–10, where Paul quotes Lev. 18:5, 'the person who does these things (i.e., the commandments of the law) shall live by them', and draws a contrast between this requirement of *doing* and the gospel requirement simply to *believe*. See also Rom. 3:27–31; Gal. 2:15–21; Phil. 3:8–9.

48. 2 Cor. 5:10.

49. 1 Cor. 3:10–15, quoting v. 15 from NRSV.

he was ticking boxes, and scoring brownie points so that God would 'recompense' him with deliverance. He was not 'working' for salvation, in that sense. Rather – and this is very clear in the stories that cover the relevant period of his life[50] – David lived the relationship with his Lord. When many pressurized him to do the 'normal' thing and murder Saul and usurp his throne, he refused, recognizing that Saul was the Lord's anointed king.[51] He constantly sought the Lord's guidance about what he should do next.[52] He sometimes behaved impulsively and vindictively,[53] but it is also true that he consistently sought to find and do the Lord's will and to act with integrity – and the psalms from this period show how he sought to keep his relationship with the Lord at the heart of his life, even through all the danger, chaos and uncertainty.[54] *His relationship with the Lord was not a quest for rightness, motivated by fear, but a careful 'keeping of his ways', motivated by love* – as we saw in his dramatic statement of love in verse 1.

And so it is for Paul, also. Justification by faith and judgment by works are fully compatible, because faith is not just about believing the gospel, but even more about walking with the Lord, being 'led by the Spirit',[55] holding onto him when things get tough,[56] knowing that nothing can separate us from his love, even when we feel like 'sheep for the slaughter'.[57]

This kind of relational faith is not easy – but it is the kind of faith that connects our experience here and now with our yet-to-be experience of the Lord, after his coming. He is the same Lord, after all! So the same story continues, linking the present to the eschatological future. It is through faith like this that each 'present moment' can become a *kairos*-moment drawing back the veil between heaven and earth *right now*, anticipating that glorious final unveiling. As we will see, how the present age relates to the 'age to come' is a profound and

---

50. From 1 Sam. 19 through to 2 Sam. 7.

51. 1 Sam. 24:4–15.

52. E.g. 1 Sam. 23:2; 2 Sam. 2:1–2.

53. E.g. 2 Sam. 1:14–16; 3:14–16.

54. One of the most vivid and dramatic is Ps. 34, written early in his experience as an outlaw, when he had made a serious mistake by seeking refuge among the Philistines (1 Sam. 21:10–15). For a beautiful study of all the Davidic psalms with historical introductions – including Ps. 18 – see J. A. Motyer, *Treasures of the King: Psalms from the Life of David* (Leicester: Inter-Varsity Press, 2007).

55. Rom. 8:14.

56. 2 Cor. 4:7–12 is a most dramatic statement of this kind of faith.

57. Rom. 8:35–39.

important point at the heart of our understanding of eschatological time. Maybe this is why the same kind of cosmic language can be used to describe God's intervention both now and then.

This leads us right into the next section.

b. The synergy principle: God's agency (vv. 28–45)

The relationship of faith, which underlies David's statement of his achievement in verses 20–27, undergirds this section too. But whereas David is the implicit agent throughout the preceding section, here God is the agent. God is the subject of most of the verbs here – and when he is not, his is the implied strength or will behind the actions described (e.g. vv. 29, 39, 41–42).

As David looks back over his life, he sees 'God and me together' as the theme tune. It's all been a story of partnership. He knows that he could not have done it without the Lord – in fact, the Lord has directed the whole operation. Different emphases swirl through David's poetic summary of this relationship.

(i) Can-do

In verses 26–33 the leading theme is the way in which the Lord supplied David's *strength* to do what he did, leading him, strengthening him and keeping him secure. At the lowest point of all, when Ziklag had been sacked and all the families captured, including David's two wives, and his men started blaming him and threatening to stone him, we read that 'David strengthened himself in the LORD his God'[58] – and an amazing (though extremely testing and exhausting) deliverance then followed.

(ii) Know-how

In verses 34–38 the focus falls on the *know-how* and *skill* which the Lord gave David: even his practical warrior skills are the Lord's training! His shield is *the shield of your salvation* (v. 35), the means by which *the Lord* keeps him safe (although of course it was David's arm which held it firm).

(iii) Back-up

In verses 39–42 the emphasis moves to the Lord's agency in the outcome of David's battles. It was not that the Lord just gave him the strength and the skills, and then left it up to David to win: *You made my enemies turn their backs to me* (v. 40). The Lord was alongside David in the battle, turning a deaf ear to the prayers of his enemies (v. 41).

---

58. 1 Sam. 30:6.

(iv) Success!

In verses 43–45 it is not surprising that David ascribes his final success to the Lord's agency. *You made me head of the nations* (v. 43). The language here is reminiscent of Psalm 2:7–11, which is likewise about the *synergy* – the concerted action – between the Lord and his anointed king.

6. Conclusions (vv. 46–50)

And so David comes back to the four themes with which he began: God as *rock* (v. 46), deliverance from *enemies* (vv. 47–48), *praise* (v. 49), and confidence for the future (v. 50). These are all themes that we can take for ourselves from this psalm, and apply to whatever enemies we face, too. David here claims a special covenant relationship with God as his *anointed* (v. 50), underlying the relationship described in the psalm as a whole. But this does not set David apart from us, giving him a special relationship with God greater than ours. Paul takes the language of the Davidic covenant promise in 2 Samuel 7 and applies it to all of us who are God's children in Christ – and God himself does the same in John's vision in Revelation 21. We are 'sons and daughters' of God, just like David![59] So this relationship, and this confidence in the face of our 'enemies', whatever they are, is open to us too.

Paul quotes verse 49 in Romans 15:9, where he gives it his own special application. *For this I will extol you, O LORD, among the nations, and sing praises to your name.* David seems to mean (probably) that he will make sure his story is not secret, so that other (Gentile) nations will know that his success is down to the Lord's agency. But Paul goes further: the *whole purpose* of God's blessing of Israel is for the sake of the Gentiles.

> Christ became a servant of the circumcised on behalf of God's truth, to establish
> the promises given to the fathers that the Gentiles will glorify God for his mercy,
> as it is written, 'For this reason I will praise your name among the Gentiles . . .'[60]

From Paul's perspective, commissioned as apostle to the Gentiles, and leaving behind his exclusive commitment to Israel as God's people,[61] the whole purpose

---

59. The promise in 2 Sam. 7:14 is quoted in 2 Cor. 6:18 and Rev. 21:7. Paul makes it both plural and bi-gender, to make it clear that we all, male and female, stand in the same covenant relationship to God as David did, if we belong to Christ.

60. Rom. 15:8–9.

61. Phil. 3:4–9.

of Israel's history, and testimony to the grace of God – culminating in the glorious grace of *Christ* – is *so that there may be a universal witness*, and the Gentiles will discover how wonderful this God is, and learn to worship him too. Finally, I think that David would have been pleased about that.

It is appropriate that we end on this universal note as we move on to our next passage in our search for the biblical theology of the second coming of Jesus Christ, for this passage takes us onto a world stage, and reveals even more of the dimensions of the *rule of God* that Jesus' coming will bring.

3. THE COMING OF 'ONE LIKE A SON OF MAN' (DANIEL 7)

1. Introduction

The book of Daniel is proportionately the most referred-to Old Testament book in the New. The most widely used edition of the Greek New Testament lists 201 allusions to, or quotations of, Daniel in the New Testament. And of these, no fewer than fifty-nine are listed for Daniel 7, including six direct quotations of Daniel 7:13–14.[1] We will meet quite a few of these in later chapters!

The New Testament interest in Daniel 7 arises especially from the fact that Jesus' favourite self-designation in the Gospels is 'the Son of Man' (he uses this expression thirty times in Matthew's Gospel alone), and a link with the 'one like a Son of Man' in Daniel 7:13 is acknowledged by nearly all. For instance in Matthew 24:30 Jesus says, 'Then the sign of the Son of Man will appear in heaven . . . and they will see the Son of Man coming in the clouds of heaven with power and great glory.' Here the accompanying references to 'the clouds of heaven' and to 'power and great glory' make the allusion to Daniel 7:13 very clear. However, when the expression 'the Son of Man' appears in the New Testament (on some eighty-two occasions in total), the definite article ('the') is

---

1. K. Aland et al. (eds.), *Novum Testamentum Graece*, 27th ed. (Stuttgart: Deutsche Bibelgesellschaft, 1994), pp. 797–798.

used with it all but once.[2] But no article is used in Daniel 7; he did not see 'the Son of Man' but 'one like a son of man'. Probably, in adding the definite article, the New Testament writers were saying, 'Now we know what Daniel's vision truly means! That figure, the one "like a son of man" – Jesus – fits that picture. He is *the* Danielic Son of Man.'[3]

This shift, between the vision itself and its use in the New Testament, is most important for us to note. Daniel, as we will see, leaves the identity of this 'one in human likeness'[4] extremely vague. He also leaves very vague the nature of the 'coming' of this humanlike figure in the clouds. So, vivid and wonderful though the vision in Daniel 7:13 is, it is not a prophecy of the second coming, nor even of the coming of Jesus – even though it is applied to both in the New Testament. *It is more significant than this*, as part of the theological framework that sits around the second coming in biblical theology. That is why we need to look carefully at the whole chapter, and ask what this vision meant for Daniel, so that we can then understand its further application to Jesus, and thus give ourselves a good foundation for understanding the meaning of the second coming for us today.

Daniel 7 records a visionary experience given to Daniel in Babylon in about 550 BC.[5] We are thus in the same time period as Psalm 89 – the time of the

---

2. John 5:27 is the sole exception.

3. This is the view – amongst others – of C. F. D. Moule, *The Origin of Christology* (Cambridge: Cambridge University Press, 1977), pp. 13–14. There is a truly vast literature on the meaning and background of the use of 'the Son of Man' in the Gospels, but the significance and influence of Dan. 7:13 is one of the core elements agreed by nearly all. More on this below.

4. This is the translation of the phrase given by John Goldingay in his commentary on Daniel (John E. Goldingay, *Daniel*, Word Biblical Commentary [Dallas: Word, 1991], p. 142). Goldingay uses the shorthand 'humanlike figure' in his exposition.

5. Dan. 7:1 gives us a very clear date. Many have suggested that the book of Daniel dates from the second century BC (rather than from the sixth century, as indicated by this and other time-notices in the book), because of the clarity of the way in which it predicts the events of 167 BC, when the Syrian king Antiochus IV Epiphanes took over the temple in Jerusalem, suspended the daily sacrifices, and set up pagan worship there. (The books of Maccabees describe the sacrificial fightback that eventually restored the temple and its worship.) We do not need to solve this question of date in order to explore how Dan. 7 provides a theological frame for the New Testament teaching about the second coming of Jesus, so we will take Daniel at face value as relating to the situation of the exiles in sixth-century Babylon. The issues were much the same in the Maccabean period!

exile, when Israel had lost her home and her temple, and seemed to have lost the covenant with her God too. The powers of the world around seemed to have overwhelmed little Israel, and swamped her special relationship with the Lord. The God of Israel, who had spoken so clearly through Moses and the prophets, and who had chosen Jerusalem to be his secure, immovable home in their midst,[6] seemed *himself* to have been overthrown by the more powerful gods of Babylon and their terrible armies. The whole book of Daniel relates to this situation – to this awful need to find a way of understanding how Yahweh, the God of Israel, has not himself been defeated, but is still in charge, and still committed to his people.

More than any other book of the Bible, therefore (except perhaps Revelation), Daniel is about the *sovereignty of God* in and over his world. He is 'the God of heaven',[7] who has *given* to King Nebuchadnezzar, the conqueror of Jerusalem, 'the kingdom, the power, the might, and the glory'[8] which he enjoys. Eventually Nebuchadnezzar recognizes this. Through losing it all, and then regaining it, he learns that 'the Most High has sovereignty over the kingdom of mortals',[9] and that 'his sovereignty is an everlasting sovereignty, and his kingdom endures from generation to generation'.[10] The Lord gives 'kingdom' to whomever he wills, even to huge pagan rulers like Nebuchadnezzar – and he takes it away when he wills also, as he does in the case of King Belshazzar in Daniel 5. He is 'the Most High God', so *his* is the judgment that finds Belshazzar 'wanting', and removes his kingdom from him.[11]

However Daniel is not just concerned to *assert* that, contrary to appearances, the power of Babylon is secondary to the power of God. There are two further vital elements that undergird this message: *revelation* and *experiential testimony*. We have just met both of these in Psalm 18, where they come together. God revealed himself experientially to David in numerous practical interventions, and David then summarizes all those experiences in that wonderful, evocative language of revelation.

In Daniel the two are teased apart, as we see (on the one hand) Daniel and his friends discovering the practical power of God to rescue them from the

---

6. See Deut. 12:5–7; and (e.g.) Pss 46:5–7; 48:4–8 (note 'for ever', v. 8).

7. Dan. 2:18–19, 28, 37, 44.

8. Dan. 2:37.

9. Dan. 4:25.

10. Dan. 4:34.

11. Dan. 5:23–27, 30.

fiery furnace[12] and from the lions' den,[13] and (on the other) God's power to 'reveal mysteries'. This latter strand is emphasized from the start in Daniel, and is connected closely to his ultimate power over kings and rulers. Daniel's blessing summarizes it:

> Blessed be the name of God from age to age,
> for wisdom and power are his.
> He changes times and seasons,
> deposes kings and sets up kings;
> he gives wisdom to the wise,
> and knowledge to those who have understanding.
> He reveals deep and hidden things;
> he knows what is in the darkness,
> and light dwells with him.[14]

King Nebuchadnezzar is the first recipient of this blessing, as Daniel recounts to him his troubling dream, and its interpretation.[15] Nebuchadnezzar saw a four-part statue, symbolizing four great kingdoms, his own included; but then the statue was completely destroyed and replaced by a stone that 'became a great mountain and filled the whole earth'.[16] This stone, Daniel tells the astonished king, is a kingdom that the God of heaven himself will set up, 'that shall never be destroyed, nor shall this kingdom be left to another people. It shall crush all these kingdoms and bring them to an end, and it shall stand for ever.'[17]

Of course, in this revelation to Nebuchadnezzar the two strands – the revelatory and the experiential – come together again, as *the pagan king* discovers by experience that 'there is a God in heaven who reveals mysteries',[18] and is saved from his perplexity and given at least the beginnings of a fuller understanding of who he truly is, in God's world.

So Daniel's response to the crisis of the exile contains these three interconnected elements:

---

12. Dan. 3.
13. Dan. 6.
14. Dan. 2:20–22.
15. Dan. 2:31–45.
16. Dan. 2:35.
17. Dan. 2:44.
18. Dan. 2:28.

(a) A glorious proclamation of the continuing sovereignty of the God of Israel over the whole world, in spite of the apparent denial of this by events.

(b) The proof of his sovereignty through wonderful acts of deliverance, albeit entailing awful hardship for the faithful people concerned. The God who acted to save Israel in the past acts still for his people, when they trust their lives into his hands. He both saves his people, and convinces their oppressors that he is truly 'the God of heaven'.

(c) Visionary revelations of the future which entail a *story* showing how God's sovereignty, currently veiled, will become much more concrete and clear on the earth.

Daniel 7 brings together (a) and (c) here. But whereas the vision in chapter 2 was given for the sake of the king, this one – although parallel in many ways – is given for Daniel's sake, at the beginning of the reign of the king who, we have already seen, is not like Nebuchadnezzar his father, and does not honour 'the God in whose power is your very breath, and to whom belong all your ways'.[19] Similarly, Daniel has just (in the structure of the book) discovered that, even when kings seem all-powerful, they are yet part of a bigger system which is corrupt and opposed to God, and before which even the king himself may be powerless.[20]

But God is not powerless. The God who has just delivered Daniel from the lions, now reveals the wider, future deliverance of his people. But before we delve into the chapter we need to note how the three elements of Daniel's message match the three focuses in our theology of time and history:

(a) *The present-as-present*: 'He is the living God!' is Darius' proclamation.[21] Whatever their circumstances, God's people can know that, right now, at this fleeting moment we call the present, God is alive and is on the throne.

(b) *The past-as-present*: The great acts of deliverance recorded here (the fiery furnace, the lions' den), taking place in exile in Babylon, invite us to prove God in our experience too, so that we too may have stories to tell of how he met us in our hardship. This is like the 'reframing' that we saw in Psalms 89 and 90.

---

19. Dan. 5:23.

20. This is the situation in ch. 6, where King Darius has to condemn Daniel to the lions' den, even with a prayer that Daniel's God may deliver him from the punishment that the king himself is inflicting! (Dan. 6:16).

21. Dan. 6:26.

(c) *The future-as-present:* Daniel's great visions, and in particular chapter 7 which sits right at the heart of the book,[22] give us a way of holding the future in our imagination right now. 'This is our world', we say, agreeing that God has truly spoken in this vision, which is a word to us too, just as it was to Daniel and his people when first given.

2. Structure

The chapter has quite a simple structure, framed by two narrative notes (vv. 1, 28) which play an important role in setting up the vision. They tell us that Daniel immediately *wrote down the dream* (v. 1), thus expressing (a) its solidity, God-givenness and significance, and (b) its 'accountability' before future events. Through writing, the dream becomes public property, so that people can evaluate it and either accept it or reject it as a word of God for them. The concluding note (v. 28) shows that, even if we accept it, this dream does not offer easy comfort for the future. It is hard to hear. Daniel's final terror matches the disturbance of spirit and terror he feels within the dream itself (v. 15).

Between these narrative notes, the vision falls into two halves: the vision itself (vv. 2–14), and its interpretation by 'one of the attendants' (vv. 15–27). A more detailed analysis runs like this:

A. Vision (vv. 2–14)
     a) The four beasts and their power – part 1 *(prose)* (vv. 2–8)
     b) The thrones of judgment *(poetry)* (vv. 9–10)
     c) The four beasts and their power – part 2 *(prose)* (vv. 11–12)
     d) Kingdom bestowed *(poetry)* (vv. 13–14)
B. Interpretation (vv. 15–27)
     a) First Q&A – the whole thing (vv. 16–18)
     b) Second Q&A – the fourth beast (vv. 19–27)

We will look at each of the main sections in turn.

---

22. Commentators agree that, structurally, Dan. 7 forms a vital centre for the whole book. The largely narrative chs. 1 – 6 give way to a series of private visions which occupy chs. 7 – 12, beginning with this vision which sets the tone for all the rest. Goldingay calls it 'the hinge of the Book of Daniel as a whole' (Goldingay, *Daniel*, p. 159).

3. The four beasts and the thrones of God: Colliding kingdoms (vv. 2–14)

The alternating prose and poetry in this section (visible in most Bibles in the print layout) underlines the structure here. In response to the awful power of the beasts, which seem to make victims of us all, *thrones were set in place* (v. 9), and poetic language replaces the stark prose with which the beasts are described. Two simple words in both the Aramaic and the Greek – 'thrones, set!' – suffice to counteract the terrifying power of the four awful beasts Daniel has just described. And then in the second prose-poetry cycle (vv. 11–14), the coming of *one like a son of man*[23] parallels the setting of the thrones. In both cases the 'beasts' more than meet their match, as the overwhelming power of heaven is revealed.

a. The four beasts (vv. 2–8, 11–12)

In fact God's power has already been at work, secretly, within the terrifying vision of the beasts (vv. 2–8). Daniel chooses passive verbs, in his descriptions of each of them. Beast One – the lion with eagle's wings – had its wings *plucked off*, and then it *was lifted up* and *made to stand on two feet like a human being.* And then *a human mind was given* to this beast (v. 4). Similarly Beast Two – the bear – *was told, 'Arise, devour many bodies!'* (v. 5), and of Beast Three – the leopard with four wings and four heads – we read *dominion was given to* it (v. 6).

Who is the agent implied by these passive verbs, the one actually doing the 'plucking off', 'lifting up', 'telling', etc.? Only one, in Daniel's universe, *gives dominion*. Daniel has chosen to phrase his description in a way which points already to the agency and sovereignty of God, lying behind the power and rapacity of the beasts.

The first beast reminds us strongly of Nebuchadnezzar himself. In his case, we have already seen this divine sovereignty at work. The plucking of the wings and the gift of a human mind reminds us of the story in Daniel 4 about Nebuchadnezzar's loss of his rule through madness, and then the restoration of his mind, now filled with a new gratitude to 'the King of

---

23. NRSV uses the expression 'one like a human being' here to translate the Aramaic *kĕbar 'ĕnāš* in Dan. 7:13, and offers the more literal 'one like a son of man' as an alternative. I prefer this more literal translation (followed e.g. by NIV and CEV) because of the connection it allows us to see between Daniel and the use of this term by Jesus in the Gospels.

heaven'[24] to replace the self-adulation that had brought him low. God has already been deeply at work in the first beast.

The second and the third, too, illustrate the truth already unpacked, that rulers only have their power in the world – *even their power to oppress with violence* – by divine permission. This does not make God the agent of their violence. In *devouring many bodies* (v. 5) the bear is only doing what comes naturally to bears. But God has allowed the bear to be, so that the devouring is happening on his watch. By this theology, Daniel allows that God did not lose his throne when the armies of Nebuchadnezzar sacked Jerusalem and carried the people into exile amid dreadful slaughter.

Similarly, in the case of the awful Beast Four, the worst of the lot, we read that *three of the . . . horns were plucked up by the roots* to make room for the little horn with *a mouth speaking arrogantly* (v. 8). Even though (we learn later) this mouth *shall speak words against the Most High* (v. 25), we should probably still see in the passive verb (*were plucked*) the implied agency of God. He is in charge, even when kings or empires become atheistic and refuse to accept any constraint on their power from divine sources.

How should we interpret these beasts? They are identified as *four kings who shall arise out of the earth* in the first Q&A exchange (v. 17), but generally inter-preters have seen them as empires, and have worked hard to identify a sequence of four world or regional empires that might be intended here, starting with the Babylonian as the first. A sequence followed by not a few evangelical interpreters – and indeed by many of the early church fathers – identifies the Babylonian, Medo-Persian, Greek and Roman empires here.[25] But the careful discussion by John Goldingay, reviewing the many suggestions made by scholars, reveals how difficult the identification is.[26] The interpreting attendant in verse 17 suggests that all *four kings* are still to come, but the first had already been around for a long time, if it is identified as Babylon – and as we have already seen, the imagery of the first beast certainly suggests Nebuchadnezzar.

---

24. Dan. 4:37. The imagery of the lion with wings could well have been drawn from the decoration on the Ishtar Gate in Babylon, where about 120 lions with wing-like extensions to their manes, in glazed brick relief on the walls, led worshippers along the processional way from the gate to the temple. It was built only about twenty years before the date given to Daniel's vision here.

25. So, for example, Joyce G. Baldwin, *Daniel: An Introduction and Commentary*, Tyndale Old Testament Commentaries (Leicester: Inter-Varsity Press, 1978), p. 147. See Goldingay, *Daniel*, p. xxxi for a summary of early church views.

26. Goldingay, *Daniel*, pp. 173–176.

The book of Daniel itself might suggest *either* that these four kings are the same as the four kingdoms represented by the parts of Nebuchadnezzar's statue in his dream in chapter 2 (but in that case, the fourth kingdom is weak and crumbling, not the most terrifying of all, as here), *or* that they are the four kings mentioned in the book so far, Nebuchadnezzar, Belshazzar, Darius and Cyrus. But three of these are not still future; Cyrus has literally only just been mentioned,[27] and Daniel's readers in any age would find it hard to identify as this fourth, terrible beast the king whom the Lord calls 'my anointed' in Isaiah,[28] and who was instrumental in bringing Israel back from exile![29] Cyrus certainly did not *speak words against the Most High* (v. 25) – quite the contrary.

This is a case for biblical theology. It is an excellent example of the way in which, when we listen carefully to the whole of Scripture, the Bible itself directs our task of interpretation. We already have a scriptural interpretation of Daniel's four beasts in Revelation 13, which gives insight into how John, the writer of another apocalyptic vision,[30] 'heard' Daniel's vision when he was searching for language to describe his own. I have no doubt that John actually saw[31] what he describes. But in writing his description, he has chosen to use language which directs our attention to Daniel 7. In turn – assuming that John is not completely misusing Daniel! – this could give us some insight into how we, too, should read Daniel.

John takes Daniel's four beasts and combines them into one, great, composite beast, which was like a leopard with bear's feet, a lion's mouth and ten horns.[32] Similarly, John's beast speaks terrible blasphemies against God,[33] and makes war on God's people and conquers them.[34] It seems that John was not concerned to preserve a tradition in which the symbolism of Daniel's four beasts needed to be 'unlocked' by discovering which empires they represented. He just wasn't reading them that way. *Together* they symbolize pagan, secular power, which can range from *not too bad*, like Nebuchadnezzar and Cyrus (Beast One), to *completely*

---

27. Dan. 6:28.

28. Isa. 45:1.

29. Ezra 1:1–11.

30. The command to John to 'write' frames the book of Revelation (see 1:11; 21:5), so that John's words become a 'book' which must be 'kept' in every sense (Rev. 1:3; 22:7, 9, 18–19).

31. Rev. 13:1.

32. Rev. 13:1–2.

33. Rev. 13:6.

34. Rev. 13:7; cf. Dan. 7:21.

dreadful (Beast Four). When Daniel says that they were all *different from one another* (v. 3), it seems that he is not just referring to their appearance. Maybe there are *four* because 'four' is the number that expresses *earthly comprehensiveness* (because of the four points of the compass and the four great winds that blow from them).[35] Wherever you look, empires and their kings will be like this – on a spectrum from 'reasonable' to 'terrible'.

This helps us to understand the mysterious verses 11–12. Daniel sees the fourth beast being completely destroyed (v. 11), but in the case of the others, *their dominion was taken away, but their lives were prolonged for a season and a time* (v. 12). It seems as though Daniel is telling us that the worst excesses of secular power – the persecutions, the blasphemies, the arrogant, atheistic self-assertion and the cruelties that always follow – will not last long. *That* beast will be destroyed. But 'secular power' as such will continue. We can't get away from that. And yet it doesn't have *dominion*, even while it lasts. This *dominion* is given in verse 6, and taken away in verse 12. The word (Aramaic *šolṭān*) means 'mastery, domineering'[36] – the kind of autocratic, tyrannical power which kings sometimes seem to have,[37] but on which there is usually some curb or restraint. Tyrants always fall, even if they seem to be invincible. They do not have ultimate *dominion* – that belongs elsewhere!

If Daniel was indeed writing at the time of the persecution by Antiochus Epiphanes, the Greek emperor who abolished the sacrifices in the temple in 167 BC and regarded himself as an 'epiphany' of God on earth, his readers would certainly have known which beast to identify him with. But even if Daniel received and wrote this vision in 550 BC, readers at the time of the Maccabees who resisted Antiochus would still have read his vision this way. And sure enough, Antiochus fell. His dominion was taken away. And readers of Revelation would have seen the awful power of Rome, especially the persecuting emperors Nero and Domitian, mirrored both in Daniel's fourth beast and in John's composite beast. But their power, too, passed away.

We too can use these visions, read this way, to interpret secular power of all kinds, and to help form a Christian world view for today. But to do this, we need to add the poetic sections to the prose analysis of secular power.

---

35. This is the symbolism associated with the number four also in Revelation: see Rev. 7:1, and the fourfold expression 'tribe, language, people and nation' (e.g. 5:9) which summarizes the whole human world. This expression occurs seven times in Revelation, but never in precisely the same form.

36. Francis Brown, S. R. Driver and Charles A. Briggs, *A Hebrew and English Lexicon of the Old Testament* (Oxford: Clarendon Press, 1972), p. 1020.

37. See Eccl. 8:4, where the equivalent Hebrew word is used.

b. The thrones of God and the gift of the kingdom (vv. 9–10, 13–14)

Daniel's vision of God is awesome indeed! In verse 9 we have the only direct description of the appearance of God himself in the Old Testament. Ezekiel gets close, but all he manages is 'a likeness, like the appearance of a human'.[38] Daniel is much more direct. There are *thrones*, and among them *an Ancient One took his throne* (v. 9) – literally 'an Ancient of Days'. God looks like the oldest and wisest you can imagine. Then attention moves to the blazing brightness of his appearance, and in particular to the *fiery flames . . . burning fire . . . stream of fire* which make up *his throne* and *flow out from his presence* (vv. 9–10). Ezekiel also saw 'something that looked like fire' enclosing God and his throne,[39] and we met 'glowing coals' that 'flamed forth' along with 'devouring fire from his mouth' in Psalm 18.[40]

In terms of physical imagery, it would be hard to find a more powerful image of *unstoppable, overwhelming destructiveness* than a pyroclastic flow from an erupting volcano. Both David and Daniel draw on this imagery. No beast can stand against it – the mighty fourth beast is simply *given over to be burned with fire* (v. 11), and its arrogant voice silenced.

But this is actually a court scene. In verses 9–10 the Ancient of Days takes his seat as judge, and around him stand myriads of attendants.[41] In the middle of these standing hosts, *the court sat*, although only the Ancient of Days has been described as sitting. *The books were opened* (v. 10) suggests several things: the laws to be applied, the evidence to be considered, and the judgments to be issued.[42] Perhaps especially that last one, because what immediately follows is a two-part judgment issued from the throne: first, the beasts are dealt with, as we have seen (vv. 11–12), and then secondly, the dominion taken from the beasts is given to another, the 'one like a son of man' who suddenly appears in verse 13. Verses 13–14 are worth quoting in full:

> *As I watched in the night visions,*
> *I saw one like a human being*
> *coming with the clouds of heaven.*
> *And he came to the Ancient One*
> *and was presented before him.*

---

38. Ezek. 1:26, literal translation.
39. Ezek. 1:27.
40. Ps. 18:8.
41. They appear again later in Rev. 5:11–12.
42. Probably not, here, the names of the saved, as in the 'other book' in Rev. 20:12.

To him was given dominion
and glory and kingship,
that all peoples, nations and languages
should serve him.
His dominion is an everlasting dominion
that shall not pass away,
and his kingship is one
that shall never be destroyed.

This is so surprising! *The Ancient of Days shares his rulership with another.* Perhaps this is why *thrones* (plural) *were set* at the start of the vision, although Daniel does not see this *one like a son of man* occupying a throne. Effectively, though, he acquires the *everlasting dominion* which Darius recognizes as God's, and God's alone, at the climax of the preceding chapter.[43]

Actually that sharing of God's rulership has been going on throughout the book. Daniel has emphasized that God alone is the giver of kingship.[44] Nebuchadnezzar had already received from God the *dominion and glory and kingship* given here to the Son of Man.[45] We have heard, too, of the coming kingdom that 'the God of heaven' himself will set up, replacing all earthly empires.[46] Now, we discover that God will do this through a regent who will receive the dominion from God as these earthly emperors did, but who will rule everlastingly as God alone does.

We need to underline the *earthliness* of this. Goldingay suggests that this judgment scene is taking place on earth. The vision starts on earth in verse 2, with the sea giving up the beasts, and there is nothing to suggest that Daniel starts looking in a different direction in verse 9. The action does not switch suddenly to heaven.[47] So when he sees this 'one like a son of man' *coming with the clouds of heaven* (v. 13), it is from the perspective of earth that he sees. The vision is therefore very like the rescue vision of Psalm 18, where the Lord himself comes down surrounded by clouds, fire and brightness, to save his servant in distress.

The difference here is the universality of it. Driven by the trauma of the exile, Daniel is receiving and writing a *universal vision* of the kingdom that God will

---

43. Dan. 6:26; cf. 4:34.
44. E.g. Dan. 2:21, 37; 4:17; 5:18.
45. Dan 2:37; 5:18.
46. Dan. 2:44.
47. Goldingay, *Daniel*, pp. 164–165.

set up on earth. The phrase *all peoples, nations and languages* (v. 14) has appeared on several occasions to underline the universality of the rule of the earthly emperors who are here being replaced.[48] Darius' letter is addressed 'to all the peoples, nations, and languages that dwell in all the earth'.[49] Never mind that Darius, king of the Medes, never actually ruled over 'all the earth';[50] he is depicted as a universal ruler, and that is what is important for the way in which the vision in chapter 7 engages with the themes of the book as a whole.

This is vital for our understanding of the New Testament passages to which we will shortly turn. When Jesus proclaims, 'The time is fulfilled, and the kingdom of God has come near',[51] and when he claims that 'the Son of Man has authority on earth to forgive sins',[52] he is asserting the arrival of this universal, earthly rule of God. Of course, there is much that is puzzling about this – not least, that the dominion of the earthly powers is not *replaced* by the arrival of God's kingdom in Jesus. The power of Rome remains very real. So ultimately Jesus says to Pilate, 'My kingdom is not of this world',[53] meaning (in that context) that his kingdom does not base itself on the same means of power as earthly kingdoms like that of Pilate – in particular, on armies and physical force. However there *will* be a day when that glorious kingdom of love will replace all earthly rule. Humiliated, about to be condemned and publicly shamed and executed on a Roman cross, a helpless victim of Jewish and Roman power in strange cahoots, Jesus says to the high priest, 'You will see the Son of Man seated at the right hand of the Power, and coming with the clouds of heaven.'[54]

And so 'the coming of the Son of Man'[55] is stretched across both comings of Jesus in the New Testament. He really exercises the authority of God in his ministry, displayed not just in the forgiveness of sins, but also in his rulership over the physical universe – in his healings and in his power over nature. But there is a further coming yet to be, 'with power and great glory',[56] when 'all the tribes of the earth will mourn' and 'he will send his angels with a great trumpet

---

48. See Dan. 3:4, 7; 4:1; 5:19; 6:25.

49. Dan. 6:25, RSV.

50. In fact, this particular King Darius is not known outside the book of Daniel.

51. Mark 1:15.

52. Mark 2:10.

53. John 18:36.

54. Mark 14:62.

55. Matt. 24:37.

56. Matt. 24:30.

call, and they will gather his elect from the four winds'[57] – when the full Danielic vision will become a reality on earth.

As we will see, Daniel gives the whole biblical theology of the second coming of Jesus *its essentially political setting and relevance*. Jesus' kingdom replaces that of the earthly powers around us. As N. T. Wright summarizes it: 'The spirit comes to equip the church for the hard and costly task of bearing witness to the overthrow of the world's powers, to the exaltation of Jesus as Lord in their place, and to the renewal of creation itself.'[58]

This witness has two focuses to it, visible in the revelatory and experiential elements of Daniel's message. He writes a word from God which proclaims the overthrow of all earthly power, however great, by the kingdom of God itself; and he lives out a practical testimony to God's power at work right now, to make his kingdom real in the lives of those who trust him. We do not yet see the overthrow of the powers, but we see beyond them to the greater, glorious power of the kingdom of God, already real among us. Ralph Davis comments, 'Seeing this secret behind history may not keep God's people from pain but should keep them from panic; we may still be fearful but should not be frantic.'[59] Daniel illustrates this for us beautifully, as he quietly prays and seeks the mercy of his God – because he knows that *his* mercy is far more important than that of King Darius.[60]

Before we move to the New Testament there is another amazing twist to be met in Daniel 7, which also sets the scene dramatically for the fulfilment of this vision in the New, and which turns out to be absolutely vital for our theology of the second coming of Jesus Christ.

4. Daniel's terror and the interpretation of the vision (vv. 15–28)

The second half of the chapter is structured around two Q&A exchanges between Daniel and *one of the attendants* (v. 16) – presumably one of the vast crowd of onlookers who surround the action and likewise watch[61] while *the*

---

57. Matt. 24:30–31.

58. N. T. Wright, *Creation, Power and Truth: The Gospel in a World of Cultural Confusion* (London: SPCK, 2013), p. 85.

59. Dale Ralph Davis, *The Message of Daniel: His Kingdom Cannot Fail*, The Bible Speaks Today (Nottingham: Inter-Varsity Press, 2013), p. 101.

60. Dan. 6:10–11.

61. The word 'watch' (Aramaic *ḥăzāh*) is used nine times in vv. 1–13.

beast was put to death (v. 11) and the dominion is given to the Son of Man. They are described as *attending* the Ancient of Days in verse 10, and the same verb is used in verse 16. The first Q&A concerns a general question about *the truth concerning all this* (v. 16), which receives a brief and general reply (vv. 17–18). The second is a much more specific question *concerning the fourth beast*, which entails a detailed redescription of the beast (vv. 19–20); and it seems that, as Daniel describes it, the vision is activated again, and a further element is added (vv. 21–22). The much fuller reply to the second question (vv. 23–27) picks up this extension of the vision also.

Why is the vision of the beast extended in this way, in the context of Daniel's second question? The answer, I suggest, is to do with the amazing twist that appears in *the interpretation of the matter* given in answer to the first question (vv. 17–18):

> *As for these four great beasts, four kings shall arise out of the earth. But the holy ones of the Most High shall receive the kingdom and possess the kingdom for ever – for ever and ever.*

Here the interpretation of the beasts as *kings* is strangely matched by the interpretation of 'one like a son of man' as *the holy ones of the Most High*. Two things are deeply puzzling here: (1) why is the Son of Man figure depicted as an individual, kingly figure in the vision, if in fact the vision is of some group – *the holy ones* – receiving the kingdom? Does Jesus misuse Daniel's vision in applying it to an individual figure – himself? And (2) who, anyway, are these *holy ones of the Most High* who receive the kingdom and possess it for ever?

It is the New Testament angle, here, which makes the first puzzle particularly pressing. Jesus clearly does not stand in a tradition of interpretation which saw the 'son of man' figure as just a corporate symbol. However it does seem that its *mysteriousness* is vital to the way in which Jesus turns it into a title and applies it to himself. It was not an obvious messianic title in the first century, and there is some evidence that, in first-century Aramaic, 'son of man' could be a slightly roundabout way of referring to oneself. So some scholars have argued that Jesus intended no particular reference to Daniel 7:13, and that all we meet, in fact, is a rather quaint and idiosyncratic turn of phrase which he liked to use.[62] Others, on the other hand, see in Jesus' use of the phrase a full-blown claim to be *the* Danielic Son of Man invested with God's kingly power.

---

62. Most notably, Geza Vermes, *Jesus the Jew: A Historian's Reading of the Gospels* (London: Collins, 1973).

We can apply to Jesus' use of 'the son of man' the same rubric that he himself spoke over his use of parables: 'If you have ears to hear, then hear!'[63] People hear what they feel inclined to hear in his usage, and this applies as much to contemporary scholars as to those who first heard him. And one vital aspect of the elusive mysteriousness of this title is the way in which Daniel's angelic attendant interprets 'one like a son of man' corporately. Does this influence Jesus' usage at all?

To get a handle on this, let us address the second puzzle – who are these *holy ones*, anyway? The term is used several times in Daniel 4 and 5 to refer to heavenly beings – not named as angels, but this could be a useful shorthand. For instance, Nebuchadnezzar writes about Daniel being 'endowed with a spirit of the holy gods' – literally, 'the spirit of the gods, the holy ones, [is] on him'.[64] And in Daniel 4:17 it seems clear that 'the holy ones' are angelic beings; the 'decision' that Nebuchadnezzar should be deprived of his power for a while has been 'given by order of the holy ones'.[65] So an obvious first candidate would be that 'one like a son of man' stands for a group of angelic beings who are invested with divine authority and dominion to replace that of the beasts.

But actually Daniel 4:17 makes it difficult to identify *the holy ones* in 7:18 as heavenly beings, for in 4:17 they *already* exercise God's power to judge. These 'holy ones', who share in heaven's decrees, reappear in Daniel 7 in the *ten thousand times ten thousand* who stand attending the Ancient of Days, and who help to constitute the *court* (v. 10) which issues the further judgment that authority and dominion should be given to 'one like a son of man'. It simply does not fit that they should also be the recipients of the gift. They surely do not award it to themselves.

So maybe *the holy ones of the Most High* are God's people – human *holy ones*, his 'holy nation',[66] the people who are 'holy to the LORD your God',[67] called to 'be holy, for I the LORD your God am holy'.[68] This interpretation is confirmed by the new visionary element added to Daniel's description of the fourth beast in verses 21–22:

> *As I looked, this horn made war with the holy ones and was prevailing over them, until the Ancient One came; then judgment was given for the holy ones of the Most High, and the time arrived when the holy ones gained possession of the kingdom.*

---

63. Mark 4:9.
64. Dan. 4:8 – see also 4:9, 18; 5:11.
65. Dan. 4:17.
66. Exod. 19:6.
67. A repeated description in Deuteronomy: 7:6; 14:2; 14:21; 26:19.
68. Lev. 19:2.

The *horn* seems to be a particularly dreadful ruler exercising the awful power of the fourth beast. What made this *horn* different in the earlier vision was its *arrogant words* (v. 11), but now Daniel sees it making war on the *holy ones* and *prevailing over them*. There is no doubt that Daniel's readers (whether in the sixth century BC or the second) would see their own experience mirrored here. The awful events of 587 BC, when God's people were annihilated and God's name besmirched, tell them (and us) how to read this vision – and indeed, how to apply it to every other situation when it becomes a commitment of public policy to persecute the people of God and to back this up with arrogant propaganda against God and his Christ. That is what is *different* about the fourth beast[69] – the persecution of God's 'holy' people.

This approach seems to be confirmed at the climax of the second interpretation, when Daniel's interpreter says that ultimately – after his defined period of rule[70] – the dominion of the beast will end and

> *the kingship and dominion*
> > *and the greatness of the kingdoms under the whole heaven*
> > *shall be given to the people of the holy ones of the Most High;*
> *their kingdom shall be an everlasting kingdom,*
> > *and all dominions shall serve and obey them.[71]*

The addition of *the people of* is suggestive here, and the best way of understanding the expression is to see the *of* as explicatory – the people *who are* the holy ones of the Most High. This must have been enormously encouraging to the exiles in Babylon (or to the persecuted people at the time of Antiochus

---

69. Ralph Davis points out that the fourth beast and the 'little horn' are described as 'different' on three occasions (vv. 7, 19, 24), so that its sheer difference from the other beasts is its chief defining characteristic (Davis, *Daniel*, pp. 95–96). And what makes it *different* is that it persecutes and overpowers God's people. It is not difficult to identify the power of the fourth beast in several regimes and cultures in today's world.

70. This seems to be the point of the *time, two times and half a time* for which he is permitted to rule (v. 25). The variation seems to say that the reign of such rulers may vary in length, but will always end. It is important that, in the Greek version of Daniel, the word *kairos* is used here, rather than *chronos*. *Kairos* expresses God's plan, his permission of dominion by the beast for a *kairos* period within his overall plan to give dominion to his people.

71. Dan. 7:27.

Epiphanes). They are still his *holy ones*, and it is not God's plan that the power of the beast will prevail over them for ever. Rather, it *is* God's plan that they themselves will one day rule the nations.

Does this help us to understand Jesus' application of the title 'Son of Man' to himself? Yes, in two ways.

First, it explains the range of his usage. Scholars have puzzled over the way in which, in some places, Jesus sees the 'Son of Man' not just as a glorious, reigning figure, but as suffering, with nowhere to lay his head,[72] criticized by the upright,[73] and destined for rejection, suffering and death.[74] A favourite solution has been to propose that Jesus combined the 'son of man' vision from Daniel 7 with the 'suffering servant' prophecy in Isaiah 53, identifying himself with both figures. There is certainly some truth in this, as we can see particularly in Mark 10:45: 'The Son of Man came not to be served but to serve, and to give his life as a ransom for many.' This is strange, in the light of Daniel's vision that *all peoples, nations and languages [will] serve him* (v. 14). It is almost as though Jesus is denying that aspect of the vision, and directing our attention instead to Isaiah 53:10–12, to which the second half of the verse clearly alludes.

But it is not an either-or. Jesus clearly draws positively on Daniel 7:14 elsewhere, as we have seen. And it is vital for us to note that a suffering Son of Man is also clearly presented in Daniel 7, because of this amazing 'twist' in the interpretation of 7:14, whereby the Son of Man becomes a corporate figure. He identifies himself totally with his persecuted people, so that they share his rule and he shares their sufferings, just like the suffering servant of Isaiah 53. To quote Ralph Davis again, 'So the servants have no kingdom apart from their King, and the King does not reign without his servants. Jesus just cannot stand being separated from his people.'[75]

Secondly, it helps explain the two sides of Jesus' identification with God's people. On the one hand, he stands alongside people in their sin, need and suffering, being baptized alongside repenting sinners,[76] feeling the pain of their helplessness,[77] bearing their sicknesses as their healer,[78] mourning with them,[79] feeling frustrated

---

72. Matt. 8:20; i.e., rejected by the people who will not offer him hospitality.

73. Matt. 11:19.

74. Matt. 12:40; Mark 8:31; 9:31.

75. Davis, *Daniel*, p. 104.

76. Matt. 3:13–17.

77. Matt. 9:36.

78. Matt. 8:16–17.

79. John 11:35.

by their spiritual obtuseness,[80] touched by their alienation[81] and angered by their suffering.[82] All through the Gospels we see Jesus' amazing closeness to people, his refusal to allow even the most rotten human condition to repulse him as it repulsed others,[83] and his insight into people's deepest needs and longings.[84]

On the other hand, remarkably, we see his proclamation of the blessedness of those who mourn, his promise of the kingdom to the poor and the persecuted,[85] his invitation to the outcasts and the rejected[86] and promise of eternal life to those who give away everything for his sake[87] – and especially his promise to his disciples who have 'left everything to follow you':

> Truly I tell you, in the new creation, when the Son of Man will sit upon the throne of his glory, then you who have followed me will also sit upon twelve thrones, judging the twelve tribes of Israel.[88]

The identification is complete – he with them in their suffering, they with him in his glory. Jesus truly does help us to understand what the mysterious Daniel 7 is really about! The twelve disciples, symbolizing the whole people of God (the twelve tribes), symbolize also the reign of God's people with their Lord. Paul will later unpack further dimensions of this 'reign'. Because of Jesus, those who believe in him are destined to 'exercise dominion in life',[89] and behind such language it is hard not to discern the influence, and promise, of Daniel 7:27.

Now we move to the New Testament. But first, let us summarize the state of play: where have we got to, as we seek our biblical theology of the second coming?

---

80. Matt. 17:17; Mark 8:14–21.

81. John 4:7–10.

82. Mark 1:41: I think 'moved with anger' is Mark's original, rather than 'moved with pity'.

83. I think especially of the demoniac in Mark 5:1–13.

84. And here I think particularly of the woman in Luke 7:36–50.

85. Matt. 5:3–10.

86. E.g. Mark 2:15–17; Luke 19:1–10; John 4:13–15.

87. Mark 10:28–31.

88. Matt. 19:28.

89. Rom. 5:17.

EN ROUTE TO THE NEW . . .

Our three Old Testament passages have laid the foundation for our exploration of a series of New Testament passages which bear on the second coming of Jesus Christ, and together give a framework for the biblical theology which surrounds that glorious expectation. Before we move on, let us check what this framework is looking like for us. We can summarize it under four points.

1. Time has a very distinct quality in the Bible

Psalms 89 and 90 bring before us the distinction between *kairos* and *chronos*, at the heart of a biblical theology of time and history. From the perspective of *chronos*, time measured by clocks and calendars, everything can look completely confused. It can appear that God makes promises and then breaks them. History leaves us breathless with puzzlement. Indeed, from the perspective of *chronos* we are made for 'nothingness', complete insignificance, and it seems that God likes it that way. We pass away under his wrath, with nothing to mark our passing.

This (literally) *chronological* perspective has been enormously confirmed by scientific studies in evolution and earth prehistory. As mentioned above,[1]

---

1. See ch. 1, note 2.

Christians disagree strongly about whether we can accept an evolutionary history for ourselves. It is not surprising that some reject it passionately, because it seems to say that for billions of years of Earth's history God was absent, just letting the evolutionary process roll on, with whole species of creatures rising and disappearing until finally humankind appears in the last few seconds of the evolutionary 'day'. What kind of theology of God's intervention now, in Christ and by the Spirit, is possible, if he was so absent for so long? How can the cross and resurrection of Jesus Christ – coming so late in the day – be the centre of such a history?[2] And how can we have anything more than just a fleeting significance, as human beings?

But this view mistakes the nature of biblical time – in fact, gives *chronos* the whip hand over *kairos*. In the biblical perspective, *chronos* does not rescue us. *Chronos* is an enemy, because it robs us of our loved ones, limits our existence on the planet, and leaves us panting with confusion because we cannot 'see the end from the beginning' as God does.[3] *Chronos* is built into our bodies, whereas *kairos* inhabits our minds and hearts. In our imagination, we plan and hold the achievements we long for, and we celebrate (or regret) the vital *kairos*-moments of the past which have shaped who we are. We can hold our whole past and our whole future in our minds simultaneously, because we hold it in the form of a story which interprets the merely chronological 'facts'.

Biblically, *chronos* provides the framework within which God reveals himself to us, but the *kairos*-moments within it are those moments of revelation which give meaning to the story, and which could be spread over a whole lifetime until they can be clearly seen and interpreted, as in Psalm 18. But even at the beginning of a lifetime, we can hold them in imagination. I cuddle my four-year-old grand-daughter and hold in love before God all that could be true for her. Some things I know for sure, and they are all *kairos*-things: that God will love her and reveal himself to her in his own way; that when she falls there will be grace to sustain her; that if she trusts Jesus and seeks to serve the kingdom, that same grace will

2. For Christian arguments against evolution and in favour of a 'young earth', see e.g. the now classic J. C. Whitcomb and H. M. Morris, *The Genesis Flood: The Biblical Record and its Scientific Implications* (Philadelphia: Presbyterian & Reformed Publishing Company, 1961); also Ken Ham, *The Lie: Evolution* (Green Forest: Master Books, 1987). For arguments in favour of a Christian evolutionary view, see Denis Alexander, *Creation or Evolution: Do We Have to Choose?*, 2nd ed. (Oxford: Monarch Books, 2014 [2008]); also John F. Haught, *Responses to 101 Questions on God and Evolution* (Mahwah: Paulist Press, 2001).

3. See Isa. 46:9–10.

make her a blessing to others; that he will meet her with comfort and courage when she loses us, her grandparents. I only know one *chronos*-thing about her future, which is that she will one day die; but as a chronological point in her future that bears no significance at all, compared to the way in which God will make that moment a *kairos*-point of grace for her, opening the door of paradise to let her in.

From this *kairos*-perspective, it matters not at all if God has shaped the earth, and the universe, over an evolutionary timescale. What a glorious testimony, in fact, to his lordship over time! He is its Creator, and it his humble servant. From the perspective of God's eternity, what matters is not the passage of the years (for God, a millennium is the slightest moment),[4] but the pursuit of the plan: the plan that will mean 'steadfast love' for his insignificant servants, whose work may actually end up meaning something, in spite of our 'nothingness'.

So those who fear that the aeons of evolutionary time undermine a Christian world view are making the same mistake as those who seek to *timetable* the events of the End, or even to give it a date, like Harold Camping, the author of the latest failed prediction.[5] In both cases, *chronos* is being given more weight than *kairos*, though the motivation could hardly be higher – to protect the glory of God and the truth of his sovereignty over the world. Like the late-mediaeval theologians who opposed Galileo and argued that God's glory would be compromised if an inch were conceded to the view that the earth is not the centre of the universe, so these two views seek to defend God against the possibilities that (a) 'evolution', not he, has been in charge of planet Earth for 4.5 billion years, or (b) that there may yet be many years of *chronos* to elapse before the final *kairos* of Christ's return.

Both fears are based on a muddling of *chronos* with *kairos*. *Chronos* obscures, as well as reveals, as we saw in Psalm 89. Poor Ethan the Ezrahite could not see

---

4. Ps. 90:4: 'A thousand years in your sight are . . . like a watch in the night'. The point is that a 'watch in the night' passes instantaneously for most people, who are then asleep. God does not *count* the passage of time as we do – his experience of it, as its Lord and Creator, is completely different.

5. Camping's prediction of the rapture, the second coming and the end of the world on 21 October 2011 was widely publicized at the time. He had previously predicted the End in 1994, so this was his second stab at biblical calculation. When it failed to occur, Camping retired from public ministry (he was then 90 years old) and was reported by his own news media to be studying Scripture 'even more fervently . . . not to find dates, but to be more faithful in understanding'. He died in November 2013.

how the terrible events that had occurred within his own lifetime (the *chronos* that he had experienced) could possibly cohere with God's covenant with the Davidic house – those *kairos*-moments of choice, rescue and promise in the deep past which had provided a framework within which to give his life security. Yet he still clung to the God who had promised – 'How long, O LORD?' – and maybe he too then felt himself directed back beyond David to Moses, and to the God who had been (and who will be!) 'our dwelling-place in all generations'. His sovereignty depends not a whit on the second coming taking place soon. As we will see, the New Testament has a particular take on the 'when' question, which approaches it completely through the *kairos* of God's plan, rather than the *chronos* of God's world.

This is worth illustrating now, from a remarkable passage in 1 Corinthians 7. Paul urges the Corinthians to change their lifestyles dramatically, in the light of the imminent End:

> I tell you, my brothers: the time has been cut short. From now on, let those who have wives live as if they did not; let those who mourn dispense with mourning, and let those who rejoice abandon rejoicing; let traders give up possessing, and business people give up thinking it matters; for the form of this world is passing away.[6]

How do we make sense of this first-century urgency, as we look out on a twenty-first-century world to which the Lord has still not returned? The 'present continuous' tense of the verb helps a little; 'is passing away' points to a process, and clearly this process in God's plan has not yet reached completion. Paul does not write 'is about to pass away'.

But even more than the fact of a *process* (which still keeps us within the realm of *chronos*), Paul rests this urgency on the remarkable opening statement here: 'The time has been cut short.' Here 'time' is *kairos*, not *chronos*. So this is not a calendar-statement ('shape up quick – he's coming next week!'), but a perspective-statement ('shape up radically – his coming is the next thing in the plan!'). The difference is like that between the school that has just received notice of an Ofsted inspection in three days' time (panic), and the school that has just been brought under the Ofsted inspection regime and knows that an inspection could happen at any time. We, too, live wholly in the light of God's *kairos*-plan for his world, and it must impact us dramatically even two millennia after Paul wrote those words to Corinth.

---

6. 1 Cor. 7:29–31.

2. God's *kairos*-plan is the establishment of his universal kingdom

This truth is ringing in our ears from Daniel as we move forward to the New Testament. And here too, we take from Daniel the observation that interpretation gets very muddy, if we seek to use *chronos* as our guide. If the fourth beast is the Roman Empire, as so many interpreters have suggested, then we are left with the difficulty that the Roman Empire was not replaced by the universal kingdom of God that Daniel saw. The same issue applies in the interpretation of the book of Revelation, where likewise the beast is often strictly identified with the Roman Empire. And there, too, the overthrow of the beast is the immediate preliminary to the marriage feast of the Lamb, and the creation of the new heavens and new earth, with the coming down of the bride prepared for her husband.[7] Why did this not happen in AD 410, when Alaric the Goth sacked Rome? Or in 476, when Romulus the last western Roman emperor was forced to abdicate by invaders? Or in 1453, when the eastern, Byzantine empire (the last successor remnant of the Roman empire) finally fell with the sack of Constantinople by the Ottoman Turks?

These questions already reveal how difficult it is to try to map biblical prophetic symbols onto *chronos*-realities 'on the ground'. Actually, the fact that the Lamb did not arrive for his marriage supper on any of those dates makes it clear that we should not identify the beast in Revelation with Rome – nor the fourth beast in Daniel. As we saw, it makes much more sense to interpret the beasts (in both books) as picturing for us the essential qualities of empire, wherever and whenever it appears. For the hearers of Revelation in the first century, this was certainly Rome. But in other times and places it will be other powers. This approach allows us to apply these Scriptures much more fully and broadly in the world, and to give full power to the vision that *God's plan is to overthrow all earthly authority, whether benign or malevolent, and to set up a glorious kingdom of peace under the rule of his Son – a kingdom in which God's people, too, will 'reign'.*[8]

What a vision to hold, as part of our imagination of the story of the future of God's world, as part of the future-as-present that all Christians can hold for

---

7. Rev. 19:6–10; 21:1–2. We will consider these passages in due course!

8. Commenting on 1 Cor. 6:2 ('Don't you know that God's people will judge the world?'), N. T. Wright remarks that 'Paul, like some other early Christians, firmly believed that the future role of the Messiah would be shared with his people', and that 'the most likely explanation of this . . . is that passages such as Daniel 7 were woven deeply into Paul's belief-structure' (N. T. Wright, *Paul and the Faithfulness of God* [London: SPCK, 2013], p. 1090).

themselves! As we move forward to explore this vision in the New Testament, we simply need to note that Daniel's voice is not alone here. We could have looked at numerous passages in the psalms and prophets that hold this expectation, in different ways, that the God of Israel is the God of all the nations, and his universal rule will one day be acknowledged, and very real.[9]

As we move on into the New Testament, we will have plenty of opportunity to see how foundational this universal vision is for a whole-biblical theology of the second coming of Jesus Christ.

3. God intervenes now to save his people

We bring this forward particularly from Psalm 18, but also from the wider story of Daniel and his three friends. Something very subtle is happening here around the notion of God's 'kingship'. God steps in to save David and Daniel, and is able to do so precisely because he is *already* King of all the earth. His *kingdom* is yet to be, but his *kingship* is a present reality, experienced by David on many occasions in his eventful life. Reacting to Daniel's deliverance from the lions, King Darius commands 'all in my royal dominion' to worship Daniel's God,

> For he is the living God,
>   enduring for ever.
> His kingdom shall never be destroyed,
>   and his dominion has no end.
> He delivers and rescues,
>   he works signs and wonders in heaven and on earth . . .[10]

So already in the Old Testament we meet the balance between the 'already' and the 'not yet' which we will find in the New. Jesus' proclamation of the kingdom, as numerous scholars have noted, contains statements which suggest that the kingdom is already present,[11] alongside statements which make it definitely future, associated with the future coming of the Son of Man.[12] And Jesus' healings are presented in the Gospels as evidence of kingdom power released

---

9. See, for instance, Pss 2; 46; 47; 96; Isa. 2:2–4 (Mic. 4:1–4); 45:22–23; 49:6–7; Amos 9:11–12; Jonah; Zech. 2:10–11; 8:20–23; 9:9–10; 14:8–9.

10. Dan. 6:26–27.

11. E.g. Luke 11:20; 17:20–21; cf. Mark 2:18–28.

12. E.g. Matt 13:36–43; 16:27; 25:1–13; Mark 8:38 – 9:1.

now because of the presence of the King.[13] Because he rules, 'even the wind and the sea obey him'.[14]

This produces a really interesting situation in the New Testament. There is a strong sense that the great confession 'Jesus is Lord!'[15] means 'Jesus is Lord, *and not* Caesar and other earthly potentates!' There is a revolutionary edge to it, and a very clear sense in which earthly powers need to feel judged by the kingdom of God. But Christianity is not a revolutionary movement, because it is *God* who brings his kingdom in, and not us. Just as Daniel lived obediently in Babylon and served its king and people,[16] so Paul calls the followers of Jesus to accept the God-given authority of 'the powers that be', and to live submissively under them,[17] while yet knowing that 'the form of this world is passing away',[18] and that one day the Lord Jesus will 'nullify every rule and every authority and power'.[19]

Our ultimate loyalty is to his kingdom, both coming and present: and his *present* kingdom may mean standing up against earthly rulers – as it did for Daniel, and indeed for Paul – and trusting in the power of the King to deliver us. Like David, we live in danger, and by faith, and we trust him for wisdom and strength, and rely on his power to rescue us as he sees fit.[20] He may *not* rescue us (as Shadrach, Meshach and Abednego knew[21]) – but if so, the New Testament has a whole new message for us about *the way in which* the Lord Jesus exercises his rule in the world, as we will see. The cross turns all 'normal' notions of power upside-down.

4. The same language can be used for both present and future kingdom

Our final legacy from these Old Testament passages concerns the way in which apocalyptic language works. We thought about this especially in connection with Psalm 18:7–15, and the way in which *any* coming of the Lord, whether

---

13. E.g. Luke 11:20; Matt. 4:23; Mark 3:22–27.

14. Mark 4:41.

15. E.g. 1 Cor. 12:3; cf. 8:6.

16. E.g. Dan. 6:1–5.

17. Rom. 13:1–7; 1 Tim. 2:1–4.

18. 1 Cor. 7:31.

19. 1 Cor. 15:24. We will look closely at this passage in ch. 9 below.

20. See Dan. 3:13–18 for this principle in action.

21. Dan. 3:18.

now in rescue or at the end of the age in glory, can be described using the same kind of apocalyptic, cosmic language – the language of cosmic impact and disruption.

This is beautifully illustrated by Peter's quotation from Joel on the day of Pentecost.[22] 'This is what was spoken of, through the prophet Joel', he says, referring to the strange events of Pentecost morning. But he continues the quotation beyond just the prediction of the outpouring of the Spirit and the arrival of prophecy[23] into the apocalyptic language that follows:

> I will give wonders in the heaven above, and signs on the earth below, blood and
> fire and swirling smoke; the sun shall be turned to darkness and the moon to blood,
> before the day of the Lord comes, that great day of revelation. And it shall be, that
> everyone who calls on the name of the Lord shall be saved.[24]

In this second part of the quotation, has Peter shifted his gaze to the future, to another fulfilment of Joel when these cosmic 'signs' will mark the coming 'Day of the Lord'? This seems unlikely, because to 'call on the name of the Lord' becomes a way of describing the *present* response of faith.[25] Peter is not describing the response of faith required when the final Day arrives. This *is* that day, the day of which Joel was writing, a day taking place now, *before* the final Day of the Lord comes. And this present day is so earth-shattering as a *kairos* in God's plan that only cosmic language is sufficient to describe it. That's what it means, that God's Spirit is poured out universally on God's people, even on slaveboys and slavegirls: it's the shaking of the heavens!

One of the 'signs on the earth below' has just been fulfilled, literally – the 'fire' on the heads of the disciples.[26] But we are not supposed to pick this out and ignore the rest of the symbolism. It is *all* fulfilled on that 'great day of revelation', both the literal fire and the symbolic darkening of the sun and the moon. As we encounter such language, we need to take care to let it be literal, or symbolic, or some combination of the two – and usually it will be pretty clear

---

22. Acts 2:17–21. Peter quotes Joel 3:1–5 (Heb. and LXX); in our English Bibles, it is Joel 2:28–32.

23. Acts 2:17–18; Joel 3:1–2 (LXX).

24. Acts 2:19–21; Joel 3:3–5 (LXX).

25. See Acts 9:14, 21; 22:16. See also the way in which Paul uses Joel 3:5 (English: 2:32) in Rom. 10:13; he too applies it to the *present* response of faith, and broadens out the 'everyone' to include both Jews and Gentiles equally.

26. Acts 2:3.

how we should read it. Of course the phrase 'the Day of the Lord' also describes the *future* day, the day of his second coming.[27] So once again we find the language stretched across the two comings of the Lord and the coming of his Spirit inbetween, with cosmic apocalyptic language equally descriptive of any great *kairos* in the plan.

So let us now turn to the New Testament! We will follow the rhythm of the New Testament itself, by looking first at three passages from the Gospels, then turning to Acts' distinctive 'take' on the second coming, then to a series of vital passages from the epistles. Finally we will look at the book of Revelation and allow that glorious text to round off our search for the biblical theology of the second coming of Jesus Christ.

---

27. See 1 Thess. 5:2; 2 Pet. 3:10.

PART 2:

NEW TESTAMENT HOPES AND VISIONS

.

4. THE COMING OF THE SON OF MAN (MARK 13)

We start in the New Testament with one of the most disturbing, and powerful, passages in the Gospels. Mark 13 has been called Jesus' 'Apocalyptic Discourse', which is the scholar-ese equivalent to calling the Ten Commandments 'Moses' Moral Reflections'. This is extremely dynamic, indeed explosive material, which – as we will see – may well have circulated independently in the early churches, before the Gospels were written. It is the longest connected piece of teaching by Jesus both in Mark's Gospel, and in Luke – for we have three versions of this 'discourse', in Mark 13, Matthew 24 and Luke 21. They run mostly parallel to each other, but there are some interesting differences which we will pick up en route. Matthew's version is quite a lot longer, because he adds material which we also find elsewhere in Luke.[1] In all three Gospels the discourse starts with Jesus' prediction of the destruction of the temple, which prompts a surprised question from the disciples, 'When will these things be . . .?'[2] – and away we go.

For many this is an absolutely key New Testament passage on the second coming.[3] This is not surprising, because at its heart is Jesus' prediction – using

---

1. Matt. 24:37–51, parallel to Luke 17:26–27, 34–35 and 12:39–46.
2. Mark 13:4; Matt 24:3; Luke 21:7.
3. So, for instance, John MacArthur, *The Second Coming* (Wheaton: Crossway, 2003), whose whole book is basically an exposition of this 'Olivet Discourse', as he calls it.

the language of Daniel 7:13 – of *the Son of Man coming in the clouds with great power and glory.*[4] In Matthew's version the disciples' question, which sparks the whole discourse, asks specifically about it: 'Tell us, when will these things be, and what will be the sign of your coming and of the end of the age?'[5] Matthew draws out what he must have regarded as implicit in Mark's version of the question, *Tell us, when will these things be? And what will be the sign when all these things are about to be fulfilled?*[6] But in spite of this, the relevance of Mark 13 to the second coming has been strongly challenged in recent scholarship. So substantial is this challenge that we need to review and engage with it. And remarkably, as we do so, we will find that we lay more foundations in our biblical theology of the second coming, because we will need to engage with Paul in order to resolve the issues.

First, however, let us have the chapter clearly in mind.

1. Structure

The outline of Mark 13 is simple and clear:

A. Introduction (vv. 1–4)
      a) The horrifying prediction (vv. 1–2)
      b) The disciples' question (vv. 3–4)
B. Jesus' response (vv. 5–37)
      a) Watch out (1) – don't be deceived (vv. 5–8)
      b) Watch out (2) – first things first (vv. 9–13)
      c) Seeing (1) – the 'desolating sacrilege' and its aftermath (vv. 14–23)
      d) Seeing (2) – the coming Son of Man (vv. 24–27)
      e) Seeing (3) – the foreseeable nearness (vv. 28–32)
      f) Watch out (3) – the unforeseeable coming (vv. 33–37)

As this outline reveals, the two verbs 'watch' and 'see' are key to the structure here (Gk *blepein* and *horan*). Each is used at three key points: *blepein* in verses 5, 9

---

4. Mark 13:26; cf. Matt. 24:30; Luke 21:27.

5. Matt. 24:3.

6. Mark 13:4. The verb 'fulfil' (Gk *synteleisthai*) is the verbal form of the noun 'end' in Matthew's version of the question (Gk *synteleia*). We consider the significance of this word below.

and 33, beginning those sections (plus also v. 23, concluding section c), and *horan* in verses 14, 26 and 28. This follows from the introduction, where the disciples, looking at the Jerusalem temple, exclaim, *Look* [horan], *Teacher – what great stones! What great buildings!* (v. 1) and Jesus replies *Do you see* [blepein] *these great buildings? Not a single stone will be left upon another – they will all be thrown down.*

By highlighting these verbs of sight, the chapter engages with one of the key themes of apocalyptic – namely, the challenge to see clearly, as God sees, and thus to be able to interpret what we see and to respond to it with wisdom. Wonderfully, the chapter underlines this challenge of sight through the very particular challenge of interpretation here. How can we 'see' the chapter clearly? This has become a matter of starkly differing viewpoints in recent years. So we need to think in broader terms about our approach to interpretation, before we get down to the detail.

2. Interpreting Mark 13

In 1971 R. T. France proposed a new way of reading Mark 13 which based interpretation on the statement in verse 30 that *this generation will not pass away until all these things have come to pass.*[7] Because the preceding verses have usually been applied to the second coming, especially the reference to the coming of the Son of Man (v. 26), verse 30 has either been understood to be an expression of Jesus' *mistaken* belief that the Son of Man will come within one generation (the option of radical scholarship), or the phrase *this generation* has been interpreted loosely to cover the whole period between the resurrection and the second coming, or maybe the last generation in this period.[8]

Neither option is really acceptable. So France revived an older view that the whole chapter preceding verse 30 refers to the event about which the disciples asked the question at the start – the destruction of the temple. It is this, after

---

7. R. T. France, *Jesus and the Old Testament: His Application of Old Testament Passages to Himself and His Mission* (London: Tyndale Press, 1971).

8. Evangelical writing has tended to adopt one of these latter approaches. E.g. MacArthur, *Second Coming*, p. 133: 'Christ is saying that the generation alive when the true labor pains begin will be the same generation that sees the delivery.' But this does violence to the word 'this'. Another option has been to make 'all these things' refer not to the coming of the Son of Man, but only to the signs of the end in vv. 5–23. This is the view of G. E. Ladd, *Jesus and the Kingdom* (London: SPCK, 1966), p. 317. But this does violence to the word 'all'.

all, which is foreshadowed by the appearance of the *desolating sacrilege* in verse 14 – where Luke, for the avoidance of all doubt, writes, 'when you see Jerusalem surrounded by armies . . .'[9] In case anyone should wonder if the *desolating sacrilege* refers to something other than what Daniel meant by this phrase – a disaster in the Jerusalem temple[10] – Luke brings us back down to earth; we are talking here about the sack of Jerusalem, and the destruction of the glorious temple buildings that the disciples admired so much.

So France argued that the apocalyptic language in verses 24–27, including the reference to the coming of the Son of Man, was actually the climax of Jesus' answer to the disciples' question, a prophecy of the destruction of the temple – which of course occurred in AD 70, within one generation of the prophecy.[11]

This case is easier to make with reference to verses 24–25, as France himself admitted.[12] The 'cosmic collapse' language in these verses is drawn from Isaiah, where it is used to refer to the fall of Babylon[13] and of Edom[14] – so France argued that it must be interpreted symbolically, not literally. Jerusalem – horrifyingly, in God's plan – has turned into Babylon, a city under God's judgment. France extended this line of interpretation to cover verse 26, also, on the ground that Daniel 7:13, quoted here, is not about the coming of the Son of Man *to earth*, but about his coming *to God*, to receive authority and power. He wrote,

> Jesus is using Daniel 7:13 as a prediction of that authority which he exercised when in AD 70 the Jewish nation and its leaders, who had condemned him, were overthrown, and Jesus was vindicated as the recipient of all power from the Ancient of Days.[15]

So the *coming Son of Man* in verse 26 is a veiled but vivid way of underlining the prediction of the destruction of Jerusalem: the Son of Man comes as Judge. Verse 30 can then bear its natural meaning, that *all these things* will occur within one generation.

---

9. Luke 21:20.

10. Dan. 8:13; 9:27; 12:11. We will return to the significance of Daniel's 'abomination' below.

11. France devoted a whole appendix to this discussion: *Jesus and the OT*, pp. 227–239.

12. *Jesus and the OT*, p. 235.

13. Isa. 13:10.

14. Isa. 34:4.

15. *Jesus and the OT*, p. 236.

France did not deny all reference to the second coming here. Basing his case particularly on Matthew 24, he argued that Jesus then prophesies his own coming after the coming destruction of Jerusalem in Mark 13:32–35,[16] where a new section begins with *But concerning that day or hour no-one knows, not even the angels in heaven, nor the Son, but only the Father.* Having given signs that will indicate the imminent coming of the destruction of Jerusalem, France argued, Jesus now begins to speak of another very different *Day*, for which there is no advance warning – the Day of his coming.

This interpretation is helped along by the fact that, as we saw, the disciples' introductory question in Matthew covers this further 'day'. France suggests that Matthew unpacks the question more clearly than Mark, and that Jesus then tackles each part of the question in turn:

a) Question 1, 'When will these things be?' Answer, Matthew 24:4–35 // Mark 13:5–31, these things will be within this generation, heralded by signs.

b) Question 2, 'What will be the sign of your coming and of the end of the age?' Answer, Matthew 24:36–51 // Mark 13:32–37, the Son of Man will just appear without warning, like 'a thief in the night'.[17]

This interpretation has quite a lot to commend it, as we will discover below, although it is by no means crystal clear that a whole new subject is introduced in verse 32. That verse seems to end a section, rather than start a new one. But the paradox that arises through giving signs to indicate the coming of something that is actually unpredictable (the contrast between vv. 28–29, on the one hand, and vv. 33–37, on the other), seems deliberate and important for our understanding of the passage.

We will return to this! But let us return now to the scholarly discussion in order to introduce the name and ideas of N. T. Wright, who has dominated recent discussion through his extremely persuasive and powerfully-argued case that *the entire chapter, including verses 32–37, is about the destruction of Jerusalem and the temple in AD 70.* He takes France's approach further, and furnishes it with arguments that must be taken seriously.

His case is presented in many publications but chiefly in his major series of scholarly works entitled *Christian Origins and the Question of God*, over twenty

---

16. Parallel to Matt. 24:36–44.

17. This is how Paul describes it in 1 Thess. 5:2, drawing on Jesus' parable in Matt. 24:43.

years in the making.[18] He includes an extensive exegesis of Mark 13 in *Jesus and the Victory of God*,[19] but his way of approaching the passage is shaped by his overall perspective on Jesus and his sense of his mission, and so needs to be seen as part of his overall argument. In a nutshell, he says:

a) We need to take great care to see Jesus within his own terms and context, that of one called by God to be the Messiah of Israel, calling Israel back to faithfulness to God, and announcing the judgment of God if Israel refused to respond.

b) Against this background Jesus thought in the terms given to him by the Scriptures, and in particular – for our purposes here – we must bear in mind that cosmic apocalyptic language was regularly used to depict great geopolitical events. As he puts it, 'this is simply the way regular Jewish imagery is able to refer to major socio-political events and bring out their full significance'.[20]

c) So to him it is no surprise that Jesus (a) uses 'cosmic collapse' language to refer to the coming judgment on Israel and Jerusalem, and (b) uses Daniel 7:13 to depict the vindication that both he and his followers, as God's people, will receive from God – a vindication signalled first by the destruction of the temple, and then by the worldwide spread of the gospel through the *messengers* who will *gather his elect from the four winds, from one end of the earth to the other end of heaven* (v. 27).[21]

d) He discerns no change of subject in verse 32, and nothing that indicates Jesus' expectation of a separate 'coming' of a 'son of man' figure floating down to earth on a literal cloud in order to bring about 'the

---

18. It comprises four major volumes so far: *The New Testament and the People of God* (London: SPCK, 1992); *Jesus and the Victory of God* (London: SPCK, 1996); *The Resurrection of the Son of God* (London, SPCK, 2003); and *Paul and the Faithfulness of God* (London: SPCK, 2013). We will have reason to refer to all four!

19. Pp. 343–367.

20. *Jesus and the Victory of God*, p. 361. Wright rests this view on an extensive treatment of apocalyptic language in his first volume: *NT and the People of God*, pp. 280–299.

21. 'The "coming of the son of man" is thus good first-century metaphorical language for two things: the defeat of the enemies of the true people of god, and the vindication of the true people themselves' (*Jesus and the Victory of God*, p. 362).

collapse or end of the space-time universe'.[22] The traditional 'second coming' is nowhere to be found in Mark 13!

Wright has exercised enormous influence with this persuasive argument that removes all reference to the second coming from Mark 13. So should this chapter contribute at all to our biblical theology? For two reasons I do not find Wright's argument compelling: one to do with his handling of apocalyptic language, and then a second, more substantial point, which arises from our concern for biblical theology here.

First, we have already seen some of the surprising ways in which this kind of 'cosmic collapse' language can be used. But one of the effects of our study so far has been to underline the flexibility of its use, and the way in which its actual referent (what it's really talking about) needs to be judged from context to context, and not presumed in advance. I would suggest that Wright makes his interpretation too rigid by making it 'a matter of genre, that apocalyptic language . . . was regularly employed as a coded way of speaking about the rise and fall of great world powers'.[23] It means that he forecloses his options, and does not allow that Jesus *could* be talking about his own literal return as the vindicated Son of Man, bearing with him the vindication of his people. We need to let this be possible, as we approach the chapter, and not decide in advance that this apocalyptic language can only have a 'socio-political' referent.

Wright's approach to this language has been strongly criticized by Eddie Adams, in a comprehensive study of the language of cosmic catastrophe in the Bible.[24] Adams makes the case that biblical writers certainly envisaged 'the collapse or end of the space-time universe', to use Wright's language – i.e., the end of the cosmos as they knew it. Using Mark 13:31 (*heaven and earth will pass away*. . .) to interpret verses 24–25, Adams suggests that the 'cosmic collapse' language in those verses should be interpreted literally: Jesus here predicts the end of the cosmos as we know it.

Personally, I think that Adams pushes the argument too far in the opposite direction. We certainly need to allow that this language of comic disruption can refer to 'earth-shaking' events, whether personal (like David's experience of

---

22. Wright often uses language like this to depict the literalistic interpretation of apocalyptic language which he is opposing: in this case the quotation is from *Jesus and the Victory of God*, p. 362.

23. *Paul and the Faithfulness of God*, p. 1289.

24. Edward Adams, *The Stars Will Fall from Heaven: Cosmic Catastrophe in the New Testament and its World*, Library of New Testament Studies (London: T&T Clark, 2007).

God's rescue) or communal (like the outpouring of the Spirit at Pentecost[25]), which nonetheless leave *terra firma* intact. But on the other hand, some 'earth-shaking events' will mess up *terra firma* substantially. We will return to Adams' discussion particularly when we look at 2 Peter 3.[26]

Secondly, however, there is another much more significant reason why I find Wright's interpretation of 'the coming of the Son of Man' in Mark 13:26 unpersuasive, and I offer this critique as one who benefits hugely from his overall vision both of Jesus, and of Paul. *From a biblical-theological perspective, we have to take seriously the onward interpretation of Mark 13 within the Bible itself, and Wright's reading of it is definitely not that of the apostle Paul.*

The situation here is similar to that which we encountered when reading Daniel 7:13–14 in the light of Jesus' use of the title 'Son of Man' for himself. It's not that Jesus tells us how to interpret Daniel 7, but that he gives us insight into how to read it by allowing us to see its impact on him. In the same way, within a biblical-theological frame, Revelation 13 gives insight into how to understand Daniel's 'beasts'. Similarly, Paul clearly shows the impact of Jesus' apocalyptic teaching on him, and this must – I think! – affect the way in which we understand it, too. After all, if Paul is not an important interpreter of Jesus, then I don't know who is!

The facts are these. Paul's writing about the second coming of Jesus in 1 and 2 Thessalonians[27] shows such significant parallels and verbal allusions to the material which we now have in Mark 13, Matthew 24 and Luke 21, that he must have been aware of this teaching of Jesus, in some form. And quite clearly, he did not interpret 'the coming of the Son of Man' as coded language for the destruction of Jerusalem, but took it much more literally. We need to get a bit detailed and technical in order to review the evidence, starting with the ways in which Paul's language echoes that of Jesus in the Gospels:[28]

---

25. Acts 2:19–20.

26. Ch. 13 below.

27. 1 Thess. 4:13 – 5:11; 2 Thess. 1:6–10; 2:1–10.

28. These connections have already been discussed, for instance by G. R. Beasley-Murray in *Jesus and the Future* (London: Macmillan, 1954), pp. 226–230, and by David Wenham in *The Rediscovery of Jesus' Eschatological Discourse* (Sheffield: JSOT, 1984). See also Ben Witherington III, *Jesus, Paul and the End of the World: A Comparative Study in New Testament Eschatology* (Downers Grove: IVP Academic, 1992), pp. 159–161. I set out the evidence more fully than I have found it anywhere else, because the debate with N. T. Wright's reading of Mark 13 gives extra significance to the connection between Jesus and Paul here.

a) *As in Matthew*
- Paul uses the distinctive word *parousia* (presence, arrival) to describe the coming of the Lord.[29]
- The Lord appears with a trumpet call.[30]
- Paul uses the metaphor of the 'thief in the night' to describe his coming.[31]
- Like Jesus he uses the metaphor of 'drunkenness' as a warning against not being ready.[32]
- The interesting phrase 'going out to greet him' is used.[33]

b) *As in Matthew and Mark*
- The use of the verb *grēgorein*, to stay awake, be watchful.[34]
- The use of the metaphor of 'birth-pangs', although Paul uses it in a slightly different sense.[35]
- The use of the word *thlipsis* (persecution), to describe what awaits the followers of Jesus.[36]
- The use of the word 'gather together', to describe the gathering of people to the Lord at his return.[37]
- The use of the unusual verb *throeisthai* in the command 'don't be disturbed'.[38]
- The performance of false and deceptive 'signs and wonders' by false prophets.[39]

---

29. Matt. 24:3, 27, 37, 39; 1 Thess. 4:15; 2 Thess. 2:1, 8. Cf. also 1 Cor. 15:23; 1 Thess. 2:19; 3:13; 5:23.

30. Matt. 24:31; 1 Thess. 4:16.

31. Matt. 24:43; 1 Thess. 5:2, 4.

32. Matt. 24:49; 1 Thess. 5:7. Cf. also Luke 12:45.

33. Gk *eis apantēsin:* Matt. 25:6; 1 Thess. 4:17. We will consider the special significance of this phrase when we look at 1 Thess. (ch. 10).

34. Matt 24:42–43; Mark 13:34–37; 1 Thess. 5:6, 10. Cf. also Luke 12:37.

35. Matt. 24:8; Mark 13:8; 1 Thess. 5:3.

36. Matt. 24:9, 21, 29; Mark 13:19, 24; 2 Thess. 1:6–7. When Paul says, in 1 Thess. 3:4, 'When we were with you, we were telling you in advance that that we will certainly be persecuted' – how did he know this?

37. Matt. 24:31; Mark 13:27; 2 Thess. 2:1. This is the only place where Paul uses this root.

38. Matt. 24:6; Mark 13:7; 2 Thess. 2:2. This rare verb occurs only here in the New Testament (and just once in the Old Testament).

39. Matt. 24:24; Mark 13:22; 2 Thess. 2:9–10.

c) *As in Mark*
- The use of the verb *katheudein* (to sleep), to describe the state of not being ready for the Lord's return.[40] This is particularly interesting because Paul also uses the verb in a different sense in the same passage, to describe those who have died ahead of the Lord's return.[41] This slightly awkward double meaning seems to be influenced by the use of the verb in the tradition that Paul is quoting.

d) *As in Luke*
- The use of the unusual word *aiphnidios* (sudden), to describe the sudden, unheralded arrival of the Day of the Lord.[42]
- The use of the compound verb *ekpheugein* (to escape), to describe flight before the coming horrors.[43] All three evangelists use the simple form *pheugein* (to flee), to describe what the Judean disciples must do in the face of the 'abomination of desolation'.[44]

e) *As in all three synoptic Gospels*
- The command not to be deceived.[45]
- The motif of 'the things that must happen first, before the day can come'.[46]
- The fact of the coming persecution and suffering.[47]
- The use of Daniel to shape both the language and the expectation.[48]
- And – I would argue – the personal return of the Lord Jesus Christ, the Son of Man.

It is fascinating that in Paul we find distinctive aspects of Jesus' teaching which parallel elements found in all three synoptic Gospels. Not all these points

---

40. Mark 13:36; 1 Thess. 5:6–7.

41. 1 Thess. 5:10 (cf. 4:13, 15 where a different verb is used).

42. Luke 21:34; 1 Thess. 5:3. The word is used only in these two places in the New Testament.

43. Luke 21:36; 1 Thess. 5:3. Paul uses it with a different referent.

44. Matt. 24:16; Mark 13:14; Luke 21:21. Wright has a brilliant section on the prophetic background to this command to 'flee': *Jesus and the Victory of God*, pp. 356–358.

45. Matt. 24:4; Mark 13:5; Luke 21:8; 2 Thess. 2:3.

46. Especially Matt. 24:6; Mark 13:7; Luke 21:9; 2 Thess. 2:3.

47. Matt. 24:9–13; Mark 13:9–13; Luke 21:12–17; 2 Thess. 1:6–7.

48. In particular Dan. 7:13 (Matt. 24:30; Mark 13:26; Luke 21:27; 1 Thess. 4:16–17; 2 Thess. 1:7–8) but as we will see, Paul is prompted to a wider reflection on, and use of Daniel, especially in 2 Thess. 2.

have equal significance – in fact, some do not bear much individual weight as indications that Paul is influenced by, and reflecting on, Jesus' apocalyptic teaching. But cumulatively the case is very strong. The dates are interesting: the letters to the Thessalonians were written close in time to each other, probably in AD 51, long before any of our Gospels existed in their present form.[49] So Paul may provide evidence that Jesus' 'Little Apocalypse'[50] circulated independently, in written Greek form, before being edited into the synoptic Gospels. Or he may illumine for us how the verbal traditions of Jesus' teaching were passed on. Something must account for the level of overlap, and the influence almost certainly ran from Jesus to Paul, rather than from Paul to the Gospels. It may even be that Paul refers to these existing traditions in 1 Thessalonians 4:15, where he says that his eschatological teaching is 'based on the Lord's word'.[51]

There is a technical discussion around this, which is not relevant to our argument here.[52] My point is simply that Paul is Jesus' first interpreter, responding to and amplifying Jesus' eschatological teaching. And it is clear that, responding to this teaching, he believed in the personal 'coming-again' of Jesus Christ. Wright agrees that this was Paul's belief: 'This, I think, is what is going on in the Thessalonian correspondence. Clearly, he is looking ahead to the ultimate "last day" when Jesus will return and the dead will be raised.'[53] But Wright does not believe that Paul got this expectation *from Jesus*. So he does a magnificent job lining up other sources and influences that could have led Paul to expect Jesus' *parousia*. Chief among these is the Old Testament and Jewish

---

49. See the careful presentation of the evidence in David J. Williams, *1 and 2 Thessalonians*, New International Biblical Commentary (Peabody: Hendrickson, 1992), pp. 9–10.

50. This was the name given to this possible document by critical scholarship when this idea was first mooted and discussed in the nineteenth century.

51. Commentators generally leave open whether Paul is referring to a 'word of the Lord' received by tradition from Jesus or through a prophetic revelation in the church (so e.g. F. F. Bruce, *1 and 2 Thessalonians*, Word Biblical Commentary (Waco: Word, 1982), pp. 98–99; Williams, *1 & 2 Thessalonians*, p. 82). But since Paul elsewhere took pains to distinguish between his own teaching and that of the Lord, where there were traditions of Jesus' teaching relevant to the topic in hand (see 1 Cor. 7:10–12), the possibility that Paul is here revealing his sense of dependence on Jesus' teaching seems stronger to me. We return to this in ch. 10 below.

52. See Wenham, *Rediscovery*, for the full technical discussion.

53. Wright, *Paul and the Faithfulness of God*, p. 1081.

expectation of the return of the Lord (Yahweh) himself to Zion.[54] He summarizes this expectation vividly:

> Central to second-Temple monotheism was the belief . . . that *Israel's God, having*
> *abandoned Jerusalem and the Temple at the time of the Babylonian exile, would one day return.*
> He would return in person. He would return in glory. He would return to judge and
> save. He would return to bring about the new exodus, overthrowing the enemies that
> had enslaved his people. He would return to establish his glorious, tabernacling
> presence in their midst. He would return to rule over the whole world. *He would come*
> *back to be king.*[55]

This is all wonderfully true, and deeply important for the New Testament, and
for our biblical theology of the second coming. And Wright does not want to
say that these Old Testament expectations of the coming of the Lord only
influenced expectations of the *second* coming of Jesus. He maintains that Jesus
himself saw himself as the fulfilment of this expectation, *in his earthly ministry.*
But for some reason – even though Wright emphasizes the vital significance of
this tradition for the whole New Testament – he does not accept that Jesus
could have been drawing on it in his teaching about the 'coming' of the Son of
Man, even though Paul himself clearly read Jesus' teaching in that way.

Let us not be reluctant. We can say with some certainty that Paul's reading
of Jesus' apocalyptic teaching led him to expect his personal return 'from
heaven' in glory. He did not read 'the coming of the Son of Man' as apocalyptic
language simply expressing the vindication of Jesus and his people in the
destruction of the temple. Within a biblical-theological frame, we must surely
receive Paul's reading of Jesus' teaching as a reliable platform on which to build.

The irony is, that this does not have to be an either-or. Wright's exposition
of Mark 13 against its Danielic background is hugely illuminating and exciting,
and of great theological significance, as we will see. His emphasis on the vindication of Jesus as the Son of Man is surely right. But to suggest that this
vindication occurs *only* in and through the destruction of the temple and the
subsequent 'gathering' of God's people through the preaching of the gospel,
is to resist the evidence of one of Jesus' first and most influential interpreters,
Paul himself.

----

54. Wright sets out the relevant prophetic passages fully in *Jesus and the Victory of God*,
    pp. 615–621. He summarizes the influence of this tradition on Paul's *parousia*
    expectations in *Paul and the Faithfulness of God*, pp. 1084–1085.
55. Wright, *Paul and the Faithfulness of God*, p. 653. His emphasis.

Whether we like it or not, Paul does seem to have believed and taught something like the 'monstrosity', as Wright calls it, that 'the supposed "heavenly son of man" ... would "come" – i.e., "return", downwards to earth, on a literal cloud'.[56] What exactly Paul believed, we will ask when we look at these passages in later chapters. For the moment we simply note (a) that Paul offers this expectation of *a personal reunion with the Lord* as a realistic answer to the problem of the current death of some believers,[57] (b) that he gives this teaching not on his own authority but as a 'word of the Lord', and (c) that the evidence is strong that Paul's belief in the personal return of the Lord was based on his reading of the teaching which we now have in Mark 13 and parallels. I do not want to imagine that Paul misintepreted Jesus,[58] or even found in Jesus' teaching radical dimensions that Jesus did not himself envisage.

Wright's case is based, as we have seen, on what apocalyptic language was supposed to do, in Jewish thought-worlds. I want to suggest that, even in apocalyptic, the language of coming, or presence, or return can include just this, whatever else it might also have meant symbolically. Indeed, if Mark did *not* understand Jesus to be talking about the physical re-appearance of the Son of Man in verse 26, then it would seem unlikely that he would have added, in explanation, a little parable that talks precisely about the absence, and then the unexpected *coming* (the same verb) of the *Lord of the household* who has been away (v. 35).

However, we have made a difficulty for ourselves, which we will have to face in due course: if Paul knew Mark 13 or something very like it, and applied verse 26 to the *parousia* of Jesus, then in all likelihood he will have expected this to happen within one generation (in line with v. 30), and in connection with the destruction of the Jerusalem temple. Indeed, to judge from 2 Thessalonians 2:4–10, it seems as though he did indeed hold this expectation. We will return to this!

So now we can turn to the passage itself. We will follow the outline given above.

---

56. Wright, *Jesus and the Victory of God*, p. 517.

57. Note 1 Thess. 4:17, 'and in this way we will always be with the Lord' – i.e., we will be united with the already-dead in Christ in personal and permanent union, because of his *parousia*.

58. Wright does not suggest this. He simply does not discuss any possible connection between Paul's teaching about Jesus' *parousia* and Jesus' apocalyptic discourse.

3. The bolt from the blue and the disciples' reaction (vv. 1–4)

Teacher— look! What stones! And what buildings! (v. 1). The disciples' admiration for
the temple is not surprising. Herod the Great began building it in 19 BC, and
Josephus tells us that the main construction was finished in eight years. He too
mentions the magnificent size of the stones used.[59] It was a staggering building,
faced with gold on the side opposite the *Mount of Olives* where Jesus and the
disciples sit to talk about it (v. 3).[60] Josephus also says that building was still
under way on the temple just a few years before it was destroyed in AD 70; and
in John 2:20 we discover that, at that point, near the beginning of Jesus' ministry,
it had been under continuous construction for forty-six years.

The magnificence, and the feeling of permanence and solidity, held theological significance. It spoke of God's commitment to Israel, of the permanence
of the covenant and therefore the security of his people. It seemed to embody
Israel's whole identity, as the people chosen by the Lord to belong to him, to
receive his word and his law, to be the company among whom he dwelt. Not
all Jews felt this way about the temple; most notably, the Qumran sect regarded
the temple and its officers as corrupt and ripe for judgment. But for the vast
majority of Jews worldwide, the Jerusalem temple embodied the solidity and
reliability of their covenant relationship with the Lord. Inspired by this theology,
one of his disciples makes the admiring exclamation in verse 1 that prompts Jesus'
bolt-from-the-blue reply: *Do you see these great buildings? There will not be left here one
stone on another that will avoid destruction!* (v. 2).

The inner circle of the disciples plus Andrew[61] then approach Jesus with a
question, as he sits looking at the temple from the vantage point on the Mount
of Olives: *Tell us, when will this be, and what will be the sign that this End is about to
come?* This translation seeks to bring out the significance of the verb used in
the second half of their question, which means more than just 'about to be
accomplished'[62] or even 'about to be fulfilled'.[63] Mark uses the verbal form of
the noun translated 'end' in Matthew's version of their question,[64] so it needs

---

59. Josephus, *Antiquities*, 15:392. http://www.ccel.org/j/josephus/works/ant-15.htm.

60. 'A mountain of white marble decorated with gold . . . an object of dazzling beauty':
    W. L. Lane, *The Gospel According to Mark* (Grand Rapids: Eerdmans, 1974), p. 451.

61. See Mark 5:37; 9:2. Was Andrew the one who made the comment in v. 1?

62. NRSV, ESV.

63. NIV, NKJV.

64. Matt. 24:3. It is a favourite word of Matthew's in the phrase 'the end of the age'
    – see also Matt. 13:39, 40, 49; 28:20.

to express the disciples' conviction – based on the theology surrounding the temple – that its destruction will mean an end in some deep and dramatic way. The previous destruction of the temple, in 587 BC, meant the end of the Davidic dynasty and of Israel's sovereignty in her own land, which had never been regained. What kind of end will this new destruction mean – awful to contemplate?

The reason for their question about the *sign* of this end is probably related to their perception of Jesus as a prophet. Prophets regularly gave 'signs', both to express their message in vivid, visual ways, and also to make clear that the message was the Lord's and not just their own. Both Jeremiah and Ezekiel gave such signs in relation to the destruction of the temple and Jerusalem by the Babylonians.[65] So the disciples' request for a sign is probably not motivated by a desire to have some advance warning of the destruction, but to know in what ways God might express the truth of this prophecy in vivid, concrete ways. In at least one famous Old Testament example, the 'sign' of the prophecy was its actual fulfilment – the concrete act of God that brought it about.[66] And in Matthew's version of the discourse, that is the case here also – 'then the sign of the Son of Man will appear in heaven'.[67] This does not signal a separate, warning event, but is part and parcel of the coming of the Son of Man, which is itself the sign that confirms the prophetic word.

This understanding of the question about *the sign* helps us with what follows.

4. Watch out (1) – don't be deceived! (vv. 5–8)

Jesus begins in a surprising place, apparently not answering the disciples' question directly, but instead warning them about things which do *not* constitute *the End* (v. 7). But before we label this paragraph as an added extra, before Jesus gets to the main point, we must bear in mind that apocalyptic is all about seeing the world clearly in the light of God's hidden purpose. Daniel's four beasts were just as much part of his vision as the Ancient of Days and the Son of Man – in fact, they were the essential backdrop to the 'dominion, glory and kingship' given to the Son of Man. Daniel's readers – us! – were being encouraged to see the dreadful things they experienced, under the power of the beasts, as *also* part of God's plan. Speaking to Nebuchadnezzar about his statue vision in chapter 2,

---

65. See e.g. Jer. 13:1–14; 16:2, 5; 19:1–15; Ezek. 4:1–8; 5:1–4; 12:1–7.
66. See Exod. 3:12.
67. Matt. 24:30.

Daniel says, 'There is a God in heaven who reveals mysteries, and who has made clear to King Nebuchadnezzar *what must happen* in the last days.'[68] The appearance of all the earlier empires, with all their greatness and corruption, was as much part of 'what must happen' as the subsequent appearance of the kingdom from God that replaces them all.[69] And that phrase 'what must happen' in Daniel 2:28 is echoed here in verse 7: *When you hear of wars and rumours of wars, don't be disturbed. These things must happen, but the End is not yet.*

In talking first about the awfulness that precedes the coming of the Son of Man, Jesus is reproducing the pattern of these Danielic visions. And so, once we have the eyes to see, the awfulness is as much a sign of God's powerful sovereignty as the kingdom that follows. The power of the beasts is always derived from him, and limited by him.

Jesus mentions three aspects of bestial power here, following his call to *watch out, lest anyone deceive you* (v. 5). Bestial power has a terrible capacity to deceive, because it always dresses itself up in party clothes.

a. Messianic pretenders

Many will come in my name saying 'I am He!' and will lead many astray (v. 6). These messianic pretenders are not putting themselves forward to be Jesus – that's not the point; they are usurping his position, and claiming to be *saviours*. This is always essential to bestial power: the benevolent face that claims to rescue and give prosperity. We see it the world over. But the promises always have the same outcome, sooner or later:

b. Wars and rumours of wars

When you hear of wars, and rumours of wars . . . (v. 7). Bestial power knows of only one means by which to secure itself and to appear to keep its promises of salvation: destroy the enemy. And often those who have been deceived will believe that it's true – there is no other way, they'll say, than to go to war to destroy the threat. Praise God, we have a Saviour who dies for his enemies and who wins them by love. He does not ape the power of the beast. When Jesus says *these things must happen*, he probably partly means that this is the inevitable consequence of bestial messianic pretence. But, as we've seen, behind it all is the hidden plan of God, which he wants his disciples to see. *The end is not yet –* there is no salvation by earthly, political means.

---

68. Dan. 2:28, translation of the LXX.

69. Dan. 2:44–45.

c. Conflict and deprivation

People will rise against people, and kingdom against kingdom; there will be earthquakes in places, there will be famines . . . (v. 8). The consequence of bestial power which only has one weapon in its arsenal – war – is always the same: conflict based on tribalism (*people against people*) or nationalism (*kingdom against kingdom*), or some toxic combination of the two. In each case the 'other' is demonized as the enemy, and salvation means elimination. And the consequence of such wars is always the same, too – *famines*. I think that the *earthquakes* here are probably not literal, but are apocalyptic earthquakes as in Psalm 18:7 and the other places where the 'shaking of the heavens and the earth' is symbolic for great, cataclysmic events that change the shape of life for us. That's what bestial empire does, eventually, in spite of all its party clothes and promises of more – it ruins its own people with conflict and deprivation. The language of verse 8 echoes two Old Testament passages where this kind of internecine conflict is described specifically for Egypt[70] and for Israel herself.[71]

These things are the beginning of the birth-pangs, says Jesus – i.e., two stages removed from the end: labour pains precede delivery, but these lashings of the bestial tail are just the preliminary contractions, not yet real labour.[72] And yet, because God is not absent when beasts cause mayhem, these are still signs that the end is on its way.

5. Watch out (2) – first things first (vv. 9–13)

How are the disciples to manage, under the reign of the beasts? *Watch out for yourselves*, says Jesus (v. 9). This means more than just 'take care of yourselves', although it certainly includes this. This is about *living a reflective life*, seeing things clearly in the light of the insight that the Lord gives. He tells them about their *mission* (vv. 9–10), their *strategy* (v. 11) and their *enemy* (vv. 12–13), using the same verb in relation to each of these – the Greek verb *paradidonai*, to 'hand over' or 'betray'. This is the verb prominently used by Mark in relation to *Jesus'* own betrayal and 'handing over' to suffering and death,[73] so the underlying point is that, as his disciples, they too will experience rejection and betrayal because of

---

70. Isa. 19:2–4.

71. 2 Chr. 15:6.

72. See Isa. 26:16–18; 66:7–9; Mic. 4:9–10 for prophetic precedent for the use of this image.

73. See Mark 3:19; 9:31; 10:33; 14:10–11, 18, 21, 41–42, 44; 15:1, 10, 15.

their commitment to bear witness to the gospel. They are not alone. This calling to *fellowship with Jesus* – and the awful difficulty of it – is signalled in the next chapter when the same inner circle of disciples are called to 'watch' with Jesus in Gethsemane, and sadly fail the test by falling asleep.[74] This 'watching out for yourselves' is tough!

a. The mission (vv. 9–10)

Jesus gives the astonished quartet of disciples a glimpse into their lives, post-Pentecost. What a vision! Like Jesus they will be betrayed and called to stand before synagogue authorities and before *rulers and kings*, all *for my sake*, so that they may *bear witness to them*. Even the *beatings* that Jesus foresees for them will serve the purpose of *witness* – we are reminded of Paul, who says that he received these synagogue beatings five times, presumably because he kept coming back for more and did not keep silent about the Lord.[75]

And all because, says Jesus, *the gospel must first be preached to all peoples* (v. 10). In context, *first* here must mean 'before the End comes'. As we will see, this is a crucial verse for us as we consider Paul's interpretation of Jesus' apocalyptic teaching in 2 Thessalonians. For the moment, we can notice the passion that Paul had to fulfil this calling. He particularly felt appointed to be an 'apostle to the nations',[76] and pursued the task of bearing witness *to all peoples* within one generation, as Jesus said. To judge from Romans 15:18–29 and Colossians 1:6, he thought he was getting pretty close to achieving the goal!

b. The strategy (v. 11)

Their strategy is simply to trust the Holy Spirit. He will be their sufficient resource as they bear witness. Interestingly Luke does not mention the Spirit here, but says 'I will give you a voice, and wisdom, which all your opponents will not be able to resist'.[77] This means the presence of Jesus himself in and with his disciples through the indwelling Holy Spirit – which is what we are

---

74. Mark 14:32–42. The same words are used as in Mark 13:35–37.

75. 2 Cor. 11:24.

76. See Rom. 1:5 (cf. Gal. 2:7–8). 'All peoples' and 'all the Gentiles' are equally possible translations of the same phrase, *panta ta ethnē*.

77. Luke 21:15. Luke includes something closer to Mark earlier (Luke 12:11–12). He illustrates what he means in Acts, in the example of Stephen, whose opponents 'could not resist the wisdom and the Spirit with which he spoke' (Acts 6:10). He still ended up being stoned – in fact, that was the only way in which his wisdom could be resisted.

hearing here. Jesus will be with them, just as he asks them to be with him in Gethsemane. Wonderfully, he will not fall asleep on the job as they did.

The whole chapter arises from the disciples' perception that Jesus is a prophet, and indeed the whole chapter has the quality of prophetic revelation. But here he reveals that they, too, will be prophets, anointed by the Holy Spirit for their task of speaking the gospel worldwide. As they speak, so the Spirit will speak.

c. The enemy (vv. 12–13)

Brother will betray brother to death, and a father his children, and children will rise up against their parents and have them executed; and you will be hated by all because of my name. This is awful. Once again, they are not alone in this: Jesus himself has already been told that he is mad by his family,[78] accused of demon-possession by the religious authorities,[79] and rejected by his home village;[80] and he will be betrayed by one of his closest friends.[81] But it is still terrible to experience the rejection and betrayal of one's own family because of one's commitment to Christ. And yet, that is what so many brothers and sisters in Christ experience today, especially in Muslim countries and families. Jesus' words are still a vivid reality in our world. Praise God, it is not always so. But Jesus reminds his disciples of what he told them in Mark 10:29–31, that they have a higher loyalty now, greater than loyalty to family and home, which is 'for my sake and for the sake of the gospel'.[82] And that means all of us, whether or not our family turns against us.

But the one who endures to the End will be saved (v. 13). This is not a stick to beat the persecuted with – unless you keep going, you won't be saved. This is a word of encouragement to sustain us in the face of the hatred of the world around. When it gets really bad, hold on – the End is at hand, when salvation will come! Salvation here means rescue, deliverance from all enemies that seek to destroy us.

When will this End come? We get closer to an answer as we turn to the first section introduced by the other verb of seeing, Greek *horan*. Whereas *blepein* (vv. 5, 9) has the connotation 'take care, watch out for', *horan* is a more literal word. There are signs of the End more literally visible than the things for which Jesus has just told his disciples to 'watch'.

---

78. Mark 3:21.
79. Mark 3:22.
80. Mark 6:2–3.
81. Mark 14:18–21.
82. Mark 10:29.

6. Seeing (1) – the 'desolating sacrilege' and its aftermath (vv. 14–23)

But whenever you should see 'the desolating sacrilege' standing where it should not (let the reader understand!), then let those in Judea flee to the mountains . . . (v. 14). We clearly move to a new level of 'sign' here – not now the general condition of the international scene (vv. 5–8) or the general experience of Jesus' followers (vv. 9–13), but something specific called 'the desolating sacrilege'. The Greek means literally 'the sacrilege of abandonment', i.e., probably 'the sacrilege that causes abandonment'. A frequent translation is 'the abomination of desolation', familiar from older Bible versions.[83]

This may allude to Ezekiel 8 – 11, Ezekiel's vision of the corruption in the temple which caused the glory of the Lord to abandon the place where he had promised to dwell. But a much closer point of reference is undoubtedly again Daniel, where the Greek phrase used here occurs three times (with slight variations) in descriptions of the desecration of the temple by pagan invaders.[84] The phrase is then also used in 1 Maccabees 1:54, to describe the pagan altar erected by the Syrian king Antiochus Epiphanes, in December 167 BC, on top of the altar of burnt offering in the temple – probably an altar to himself, because he regarded himself as a manifestation (*epiphany*) of God on earth. The description in 1 Maccabees of the persecution and suffering surrounding this, makes it clear that the author of 1 Maccabees saw this event as the fulfilment of Daniel's prophecy.

So the reappearance of this phrase in Mark 13, within Jesus' prophecy of the destruction of the temple, makes us pause and ask about the nature of Daniel's prophecy and its fulfilment. There are further allusions to the Maccabean story here – most notably the encouragement to *flee to the mountains*, which actually makes no (literal) sense as a command to people in Jerusalem, since Jerusalem lies higher than the surrounding countryside. But it makes perfect sense as a reminiscence of 1 Maccabees 2:28, where we read that 'then [Mattathias] and his sons fled to the hills and left all that they had in the town', and all who wanted to remain faithful to the Lord and the law, like them, fled too.

We can summarize the situation like this. However precisely Antiochus Epiphanes may have fitted the description of the fourth beast and its 'little horn'

---

83. So KJV and NKJV, also NASB. NIV 1984 and 2011 have 'the abomination that causes desolation'.

84. Dan. 9:27; 11:31; 12:11. In Matt. 24:15 Jesus specifies that this is the sacrilege 'spoken about by Daniel the prophet'.

– trying to 'change the sacred seasons and the law',[85] abolishing the sacrifices,[86] persecuting God's people,[87] speaking blasphemy and setting himself up as god on earth[88] – the significance and power of Daniel's prophecy has not been exhausted by its fulfilment in 167 BC and the following Maccabean war, which eventually led to the restoration of the temple and the sacrifices three years later. This is, actually, what we would expect, because it is part of the power of apocalyptic imagery to speak beyond the particular, and to create a reservoir of symbolism that can address many situations. The 'beasts' are an excellent example of this – and here in Mark 13 we see Jesus working with precisely this understanding of apocalyptic imagery. 'The abomination of desolation' is about to come to life again.

Actually, Daniel's prophecy expected the destruction of the city and of the temple by the coming blasphemous king.[89] This never happened under Antiochus Epiphanes. So maybe this was partly what prompted this further use of Daniel in connection with a prophecy which certainly does envisage this destruction.

Mark's little interjection – *let the reader understand* (v. 14) – is an invitation to go on the journey that we have just been on. Prophecy asks us to wrestle with the interface between text and world. Mark invites his readers to consider what they have seen, and to decide for themselves whether it constitutes 'the abomination' or not. Maybe, if he was writing his Gospel before the events of the Jewish War, he himself did not know precisely what this 'abomination' would be. But his readers would know more. Luke – very probably writing after it – leaves us in no doubt: 'When you see Jerusalem surrounded by armies, then know that her desolation[90] is near.'[91]

What might Mark's readers identify as *the abomination of desolation?* What might *we?* Actually, this flexibility of reading is a crucial key to the interpretation of this whole chapter. It should not be *fixed*, either by limiting its reference to the future or by limiting its reference to the first century as Wright does. Building upon Daniel, Mark 13 invites us into a debate about multiple applications and fulfilments. We too live in a world accurately described by verses 5–13. Where

---

85. Dan. 7:25.

86. Dan. 8:11–12; 9:27; 11:31; 12:11.

87. Dan. 7:21, 25.

88. Dan. 7:11; 11:36–37.

89. Dan. 9:26.

90. Luke uses the same Greek word, *erēmōsis*.

91. Luke 21:20.

might we also see verses 14–23 – the most awful outbursting of bestial power, leading to the most terrible suffering for God's people?[92]

Mark's openness is signalled by an interesting grammatical quirk in verse 14. Technically, the noun *abomination* is neuter (Gk *bdelygma*), but the participle *standing*, which is meant to agree with it in gender, is in masculine form, not neuter. So deliberately Mark leaves open whether we might identify the *abomination* as a thing or a person.[93]

The period of the Jewish War leading up to the final destruction of the city and temple by Roman forces in AD 70 was a period of terrible suffering, aptly summarized by Jesus' words here (vv. 17–20). Writing in the early fourth century, Eusebius summarizes what he found in Josephus, the Jewish historian:

> But the number of calamities which everywhere fell upon the nation at that time; the extreme misfortunes to which the inhabitants of Judea were especially subjected, the thousands of men, as well as women and children, that perished by the sword, by famine, and by other forms of death innumerable: all these things, as well as the many great sieges which were carried on against the cities of Judea, and the excessive sufferings endured by those that fled to Jerusalem itself, as to a city of perfect safety, and finally the general course of the whole war, as well as its particular occurrences in detail, and how at last the abomination of desolation, proclaimed by the prophets, stood in the very temple of God, so celebrated of old, the temple which was now awaiting its total and final destruction by fire – all these things any one that wishes may find accurately described in the history written by Josephus.[94]

Eusebius is applying 'the abomination of desolation' to the final erection of the Roman legionary standards in the Holy of Holies, to which the Roman soldiers then offered sacrifice.[95] However I think that if Josephus himself had been asked when the temple was desecrated, he would have replied that this took place at a much earlier stage in the war when two Zealot factions themselves

---

92. As I write, in August 2014, I am thinking of Mosul and other cities in northern Iraq, where the forces of the self-proclaimed Islamic State in Iraq and Syria have banned all Christian worship and are apparently enforcing conversion to Islam on pain of immediate death or banishment.

93. Matthew tidies the grammar up and does not reproduce this grammatical oddity (Matt. 24:15).

94. Eusebius, *Ecclesiastical History*, 3:5:4. http://www.ccel.org/ccel/schaff/npnf201.iii.viii.v.html.

95. Josephus, *Jewish War*, 6:316. http://www.ccel.org/j/josephus/works/war-6.htm

fought over the temple, leading to huge bloodshed, including the blood of worshippers who were killed at the altar while offering sacrifice.[96] And interestingly Eusebius tells us that the Christian community in Jerusalem did not wait for Jerusalem to fall, but in response to a prophecy (not that of Jesus, it appears, but undoubtedly in obedience to Mark 13:14), they fled from the city after the start of the war and moved to Pella, a city on the other side of the Jordan about thirty miles north of Jerusalem.[97] Maybe they, too, saw the 'abomination of desolation' in the Zealot desecration of the temple. Sometimes, all God's people can do is flee. Wright brilliantly summarizes the prophetic passages in the background behind this command to *flee*,[98] commenting: 'When Babylon is destroyed, there is only one proper response for YHWH's people: get out and run.'[99]

The description of the suffering as *like nothing that has happened since the beginning of God's creation until now, and nothing like it shall occur again* (v. 19) is not prophetic hyperbole. Daniel used this language in his prophecy, and the Maccabees applied it to their sufferings.[100] Jesus reuses the image for this new crisis, in the first century – and we too can apply it in sympathy to the sufferings of Christians today. This is another point at which we need to step out of *chronos*, and look at things from a *kairos* perspective. As far as *chronos* is concerned, there can of course be only one period of suffering which is the 'worst' in world history. There may be rival candidates, but one will be the winner. But by reapplying this language of 'the worst since creation', Jesus allows us to sit with the reality of each moment, and to be able to say 'This is *absolutely* dreadful. How could things get worse?' – and for this feeling not to be self-deception or untrue.

Of course, for it to qualify as a fulfilment of this prophecy, there needs to be (a) an experience of terrifying *corporate, societal* collapse, accompanied by (b) some absolute desecration of the name of the Lord. If these are both in place, then we can be sure that 'he is near, just outside the doors' (v. 29). Ethan the Wise was experiencing just such a time, when he wrote Psalm 89. Daniel was facing it in Babylon, and under Darius. The Maccabees faced it under Antiochus Epiphanes. The seven churches knew it in Asia Minor, under the power of

---

96. Josephus, *Jewish War*, 5:5–20. 'The temple on every side was defiled with carnage' he writes (5:10), and complains that the temple could no longer continue to be 'God's place', having been made a tomb for the bodies of God's own people (5:19). http://www.ccel.org/j/josephus/works/war-5.htm

97. Eusebius, *Ecclesiastical History*, 3:5:3.

98. Isa. 48:20; 52:11–12; Jer. 50:8; 51:6, 45, 50; Zech. 2:6–8; 14:5.

99. Wright, *Jesus and the Victory of God*, p. 358.

100. Dan. 12:1.

Rome and the imperial cult.[101] Everywhere, where the beast raises its horns and starts trampling and crushing, there we *the reader* can *understand* that the *abomination* has crawled out of the abyss, yet again.

But God is sovereign! – he will *limit* the suffering (v. 20), and very soon the Son of Man will come to displace the power of the beast with his own beautiful, peaceful authority (v. 26). How often have we seen this happen, in preliminary ways, in the experience of the church of Jesus Christ through the centuries?

Morna Hooker thinks that, in verse 21, we move into the period *after* the destruction of the temple.[102] Without commenting on it, she seems to take *And then* ... (v. 21) in a strictly chronological sense, 'and next, after that ... ' But 'then', both in Greek and in English, can also mean 'at that time', and this seems more likely here.[103] Part of the *abomination* is the appearance of extreme deception, false 'messianic' figures and charismatic leaders who seem blessed with extraordinary, even miraculous powers. Times of societal collapse are the seed-ground for the appearance of figures like this. *Watch out*, says Jesus (v. 23): remember that there is but one Saviour! God's people have always needed to be warned against false prophets,[104] and the warning still stands.

Jesus is certainly telling Peter, James, John and Andrew that they must expect a period of terrible suffering in the immediate run-up to the fulfilment of his prophecy of the destruction of the temple – and indeed it was horribly so. But should we also expect a period of great tribulation before Jesus finally comes again? This is where we need to consider the strange tension in this passage – key to France's reading of the whole chapter – between an event heralded by signs, on the one hand (vv. 28–29), and a 'coming' for which there is no warning at all, on the other (vv. 32–37). We will tackle this question when we get there!

7. Seeing (2) – the coming Son of Man (vv. 24–27)

But in those days, after that tribulation ... (v. 24). This does not mean that there is to be a gap between the *tribulation* and the coming of the Son of Man. Rather, the Son of Man is the answer to the tribulation, so that it can no longer continue after he has come. He is the one who delivers us from the power of the beast,

---

101. Rev. 13.

102. Morna D. Hooker, *The Gospel According to St Mark*, Black's New Testament Commentary (London: A&C Black, 1991), pp. 316–317.

103. So for instance in NIV and NRSV.

104. Deut. 13:1–4 is lurking in the background here.

so the beast's power to oppress decisively ends, once he appears. Like Aslan returning to a Narnia in the grip of the White Witch, winter melts before his gaze . . .

The sun will be darkened, and the moon will not give her light, and the stars will be falling from heaven, and the powers in the heavens will be shaken . . . (vv. 24–25). The case has been sufficiently well made by France and Wright and many others that we are meeting apocalyptic language here, which functions by its own rules. To interpret it literally would be as silly as believing that heaven is really Narnia, and Jesus is really Aslan. Nobody mistakes the genre of Lewis' Narnia stories – beautiful presentations of Christian truth (albeit with a good overlay of medieval cosmology, if Michael Ward is to be believed[105]). Lewis was not setting out to write theology. Similarly Isaiah was not setting out to predict strange astronomical events, when he used just this language to predict the downfall of Babylon[106] and of Edom.[107] In both cases, as Wright argues so powerfully, 'this language denotes socio-political and military catastrophe'.[108]

We do not need to go along with Wright's insistence that it can *never* have any literal connotation, to recognize that he is fundamentally right here.[109] There was no darkening of the sun when the city finally fell, no more than there was on the day of Pentecost when the Spirit came. But both events were of earth-shattering, world-reshaping significance, after which the cosmos was lit by a different light. The era of the temple ends, the literal, physical presence of God served most closely by those who could be there with him; and the era of the Spirit begins, in which God is served by all who know him by faith and host his presence in their hearts.

And then they will see the Son of Man coming in the clouds with great power, and glory (v. 26). This is the End that the disciples asked about (v. 4), heralded by all the preceding signs. Of course, we were expecting Jesus to say something much more literal about the casting down of the massive stones of the temple. Instead, we get these glorious words drawn from Daniel 7:13.

There are some passages of Scripture that defy commentary, and this is one of them. The rabbis believed that the greatest mysteries should not be taught

---

105. Michael Ward, *Planet Narnia: The Seven Heavens in the Imagination of C. S. Lewis* (New York: Oxford University Press, 2008).

106. Isa. 13:10, quoted here in v. 24.

107. Isa. 34:4, quoted here in v. 25.

108. Wright, *Jesus and the Victory of God*, p. 361.

109. I've already suggested that, when this language is used in Heb. 12:26, it does have literal significance.

publicly, but only discussed quietly, after dark and in private, among learned friends. This is one such passage. What words can replace it, or explain it? It feels like we step onto holy ground here, and reverent silence, not noisy commentary, is the appropriate response. Here faith comes face to face with its opposite, the bestial arrogance[110] which says that death is the end, and we are alone in the cosmos, and man is the measure of all things, that love is weakness and power is all. Against all this, faith simply says *they shall see the Son of Man coming in the clouds with great power, and glory*. It refers all questions to Jesus Christ, the Son of Man, ascribes all power to him, locates the future in him, makes him the measure of all things, and calls him the Lord of life and of death, and of all the cosmos.

So a big part of me does not even want to try to interpret this verse, because no words can replace or improve it. It is absolutely at the heart of the *confession* of a Christian world view. The whole world is qualified by it. It is the capstone of all Christian theology, the belief that all history, the whole stuff of this vast and wonderful universe, every corner and cranny of space and time in all its magnificence, mystery and pain, is focused on the moment when *they shall see the Son of Man coming in the clouds with great power, and glory*. This is *kairos* bursting into *chronos* and transforming it, moving us from the pain of Psalm 89 into the eternity of Psalm 90, and from the power of the beast to the glory of the new creation. No other words in Scripture are more important than these for shaping the world view of the disciples of Jesus Christ.

This statement fires our imaginations as we inhabit our lives on planet Earth, and becomes the absolutely key element in in our future-as-present. Key to Augustine's view of time was his notion of 'extension' (Lat. *distentio*), by which he expressed the idea that we are stretched between the past and the future. On the one hand we are rooted in the past, with all its complexity. But like Paul in Philippians 3, we seek to 'forget what lies behind', because it does not constitute the final judgment on us, and instead we 'strain forward to what lies ahead', which is 'the upward call of God in Christ Jesus'.[111] As we hold this imagination of ourselves in the present, we are *extended* over past, present, and future – and the most vital bit of this is the imagination we hold of the future, when we will 'be found in Christ', knowing 'the power of his resurrection'.[112] When it comes to inspiring this future-as-present vision, no words are more significant or powerful than *then they will see the Son of Man coming in the clouds with great power, and glory*. It inspires Paul in Philippians:

---

110. Dan. 7:11.

111. Phil. 3:13–14.

112. Phil. 3:9–10.

We expect and wait for a Saviour from heaven, Jesus Christ the Lord, who will re-form our lowly bodies so that they con-form to his glorious body, as he exerts the power which enables him to subject everything to himself.[113]

But even if commentary is inappropriate – because it can't truly be said better, or more clearly, in other words – nonetheless verse 26 raises questions to discuss. Most notably:

- What kind of 'seeing' is this? And who's doing it?
- And how does this 'coming' relate to the destruction of the temple in AD 70?

a. 'Then they will see . . .' – what kind of seeing?

This follows from 'whenever you see' in verse 14. There, the 'seeing' is a seeing-by-faith, because it is based on interpreting and applying the prophetic word about the *abomination of desolation*. France and Wright would also want us to understand the 'seeing' in verse 26 to be the same kind of 'seeing-by-faith'. Inspired by the (same) prophetic word, we 'see' the destruction of the temple as the wonderful coming-to-power of the Son of Man, as (in Wright's terms) his public vindication and exaltation. 'Jesus staked his reputation on his prediction of the Temple's fall within a generation; if and when it fell, he would thereby be vindicated.'[114] But this vindication would not just be as a prophet (after all, Rabbi Johanan ben Zakkai also predicted the destruction of the temple), but as the Danielic Son of Man. So the 'seeing' is that seeing which is willing to grant that Jesus' vindication has this 'Daniel' dimension.

Actually, Wright's case would be easier to defend if verse 26 said 'then *you* will see', using the second person, as in verse 14. The movement into the third person gives it the quality of a much bigger seeing, beyond the bounds of those who see by faith. It leads on to the 'you will see' in the next chapter, addressed to the whole Sanhedrin:

Again the high priest questioned him, and said, 'You are the Christ, the Son of the Blessed One?' And Jesus said, 'I am; and you [plural] will see the Son of Man sitting at the right hand of the Power, and coming with the clouds of heaven.'[115]

---

113. Phil. 3:20–21.

114. Wright, *Jesus and the Victory of God*, p. 362.

115. Mark 14:61–62. Jesus combines words from Dan. 7:13 with words from Ps. 110:1.

This has to be a public 'seeing' which will vindicate Jesus in the eyes of those who are now condemning him – a seeing which transforms him from victim to judge, so that the authority which now condemns him will find itself over-thrown along with the beast, and replaced by the kingdom of God.

I think that the 'seeing' in 13:26 has to be of the same kind. This is clearly how Paul read Jesus' prophecy, and I think that he gives us the right approach. It is also how Matthew understands it. He has an expanded version of Jesus' words here:

> And then the sign of the Son of Man will appear in heaven, and then 'all the tribes of the land will mourn', and then they will see 'the Son of Man coming upon the clouds of heaven' with power and great glory . . .[116]

The reference to 'the tribes of the land' comes from Zechariah 12:12, and makes it unmistakable that the 'seeing' is a public one, leading to the repentance of 'those who pierced him'.[117] There is no way, I would contend, that the meaning of this 'seeing' can be exhausted by the seeing-by-faith which might discern a fulfilment of the Daniel vision just in the destruction of the temple alone. But it is not just a public, visible 'seeing' – it is a sharing of Daniel's vision, so that this seeing includes the meaning that Daniel 'saw': this Jesus comes as Lord, trailing kingdom through the clouds!

This leads to our second question.

b. The 'coming' of the Son of Man and the destruction of the temple

How do these two relate? There are three possible answers:

1. Jesus has left the disciples' question about the temple behind, and is now (in v. 26) talking about something separate and different, the coming of the Son of Man.
2. Jesus has not left the disciples' question behind, and is referring to the destruction of the temple using apocalyptic and thus interpretative language.

---

116. Matt. 24:30.

117. Zech. 12:10. Zechariah is definitely talking about the 'tribes' of Israel, and so we should probably translate gē as 'land' here, rather than 'earth' (against all the leading translations). In Matthew the 'seeing' is one specially for Israel. In Rev. 1:7, however, where Zech. 12:10 is again quoted, the reference seems to be broadened out beyond Israel.

3. Jesus is still addressing the disciples' question, and the fall of Jerusalem and the temple was indeed a significant overthrow of the power of the beast, a milestone on the road to the enthronement of the Son of Man. But his 'coming' is much bigger than this, and there is much more yet to be!

As will by now be apparent, I want to argue for the third approach. The first is that represented by traditional exegesis here (see, for example, Hooker above), and the second is the radical approach of France and Wright, especially the latter. I think that the first does not respect the consistency of the chapter and the focus of Jesus' response, and the second leaves us with a pale, pale reading of the coming of the Son of Man. How could the significance of Daniel 7:13 possibly be exhausted by the destruction of the temple, of huge significance though that was? Daniel envisages a *world transformed* by the coming of God's kingdom in and through this 'one like a son of man', a coming into which all God's people are caught up to share the reign. Did we see this in AD 70?

The interpretation of verse 27 is important here. Wright applies this to the gathering of the people of God through the preaching of the gospel, carried by the 'messengers' who go out with the glad news of the vindication of the Son of Man. This may well be *part* of its meaning. There are comings, not just a coming! Those who had already called Jesus 'Lord' were undoubtedly comforted and strengthened by the message of the gospel, when Jerusalem fell. But when Matthew uses this imagery earlier in his Gospel, it definitely refers to the *end-time* 'gathering' of 'the sons of the kingdom' involving the final judgment when the 'weeds' are sifted out and burned.[118] At least as far as Matthew is concerned, it seems inappropriate to give the same symbolism a radically different meaning in 24:31. And the same applies to Mark 13:27, I suggest.

8. Seeing (3) and watch out (3) – the foreseeable nearness and the unforeseeable coming (vv. 28–32, 33–37)

We take these last two sections together, since we need to expound them in relation to each other because of the strange contrast between them. Many commentators point to the 'apparent tension' (Hooker[119]) between the two

---

118. Matt. 13:37–43, especially vv. 40–41: 'So will it be at the end of the age: the Son of Man will send out his angels . . .'

119. Hooker, *Mark*, p. 322.

parables here. First we have the little parable in verses 28–29, which invites the disciples to be encouraged by the signs Jesus has given, because when they see them, they can *know that he* [or 'it'] *is near, right at the door* (v. 29). But in the second parable in verses 33–37 Jesus invites them to be ready for something that might happen at any moment, without warning: *For you do not know when the Lord of the house will come, whether in the evening, or the middle of the night, or at cock-crow, or early in the day* (v. 35). How can the coming of the Lord be both heralded and completely unexpected?

Hooker comments that 'it is possible to be confident that an event will occur within a certain span of time without being certain of the precise day or hour'.[120] True. I recall the many occasions when various relatives waited for us to arrive for a visit, knowing that we'd come at some point during the day, but never knowing whether the ETAs we provided would bear any relation to fact, such is the level of our disorganization around packing and travelling.

Hooker's comment is helpful, but I think that more can be said about this strange double vision in Mark 13. It arises from the way in which Daniel 7:13 works as a prophetic vision by which we live. We believe in a God, and a Christ, who hears when his people call and who 'comes down' to deliver. We saw this in Psalm 18, and Daniel and his friends experienced this dramatically on several occasions. The three friends in the furnace, and Daniel in the lion's den, knew what it was to trust in a God who might, or might not, turn up to save them – but who, either way, was the supreme God of all the earth, the holder and giver of all authority and power, whom they were committed to acknowledging, come what may. David looked back on a life of danger and desperation, with the Lord's 'steadfast love' appearing often at the last moment to deliver him.

For all these, and for all of us as followers of Jesus Christ today, that very danger and desperation are the signs of his coming – as here in Mark 13. When the beast lashes his tail, when abominations surround and flight is the only option and we seem to have no other resource, then *these things* can assure us that he is at the door. He will not leave us helpless, because he is the Son of Man in whom 'the saints of the Most High' receive and possess the kingdom.[121] But we do not know how, or when, this may become true of us. We do not know how, or when, the cross may be succeeded by resurrection for us. All we know is that the suffering is a sign of his coming.

And what about the final End – the final coming of the Son of Man, when at last the powers of the beast will be overthrown and God will be 'all in

---

120. Ibid., p. 323.
121. Dan. 7:18.

all'?[122] We have no idea when *this* will be. A *little* more can be said than just that we don't know, as we'll see. But for sure, he will come; and for sure he will come *now* when we call upon him in time of need, as he did for Peter, James, John and Andrew in the years that followed that day on the Mount of Olives.

This stance – the signs of his coming are the sufferings that oppress us, but we have no idea how he might come to deliver us, or when he will finally come to deliver the world – is the stance appropriate to the inhabitants of *chronos* whose future-as-present is shaped by the *kairos* of the coming of Jesus Christ.

These thoughts are powerfully carried forward as we turn to our next passage, Luke 17:20 – 18:8, which we will be able to consider more briefly.

---

122. 1 Cor. 15:28.

5. 'WILL HE FIND FAITH ON THE EARTH?'
(LUKE 17:20 – 18:8)

1. Stocktake

Before we plunge into this next passage, let us pause and review where we've got to in our search for the biblical theology of the second coming of Jesus Christ. We have yet to look at the rest of the New Testament, but we have looked closely at an absolutely key Gospel passage against the background of the framework provided by the Old Testament. We have laid four foundation stones, so far.

a. The Son of Man and the kingdom
First, we have discovered the intimate connection between these two. The Son of Man in Daniel 7 comes before the Ancient of Days in order to receive the kingdom – the kingdom which will replace all the dreadful or not-so-dreadful powers of the world with the glorious rule of God himself. This political relevance of the kingdom of God is vital to its meaning. Indeed, under some circumstances the coming of *the kingdom* and the coming of *the Son of Man* are interchangeable – as for instance in the saying which introduces the story of the transfiguration, where Mark has 'Truly I say to you, there are some standing here who will not taste death until they see the kingdom of God come in

power', and Matthew has '. . . until they see the Son of Man coming in his kingdom'.[1]

This is why N. T. Wright cannot be wholly wrong to interpret Mark 13:26 with reference to the destruction of the temple in AD 70. He has done us a wonderful service by emphasizing so much the political relevance of the kingdom of God. We should not have forgotten it, anyway – it's all there in Daniel. It is indeed truly horrifying, as he emphasizes, that Israel steps into the role of Babylon in Jesus' language, and finds herself aligned with the enemies of God's kingdom.

b. Judgment and salvation

These go together, too! The Son of Man comes to exercise both – to bring salvation to the persecuted people of God, who receive and share the kingdom with him, and to bring overthrow and judgment to the beasts who have oppressed them and the world. We can see this double meaning also in Mark 13, once again affirming the rightness of Wright's reading to some extent (his coming in judgment on Jerusalem and the temple), but adding that the Son of Man comes also to rescue his suffering people, 'the elect' for whose sake he has 'shortened the days'[2] of suffering. This parallel experience of salvation and of judgment in the destruction of Herod's temple takes us back to the destruction of Solomon's, the awful theological questioning in Psalm 89, and the balance to this, the bigger vision of God's lordship over time, in Psalm 90.

We sit in the same place – creatures of *chronos* who cry out to the Lord of time to visit us with the *kairos* of his steadfast love. The destruction of Herod's temple, and the rescue of God's people in and from that disaster, is not the end of the story of the coming of the Son of Man. We cry to him still, to receive the dominion and to extend it to the suffering people of his world.

And this leads us to the vital third foundation stone.

c. Multiple comings, and final coming

Psalm 18 has already guided us in this direction. And it was not just that David experienced many individual moments of *kairos*-deliverance about which he could say 'he bowed the heavens, and came down',[3] but even more that his

---

1. Mark 9:1; Matt. 16:28. Jesus may be referring to the transfiguration that follows, or to the resurrection, or to Pentecost, or to the initial expansion of the church, or to the destruction of the temple, or indeed to all of these.

2. Mark 13:20.

3. Ps. 18:9.

whole life was spent under the superintendence of the Lord, who trained him, strengthened him, protected him and gave him victory, so that his whole experience, in sum, was of the 'coming' of the Lord to him. 'From his temple he heard my voice, and my cry to him reached his ears.'[4]

The basic principle is that *the Lord is a God who comes to his people*, and this is still gloriously true. Wright has so helpfully emphasized the significance of this for our whole understanding of Jesus in the New Testament. The smaller 'comings' we experience all point forward to a final coming, when it will not just be an individual David or a group to whom he comes, but the whole cosmos, and the salvation and judgment will be total. The change from 'you' to 'they' in Mark 13:26 points in this direction. Yes, he came in AD 70, so that his words were fulfilled within one generation. But the fullness of the coming of the Son of Man, as envisaged in Daniel, did not happen then. And has not happened yet.

At the heart of this principle – not to be forgotten – is the *relational connection and commitment* between God and his people. We saw this so vividly in Psalm 18, and we are yet to discover how absolutely vital this is for our biblical theology of the second coming.

d. The special significance of apocalyptic language

This has turned out to be a vital principle, too. Maybe this language does go back to the phenomena that accompanied the Lord's 'coming down' on Mount Sinai – rumblings, flashings, quakings, smokings, clouds and 'a trumpet so loud that all the people who were in the camp trembled'.[5] The author of Hebrews certainly understood these to be literal manifestations of God's terrifying presence.[6] But from that point onward, this kind of language – plus the shaking and falling of the heavenly bodies – could be used to *symbolize* God's awesome coming, as we saw in Psalm 18.

Apocalyptic language is very flexible, and works by *evocation* – that is, by its *impact* on readers and hearers who are trained in biblical language and in the ways in which such symbolism has been used before. This is an absolutely vital principle in the interpretation of the book of Revelation, and indeed in many of our 'second coming' passages, as we have already seen. There is a lot of overlap between apocalyptic language and the language of the parables, which likewise use vivid symbolism and seek to make an emotional, as well as a cognitive, impact on hearers.

---

4. Ps. 18:6.

5. Exod. 19:16.

6. See Heb. 12:18–21.

But with Sinai in the background, we always need to be alert to the ways in which apocalyptic language might have a 'literal' edge to it. We will certainly come back to this when we look at 1 Thessalonians 4:13–18 and 2 Thessalonians 2:1–12.

2. The present and the future

Luke tends to scatter Jesus' eschatological teaching around, rather than concentrating it chiefly in one climactic chapter, like Matthew and Mark. Much of Luke 17:20 – 18:8 is unique to Luke, though we meet some parts of it also in Matthew; chiefly in Matthew 24,[7] but also in Matthew 10 and 16.[8] The introduction is unique to Luke (17:20–22), as are the words about Lot (17:28–30) and the amazing parable with which our passage comes to a climax (18:1–8). One small section here runs parallel to Matthew 24 and Mark 13 – Luke 17:31.[9]

This passage falls within Luke's so-called travel narrative, the long central section of his Gospel which contains much material unique to Luke, and which is structured around Jesus' journey from Galilee to Jerusalem. This begins in Luke 9:51, and we are reminded periodically that he is on his way towards that destination, where he is going to die.[10] The great twin themes that interweave through this central section of Luke are (a) the practical discipleship difference that it makes (b) to believe in the coming judgment of God, to whom we must give account. And as these themes are woven together, a sub-theme develops underneath them, which is (c) that Jesus himself is both the agent and the focus of that coming judgment of God, and indeed of the kingdom of God itself. He is the one who teaches how we should live, in the light of the End, and it is in and through him that 'the kingdom of God has come upon you'.[11]

Sayings like this, emphasizing the *presence* of the kingdom, were in stark contrast to contemporary Jewish expectation of the kingdom of God, which was of a coming era in which God would vindicate his people, deliver them

---

7. Matt. 24:26–28 (parallel to Luke 17:23–24, 37), and Matt. 24:37–41 (parallel to Luke 17:26–27, 34–35).

8. Matt. 10:39 and 16:25, both parallel to Luke 17:33. This verse is also paralleled in Mark 8:35 and indeed earlier in Luke (9:24).

9. Cf. Matt. 24:17–18 and Mark 13:15–16.

10. See Luke 13:22, 33–35; 17:11; 18:35; 19:11, 28.

11. Luke 11:20; cf. 10:9, 11.

from their enemies, and establish them securely in the earth. The exclamation of one of Jesus' fellow dinner guests, 'How blessed the one who will eat bread in the kingdom of God!'[12] expresses the kind of pious hope and expectation evoked by talk of the kingdom – and Jesus was talking about it all the time.

It was natural, therefore, that Jesus would find himself being asked the question in Luke 17:20: *When will the kingdom of God come?* And Jesus' answer to this question takes us deep into the relationship between *present* and *future* in our experience of the kingdom.

3. Structure

The structure of this section of Luke's travel narrative runs like this:

A. The question and Jesus' reply: the presence of the kingdom (17:20–21)
B. Unpacking the reply for the disciples (17:22–35)
    a) The suffering presence of the coming Son of Man (vv. 22–25)
    b) The Day no-one foresaw and no-one will want (vv. 26–30)
    c) The terrible division and the reason for it (vv. 31–35)
C. The disciples' puzzled response and Jesus' puzzling reply (17:37)[13]
D. Prayer: the presence of the kingdom (18:1–8)

As these headings reveal, I want to suggest that the theme of the question, and especially of Jesus' reply in 17:20–21, is picked up and unpacked further in the parable of the unjust judge in 18:1–8. This amazing little parable draws out the essence of what it means, practically, to believe in the presence of the kingdom of God. But of course much of this passage overall is not about the presence of the kingdom, but about its future (which is what the Pharisees ask about in 17:20). So the passage as a whole develops these twin themes of the presence and the future of the kingdom, and of the relationship between these.

Because of the way in which the parable in 18:1–8 engages with the theme of the Q&A at the start, we will look at them together.

---

12. Luke 14:15.
13. It is worth noting that v. 36, which is in the so-called 'received text' and therefore in NKJV, is actually only in one ancient manuscript tradition and is certainly not original.

4. The presence of the kingdom (17:20–21; 18:1–8)

Jesus' reply to the Pharisees' question is both striking and puzzling. He tells them that the kingdom of God does not come with watching and observation. *People won't be able to say 'here it is!' or 'there it is!'* – for if you look carefully, you'll see that *the kingdom of God is in your midst* (vv. 20–21). The phrase translated 'in your midst' is an interesting one, used only here of the kingdom of God. There is some evidence that a better translation would be 'within your reach' or 'within your grasp', giving a more active sense: it is not that the kingdom of God is present but hidden, but that it is present and available to all who will reach out for it.[14]

We have seen many people doing this in Luke's Gospel so far – not least in the immediately preceding passage, where ten Samaritan lepers cry out in faith, 'Jesus, Master, have mercy on us!',[15] and then obey him when he tells them to go as they are, bearing their leprosy, to the priest in order to be declared clean. En route, they are healed – because they reached out and grasped the kingdom of God present in and around Jesus. You can, too! says Jesus to the Pharisees, who seem to be interested just in the traditional theological question, *When will the Kingdom of God come?* For Jesus, this cerebral interest in 'when?' is a diversion from the real point of the kingdom, which – if we will let it – will have a dramatic impact on our life *now*.

This present *grasping* of the kingdom of God is the theme of the parable in 18:1–8. *He began to tell them a parable, to make the point that they ought always to pray, and not give up in weariness* (v. 1). The point of the parable is that even in the most unpromising-looking circumstances, it's vital to keep persisting in prayer, like the grumpy, obstreperous widow who refuses to leave the hard-hearted judge alone but keeps threatening to give him a black eye unless he takes action for her.[16] Jesus' parables – especially in Luke – do not hesitate to use disreputable characters even to represent God. The argument in verse 7 has a 'How much more . . . ?' shape to it, even though it is not phrased in that way. If even a cold-hearted judge, untouched by human pain, will eventually respond to the pleas of a persistent widow, how much more will God *act to bring justice for his elect who*

---

14. So N. T. Wright, *Jesus and the Victory of God* (London: SPCK, 1996), p. 469. Also I. H. Marshall, *The Gospel of Luke: A Commentary on the Greek Text* (Exeter: Paternoster Press, 1978), p. 655.

15. Luke 17:13.

16. The word *hypōpiazein* in v. 5, translated 'wear out' (NRSV) or 'attack' (NIV), literally means 'to give a black eye'!

cry to him day and night, while his patience looks like delay? I tell you, Jesus goes on, *he will act to bring them justice quickly!* (vv. 7–8).

The last clause in verse 7 – *while his patience looks like delay* – is difficult to translate. Howard Marshall lists nine different interpretations of this phrase, some much less likely than others.[17] But the translation here is probably the best bet, because it allows for the influence of a passage in Ben Sirach (Ecclesiasticus) where also the topic is God's readiness to hear and answer the persistent prayer of the humble, and the same Greek phrase clearly means 'he will not delay'.[18] This actually takes us to the heart of the passage, because God's *elect* – his chosen people who belong to him – know that he is the one with the real power, whatever appearances might suggest to the contrary; and therefore it is worthwhile, indeed *vital*, to appeal to *him* for justice rather than expecting justice from any earthly power; just like David, in fact,[19] or like Daniel, who insisted on 'praying and seeking mercy before his God' in spite of royal edicts forbidding it.[20]

So it turns out that *prayer* is the vital activity that recognizes the presence of the kingdom of God when it seems to be absent. It's not about 'watching' for the coming of the kingdom like doctors watching for spots (17:20), but of acting passionately now out of faith in the *presence* of the kingdom – even though God seems to be delaying. (But what looks like delay to us, looks like patience from the perspective of others.[21]) The faith of a Daniel knows this, and persists in prayer to the God who dispenses all authority on earth, even when it is misused to produce oppression and corruption. *If you will look for it, the kingdom of God is within your grasp!* says Jesus (17:21).

The alternative to prayer is the disengaged, academic attitude of the Pharisees who simply want to know *when will the kingdom of God come?* This is a hands-off, intellectual sort of question that makes no difference to the way we live now. For Jesus, the kingdom *is* a present reality with a huge impact on the way we live: this has been the great burden of his teaching in the chapters preceding this one. To *cry to him day and night* for justice (18:7) is the stance of those who believe both that the kingdom is truly present – he is the one with the power! – and that the kingdom is not yet here, because justice is still a longed-for hope, and power lies in corrupt, human hands.

----

17. Marshall, *Luke*, pp. 674–675.

18. Ecclus. 35:19 (22). In both places the verb *makrothymein* is used, literally 'he is patient towards them'.

19. Ps. 18:6, quoted above.

20. Dan. 6:11.

21. See Rom. 2:4; 9:22; 2 Pet. 3:9.

But when the Son of Man comes, will he then find faith on the earth? (v. 8). With this question of his own, Jesus brings the whole sequence to a climax. Actually, I think, this question looks back over all the material in Luke 16 and 17, and not just over the section we are studying. Faith is what led the unjust steward to 'make friends using the mammon of unrighteousness', because he saw a bigger goal beyond the disaster of being dismissed by his master.[22] Faith in small things will strengthen faith for bigger tasks, and will save us from trusting in deceptive money.[23] Lazarus had no money, so his faith burned bright, while the rich man at whose gate he lay was deceived until death revealed the truth. But then it was too late.[24] Faith means constant, generous forgiveness, and never causing another to stumble[25] – but so impossible is this, that 'the apostles said to the Lord, "Increase our faith!"',[26] and Jesus encouragingly tells them that they only need mustard-seed faith to qualify as real believers, serving the Lord as he wants.[27] Faith led the leprous Samaritans to cry out to Jesus, and to find his steadfast love and power in a wonderful *kairos*-encounter of healing grace.

This is the faith for which the Son of Man will look when he comes! – faith that cries out in weakness, desperation and glimmering trust, the day-and-night prayer of our hearts that engages the whole of us. The language of 18:7 is drawn from Psalm 22:1–2:

> My God, my God, why have you forsaken me?
>> Why are you so far from helping me, from the words of my groaning?
> O my God, I cry by day, but you do not answer;
>> and by night, but find no rest.

This is the cry of those who hold on to faith in the *presence* of the *absent* God, and in the *reality* of God when he is *silent*. Faith is what sustains persistent prayer, and keeps us *crying day and night* to the God whom faith sees as sovereign, even though other powers seem stronger and he seems to delay.

This perspective will help us enormously as we look at the verses that lie in between the opening question and the closing parable, because they contain

---

22. Luke 16:9.
23. Luke 16:10–15.
24. Luke 16:19–31.
25. Luke 17:1–4.
26. Luke 17:5.
27. Luke 17:6–10.

some bleak and difficult material. Here faith is truly tested, and we need that cry of desperate trust.

5. The future of the kingdom (17:22–35)

We encounter a familiar pattern in verse 22, that having said something publicly Jesus now explains what he has said privately to his disciples.[28] So we expect what follows to unpack the notion of the presence of the kingdom. It is not surprising, therefore, that commentators scratch their heads over what follows, because it seems precisely *not* to pick up that idea, but instead to address more directly the Pharisees' question about the future coming of the kingdom.

But appearances are deceptive! As we look more closely at Jesus' words, we find here exactly that subtle balance between present and future which is then so vividly unpacked in the parable. The passage falls into three sections.

a. The suffering presence of the coming Son of Man (vv. 22–25)
Verse 22 is a beautiful recasting of the Pharisees' question, giving it a much more realistic quality. This is the form of the question that most of us can relate to: not an abstract, intellectual 'When will it come?', but a passionate, heart-felt, need-driven 'When will it come?' This is the lover waiting for the letter, or the three-year-old waiting for Christmas, rather than the scholar waiting for an answer.

Days will come, says Jesus, *when you will long to see one of the days of the Son of Man, and you will not see them* (v. 22). Some think this is backward looking, so that Jesus is suggesting that, in the future, the disciples will look back with longing to the glorious days they experienced with Jesus during his ministry, but they will not be able to re-experience them. But this reading runs against the grain of the whole passage. Jesus is imagining his disciples in precisely the position of the *widow* in 18:3 and *the elect* in 18:7, crying out to God for vindication. They are in the position of 'the people of the holy ones of the Most High' in Daniel 7, given over to the power of the beast and longing for deliverance – longing for *the days of the Son of Man* when the beast will be overthrown and they too will receive 'the kingship and dominion and the greatness of the kingdoms under the whole heaven',[29] no longer trampled under beast's terrible feet or abused by its arrogant 'horn'.

When suffering such persecution, of course the temptation is to look for signs of deliverance. Resist the temptation! says Jesus (v. 23). All *suggested* candidates

---

28. See e.g. Mark 4:10; Luke 10:23.

29. Dan. 7:27.

cannot possibly be the Son of Man, because there will be no mistaking his arrival when he appears. *For as lightning flashes brightly from one side of heaven to the other, so will the Son of Man be, in his day* (v. 24). Both France and Wright argue for their reading of Mark 13:26 on the ground that, in Daniel 7:13–14, the figure 'like a son of man' comes not to earth but to God, presented before the Ancient of Days to receive dominion and glory and kingship. So, they argue, the 'coming' of the Son of Man in Mark 13 must be to God, rather than to earth.[30] Luke 17:24 gives the lie to this rather strange distinction based on the direction of the 'coming'! It is both, of course. Because the 'dominion, glory and kingship' given to the Son of Man is *earthly* kingship, it must of course mean a coming to earth as well as a coming to God. How could it not? And when he comes, says Jesus, it will be as visible and obvious as a massive lightning bolt covering the entire sky.

The connection of thought in this passage depends on an unspoken connection between 'the kingdom of God' (the topic from v. 20) and 'the Son of Man'. Only those with Daniel 7 in mind are ready for this – and so Daniel 7 gives us the tools to read this passage aright. The Son of Man receives and brings *God's* kingdom. But he has it already, in his earthly ministry. He is already the 'strong man' plundering the kingdom of Satan by his exorcisms, casting out demons 'by the finger of God', so that 'the kingdom of God has come upon you'.[31] This is how the kingdom of God is already *in your midst* and available to all who will see it (v. 21). But the current presence of the kingdom in Jesus is not the complete fulfilment of Daniel 7, because – as in that passage – the power of the beasts has been extended.[32] They have not yet been finally overthrown. Hence the longing for deliverance in verse 22!

So verse 24 must be about the day when the vision of Daniel 7 of the replacement of the corrupt and oppressive kingdoms of earth by the just and glorious rule of the Son of Man actually becomes a full reality on planet Earth. Granted the progression of thought here, it cannot be about one of the pre-liminary *kairos*-comings on the way to that glorious End.[33] This is *the Day of the*

---

30. R. T. France, *Jesus and the Old Testament: His Application of Old Testament Passages to Himself and His Mission* (London: Tyndale Press, 1971), pp. 169, 235–236; Wright, *Jesus and the Victory of God*, p. 361.

31. Luke 11:18–22.

32. Dan. 7:12, 25.

33. I say this with N. T. Wright in mind, who suggests (as expected) in his *Luke for Everyone* (London: SPCK, 2001), p. 210, that 'the day of the Son of Man' is his vindication in and through the destruction of the city that has rejected him.

Son of Man for which the oppressed people of God have been longing, the moment when the Daniel 2 vision of the kingdom of God expanding to fill the whole earth, finally becomes a reality[34] – or, as N. T. Wright puts it, the day 'when God finally overcomes sin and death for good and remakes the heavens and the earth'.[35]

But actually – glorious though it is – verse 24 is not the most significant verse here. That privilege is reserved for verse 25: *But first it is necessary for him to suffer much, and be rejected by this generation.* Jesus gives a reason for the delay in the arrival of the Day of the Son of Man: it cannot come until he *too* has suffered. Once again, the dialogue between these words and the Daniel 7 vision gives them depth and bigger meaning. One of the most fascinating – not to say puzzling – things about Daniel 7, as we saw, is the connection between the Son of Man and 'the holy ones of the Most High', who both receive the kingdom, and who by implication therefore also both suffer under the terrible power of the beast. Daniel doesn't actually say that the Son of Man will be subjected to the beast 'for a time, two times, and half a time', along with the people of the Most High,[36] but we can well understand how the vision could be read to imply this – and this certainly seems to be how Jesus himself read it. So suffering comes as part of the 'Son of Man' package, not just glory.

In Luke the little Greek word *dei*, translated here *it is necessary*, usually points to a necessity that rests in the will of God and in the fulfilment of Scripture.[37] The suffering of the Son of Man is foreseen not just in Daniel 7, but even more clearly in all the passages that envisage the suffering and rejection of the Messiah or the Davidic king.[38] The Son of Man *must* suffer – there's no way round it.

And *this generation* is not really a time-expression here. Whereas in Mark 13:30 the primary significance of this phrase was as a time-notice, Luke tends to use it, as Earle Ellis observes, as 'a derogatory expression referring primarily to a

---

34. Dan. 2:44–45.

35. Wright, *Luke for Everyone*, p. 211. This is what Wright says Luke 17:24 is *not* about! Daniel doesn't quite say all this, but it's not bad as a summary of the *hope* of the kingdom of God.

36. Dan. 7:25.

37. Luke uses it twelve times in his Gospel. See for instance Luke 4:43; 9:22; 13:33; 22:37. We have already met this term in the 'these things must happen' of Dan. 2:28–29 which Luke himself echoes in 21:9.

38. E.g. Isa. 53; 50:6–9; Pss 22; 69.

class of people and only secondarily to a chronological period. It is an ethical rather than a physical generation'.[39] We can see this in Luke 11:29, where Jesus exclaims 'This generation is an evil generation!' and compares them unfavourably to the Ninevites at the time of Jonah – and perhaps even more clearly in 16:8: 'The sons of this age are wiser than the sons of the light, in their generation.' Here 'this age' and 'their generation' seem to be parallel expressions.

So it seems unlikely that Jesus is saying that *this generation* must reject him, while other generations might not. *This generation* probably means 'the generation in which the beast reigns still, the generation in which God's elect need to cry to him day and night for justice'. *This generation*, in this fuller sense, will only pass away when the Son of Man comes.

So here too the Son of Man and 'the saints of the Most High' suffer together. The disciples long for the Son of Man to come, but in the meantime he suffers with them at the hands of this 'unbelieving and perverted generation', as he put it earlier.[40] He too will cry for justice to the God whose kingdom will one day fill the earth, and he too will experience rejection just as they do. This prediction of his suffering looks back to Luke 9:21–22 where the language is almost identical:

> He warned them, telling them not to pass this on to anyone, saying, 'It is necessary for the Son of Man to suffer much, and to be rejected by the elders, the high priests and the scribes, and to be killed, and on the third day to rise.'

And in Luke 9 this prediction of Jesus' own suffering is immediately followed by a prediction of the suffering of his followers:

> He said to them all, 'If you want to come after me, you must deny yourself, and pick up your cross daily, and follow my example. For all who want to save their life will lose it; but those who lose their life for my sake, will save it. For what does it benefit you, to gain the whole world but to suffer the loss of yourself? For if you are ashamed of me and of my words, the Son of Man will be ashamed of you, when he comes in his glory and in the glory of his father and of the holy angels. But I tell you truly, some of you standing here will not taste death until you see the kingdom of God.'[41]

---

39. E. Earle Ellis, *The Gospel of Luke*, New Century Bible (London: Marshall, Morgan & Scott, 1974), p. 211.
40. Luke 9:41.
41. Luke 9:23–27.

This too feeds into Luke 17: particularly into verse 33, but more generally into the underlying connection between the sufferings of Jesus and those of his followers, supported by Daniel 7. Their suffering *together* is vital to their vindication when the Son of Man comes in glory. While they long for vindication, feeling deeply the pain and injustice of the world, they are walking in the footsteps of their Master who has suffered before, and with them, and who will one day come with glorious salvation.

b. The Day no-one foresaw and no-one will want (vv. 26–30)
Jesus uses two scriptural examples to illustrate the coming of the Son of Man: Noah and the flood, and Lot and the destruction of Sodom. His purpose is *warning*. And interestingly he seems to lump together his disciples with the Pharisees as the focus of this warning. It would be possible to say that, though he is addressing his disciples, the real object of this warning is the Pharisees, because they are the ones who are looking forward piously to the coming of the kingdom in blithe assurance that they will be OK – like those who 'desire the Day of the LORD' in Amos, only to be told that

> It is darkness, not light!
>> as if someone fled from a lion,
>> and was met by a bear;
> or went into the house and rested a hand
>> against the wall,
>> and was bitten by a snake.
> Is not the day of the LORD darkness, not light,
>> and gloom with no brightness in it?[42]

But of course the Pharisees are not the only ones who are desiring the coming of the kingdom. Jesus is envisaging that his disciples, too, will long for the Son of Man to appear. And elsewhere, as we saw in Mark 13, it is the disciples who are warned not to fall into complacency or to get distracted, but to 'stay awake'.[43]

When Jesus makes a similar prediction of the unexpectedness of the coming of the Son of Man in Luke 12, Peter responds with the question, 'Lord, are you telling this parable for us or for everyone?',[44] and Jesus leaves him in no

---

42. Amos 5:18–20.
43. Mark 13:32–37; cf. Matt. 25:1–13.
44. Luke 12:40–42.

doubt about the answer: the *disciples* could easily allow themselves to be distracted from their focus on faithfulness to their coming Lord, when his appearance is delayed. They could easily be like the 'unfaithful' servant who started to 'beat the other servants, male and female, and to eat and drink and get drunk'.[45]

So here, too, it is not just the Pharisees but also the disciples who could lose their passion in the business and distraction of *eating and drinking, marrying and giving in marriage . . . buying and selling, planting and building* (vv. 27, 28) – all good things in themselves, but terrible if they sap that passionate longing for the coming of the Son of Man. The activities Jesus lists are all about *making home here*, as if the future were about this life only.

Jesus' language is uncompromising. For all who live in complacent negligence of his coming, *the day that the Son of Man is revealed* will mean destruction. Jesus uses the same word as in Luke 9:24–25 quoted above, referring to those who seek to save their lives but instead lose them.

What a terrible warning this is for the church in our age – but also a glorious encouragement! Distracted by wealth, either the possession of it or the desire for it, we can lose our love for Jesus Christ, and thus lose *his* passion for justice and redemption in his world. But at any moment, Jesus is telling us, the Son of Man may come, bringing that justice and redemption with him. If we don't really want it, because we are too comfortable here already, then we won't be ready to receive him. But if we are passionately longing for that setting-right of all things, which is the kingdom of God – knowing that things are *not* all right in the ordinary business of the world – then we will welcome him with huge joy.

It is important to ask here, too, what kind of coming Jesus is referring to. One of the features of our developing biblical theology is that he comes in all sorts of preliminary ways, including many *kairos*-moments that anticipate his final appearance, and that the same kind of language can be used to describe either sort of 'coming'. The 'coming' to rescue Noah and Lot, which also meant the destruction of those around them, were two such *kairos*-moments. We argued that the language in verse 24 applies most appropriately to the full and final appearance of the Son of Man, since that is what the Pharisees were asking about. But all this language describing *the days of the Son of Man* can apply equally to his final coming, or to those comings in which we gloriously gain foretastes of his final redemption of all things. In fact it could be that the strange plural, *days*, used in verses 22 and

---

45. Luke 12:45.

26, hints at these multiple 'comings'.[46] How encouraging! He might come at any moment!

c. The terrible division and the reason for it (vv. 31–35)

Verses 22–25 focused on the *obviousness* of the coming of the Son of Man, and verses 26–30 on its *unexpectedness*. Now the focus shifts to its *violence*. Jesus' language is really grim here. His emphasis falls on the horror of the coming of the Son of Man, not the delight.

We are reminded of something only too dreadfully real to the author and the readers of Revelation, that 'the beast' is not some disembodied entity or vague spiritual power, but a terrible political, social, emotional and therefore spiritual reality that holds people in its grip, and from which they escape only by great hardship and sacrifice. The readers of Revelation – the members of the seven churches of Asia Minor – were called to 'Come out from her, my people, so that you do not get implicated in her sins, and so that you do not get caught up in her plagues of judgment'.[47] But they lived in the empire, and the whole economic, social and religious life of the communities around them was bound up in the fabric of Roman rule and power. How could they 'come out'? It was impossible to engage in trade without belonging to a trade guild dedicated to the worship of the trade deity. And the Roman imperial cult, which worshipped 'Roma' as a goddess, was extremely popular and pervasive, and to stand back from it looked like ungratitude and disloyalty, even treachery.[48]

But that is the call! – because Jesus Christ, not the Roman emperor, is 'Lord', and the days of the beast are numbered. Here in Luke 17 we meet just the same idea, and the same urgency. The structure of these verses runs like this:

- the terrible urgency – two examples (v. 31);
- the awful decision – a case and a principle (vv. 32–33);
- the dreadful division – two illustrations (vv. 34–35).

---

46. It is more likely that there is no great difference between the plural in vv. 22 and 26, and the singular in vv. 24 and 30, and that the plural is formed on analogy with the phrase 'the days of Noah' and 'the days of Lot'. The rabbis also used the expression 'the days of the Messiah' to refer to the whole period of the Messiah's reign. But even so, behind Jesus' language may lie his perception that the Son of Man comes in *many* unexpected ways when God's elect cry out to him for deliverance, day and night.

47. Rev. 18:4.

48. See Nelson Kraybill, *Imperial Cult and Commerce in John's Apocalypse* (Sheffield: Sheffield Academic Press, 1996).

The urgency creates action that looks like absolute folly. What sense does it make to take *nothing* from inside the house, if you have to flee suddenly – even if you are sitting on the roof of the house at the moment the danger appears? Not even a small supply of food or better shoes? The point is that the disciples of Jesus Christ have *already* left everything behind. Sent out on mission by Jesus, they took *nothing* with them.[49] They heard him call people to homelessness,[50] to renounce family for the sake of the kingdom,[51] to sell their possessions because they trust their Father to give them the kingdom,[52] and to make their love of family look like hatred in comparison with their devotion to Jesus.[53] 'None of you can be my disciple', he said, 'unless you wave farewell to all your possessions!'[54]

Already home and possessions hold no security for the disciples of Jesus Christ. Like the churches of Asia Minor, they live under a different lordship, because they have taken the decision implicit in verse 33. Unlike Lot's wife, who looked back because she was attached to the security of Sodom,[55] these disciples flee because they do not want to be caught up in the disaster about to fall when the Son of Man comes. They know that to seek to keep their life in Sodom will be to lose their lives. But to abandon Sodom will mean salvation.

So how should we understand Jesus' words describing the dreadful division that follows the coming of the Son of Man (vv. 34–35)?

> *I tell you, that night there will be two on one bed, and one will be taken and the other left; there will be two women milling grain together, one will be taken, and the other left.*

Once again, ordinary life is suddenly broken apart by the coming of the Son of Man. What is more ordinary than sleeping and preparing food? The surprising thing here is the emphasis on separation, this cutting into the intimate heart of family life. There are three ways of reading this.

The first is the obvious and now widespread *literal* reading, which finds here the sudden delicious rapture of believers into heaven by the Lord, leaving unbelievers only on earth – and causing absolute chaos as suddenly planes are pilotless and plunge to earth; cars are driverless so huge pile-ups ensue; patients

---

49. Luke 9:3.
50. Luke 9:57–58.
51. Luke 9:59–62.
52. Luke 12:29–33.
53. Luke 14:26.
54. Luke 14:33.
55. Gen. 19:15–26.

on operating tables are suddenly left without surgeons or anaesthetists; children worldwide suddenly have no parents; and, most remarkably of all, all infants disappear, leaving their parents in an agony of unexplained loss.[56]

Within the 'Left Behind' scenario, this chaos is the catalyst for the appearance of the antichrist and the consequent great tribulation – the terrible seven-year period which ends with the battle of Armageddon and the victorious coming of Jesus in glory. Overall, I confess that I find this picture ethically horrifying, particularly the gruesome way in which the rapture is portrayed. But the question for us is whether it is a good reading of Luke 17:34–35. One of the interesting consequences, drawn out explicitly by Dave Hunt, is that *two* comings of Jesus are needed, because the Luke 17 coming which precipitates the rapture needs to be different from the Mark 13 coming which *follows* the great tribulation seven years later, and precipitates the final judgment.[57]

Once again we see how the texts are being squeezed into an interpretative framework which is the construct of the interpreter, rather than just being allowed to speak for themselves. If they dance their own dance, it is surely clear that Luke 17 and Mark 13 are drawing on the same Daniel 7 traditions and applying them to Jesus. Their steps may be a little different, but they are wheeling round the floor together and envisaging one great 'coming' of the Son of Man – albeit possibly anticipated by other moments when he comes to his people in power. And within the Daniel 7 tradition, it is clear that the coming of the Son of Man is about victory over the powers of earth and the creation of a new kingdom under him – it is *not* about the privileged rescue of the 'saints', leaving earth's powers untouched.

There are two other ways of hearing Jesus here, and possibly both are in mind. This division between intimates is an awful image drawn from war, which

---

56. See e.g. Dave Hunt, *When Will Jesus Come? Compelling Evidence for the Soon Return of Christ* (Eugene: Harvest House, 1993), pp. 151–152. It is all portrayed with horrible realism in the film *Left Behind*, starring Nicholas Cage (directed by Vic Armstrong, released 2014). This high-profile remake of an original (2000) *Left Behind* film (followed by *Left Behind: Tribulation Force* in 2002 and *Left Behind: World at War* in 2005) testifies to the extraordinary popularity and strength of this theology in the United States.

57. E.g. Hunt, *When Will Jesus Come?*, pp. 80–83, 132–133, 147ff. Hunt suggests that the coming for the rapture is not publicly visible, but the final second coming 'will be like lightning flashing across the sky, visible to every eye' (p. 149). But that is the language Luke uses here (17:24), to describe the coming which leads to this terrible division between intimates.

always leads to the separation of families and friends. The closest companions lose each other, so extreme is the emergency that sweeps down upon them. Neither is safe, neither the one who is left nor the one who is taken. All are *in extremis*, with no resource against the disaster. Or maybe the image has a further element within it, following on from the decision in verse 33: when the moment of disaster comes, people have to choose where their loyalty lies. Will they stay, trusting in the place of earthly security, or will they go? To whom do they most deeply belong?

Luke pictured this kind of family division earlier, in words of Jesus just as sobering:

> Do you think that I came to give peace on the earth? No, I tell you – rather, division. For *from now on* five in one house will be divided, three against two and two against three. The family will be divided – father against son, son against father, mother against daughter, daughter against mother, mother-in-law against daughter-in-law, daughter-in-law against mother-in-law.[58]

Whenever the Son of Man comes, he creates division – notice 'from now on', which I've highlighted in this passage. The division at his coming echoes divisions already experienced around loyalty to him.

However we read this imagery, it's worth asking: Why does Jesus use such horrible pictures? Might we not expect him to use images of salvation, rather than of destruction, in connection with his coming? There may be several reasons for this. To some extent this may be shock tactics, jolting both the disciples and the Pharisees out of their warm, fuzzy feelings about the coming kingdom of God. The destruction of the beast cannot be nice or easy. This 'war' scenario also represents just the kind of situation within which God's elect cry for deliverance – so it is precisely within such situations that the Son of Man will come *speedily* to deliver (18:8). But we must also reckon with the fact that Jesus took judgment very seriously, as we have seen. If there is going to be *ekdikēsis*, vindication, justice,[59] setting right what is wrong in the world, then there must be a process of purging and destruction of all that is contrary to right.

It is so vital that we leave this to him! The world right now is deeply hurt by the actions of some who believe that God has called them to be the arm of his

58. Luke 12:51–53. The language deliberately echoes Mic. 7:6, which pictures the social confusion which *precedes* the coming of the Lord to rescue.

59. This is the word used three times in the parable – that for which the widow pleads (18:3) and the elect cry (18:7) and God acts (18:8).

righteous judgment against wickedness. The suffering in Syria and Iraq, as I write, is immense. But for us Christians, woe betide us if we ever forget the principle that 'vengeance is mine, I will repay, says the Lord'. In this line from Romans, Paul quotes words from Deuteronomy and uses the same Greek word, *ekdikēsis*, as we have here in Luke 18.[60] God alone is the worker of vindication, vengeance and justice. And while he may step in at any time to respond to the cry of his elect, the 'big' work of vengeance – the destruction of the beast – is for the End, when all things are made new.

We can imagine a stunned silence after verse 35. How can the disciples respond to this appalling imagery?

6. The disciples' puzzled response and Jesus' puzzling reply (17:37)

Their question is understandable! 'Where, Lord?' implies a desire to find out where this disaster will occur, so that they can organize not to be there at the time. Which bit of planet Earth is going to be inflicted in this way, the focal point of the coming of the Son of Man?

It is very interesting to me that Jesus does not reply 'in Jerusalem' or drop some enigmatic hint that this is all coming Jerusalem's way.[61] Some find just such a hint in the fact that the Greek *aetos* means both 'vulture' and 'eagle', and suggest that these 'eagles' are the Roman legionary eagles, the standards that were carried into battle at the head of the Roman armies, and which were presumably present when the armies of Titus surrounded Jerusalem.[62] This seems far-fetched. Jesus responds to the disciples' direct question with an enigmatic proverbial utterance which seems to say, 'Judgment will occur where it is required.'[63] Vultures might start to circle over a corpse anywhere – the location is random. Like the vengeance, so the place is left to God alone. But the imagery in verse 24 has already suggested a vast location: 'From the land under the heaven to the land under the heaven' the lightning will flash. Translations tidy this up – as I did above – by introducing the word 'side'. But the wording is more vague than this. Everywhere where

---

60. Deut. 32:35; Rom. 12:19.

61. That, of course, is the standard view in premillennial schemes. In effect they discount Jesus' enigmatic reply here and make him give a straight answer!

62. So Wright, *Jesus and the Victory of God*, p. 360; *Luke for Everyone*, p. 209.

63. This is Ellis' summary of the meaning (Ellis, *Luke*, p. 212). He adds 'i.e., universally'.

there is land under heaven, there the lightning will flash, and the vultures will circle.

After this deeply sobering passage, we turn to one where we meet the same balance between present and future, but in a very different way.

6. AT HOME WITH THE LORD (JOHN 14:1–31)

1. Introduction: The same Jesus?

We turn to a very different passage indeed. So different, in fact, that many scholars argue that we cannot be meeting the same Jesus in both Luke 17 and John 14. This is part of a bigger argument about the different presentations of Jesus in the Gospels, beyond our focus here, but to my mind the enormous differences in style and content between (e.g.) Luke and John testify to the inexhaustible richness and creativity both of Jesus himself, and of the Gospel-writers. He was not one who could be pigeonholed in one quick presentation or summary. We need four Gospels, and in particular we need John's Gospel alongside the other three, in order to give something approaching a full picture. But even so, John concludes with a moving reminder that every picture of Jesus is incomplete: 'There are many other things that Jesus did, and if they were all written down one by one, I don't think the world itself would contain the books that would be written.'[1]

John is very aware of the selectivity with which he has operated,[2] and therefore we too need to be aware of the care with which he has edited his

---

1. John 21:25.
2. See also John 20:30–31.

picture of Jesus in order to make it as truthful as possible. He wants to bring us as close as he can to the real Jesus whom 'we beheld'.[3] So, beyond the differences between the Jesus of John 14 and the Jesus of Luke 17 and Mark 13, we need to ask and look for the similarities also. Can we see how we are meeting the same person in all three passages? Is it believable that the differences are a result of the sheer glorious creativity of one person, mediated through the secondary creativity of the three evangelists?

One interesting feature of this chapter immediately pops up when we ask this question. We find ourselves facing the same issue here, as to whether references to the 'coming' of the Lord are about his *second* coming, or some other coming – or about both. In fact, many scholars again have argued that there are no references to the second coming in John 14. So once again I find myself needing to justify my choice of passage!

2. Is John 14 about the second coming?

There are four references to the 'coming' of Jesus in John 14. Verse 3:

And if I go and prepare a place for you, I will come again and will take you to myself, so that where I am, you may be also.

Then verses 18–19:

I will not leave you like orphans, I will come to you. In a little while the world will no longer see me, but you will see me, because I will live and you also will live.

Also verse 23:

Anyone who loves me will keep my word; and my Father will love him, and we will come to him and make a dwelling for ourselves with him.[4]

---

3. John 1:14. For a brilliant analysis of the eyewitness theme underlying John's presentation of Jesus, see Richard Bauckham, *Jesus and the Eyewitnesses: The Gospels as Eyewitness Testimony* (Grand Rapids: Eerdmans, 2006), chs. 14 – 17.

4. The best way to make the language of this translation gender-inclusive – as it should be – would be to make it plural ('Those who love me . . .'). But there is something important about Jesus' use of the singular here, so the best approach is to use masculine singular pronouns and to apologize in a footnote!

And finally verse 28:

> *You heard me say to you, 'I am going, and I am coming to you'. If you loved me, you would rejoice that I am going to the Father, because the Father is greater than me.*[5]

It is clear that in verse 28 Jesus is looking back to the previous references, and that in verses 18 and 23 he is talking about a 'spiritual' (for want of a better word) coming – associated in both places, as we will see, with the gift and the coming of the 'Paraklete', the Holy Spirit. A reference to his resurrection also seems clear in verse 18. But what about the 'coming' in verse 3? Many argue that this, too, is about a spiritual coming back, in the resurrection or at Pentecost or both.[6]

I resist this view, because it is clear that this coming has different consequences. In verses 18 and 23 the consequences of the coming are that the disciples will be strengthened in their understanding (v. 20) and in their obedience and love (v. 21), and – as we'll see in due course – in their witness to the world (v. 23). But in verse 3 the consequence is first that Jesus *will take you to myself*, and then that *where I am, you are also*. Connected to the reference to the *many dwellings in my Father's house* where Jesus says he will *prepare a place for you* (v. 2), it seems to me to be obvious that this coming is different in kind. It does not leave the disciples better equipped for witness in the world, but removes them to a different *place*, which they share with the Lord. Paul's words in 1 Thessalonians 4:17 seem close ('and so we will be always with the Lord'), likewise expressing the *consequence* of his second coming.[7]

So here too we meet the beautiful connection between the coming *now* and the coming *then* of the Lord, which we have met in Mark 13 and in Luke 17. John gives it a particular twist, as we'll see, both by his fascinating use of the Greek word *monē*, 'dwelling place', in verses 2 and 23, and also by his presentation of Jesus as the *way* (vv. 4–6, a theme that then shapes the whole chapter). Wanting to prepare his disciples for his departure – the agenda of the whole chapter – Jesus encourages them first by talking of his second coming and its consequence for them, and then of the anticipatory 'comings' of himself, of

---

5. In all four places the same Greek word is used, *erchesthai*.

6. So, for instance, B. Lindars, *The Gospel of John*, New Century Bible (London: Marshall, Morgan & Scott, 1972), p. 471.

7. This view is taken by D. A. Carson, *The Gospel According to John* (Leicester: Inter-Varsity Press and Grand Rapids: Eerdmans, 1991), p. 488.

his Father and of the Paraklete-Spirit by which they will be sustained until that glorious End arrives.[8]

3. Structure

This chapter is so rich that, unfortunately, we cannot undertake a full study of it. We need to focus on the issue in hand for us, the biblical theology of the second coming. However an overview is essential. We can analyse the chapter like this:[9]

A   The untroubled heart: Jesus the Way (vv. 1–7)
   B   Indwelling (1): Jesus and the Father (vv. 8–11)
      C   Active in the world: prayer (vv. 12–14)
   B' Indwelling (2): Jesus, the Father, the Spirit and the disciples (vv. 15–21)
      C' Active in the world: the word (vv. 22–25)
A' The untroubled heart: Jesus the Way (vv. 27–31)

The opening and closing paragraphs balance each other, focusing on the themes of Jesus' departure and return, and on Jesus' encouragement of the disciples to believe, and not to be troubled in heart. The theme of Jesus as the Way runs throughout the chapter, as we'll see shortly – and underlies the final rather surprising words, *Rise, let us go from here* (v. 31).[10]

---

8. Some scholars seem to get quite muddled over this balance between the final coming and earlier anticipations. For instance, Rudolph Schnackenburg says that 14:3 'should not . . . be in any way interpreted as referring to the parousia', but then comments that 'The "I will take you to myself" *begins* after Easter, in the existence of the believers . . . but it is *completed* only after death (or after the parousia)' (Rudolph Schnackenburg, *The Gospel According to St John*, vol. 3 [Tunbridge Wells: Burns & Oates, 1982], pp. 62–63, his emphases). We will ask below whether the primary reference to the *parousia* in 14:3 also carries overtones of what happens to believers at death.

9. The letters added to the analysis (A–A' etc.) mark the basically chiastic structure of the passage, although the central paragraphs balance each other in parallel. A 'chiasm' is a literary structure within which the elements of the text balance each other in pairs around a mid point.

10. The surprise, of course, is that Jesus and his disciples do not leave at this point: three chapters are yet to pass until we read 'Having said this, Jesus went out, with his disciples . . .' (18:1). See below for discussion of this fascinating point.

In between these opening and closing paragraphs, we have paired paragraphs that similarly balance each other. The B paragraphs focus on the inner, 'indwelling' relationships that bind Jesus and his Father (vv. 8–11), and then all the actors in the drama: Jesus, his Father, the Paraklete and the disciples (vv. 15–21). But this is not abstract theology, it is all deeply related to the concern of the chapter to prepare the disciples for Jesus' departure, and specifically for their mission in the world. So the two C paragraphs focus on this outward-looking mission in different ways.

Let us now plunge straight in with Jesus' promise of his return.

4. 'I will come again and will take you to myself'

The theme of Jesus' departure has been prominent since the beginning of chapter 13,[11] and becomes explicit at 13:33, 'Little ones, I am with you for only a little longer . . .' This prompts Peter's question, 'Lord, where are you going?' and Jesus' enigmatic response, 'Where I am going, you cannot follow now – but you will follow me later.'[12] Peter's anguished cry of grief and devotion, 'Lord, why can I not follow you now? I will lay down my life for you!', then evokes Jesus' very sobering prediction of Peter's denial of him before that very night ends.[13]

Within the drama of the Last Supper we can imagine a horrified silence at this point. Not unnaturally, with the 'betrayer' having been identified and having departed,[14] the remaining disciples might have thought 'Well, we're OK then!' The prediction that *Peter* will deny Jesus was a horrifying bolt from the blue. If Peter, then how not all of them?

Into this stunned silence Jesus' words come, addressing all of them:

> *Do not let your heart be troubled. Believe in God, and believe in me. In my Father's house are many homes. If there were not, would I say to you that I am going to prepare a place for you? And if I go*

---

11. See John's introduction to the whole passion narrative in 13:1.

12. John 13:36.

13. John 13:37–38. Carson suggests that the farewell discourse begins at 13:31, and treats 13:31 – 14:31 as a discrete section (Carson, *John*, pp. 476–477). This is not inappropriate, but I think that it downplays the way in which ch. 14 has an *inclusio* structure (a balance in themes between the opening and closing paragraphs, indicating a discrete section), and also the ways in which 13:31–38 picks up and rounds off themes which have been important in ch. 13.

14. John 13:21–30.

and prepare a place for you, I will come again and take you to be with myself, so that where I am,
you too may be (vv. 1–3).

Jesus does not take back or soften the prediction of denial, following hard on
the heels of the prediction of betrayal. But he answers Peter's question of 13:36
– connecting it with the more important allied question '*Why* are you going?' –
with this glorious promise made without hesitation to disciples who are about
to deny him.

Essential background here relates to the use of both the word *house* (Gk *oikia*)
and the word *place* (Gk *topos*) to refer to the temple, and the belief that the earthly
temple was but a copy or shadow of the real, heavenly temple where God dwells.
This conviction concerning the relationship between the earthly and the heavenly
temples is vital for the theology of Hebrews, and pops up elsewhere too. The
earthly temple is also 'my Father's house',[15] the place where his name and his
glory dwells,[16] the place that the Sanhedrin feared might be taken away by the
Romans – as indeed it was.[17] Jewish theology regularly pictured heaven as a
temple, and we meet this symbolism also in Revelation.[18] Jesus tells his disciples
that he is going home to his Father's heavenly temple-dwelling, and that he will
make it a home for them, too – and then return to take them there. Revelation
fills out this vision for us in due course: this is not about God's people inhabiting
some ethereal, 'heavenly' space with the Lord, but about the coming-down of
the heavenly city, God's dwelling, to earth, in a new creation which unites heaven
and earth because *God himself* now dwells with us, and we with him.[19]

That is a bigger topic that takes us beyond our focus on the second coming
of the Lord! For the moment, let's reflect on the amazing difference in tone and
content between this expectation of Jesus' return and the 'revealing of the Son
of Man' in Luke 17. If that passage is grim and sobering, this one is peaceful
and encouraging – it seems. The awful violence with which the coming of the
Son of Man is compared to an invading army, bringing destruction and division,
separating friends and lovers as God did when Sodom was destroyed by fire

---

15. John 2:16.

16. See e.g. 1 Kgs 8:27–30, Solomon's dedicatory prayer, using both 'house' and 'place'
    to refer to the temple, and connecting the earthly temple to the heavenly 'dwelling'
    of God. *Prayer* is what connects the two.

17. John 11:48: the irony is deep and full of pain.

18. See for instance the temple symbolism in Rev. 4, climaxing with the cry of worship
    that echoes Isaiah's temple vision (Isa. 6:3).

19. Rev. 21:1 – 22:5.

and sulphur, becomes here a glorious promise of a reunion in the heavenly temple itself. How do we tie this up?

The interesting thing is that the same verb is used in both places. 'One will be taken (Gk *paralambanein*) and the other left'[20] summed up the awfulness of his return in Luke. But here *I will take you to myself* – the same verb – is at the heart of this glorious promise to disciples who are about to deny their Lord.

It would be wrong to make too much of this, because the verb is not uncommon in the New Testament. But these are the only places in the New Testament where it is used in connection with the second coming, and Luke 17:34–35 (with the parallel in Matthew[21]) is the only place where it is used in the passive. In all other places it is active, and so it is clear who is doing the 'taking'.[22] Usually, too, it is a 'nice' word, connoting not a cruel or violent 'taking' but an encouraging 'taking along'. The word is used out of its normal character in Luke 17. But here in John 13 it is back in character, referring (I suggest) *to the same taking, viewed from a different perspective.* The beast cannot be overthrown peacefully, and we will certainly experience the violence of his overthrow, when the time comes. Even now, the lashings of the beast's tail bring destruction and anguish, and God's people are 'taken' by such events. But from the perspective of the rule of Daniel's God, who allows his people into the furnace only to stand alongside them, and into the lions' den only to shut their mouths, this is a 'taking' that means a homecoming, a deliverance from the beast's power.

We meet just such a double significance of a similar verb earlier in John. In John 9:34 we read that the synagogue authorities 'throw out' (Gk *ekballein*) the man born blind, now with his sight restored. But in this dreadful alienation Jesus finds him, opens his spiritual eyes some more,[23] and then starts to talk about the Shepherd who comes to his sheep, and calls them by name, and 'leads them out' (Gk *ekballein*, the same verb), going before them to find pasture.[24] In Jesus' hands, what had been a 'throwing out' becomes a 'leading out' to a new life. This is how he turns cross to resurrection in our experience. And this is how the ghastly 'takings' that afflict God's people as they labour under bestial power-under-judgment become glorious 'takings' that welcome them home to the Father's house.

---

20. Luke 17:34–35.

21. Matt. 24:40–41.

22. It is used with a personal object, meaning 'to take someone along' on thirty occasions: e.g. Mark 5:40; 9:2.

23. John 9:35–38.

24. John 10:1–4.

5. Jesus, the Way! – because he is the Truth, and the Life

I think this title reflects the best way to understand the relationship between the three terms in the 'I am . . .' list in 14:6. *I am the Way* is the primary one, because this has been the focus of the discussion between Jesus and Thomas in verses 4–5. But what *qualifies* Jesus to be the Way is that he is also *the Truth and the Life*, and these terms are also important for what follows.[25]

I am the Way is a dramatic and striking claim. Thomas is thinking in terms of maps, routes and destinations when he says, *Lord, we don't know where you are going. How can we know the way?* (v. 5). To be told that Jesus himself *is* the map and the route they must follow, is one of those paradigm-shifting moments that takes us out of the realm of *law* (this is what you've got to do, to follow the route) into the realm of *relationship* (this is who you need to be with). All the material that follows on the intimate relationship between Jesus and his disciples develops from this point. They need to 'go Jesus', like baby grebes on the back of their mother.

It is at this point that we need to mention the work of Jürgen Moltmann, the great German theologian who did so much to reintroduce eschatology into Christian theology in the last century. His epoch-making book *Theology of Hope* was first published in German in 1964, and its emphasis on the vital importance of *hope* grew out of his own experience as a twenty-year-old prisoner of war in Britain in 1945-47, when first he lost all hope because of his remorse over what Germany had done during the war, but then gradually found new hope through the witness of chaplains and other Christians, and as he read Mark's Gospel in the Bible he had been given. 'I summoned up the courage to live again, and I was slowly but surely seized by a great hope for the resurrection', he wrote.[26]

His *Theology of Hope* begins with these words:

> Eschatology means the doctrine of Christian hope, which embraces both the object hoped for and the hope inspired by it. From first to last, and not merely in the epilogue, Christianity is eschatology, is hope, forward looking and forward moving, and therefore also revolutionizing and transforming the present. The eschatological

---

25. 'The truth' is picked up in the emphasis on the reliability and importance of Jesus' words and commandments (vv. 10, 15, 21, 24, 29), and for 'life' see v. 19. But both these themes sit under the presentation of Jesus as the 'way' which the disciples must go. Carson has a nice discussion of the relationship between the three terms: Carson, *John*, p. 491.

26. See Jürgen Moltmann, *A Broad Place: An Autobiography* (London: SCM Press, 2007).

is not one element *of* Christianity, but it is the medium of Christian faith as such, the key in which everything in it is set, the glow that suffuses everything here in the dawn of an expected new day. For Christian faith lives from the raising of the crucified Christ, and strains after the promise of the universal future of Christ.[27]

For Moltmann, we cannot be truly Christian unless we are living in hope and expectation of the second coming and of all that that means for us and for the world. Notice how this fits with our reflections on the future as a 'future-as-present' – the vital thing is our holding of the future *now* in a way which inspires present hope. And Moltmann has a particular take on how this hope arises from our relationship with the risen Lord. Christian eschatology, he says, is not about looking into the future and predicting certain things that will happen. It is about looking into the *past* – the past of Jesus Christ – and then looking forward to Jesus' own future.

> Christian eschatology speaks of Jesus Christ and *his* future. It recognizes the reality of the raising of Jesus and proclaims the future of the risen Lord. . . . [The descriptions of Jesus in the New Testament] point believers in him towards the hope of his still outstanding future.[28]

His still outstanding future – that's Moltmann's distinctive point. The resurrection is not the end of *Jesus'* story. The resurrection means that there *has* to be hope for us, and for the world, because *his* story is not yet complete. 'The Christian hope for the future comes of observing a specific, unique event – that of the resurrection and appearing of Jesus Christ.'[29] Note how Moltmann combines 'resurrection' and 'appearing' here as two poles of *one* event: the person of Jesus Christ and his story as the crucified, resurrected and to-be-glorified Son of God holds the two together, and means that we then have a unique perception of our story, too, as those who believe in him. We have to live his story, as well, because he is not absent from the world and the church while awaiting the next instalment of his story. He is actively involved in his church and its mission, by his Spirit, sharing its story as his.

This is exactly what we find in John 14! It is built into Jesus' identification of himself as 'the Way'. He invites his disciples to 'go' him, to live out his story

---

27. Jürgen Moltmann, *Theology of Hope: On the Ground and Implications of a Christian Eschatology* (London: SCM Press, 1967), p. 16, his emphasis.

28. Moltmann, *Theology of Hope*, p. 17, his emphasis.

29. Ibid., p. 194.

in the world as they walk the way which is Jesus himself, obeying and loving him, living in intimate fellowship with him, doing his works, keeping his words, experiencing the peace which he alone gives, and living in the fellowship of the Paraklete whom the Father sends in his name.

So Christian eschatology has no substance apart from Jesus Christ. *He* is the way we walk, both now and on the Day when he comes again and takes us to be with him – and thereafter, too. There is no other way by which we may *come to the Father* (v. 6). This is implicit in Mark and in Luke, too, for all their differences from John. The destruction of the temple in Mark 13 and the coming of the kingdom in Luke 17, are both caught up into the coming of *the Son of Man*. They become part of the story of Jesus Christ as he fulfils his destiny as the Son of Man who *already* brings the kingdom, but in whom the kingdom has a much more glorious future yet to be.

Let's now unpack how John 14 shows this, by looking in turn at the paired paragraphs we identified above – the B paragraphs on relationship, and the C paragraphs on mission.

6. Living in fellowship with the Lord (vv. 8–11, 15–21)

If Jesus himself, in person, is the way we must go – not a set of instructions or rules – then it is not surprising that the emphasis in this chapter falls on intimate relationship with him. How easily we forget this! The temptation to substitute relationship with regulation has been one to which the church has constantly fallen prey. Regulation is so much easier to manage! If there are clear rules, then everyone knows where they stand; sin can be punished and virtue rewarded. The subtlety of this temptation lies in the fact that these are often rules about how the relationship with Jesus Christ is to be managed. You'll stay in fellowship with him, we are told, if you have a daily Quiet Time, say three Hail Mary's before breakfast, attend the church prayer meeting or Mass and confession regularly, tithe your income and pray for foreign missions. Some of this may be all right – but is it what *Jesus himself* commands (v. 1 5)? What *does* he command?

These two paragraphs unfold for us the basis of theology and action in the church of Jesus Christ.

a. The total sufficiency of Jesus (vv. 8–11)
Philip wants to *know*. He wants to dig deep into the truth, to plumb mysteries, and if possible to have an apocalyptic vision of God himself. This is probably the import of *Lord, show us the Father, and that will be sufficient for us* (v. 8). This is

his slight put-down in response to Jesus' amazing claim in verse 7, *If you know me, you will know my Father also. In fact, right now you know him, and have seen him!* Philip is sceptical about this. Or maybe he just fails to take in what Jesus is saying. Like many others in his day (and ours), he looks for answers to the great existential questions through experiencing God directly. If only we could see God, how wonderful that would be! Would that not be sufficient to explain the questions we have and the mysteries we face? At the time when John was writing his Gospel, almost certainly after the destruction of Jerusalem and the temple in AD 70, this desire for direct answers from God to the great 'Why' questions was very strong, and many Jewish readers of the Gospel, both Christian and non-Christian, would have empathized strongly with Philip here.[30]

But what an answer he gets! *Have I been with you all for so long, and you don't know me, Philip? Whoever has seen me has seen the Father. How can you say 'Show us the Father'?* There is no need for separate apocalyptic access to God, for he is already visible in Jesus Christ; and – by implication – all the great existential questions find their answer in him, too. All *truth* is in him. Look at me, says Jesus to Philip, and you will hear God speak, and see him act, because *I am in the Father, and the Father is in me* (v. 10).

This language of mutual indwelling is very important, and is even more vital in the next paragraph (vv. 15–21) where the Holy Spirit and the disciples themselves are drawn in as well. What does it mean for one to be 'in' another, in this way? Jesus' own explanation here is that it means a complete mutuality of speaking and acting. The words and acts of one become those of the other, so closely united are the two in mind, heart and intention: *the words that I speak to you I do not utter from myself, but the Father who dwells in me does his works.* As in speaking to the sceptical Jews in John 10, Jesus can point to his 'works' as evidence of the nature of his relationship with the Father: 'If I do not do the works of my Father, do not trust me; but if I do them, then even if you don't want to take my word for it, trust the works themselves, so that you might recognize and know that the Father is in me, and I am in the Father.'[31]

Jesus represents his Father, in the fullest sense: *re-presents* him so completely, that God's words and actions are fully displayed in him. So we need no further or different revelation of the mind and heart of God, and of his action in the world, than we have in Jesus Christ. Jesus challenges Philip especially to believe this *because of the works themselves* (v. 11). *Works* here are not just his miracles, but

---

30. Several great Jewish apocalypses date from this period – not least the greatest of them all, the book of Revelation.

31. John 10:37–38.

include his *words*, and thus embrace his whole ministry. When you look at the whole picture, Philip, what do you see? Do you see 'glory as of the only Son from the Father, full of grace and truth'?[32]

But of course the problem of Jesus' departure becomes even more acute, if there is no separate access to God, apart from him. How can Philip – not to mention people like us! – clearly *see* Jesus in order to see the Father, once he has gone? This is where the Paraklete comes in.

b. The special sufficiency of the Holy Spirit (vv. 15–21)

This paragraph sits at the heart of the chapter, and is framed by its own little *inclusio:* compare verses 15 and 21 and notice how they balance each other. Love and obedience go together, each preceding the other – because obedience is not about slavishly following rules, but about gladly embracing the constraints of the relationship with the loved one. *If you love me, you will keep my commandments* (v. 15), . . . *the one who has my commandments and keeps them, that's the one who loves me!* (v. 21). *Commandments* in this sense are not authoritative rules laid down and demanding conformity, with penalties attached, like traffic regulations. Rather, they are welcoming guidelines that prioritize relational connection, like 'Feel free to stay after the service, have a cup of coffee and chat – but remember we have to be out by 1 pm because the caretaker needs to lock up!' No rule demands that I will stay or go, talk to Mrs Smith or Mr Jones, have a coffee or not; and no regulation prescribes what I will say as I drift around the church hall. But all my action will be shaped (or not) by the constraints of the relational connection I have with the people there, and with the caretaker.

This meaning of *commandment* is illustrated by chapter 13, which lies in the background here. In fact this passage (14:15–21) builds on the great words in 13:34, 'A new commandment I give you, that you love one another; that you too should love each other as I have loved you', and these words in turn build on Jesus' action in washing his disciples' feet and giving them 'an example, that you also should do as I have done to you'.[33] Such action is not ruled by regulation, but required by relationship – by the *love* that Jesus commands us to have.

Between verses 15 and 21 lies the first promise of the Holy Spirit:[34] *I will ask the Father, and he will give you another Paraklete, to be with you for ever – the Spirit of truth whom the world cannot receive, because it neither sees him, nor knows him. You know*

---

32. John 1:14.

33. John 13:15.

34. There are four such promises in the course of the farewell discourse, with a beautiful sequence between them: 14:16, 26; 15:26; 16:7.

him, because he dwells with you, and will be in you (vv. 16–17). Calling the Spirit *another Paraklete* suggests, as many have pointed out, that Jesus himself is already a Paraklete with them – that is, an advocate on behalf of his Father, representing him in word and deed. This perception led R. E. Brown, one of the leading commentators on John, to his famous description of the Paraklete, the Holy Spirit, as 'the presence of Jesus when Jesus is absent'.[35] This is confirmed when, immediately after promising this wonderful gift, Jesus says *I will come to you* (v. 18) and adds that on that day – presumably the day when the Spirit-Paraklete is given – *you will know that I am in my Father, and you are in me, and I am in you* (v. 20).

This is the crucial point, and the answer to the problem of Jesus' departure: though still departed, he yet *comes* in the person of the *Spirit of truth*, and as a result the disciples themselves are caught up into the amazing relationship of mutual indwelling shared by the Father and the Son in verses 10–11. What a move! The language could hardly be stronger, or more compelling and moving: *The one who loves me will be loved by my Father; and I will love him too, and reveal myself to him* (v. 21).[36] Philip's longing for direct apocalyptic access to God is trumped by this glorious promise of revelation to everyone to whom the Spirit comes – revelation of and from the (now risen) Jesus himself. This is precisely Moltmann's vision of an eschatology which is rooted in the continuing story of Jesus Christ, crucified, risen, present in his church by his Spirit, and coming again in glory. The End is not the climax of a sequence of world events, as if it were the natural climax of the story of 'history' told from within its own terms. Rather, the End is the climax of the story of Jesus Christ, who is already the Lord, the Son of Man, and who moves with his church towards that glorious point when 'the kingdom of this world has become the kingdom of our Lord, and of his Christ – and he shall reign for ever and ever!'[37]

Love and obedience are the inner dynamic of this Paraklete-enabled mutual 'indwelling' of Christ and his people, expressing relational *attachment* (love) and relational *action* (obedience). And that leads us on to think about the two C paragraphs in our analysis of the chapter, which focus in different ways on 'the church in the world' – a theme which becomes much more significant and prominent in chapters 15 and 16, where we will cast a couple of glances en route.

---

35. R. E. Brown, *The Gospel According to John*, vol. 2, Anchor Bible (London: Geoffrey Chapman, 1971), p. 1141.

36. Apologies again for the masculine pronouns in this translation! The fact that Jesus' promise is in the singular is significant, because he is addressing Philip's concerns.

37. Rev. 11:15.

7. Active in the world (vv. 12–14, 22–26)

I think that John 14 is structured as it is because of the way in which the *mission* of the church is constantly woven into the theology and message of these chapters. This is why the paragraphs on relationship are interwoven with paragraphs on mission. Jesus is heading towards the moment when he will say to his disciples, 'As the Father has sent me, so I am sending you' and will breathe on them, to impart the Spirit for the task.[38] We will look at each mission paragraph in turn.

a. Working and praying (vv. 12–14)

The interweaving of the paragraphs is particularly significant for verses 12–14, for actually we need the message of verses 15–21 to make sense of the thought that the disciples, too, will start doing the actions of the Father himself, like Jesus the Son.

That is indeed what verse 12 says! Jesus' claim to speak the words of God, and do the deeds of God, is dramatic enough (v. 10). To then add that *the person who believes in me – that person will also do the works that I do, and indeed will do greater works than these, because I am going to the Father*; this has to be one of the most surprising statements, certainly in John's Gospel, maybe in the New Testament. The disciples too, qualified just by their faith in Jesus, will also perform God's actions in the world, and in a way that makes their actions *greater* even than Jesus'. Fortunately for our purposes we do not need to decide exactly what *greater* means here,[39] because for our theology of the second coming what matters here is the way in which the work of Jesus, representing his Father in the world, is carried forward and *developed* by those who are left behind, *because I am going to the Father.*

The *because* in verse 12 is interesting: note that Jesus does not say 'after I have gone'. There is some causal link between his departure, and the empowering of the church to do the works of God. We can look ahead to John 16:7 and explain the *because* on the ground that, because Jesus goes, the Spirit comes. But there must be more to it than just that, because we need some reason why it has been planned this way. Why is it better for the works of God to be done by a church empowered by the Spirit, than for them to be done by the Son of God himself? The answer must be what emerges in verses 15–21 and indeed elsewhere in the Gospel – namely that the Father achieves salvation by drawing the saved

---

38. John 20:21–22, anticipated in 17:18.

39. There is a very good discussion of this in Carson, *John*, pp. 495–496.

into the relationship of love between the Father and the Son. The obedience of the Son to the Father, including his obedience in laying down his life for the sheep, is the supreme 'work' in which the Father is seen, and that is the place where the sheep land up, caught up into that loving obedience as they nestle in the hands from which they cannot be plucked.[40] So the *because* in verse 12 is about the completion of the work of salvation – so that, sharing the life of the Father and the Son in the power of the Spirit, the church of Jesus Christ may take forward the works of God himself in the world. It is *desirable* that he leaves, so that the church may step up to the plate in this way.

It is not surprising that an emphasis on prayer follows (vv. 13–14). And here the comparison with Luke 17 is important, for we saw there that prayer is the stance of those who believe in the *presence* of the kingdom of God when as yet the kingdom has not finally come. It is the resource of the afflicted who know that God rules in an alienated and unjust world that denies his rule. And here too, prayer is the resource of the church facing the world, although these verses seem bland compared to the desperate day-and-night cry of the 'elect' for justice, and of the disciples who 'long to see one of the days of the Son of Man':[41] *Whatever you ask in my name, I will do it, so that the Father may be glorified in the Son. If you ask anything in my name, I will do it.*

But this is where it is so important to see John 14 as the first of three chapters that form a unity, rather than as complete in itself. Quite apart from the terror of just having been told that they will perform works greater than Jesus', this little band of anxious disciples is about to be told that they will face the hatred and persecution of the world[42] – indeed that 'everyone who kills you will think that they are offering service to God'.[43] Sharing the life of Jesus means that the promise of love, joy and fruitfulness is set into the context of suffering and death – because that is how it is for him. The servant is not greater than his master.[44] And in that context where the coming suffering is explained, this powerful promise about prayer is repeated (see 16:23–24).

So prayer in John, too, is the resource of the church in the overlap of the ages, when we know that God reigns and can do anything in his world, but

---

40. See John 10:14–30 (esp. 14–15, 17–18, 25, 27–30); also 6:39–40; 12:28–32; ch. 17 *passim*!

41. Luke 17:22; 18:7.

42. John 15:18–20.

43. John 16:2.

44. John 13:16; 15:20.

the final judgment and deliverance has not yet come; and in the meantime we are called to 'do his work' of facing the hatred of the world and absorbing it as Jesus did.

b. Living and speaking (vv. 22–26)

As in verse 8 a new section is introduced by a question from a puzzled disciple: *Lord, what's going on? – why is it that you are intending to reveal yourself to us, and not to the world?* (v. 22). I think that when the awards are handed out on judgment day, the prize for 'Most Theologically Astute Question' should definitely go to *Judas (not Iscariot)* for this corker. Why do we have all this rigmarole? Why don't we just cut to the final day, to the overthrow of the beast and the glorious coming of the Son of Man into his kingdom? Why does Jesus apparently intend to delay this revelation to the world, when actually that would not only solve all our problems but also be the proper fulfilment of the prophecy? Putting this question in the terms of Daniel's vision, it would be 'Why on earth is the power of the beasts extended for a while, so that they can persecute the poor people of God some more?'[45]

And it has to be said, Jesus does not obviously give this theological corker a direct reply. We have to read between the lines somewhat, to see how verses 23–26 address the question. But actually an answer emerges if we presuppose that Jesus *is* answering the question, as John says (v. 23), and not simply going off on an agenda of his own.

Anyone who loves me will keep my word . . . (v. 23). The 'anyone' is all-inclusive, and takes us beyond the immediate circle of the disciples. It implies the offer of the word and the Jesus of whom it speaks, and envisages that the word is welcomed with love.[46] And then, says Jesus, all heaven will break loose: *And my Father will love him, and we will come to him and make a dwelling for ourselves with him.*[47]

---

45. Dan. 7:12, 21–22, 25.

46. Cf. John 15:20, looking out to the world: 'If they keep my word, they will keep yours also.'

47. In a (proper) interest for gender inclusivity, NRSV makes the translation plural: 'Those who love me . . . my Father will love them . . . we will come to them.' Greek masculine singular pronouns were inclusive in the same way that 'he' and 'him' used to be in English. Here it is important that we retain the singular, because this 'indwelling' is definitely not just a *corporate* gift and experience. Israel had that experience, through the temple as a focus of God's presence at the heart of the people. Something more intimate, personal and *individual* is being offered to the church of Jesus Christ.

It really seems that God – Father and Son – loves hanging out with repentant sinners who embrace the word with faith. The dramatic thing here is the use of the word *monē*, dwelling, which Jesus used in verse 2, *in my Father's house are many dwellings*. There, it was about the *dwelling* which is awaiting repentant disciples in the heavenly temple, and to which Jesus will *take* them when he *comes again*. But that *dwelling* is anticipated by another, shared by exactly the same divine occupants, here on earth, *with* the person who hears the word and loves its Subject.

Wow! is the best response to this (though not very literary). We have to conclude that God so loves sharing human life with human beings – even amid all our mess and murk – that he is willing to postpone the moment when the Son *reveals himself to the world*. He would rather reveal himself now *to us* – but of course this 'us' is going to expand, as the gospel goes out through the church that speaks the words of God (and does his works), and countless more people qualify to have heaven break loose upon them.[48] *The one who does not love me does not keep my words* (v. 24) – the response is not guaranteed. *But the word which you hear is not mine, but the Father's who sent me*. Even if people reject the word, it is still the word of the Father mediated to the church by the Holy Spirit.

Which brings us naturally to the second Paraklete-promise in verses 25–26. This one majors (not surprisingly) on the Spirit as *teacher*, the one who will equip the church to go on speaking the words of Christ in the world. *He will teach you all things* certainly envisages that the Holy Spirit will continue to speak truth to the church of Christ, beyond the content of the teaching he gave during his ministry, even though the Spirit is also concerned to *remind you of everything I said to you*. The two go together – the words of the earthly Jesus and the words of the risen Christ mediated to the church by his Spirit.

So the answer to Judas' great question seems to be: 'I *am* going to reveal myself to the world, but *through you*: not through a massive visible-to-all revelation (at least, not yet), but through the testimony of a church equipped to speak my words with real truth, because I have come with my Father to take up residence among you, and the Spirit is among you as your Teacher.' It seems that the role and mission of the church is essential to the history of planet Earth en route to the kingdom of God.

---

48. See Jesus' prayer in John 17:20–21. It is really extraordinary that scholarship still tends to regard John's Gospel as world-denying and intent on cultivating a purely inward-looking, private piety.

8. 'Rise, let us go from here!' (v. 31)

As we noted above, the last paragraph of this glorious chapter ends with these puzzling words. They seem to indicate the end of the conversation, which has three chapters yet to run. Consequently many speculate either about literary disruptions (this should mark the end of the conversation, but it has been displaced), or about editorial ineptitude (this marked the end of the conversation in a source, or in an earlier edition of the Gospel, and was never edited out), or about the route from the Last Supper to Gethsemane (we should imagine Jesus continuing to talk as they pack up and walk through the city), or about meal-table dynamics (how often to do guests say 'we really must be going' long before they actually leave?).

All these options miss the point, I think. Jesus returns to the themes with which the chapter began – particularly his departure, and the encouragement to believe, and not to be troubled in heart. But there is a dramatic difference here, at the end. Previously Jesus told them that they could not go where he is about to go – they could not follow him.[49] Now, however, he invites them to *go from here* with him. He is not, of course, rescinding his previous reply to Peter. He will return in chapter 16 to the necessary separation which is coming.[50] In one vital sense, they cannot go with him. But now, in another sense, they can and must. What has made the difference?

An answer begins to emerge when we notice that the great opening theme of the *place* that he is preparing for them, the focus of verses 1–4, is *not* picked up in this closing paragraph. Why not? The reason for this strange absence, I believe, is that the whole notion of their *home* (Gk *monē*, vv. 2 and 23) has moved on dramatically. Yes, they have the prospect of a 'heavenly' home after Jesus' coming again, but much more immediately they will enjoy this same *home* with the Father and the Son as soon as the Paraklete brings them into the intimate relationship of love and obedience with him which Jesus holds before them. And the theme of that relationship is certainly here, in this closing paragraph. We see it in several ways.

a. The gift of peace
Peace I leave with you, my peace I give to you: I give it to you not as the world offers it (v. 27) is an addition to the bare encouragement not to be troubled in heart (v. 1). The world offers *peace* in a superficial, external way – and John's first readers would

---

49. John 13:33, 36 (cf. 7:33–34).
50. John 16:16–24.

surely have been reminded of the much-vaunted *Pax Romana*, the so-called 'world peace' which Roman imperial propaganda claimed as the great benefit of Roman rule. But because Jesus is to be *in* them, and they *in* him (v. 20), they can experience his peace directly. They do not have to try to boost their feelings into a state of non-anxiety, because he will give them his peace directly.

b. The gift of courage

And do not let your heart be timid (v. 27) is also an addition to the opening exhortation. Jesus did not mention the need for courage before – indeed, having just predicted Peter's denial of him, in spite of his protestations of devotion, it seems as though lack of courage was hanging heavy in the air. But now courage is possible – and the reason given for this in verse 28 is fascinating: *You heard me say to you 'I am going, but will come to you'. If you loved me, you would rejoice that I am going to the Father, for the Father is greater than I.* Most commentators take this as a gentle rebuke, to 'see it from my point of view – if you truly loved me, you'd be glad for me, going back to my Father: your loss is my gain!'[51]

But this explanation does not fit the flow of the paragraph. Chiding the disciples for their lack of empathy hardly supports an encouragement to know peace and be courageous. Rather, *greater* means 'greater for you', I think: Jesus' statement *the Father is greater than I* is not a comment about their relative ontology, but about their relative impact for the disciples. If they truly loved Jesus – shown by believing the words he has just spoken to them – they would rejoice at the prospect of something even greater than his physical presence with them, namely fellowship with the Father himself who will make his *home* with them after Jesus has gone.[52] That will make them courageous!

c. The gift of faith

And now I have spoken to you before all this happens, so that you may believe (v. 29). Jesus could be referring just to his prediction of Peter's denial, or of his own betrayal, but more probably he means his departure and return, with all that this will entail for his disciples. He has told them in advance of his imminent departure, and of the coming of the Paraklete with whom both he and his Father will come to them, and of the *greater works* they will do, and of their immediate

---

51. So e.g. Carson, *John*, p. 508; also Rodney Whitacre, *John*, IVP New Testament Commentary (Downers Grove: InterVarsity Press, 1999), p. 366.

52. I think this is the explanation Schnackenburg offers (*John*, p. 86), though it is rather unclear.

access to God in prayer, and of the ongoing revelation they will receive; all so that when it happens, their faith may be strengthened for the task.

d. The gift of victory

In a suggestive, yet-to-be-explained way, verses 30–31 allude to the dark hour coming for Jesus (*the ruler of this world is coming*) and his sense of ultimate invulnerability before the powers of evil (*he has no hold over me*), because he is about to do something in obedience to his Father which *will* bring revelation to the whole world (*so that the world may know that I love the Father . . .*[53]). And then his final words – *Rise, let us go from here* – invite all the disciples to join him on this path of suffering, sacrifice, obedience, love and victory. Now he calls them to *go* with him, using the same Greek verb as in 13:36 (*hypagein*). The plural form – *let us go* – is deeply significant.

This is more than just a *going* from their supper through Jerusalem to Gethsemane – in fact this is hardly what it means at all. The *going* predicted in this chapter is a going together in mutual indwelling. Jesus wants to make his disciples inseparable from himself, even though actually he must depart from them for a while because of the unique journey he alone must take, through cross and resurrection. Their story is to become his story, and his theirs, until the Day when he finally *comes again* to take them to be with him where he is. But the 'we' of the going begins now! They too must travel through rejection, pain and death to the victory that they will reach *in* Jesus.[54]

This is precisely Moltmann's vision of New Testament eschatology. It is about the ongoing story of Jesus Christ himself, and of our participation in it.

---

53. This looks back to Judas' theological corker in v. 22.

54. Very few have attempted to find a meaning for 'Rise, let us go from here!' that allows it to make sense in its context. C. H. Dodd famously interpreted it spiritually, connecting it to the coming of *the ruler of this world*: 'Up, let us march to meet him!' was his suggested translation (C. H. Dodd, *The Interpretation of the Fourth Gospel* [Cambridge: Cambridge University Press, 1953], p. 409). Dodd ignores the significant way in which the word 'go' (Gk *hypagein*) has been used in the preceding passage. Mark Stibbe similarly looks for a literary, contextual meaning and interprets it with reference to the theme of the elusiveness of Jesus throughout the Gospel: let's be off, says Jesus, 'in order to evade his captors for one last time' (Mark W. G. Stibbe, *John*, Readings Commentary [Sheffield: Sheffield Academic Press, 1993], p. 159). But this explanation does not root it in the themes of the chapter itself. I am not aware of any other attempts to see it as more than just a puzzling stage instruction.

John has thus added something special to our biblical theology of the second coming; this deep emphasis on the 'home' that is shared *now* with Jesus, anticipating the 'home' that we will share with him when he comes and 'takes' us to be with him. We saw this foreshadowed in Psalm 18, in the powerful emphasis there on David's *relationship* with his Lord. Now this receives a distinctive New Testament shape.

John 14:1–6 is often read at funeral services, with the implication that death is the moment when the departed is met by Christ, who takes him or her to the heavenly home already prepared. Is this a misuse of the passage? If (as I've argued) John 14:3 is a reference to the *parousia*, the second coming of Jesus, then it is indeed a misapplication of the passage to read it at funerals. *However* the whole chapter teaches us that we can be 'at home' with him long before death closes our eyes: our *monē* (dwelling place) with him then is continuous with our *monē* with him now. He is our dwelling place now, and at death, and in the new creation.[55] So a secondary, wider application of 14:1–6 seems appropriate. In fact, maybe the moment of our death is the moment of his *parousia* for each of us . . . we will return to this thought!

---

55. Cf. Rom. 14:7–9; Phil. 1:23.

7. REFRESHMENTS TO FOLLOW (ACTS 1:6–11; 3:11–26)

1. Acts and the second coming

We turn now to the book of Acts, which begins with the prediction and promise of the second coming of Jesus made to the disciples at the very moment of his ascension, by two angels who suddenly pop up beside them: *Men of Galilee, why are you standing looking into heaven? This Jesus, who has just been taken from you into heaven, will come in the way in which you saw him go into heaven* (1:11). Remarkably, although Acts begins with this resounding promise, the only other reference to the second coming in the book occurs in 3:20, in the other passage at which we will look in this chapter. That immediately poses an interesting question for us: Why, after this emphatic start, does the theme disappear? And what is the significance of this for us?

A slight strangeness in the angels' words points us towards an answer. What is the connection between the question they ask, and the promise which follows it? We might have thought that if Jesus is to come again in the same way as he has just departed, that would in fact be quite a good reason for standing looking into heaven! But clearly these *two men in white garments* assume the opposite. To believe that Jesus is coming again means not *looking into heaven*. Why is this?

In fact the book of Acts, both here at the beginning and throughout its story, directs us away from a focus on the second coming as such, and calls us to focus not on heaven but on earth; as Jesus has just said to his disciples: *You will receive power when the Holy Spirit has come upon you, and you will be my witnesses in Jerusalem, and in all Judea and Samaria, and to the end of the earth* (1:8). That is where the focus of the ascended Lord Jesus rests, and so ours must also. As is well known, the concentric circles of this programme provide a structure for the book: Jerusalem (chs. 1 – 7), Judea and Samaria (chs. 8 – 12),[1] and the rest of the earth (chs. 13 – 28).[2] So the focus on Paul in the second half of the book, and on his journey to Rome, the centre of the rest of the world, is not because Paul was more significant than the other apostles, but for the sake of showing the fulfilment of Jesus' earthly commission.

So Jesus himself calls us to focus, not on his return, but on his call to be witnesses to him. And – if we are to follow the example of Acts – the *fact* of his return is not a key part of our witness. We do not see the church proclaiming his coming again in Acts (except just the once, in Acts 3:20–21). It makes a fascinating study, to survey the focuses within their witness and to notice where the emphasis falls. It is not that *eschatology* has disappeared from view. Quite the opposite. The fact of coming judgment is everywhere presupposed, and is now focused on Jesus: he is 'the one set apart by God to be Judge of the living and the dead'[3] on the 'day on which God will judge the world in righteousness by a Man whom he set apart'.[4] This is deadly serious – literally – because *anyone who does not listen to that prophet will be utterly destroyed from among the people* (3:23).[5] But this coming judgment is but the background to the call to repentance and the offer of forgiveness and of salvation through Jesus, which is where the emphasis overwhelmingly falls.[6] The basis of this call – the energy behind it – is not the coming judgment but the fact of the resurrection, which is everywhere the focus of the witness to Jesus in Acts.[7] The connection between the two – resurrection and judgment – appears explicitly in 17:31, where Paul presents the resurrection as 'establishing the reliability'[8] of the whole package (God's call to everyone to repent because of the coming judgment through Jesus the resurrected one).

---

1. See the movement marked in Acts 8:1.
2. And similarly, the new Spirit-led movement marked in Acts 13:1–2.
3. Acts 10:42, Peter to Cornelius.
4. Acts 17:31, Paul to the Athenians.
5. Peter to the Jerusalem crowd, quoting Deut. 18:19 and Lev. 23:29.
6. See 3:26; 4:12; 5:31; 8:22–24; 10:43; 11:18; 13:38–39; 16:31; 17:30–31; 20:21; 26:18–20.
7. See e.g. 2:24; 3:3–15; 4:10; 4:33; 5:30, etc.
8. NRSV has 'given assurance' for this phrase.

So the second coming, as such, just fades from view in Acts. This is a salutary reminder for us. It's OK to read (and write) a book on it, but having read, we need to move on to other things, especially to ministry for the sake of the kingdom. The focus of Jesus himself, as he *continues* 'to act and to teach' through his church, is not on his return but on the earth that so needs to hear the message of forgiveness and new life in his name. Luke's opening – in good Moltmann-esque style![9] – connects the story of Acts with the story of the life and ministry of Jesus in his Gospel by saying that the latter was about 'what Jesus *began* to do and to teach'.[10] Acts, therefore, tells the story of the *continuing* acting and speaking of Jesus himself, on earth, in and through his church. It's almost as though Luke had been reading John 14.

But there is a fascinating sub-theme in Acts which is of great importance for the two references to Jesus' return at which we're looking in this chapter.

2. The kingdom and Israel

The disciples' question to the risen Jesus in 1:6 introduces this theme: *When they met with him, they asked him, 'Lord, is this the time* [chronos] *when you will restore the kingdom to Israel?'* At the other end of the book, Paul tells the Jewish elders in Rome that 'it is because of the hope of Israel that I am bearing this chain'.[11] Between these two bracketing references, Acts has a constant interest not just in Israel's 'hope',[12] but also in the related theme of the kingdom, which likewise forms a theme that brackets the whole book.[13] Underlying both these themes is the fulfilment of Scripture, to which Luke keeps returning in his narrative, as we will see. The promises of Scripture focus upon Israel, the covenant people, and so if salvation is on offer through one who is proclaimed to to be the Christ, the Messiah of Israel, then Israel's salvation must be somewhere in the frame![14]

---

9. See the previous chapter on John 14.

10. Acts 1:1.

11. Acts 28:20.

12. See Acts 23:6; 24:15; 26:6–7.

13. See Acts 1:3 and 28:31; and in between, 8:12; 14:22; 19:8; 20:25; 28:23.

14. 'The Christ' (i.e., 'the Messiah') is used as a title twelve times in Acts (e.g. 2:31; 3:18; 17:3; 18:5), but even when 'Christ' seems to have become just part of an expanded name for Jesus (as in the phrase 'the name of Jesus Christ', which appears seven times), it must still retain something of its technical meaning.

The disciples' question in 1:6 is thus very important indeed. When will the promises of Scripture be fulfilled? – the promises that, for instance,

> ... those who were cast off [I will make] a strong nation;
> and the LORD will reign over them in Mount Zion
> now and for evermore.[15]

Even though pagan nations plot against Israel and seek to destroy her,

> they do not know
> the thoughts of the LORD;
> they do not understand his plan,
> that he has gathered them as sheaves to the
> threshing floor.
> Arise and thresh,
> O daughter Zion,
> for I will make your horn iron
> and your hoofs bronze;
> you shall beat in pieces many peoples,
> and shall devote their gain to the LORD,
> their wealth to the Lord of the whole earth.[16]

This example from Micah is just one of many passages that illustrate the Old Testament prophetic vision of the restoration of Israel among and *over* the nations. Still firmly under Roman rule, Jews in the first century (including the disciples) knew that this vision had not yet been realized, even though they were living in their own land around the temple.

This national expectation was still powerfully alive in the first century. But the disciples have just – in fact just a few days previously – been given a powerful personal expectation to add to this national one. At the Last Supper, Luke tells us, Jesus said to them:

> You are those who have stuck by me in my trials. And I bequeath to you, just as my Father has bequeathed to me, a kingdom! So you will eat and drink at my table in my kingdom, and you will sit on thrones, judging the twelve tribes of Israel.[17]

---

15. Mic. 4:7.

16. Mic. 4:12–13.

17. Luke 22:29–30.

Matthew's parallel phrases the promise like this:

> Truly I tell you, in the regeneration, when the Son of Man shall sit upon the throne of his glory, then you who have followed me will also sit on twelve thrones judging the twelve tribes of Israel.[18]

Jesus unites *his* coming kingdom with that of Israel, and offers the disciples a starring role. It is not surprising, therefore, that the disciples are keen to know whether this is the *time*, the *chronos*, when this great vision of the restoration of Israel will be fulfilled. Thrones are around the corner! It may well be that this is part of the underlying agenda in their keenness to appoint a replacement for the fallen Judas in Acts 1:15–26. How can they judge the twelve tribes if there are only eleven of them? It seems to be part of *Luke's* agenda, too, in that he pointedly lists the apostles' names – all *eleven* of them – in 1:13.

Jesus' response to their question does not discourage this enthusiastic hope. *It is not yours to know the dates* [chronos] *or the moments* [kairos] *which the Father has appointed, in his authority: but you will receive power when the Holy Spirit comes upon you, and you will be my witnesses* . . . (vv. 7–8). Jesus uses both the time words here, in the plural. The restoration of the kingdom has dates and moments attached to it, in God's plan: not one great *kairos-and-chronos* moment of restoration, but (we infer) an ongoing chronology, with several or many days marked in the diary. And the first – clearly – is going to be the gift of the Holy Spirit and of power, and the appointment of the disciples as witnesses.

This gives a dramatic and wonderful twist to the Pentecost story in Acts 2. Down comes the Holy Spirit, rushing upon the disciples and filling them with the capacity to speak 'the greatnesses of God' in the home languages of all the Pentecost visitors to Jerusalem,[19] the language that will communicate with the visitors' *neighbours back home*, not just with the visitors themselves. This truly is good news for the world! But then 'Peter, standing up *with the eleven*, raised his voice and gave utterance before them, "Men of Israel and all inhabitants of Jerusalem . . ."'[20] Luke's emphatic language underlines the significance of this: the first of the *kairos*-moments has arrived, this is its *chronos*, and in this standing and speaking to Israel Peter and the eleven are beginning to enter into their kingdom. They are *standing* – not yet sitting – but the restoration has started!

---

18. Matt. 19:28. The word 'regeneration' suggests new creation, and is another way of referring to the 'restoration of all things' in Acts 3:21.

19. Acts 2:11.

20. Acts 2:14.

This is all very important for the second of our passages, where Peter not only explains, authoritatively, what Moses was talking about in Deuteronomy 18:15–20, but also – even more significantly – reinterprets the expectation of the restoration of Israel around the person of Jesus, who will bring it about when he comes again from the heaven that has now for a while received him. We will return to all this shortly!

3. Going and coming and not looking (1:6–11)

From the perspective of the biblical theology we are developing, this presentation of the twelve already entering their 'kingdom', and sharing the kingdom with Jesus the Son of Man, has great overtones. The roots of it are in Daniel 7, with the vision of the shared rule of the 'one like a son of man' and the 'holy ones of the Most High'. So we are attuned to notice other language typical of this theology – and we spot straightaway the references (a) to the Father's *authority* to determine *times* in verse 7, (b) to the gift of *power* to the disciples in verse 8, and (c) to the universal extent of their witness (*to the end of the earth*, v. 8). The divine authority to determine 'times and seasons' is essential to the Daniel view of the world, and the gift of *power* is a real anticipation of the restoration, even if the full thing is not yet. Here too we are talking about a kingdom which will spread to cover the whole earth, in due time. But there's another connection with Daniel 7, also: *Having said this, while they were watching, he was lifted up, and a cloud took him out of their sight* (v. 9).

A cloud! Once again the cloud that marks the divine presence and power makes its appearance, and reminds us of the cloud that surrounded the approach of the Son of Man to God to receive kingdom, authority and dominion. But here the cloud takes him *away* (though no less to God), and the power is left behind with those whom he has just appointed as *witnesses*.

It is important to note that Jesus disappears into the cloud in verse 9. His entry into the glory of God and the power of his kingdom is veiled from our sight. So when we read in verse 10 that the disciples were *gazing into heaven as he departed*, the idea is not that they are watching him rise. They are simply looking at the spot where they last saw him. Will they glimpse him again, maybe if the cloud thins for a moment? No. The angels tell them not to keep gazing upward, for *this Jesus . . . will come in the way in which you saw him go into heaven*. In other words, just as he was suddenly and unexpectedly taken from them, disappearing quickly into the cloud of God's presence and glory, so he will suddenly and unexpectedly reappear from the same cloud. *The way in which you saw him go* is not so much 'upwards into a cloud' as 'suddenly and unexpectedly, in the middle of a conversation'. There is no point in watching for him to come, because when the *chronos* and *kairos* are right he will be there – just like that.

We so need to hear this word from these angels! Actually we need to seek a balance, between on the one hand forgetting altogether about his return, and on the other hand focusing on it with too-passionate zeal. The first is the error of liberal Christianity, which fails to hear the *promise* of the angels. The second is the error of millenarian Christianity, which fails to hear the *warning* of the angels. We need to hear both the promise (yes, he really is coming again, to take up his kingdom and reign), and the warning (but in the meantime forget about the timing, and get on with the job of spreading the good news of repentance and forgiveness in his name). These angels will guard us from both errors.

4. The restoration of all things (3:11–26)

Now we move on to the reference to the second coming in Acts 3. I am really encouraged to note that David Gooding, in his excellent exposition of Acts, uses the title 'Christianity and the Restoration of All Things' as the headline for the whole opening section, Acts 1:1 – 6:7.[21] The phrase 'restoration of all things' is taken from 3:21, which Gooding suggests (with the reference to the second coming in 3:20) is one of the three 'towering peaks' that dominate the opening section of the book. The others are the ascension of Jesus and the gift of the Holy Spirit: taken together, these all anticipate the coming of 'the great and resplendent day of the Lord' (2:20).[22]

The role played by the sermons and speeches in Acts is important for this analysis. These are interspersed through the storyline of the book, and form the vital theological commentary that we need in order to understand what happens. Stephen's speech, for instance (the longest of them[23]), is an important carrier of the theology of Acts in relation to the central theme of the place of Israel in God's plan, and the relationship between the covenant with Israel and

---

21. David Gooding, *True to the Faith: A Fresh Approach to the Acts of the Apostles* (London: Hodder & Stoughton, 1990). It has recently been republished by the Myrtlefield Trust (Coleraine, 2013), under the same title but with different pagination. The page numbers in footnotes here are to the 1990 edition.

22. Gooding, *Acts*, p. 19.

23. Acts 7:2–53.

the extension of the gospel to the Gentiles. It paves the way for the expansion beyond Jerusalem which begins in the next chapter.[24]

However Luke has clearly not put into the mouths of his characters just the thoughts and theology he wants them to express, important though these speeches are for the message of Luke's book. The early sermons in Acts contain some unique ideas, which we meet nowhere else in the New Testament, and this must be down to Luke's desire to reflect accurately what was said and believed in those early days – even features of early language and thinking which did not catch on. We meet several such points in this second speech of Peter:

- The use of the term 'servant' to describe Jesus (Gk *pais*).[25]
- The use of the term 'the righteous one' to describe Jesus (Gk *ho dikaios*).[26]
- The use of the Greek term *archēgos* ('champion', 'author', 'pioneer') to describe Jesus.[27]
- The idea that Jesus was raised from the dead first and specially for Israel.[28]

And, of particular significance for our topic:

- The glorious expression 'times of refreshment' to describe what the second coming will mean.[29]
- The association of the second coming with the idea of the coming of the Messiah to Israel.[30]

---

24. Luke is not alone in using speeches in this way, he inherits this practice from Greek historians, most notably the historian Thucydides (fifth century BC) who first explained the theory behind including speeches by significant characters in the events he related.

25. Acts 3:13, 26; cf. 4:27, 30. Since this is the term used in Isaiah for the Servant of the Lord (e.g. Isa. 52:13), it is extraordinary that we don't meet it elsewhere in the New Testament applied to Jesus.

26. Acts 3:14; cf. 7:52; 22:14.

27. Acts 3:15; cf. 5:31. We meet this term twice in Hebrews (2:10; 12:2), but the full expression 'author of life' occurs nowhere else.

28. Acts 3:26.

29. Acts 3:19; but see below – 'times' may have a wider meaning.

30. Acts 3:20.

- The (apparent) idea that the repentance of Israel would prompt or hasten the second coming of her Messiah Jesus.[31]
- Another glorious expression – 'the restoration of all things', which occurs only here in the New Testament.[32]

So there are plenty of fascinating points about this unique sermon.

a. Structure

The sermon falls into two halves, with the movement from the first to the second marked by *And now, brothers* . . . in verse 17. The occasion of the sermon, of course, is the miraculous healing of the lame man by the Beautiful Gate of the temple.[33]

(i) It's all down to Jesus (vv. 12–16)

These verses have a chiastic structure:

A Not down to us (v. 12)
  B God glorified Jesus (v. 13a)
    C whom you rejected (vv. 13b–15a)
  B' but God raised him (v. 15b)
A' and so it's all down to him! (v. 16)

(ii) The required response (vv. 17–26)

Here the main idea – it's time to repent! – is underlined by an *inclusio* between verses 19 and 26, which also encloses a basically chiastic structure:

In mitigation (vv. 17–18)
  a) You acted in ignorance (v. 17)
  b) God was fulfilling prophecy through your sin (v. 18)
A So all the more reason to repent! (v. 19)
  B So that God may send refreshment for you in the Messiah (v. 20)
    C and so give universal restoration (v. 21a)
      D in fulfilment of prophecy (v. 21b)
        a) of Moses (vv. 22–23)
        b) and of all the prophets (v. 24)

---

31. Acts 3:19–20.

32. Acts 3:21; but the related verb 'to restore' is used by the disciples in their question in Acts 1:6. Cf. Matt. 17:11; Mark 9:12.

33. Acts 3:1–10.

> D' They are your prophets (v. 25a)
>   C' who prophesied universal blessing (v. 25b)
>   B' so God raised Jesus for you (v. 26a)
> A' so that you would turn from your sins! (v. 26b)

The appeal to repent (A–A') brackets two statements about God's action for Israel (B–B', vv. 20, 26a), which in turn bracket the central section (CD–D'C') which is wholly concerned with the fulfilment of prophecy. Because these are *Israel's* prophets (v. 25a, *You are the sons of the prophets and of the covenant*), Peter hopes to reinforce the appeal to repentance with prophetic authority. But because the sin of which they need to repent is that of crucifying the Messiah just a few weeks previously – underlined with vigorous directness in verses 13–15 – Peter sweetens the bitter pill (a) by allowing some 'mitigating circumstances' to apply (vv. 17–18), and (b) by telling them that their repentance will call forth a wonderful response from God; in fact, the fulfilment of all the glorious prophecies of the Old Testament about the renewal and blessing of the earth. The C–C' parallel between verse 21a (universal restoration) and verse 25b (universal blessing) is very important in this respect.

We will now focus on this second half of the sermon (vv. 17–26) in order to tease out its distinctive teaching about the second coming.

b. It's time to repent! (vv. 17–26)

The repeated 'so that' in verses 19–20 is really interesting: *repent, therefore, and turn around, so that your sins may be wiped out, so that times of refreshment may come from before the Lord, and so that he may send the Messiah appointed for you, Jesus . . .* The distinction between 'purpose' and 'result' clauses is sometimes blurred in Greek, but in English, too, so that can express either idea. The first 'so that' in verse 19 clearly expresses purpose. But the two in verse 20 seem to express result, rather than purpose.[34] Peter is not so much telling them to repent in order to call down these blessings from heaven, but encouraging them that, if they repent, these blessings will follow because God is at work to fulfil prophecy. But whether purpose or result, the repentance of Israel leads to wonderful blessings from God: (a) *times* [kairos] *of refreshing*, and (b) the sending *of the Messiah appointed for you, Jesus, whom heaven must receive until the times* [chronos] *of the restoration of all things* (vv. 20–21).

---

34. So, e.g. I. H. Marshall, *Acts*, Tyndale New Testament Commentary (Leicester: Inter-Varsity Press, 1980), p. 93. However C. K. Barrett finds purpose here: *The Acts of the Apostles*, vol. 1, International Critical Commentary (Edinburgh: T&T Clark, 1994), p. 203.

Here we meet both our 'time' words in the plural, as in 1:7. It seems that Peter is giving at least a partial answer to his own question in 1:6! But do they refer to the same thing? Commentators are divided between those who identify the *times of refreshing* with the *times of restoration*, saying that both phrases refer to what happens when Jesus comes again,[35] and those who distinguish between them – usually saying that *times of refreshing* are repeated 'refreshments' from the Lord, like the miracle just performed on the lame man, while the *times of restoration of all things* (or *of all people*[36]) is a much grander, universal idea, associated definitely with the second coming of Jesus.[37] Because of the two plurals, the latter view is almost certainly right – but we have learned already not to be dogmatic about distinguishing between different 'comings' of the Lord, or between gifts of grace that *anticipate* the End, and the gift of grace that *will be* the End. The same is surely true here: God acts to refresh his world and his people in many ways before the final *refreshment* which will be the *restoration of all things* in Christ.

However we need to pause on the way in which Peter ties these blessings to *Israel's* repentance. Notice his repeated *you* and *to you* in these verses, signalling his focus on Israel and the Jews:

- *Jesus, the Christ appointed for you* (v. 20).
- *The Lord your God will raise up a prophet for you from among your brothers* (v. 22).
- *You will listen to him, in whatever he should say to you* (v. 22).
- *You are the sons of the prophets, and of the covenant which God established with your fathers* (v. 25).
- *For you first, God raised up his servant and sent him to bless you . . .* (v. 26).

---

35. So e.g. John Calvin, *Acts*, Crossway Classic Commentary (Wheaton: Crossway Books, 1995), p. 56; F. F. Bruce, *The Acts of the Apostles: The Greek Text with Introduction and Commentary* (London: Inter-Varsity Fellowship, 1952), p. 111.

36. It is worth noting Barrett's preference for the translation 'restoration of all men' rather than 'of all things' (Barrett, *Acts*, p. 207). He thinks that this fits better with the background in Mal. 4:6, where the Septuagint uses the verbal form of the noun 'restoration' and says that the coming Elijah will 'restore the heart of the father to his son and of each to his neighbour' (Mal. 3:23, LXX). But when Jesus quotes this verse in Mark 9:12 (Matt. 17:11) he uses 'everything' to summarize what Elijah will restore – and then adds that the restoration did not take place through John the Baptist, even though he was Malachi's Elijah. It remains to happen yet!

37. So e.g. Barrett, *Acts*, p. 205; William J. Larkin, *Acts*, IVP New Testament Commentary (Downers Grove: InterVarsity Press, 1995), p. 69.

This is all for you! he says. The 'raising up' of the prophet like Moses *for and from* Israel has now happened *for you first* in the 'raising up' of Jesus from the dead.[38] What should we make of this? Is this still true – that the conversion of Israel is a vital prerequisite for the *refreshment* and *restoration* of the world? Or – as Dunn suggests – is Peter simply getting a little overexcited in his language here?

> All told, the language catches rather effectively a sense of trembling, expectant
> excitement at the prospect of the Christ recently departed but ready to return soon
> to bring history to its ordained climax.[39]

This is more than just excitement. Peter is speaking (I think) out of the Lord's promise that 'you will not finish going through the cities of Israel before the Son of Man comes'.[40] This was part of Jesus' commission to the Twelve when sending them out on mission during his ministry – when he also said to them, 'Don't go away down Gentile roads, and don't enter any Samaritan town: rather, go to the lost sheep of the house of Israel.'[41]

Jesus himself encouraged this focus on Israel, and Peter is living within that world view as he preaches this sermon in Acts 3. Joachim Jeremias, in his classic study *Jesus' Promise to the Nations*, explored this theology and the strange apparent contradiction here, between Jesus' limitation of his and the disciples' ministry to Israel, on the one hand, and his promise of universal blessing for the Gentiles, on the other.[42] The resolution of the problem, suggested Jeremias, was in the Old Testament expectation of the restoration of Israel *as the means of* universal blessing. When Israel rises again, restored by her God, the nations stream to holy Mount Zion, drawn by the light of revelation.[43] Israel becomes a magnet that draws the rest of the earth into the circle of her renewed life:

> In the days to come
> the mountain of the Lord's house

---

38. Peter uses the same verb 'raise up' (Gk *anistēmi*) in v. 26, as appears in the quotation of Deut. 18:15 in v. 22.

39. J. D. G. Dunn, *The Acts of the Apostles*, Epworth Commentary (Peterborough: Epworth Press, 1996), p. 47.

40. Matt. 10:23.

41. Matt. 10:5–6. See his own very similar self-imposed restriction in Matt. 15:24.

42. Joachim Jeremias, *Jesus' Promise to the Nations* (London: SCM, 1958).

43. Key texts are Isa. 2:2–4; 45:20, 22; 51:3–5; 60:1–16; Mic. 7:10–17; Zech. 8:21–23. Jeremias, *Nations*, pp. 55–60.

shall be established as the highest of the mountains,
    and shall be raised up above the hills.
Peoples shall stream to it,
    and many nations shall come and say:
'Come, let us go up to the mountain of the LORD,
    to the house of the God of Jacob . . .'[44]

Jeremias comments:

> The movement is always thought of as 'centripetal'; the Gentiles will not be
> evangelized where they dwell, but will be summoned to the holy Mount by the
> divine epiphany. Zion is always the appointed centre for their gathering.[45]

Peter is clearly inhabiting this theology, as he preaches this sermon. The word
restoration, used only here in the New Testament, is the noun of which the verbal
form appears in the disciples' question in 1:6, *Will you at this time restore the kingdom
to Israel?* As we saw there, this *kingdom* connotes the Daniel vision of a universal
kingdom filling the whole earth and replacing the bestial occupants of the office
of universal ruler. No wonder Peter felt excited, and ready to face his Jewish
hearers boldly with the reality of their sin, so that they might repent, and all this
might roll forward! These are the *days* of which *all the prophets, from Samuel and
his successors, spoke* (v. 24).

But interestingly Luke is heading somewhere different, as he develops the
story in Acts. He knows that the mission will become *centrifugal* – and that
ironically Peter himself will spearhead this new mission, moving out from the
bounds of Israel, and undergoing a dramatic shift in his own thinking and
practice. The *restoration of all things* will not be achieved simply through the conversion of Israel. It took a dramatic intervention by the Holy Spirit to convince
Peter that God was intending to create Gentile believers whose faith in Israel's
Messiah would *not* require them to be circumcised and become Jewish proselytes.
In the process, Peter himself went away down Gentile roads, entered and ate
in Gentile houses – and all because the Holy Spirit left him no alternative.[46]
There is possibly a little irony, therefore, in Peter's quotation of Genesis 22:18
in verse 25, God's promise to Abraham that *in your seed all the households of the earth*

---

44. Mic. 4:1–2.

45. Jeremias, *Nations*, p. 60.

46. I'm referring, of course, to the Cornelius story in Acts 10:1 – 11:18, and the huge
    shift this entails in Peter's theology.

will be blessed. Luke knows that Peter himself will change his mind about how this will be fulfilled.[47]

Much of the rest of the New Testament is devoted to wrestling with this shift from an Israel-focus to a world-focus. Luke faithfully traces the conflict it caused, between those who supported Peter's new approach and Jewish believers who could not. We meet its rumblings in Paul's letters, too (especially in Galatians, Romans and Philippians), and Hebrews is devoted to it. Paul became the champion of the new approach, which saw the *restoration of all things* in much bigger terms – involving the universal preaching of the gospel, a universal appeal for repentance and faith, and the universal out-pouring of the Holy Spirit on all who believe, without requiring obedience to the law.

Within Acts, Peter's new acceptance of Gentile evangelism separate from Jewish proselytism leads to the Apostolic Council in Acts 15, convened to debate whether Gentile converts 'should be circumcised and ordered to keep the law of Moses'.[48] Essentially, the issue was whether Paul's law-free missionary work, offering the Christ of Israel to the Gentiles without requiring them to become members of Israel, was to be embraced or condemned. At the heart of the debate was the interpretation of the Old Testament, and of Old Testament prophecy in particular. Luke reports that they were silenced by the impact of hearing what God was doing among the Gentiles through Barnabas and Paul.[49] And then James spoke:

> Men and brothers, listen to me. Simeon [i.e., Peter] has related how God first graciously planned and took steps to take a people for his name from among the Gentiles. And the words of the prophets concur with this: as it is written,
>
>> After this I will return,
>>   and I will build up the fallen tent of David,
>> and I will build up its ruins,
>>   and restore it,
>> so that the rest of humankind may seek the Lord,
>>   and all the Gentiles over whom my name has been called –
>> says the Lord, who does these things known from long ago.

---

47. BUT (a whispered footnote at this point), in a remarkable way, Paul will bring us round full circle back to Peter's theology in Rom. 11, as we will see.

48. Acts 15:5.

49. Acts 15:12.

Therefore I judge that we should not burden these Gentiles who are turning to the Lord . . .[50]

One of the most remarkable words here is the little word 'first' in verse 14, ascribed to Peter by James. This 'first' answers to the earlier *first* that Peter uses in Acts 3:26. In Acts 3, Israel comes first, and the restoration of all things follows. In Acts 15, the conversion of the Gentiles come 'first', and the restoration of Israel follows 'after this'. This is an amazing change of focus, especially since the passage James then quotes[51] is precisely one of those 'Israel first' passages that is covered by Peter's reference to *all the prophets* in 3:24. The 'so that' in the middle of the Amos quotation could be heard to imply that the restoration of 'the fallen tent of David' *precedes* the conversion of the Gentiles. But James reads Amos as 'concurring' with the view that it happens the other way round. The reason behind this reading is not hard to find: tragically, Israel has not embraced her Messiah, and now – amazingly – the Holy Spirit has poured himself out on the Gentiles who believe the gospel.

So the little word 'first' in Acts 15:14 seems to carry the overtone, 'before the Son of Man comes, before the restoration of all things occurs . . .' Before that can happen, a *Gentile* mission needs to be pursued. But actually this is what Jesus himself said in Mark 13:10: 'first the gospel must be preached to all the nations'.[52]

5. Christians, Jews and the Messiah

But even if we follow Peter himself away from the reading of prophecy which underlies his Acts 3 sermon, we must not lose his passionate excitement about the significance of the resurrection, nor his passionate desire to preach repentance, nor his passionate love for Jesus *the author of life*, nor his passionate delight

---

50. Acts 15:13–19.

51. Amos 9:11–12.

52. As we noted above, the Greek word *ethnē* means either 'Gentiles' or 'nations', and the context determines which is the more appropriate translation. In Acts 15 the discussion is about the basis on which the faith of non-Jewish (Gentile) believers can be affirmed. In Mark 13:10 the focus is on the universal proclamation of the gospel, so probably 'nations' or 'peoples' is a better translation. Israel is included in the 'peoples' who must hear, before the Son of Man comes.

in the *times of refreshment* and *the restoration of all things* to be expected in Jesus. He rested on the prophets, as he proclaimed all this to his fellow Jews. In conclusion it is worth wondering how Peter would encourage us to relate to Jewish people today, and in particular how Peter's belief in Jesus' second coming might be important in that relationship.

There is so much to regret about relationships between Christians and Jews, most particularly of course the terrible history of Christian anti-Semitism, about which Peter could have no inkling, as he addressed this Jewish audience as his *brothers* (v. 17). Christians have generally treated Jews as anything but brothers over the centuries, with a few notable exceptions.[53] As we reflect on Peter's undoubted sense of kinship with those to whom he was preaching, this passage raises three particular issues, which will also serve to move us in the direction of Romans 11, our next port of call.

a. Roots and origins

The movement through the story in Acts takes us along the route outlined in 1:8, as we've seen; and this is not just a geographical but also a theological journey, as we've also seen. The 'law-free'[54] Gentile Christian church emerges in the second half of the book, and from then onwards the issue of relationships between Jewish and Gentile Christians becomes a 'hot potato'. But there is no way that Peter, preaching here in Acts 3, will allow us to forget the start of the story. He probably actually had this partly in mind, when he encouraged Paul to 'remember the poor' in the Jerusalem church.[55] From his vantage point in Acts 3, Peter would say to us:

> Do not forget the Jewish cradle that nursed you in your infancy! The Christ was born of Israel, and limited his mission to Israel. Our initial vision was for the restoration of Israel *first* – and then the world! Christ first rose *for Israel*. The Holy Spirit first fell so that *Jews* 'from every nation under heaven'[56] could hear the good news. Yes, this baby

---

53. On this, see Graham Keith, *Hated Without a Cause? A Survey of Anti-Semitism* (Carlisle: Paternoster Press, 1997).

54. This expression is widely used, but I use it here with reluctance. The New Testament Gentile church abandoned neither the Old Testament in general, nor Old Testament law in particular. We meet this only in the second century, in Gentile churches influenced by Marcion, who regarded the God of the Old Testament as different from 'the God and Father of our Lord Jesus Christ'.

55. Gal. 2:10.

56. Acts 2:5.

faith became a teenager who grew up and left home, and became something we never envisaged when we first preached in Jerusalem: but don't forget where you were born! Pop home and visit now and then!

b. The fulfilment of Scripture

This is the great focus of Peter's sermon; not just in that he quotes three passages directly,[57] but even more in that the Old Testament supplies him with the vision of *the restoration of all things* which shapes his understanding of Jesus' messianic ministry. And here's the rub: Peter believed the Scriptures *as a Jew*, not as a Christian. Becoming a 'Christian' (though he would not have called himself that in Acts 3 – see Acts 11:26) simply gave him a dramatic new way of *reading* the Scriptures, around a glorious new sense of their fulfilment in Jesus. We see the fruits of this in both his early sermons (Acts 2 and 3). And of course there was huge potential for disagreement here, with Jews who did not accept (for instance) that Jesus was the 'prophet like Moses' of Deuteronomy 18:15. Sadly the dispute became quite acrimonious in the second century and later, with Christians accusing Jews of wilful obtuseness in not accepting the Christian reading of the Scriptures – which they said was *obviously* the right reading. But there is nothing obvious about it, in fact.

Once you're on the inside, the Christian readings of the Old Testament (indeed, the Christian practice of *calling* it 'the Old Testament') seem well-founded and powerful. They *are*. But while you're still outside the circle of Christian faith, they don't seem compelling at all. Within this sermon, for instance, why should Jews accept Peter's application of the threat expressed in Leviticus 23:29, *he will be utterly cut off from the people*, to all who refuse to believe in Jesus? In Leviticus, it's a threat directed at those who refuse to participate in the Day of Atonement. If you believe that the cross of Christ is God's ultimate atonement for sin, Peter's reading is more possible – but to see it that way you've got to be 'in', first!

So today there needs to be respectful handling of the Old Testament Scriptures, recognizing that Christians cannot claim a monopoly on interpretation. Actually, in the world of scholarship this has been the case for many years now, with both Christian and Jewish scholars contributing to scholarship in a spirit of mutual respect.[58]

---

57. Deut. 18:15 and 19 (v. 22–23); Lev. 23:29 (v. 23b); Gen. 22:18/26:4 (v. 25). We will return to the quotation from Lev. 23 below, in ch. 12 on Heb. 9: 23–28.

58. The Scriptural Reasoning movement is helpfully opening up real possibilities for this kind of mutual, respectful handling of each other's Scriptures.

c. The coming Messiah

Maybe this is the most poignant and powerful thing that Peter would say to us. In verses 20–21 he is re-presenting standard Jewish messianic expectation around the person of Jesus. Jews expected Messiah to come! Messianic expectations took many forms in the first century – there was no single understanding among Jews of what it meant to believe that God would one day send an Anointed One to deliver his people.[59] *Peter takes this messianic expectation and applies it to the second, not the first, coming of Jesus.* He does not frame his sermon around the argument – which became the focus of the debate in the second century – as to whether Jesus *was* the expected Messiah. Rather, he stands with his fellow-Jews in their messianic expectation and longing, and says: Yes, Messiah is coming! – and when he comes, he will be Jesus.

This is a different stance, and one that we can share today. Messianic expectation is still very varied in Judaism, but with all who place their hope as Jews still in the gift of a coming deliverer, in the face of all the horror and torment of the modern world, we can say: Yes, we agree that we cannot cope without divine intervention in our shared globe, and with you we cry in hope to God for his salvation. And we believe that when God gives that Saviour to the world, he will be Jesus.

---

59. N. T. Wright provides a very helpful brief overview of Jewish messianism in this period, in *The New Testament and the People of God* (London: SPCK, 1992), pp. 307–320. See also William Horbury, *Jewish Messianism and the Cult of Christ* (London: SCM, 1998).

8. THE DELIVERER FROM ZION (ROMANS 11:25–36)

1. Introduction

We turn to this great passage from Romans 11, which – with the preceding 'olive-tree' passage in 11:17–24 – is the climax and conclusion of three glorious chapters in which Paul has wrestled intensely with 'the question of Israel'. And at the heart of this climax and conclusion stands a powerful statement which features prominently in many eschatological schemes, and includes a unique description of the second coming, based on a composite quotation from Isaiah and Jeremiah:

> *For I do not want you to remain ignorant of this mystery, brothers, so that you may not be boastful in yourselves: a hardening-in-part has happened to Israel, until the fullness of the Gentiles comes in; and in this way all Israel will be saved – as it is written:*
>
> *The Deliverer will come from Zion,*
> *he will turn away ungodliness from Jacob.*
> *And this will be my covenant with them,*
> *when I take away their sins (vv. 25–27).*[1]

---

1. The quotation is mainly from Isa. 59:20, with lines added from Jer. 31:33 and Isa. 27:9. Paul often uses composite quotations like this.

Here the coming of the Lord (*the Deliverer will come from Zion*) seems to be especially for the sake of Israel. We are reminded immediately of Acts 3:20, where Peter tells his Jewish audience that the coming Jesus is 'the Messiah appointed for you'. Here Paul seems strongly to affirm Peter's Israel-focus, connecting the second coming to the salvation of *all Israel*. But he expands it, too, taking into account the change in order of events that we saw in Acts 15: the Gentiles are to be saved first, and when their *fullness . . . comes in* (presumably, the full number of those to be saved), then *all Israel will be saved*, too, apparently by the returning Lord Jesus who will *turn away ungodliness from Jacob*.

Paul certainly seems to attach the second coming to a timetable here, reversing the implicit timetable that underlay Peter's vision of the future. While Israel is 'hardened', the gospel goes to the Gentiles, and when the process of Gentile evangelism is complete, Jesus will come again and *all Israel will be saved*. Not surprisingly, this has become the centrepiece of many premillennial accounts of the 'last things', usually connected with the rapture, the great tribulation and the battle of Armageddon. A standard view is that the church is raptured away to heaven, the great tribulation ensues, climaxing in the battle of Armageddon, at the height of which Jesus comes to rescue Israel from destruction. Israel then embraces him as Lord, and Jesus sets up his millennial kingdom in Jerusalem. A complication is injected by Romans 11:15, where Paul seems to suggest that the 'acceptance' of Israel will be the cause of further spiritual blessing for the rest of the world: 'If their rejection has meant the reconciliation of the world, what will their acceptance mean but life from the dead?' And so some argue[2] that *after* the 'fullness of the Gentiles', and *after* the salvation of Israel, the Jews become the spearhead for a further spiritual revival ('life from the dead') for the rest of the world. In all these schemes *all Israel* means 'all Jews of the last generation, alive immediately preceding the coming of Jesus'.

I want to let Paul speak for himself, rather than putting together a scheme which then provides a template for interpretation here. For instance, Paul makes no references to the rapture or to a great battle. According to these schemes, the Gentile church, whose *fullness* has been reached, has been raptured away to heaven at least seven years before 'all Israel' is saved. And there is no indication that by 'saved' he means – even in part – 'rescued from destruction in battle'. What happens if we simply approach these verses within their setting in Romans, and against the background of the biblical theology we have already discovered?

_____

2. E.g. John Murray, *The Epistle to the Romans*, vol. 2, New International Commentary on the New Testament (Grand Rapids: Eerdmans, 1965), pp. 82–84, 95–96.

To do this, we will need to glance back at the intense argument that precedes this glorious conclusion in 11:25–36.

2. The question of Israel

The book of Acts leaves us with 'the question of Israel' dramatically unresolved. As we saw, Luke traces for us the *theological* movement which is entailed by the *geographical* movement of the gospel outward from Jerusalem to the Gentile world, orchestrated by the Holy Spirit himself. Luke makes it clear that the Spirit is poured out by the risen Christ, so that this extraordinary movement into Gentile mission is the work of Jesus the Lord.[3] But the theological question, *How can the Holy Spirit act in this way, without abandoning faithfulness to the covenant with Israel?* remains unaddressed in Acts. It remains, in fact, for Paul to tackle, especially in Romans and in particular in Romans 9 – 11, where the whole argument revolves around and responds to the question implicitly answered in Romans 9:6, 'It is not as though the word of God has failed!' No, says Paul – God's covenant 'word' to Israel has *not* been abandoned.

It looks as though Paul is especially addressing Gentile Christians who were inclined to argue that God's word to Israel had indeed 'failed'. They were inclined to write Israel off, and to 'boast over the branches', as Paul puts it.[4] The idea was simple, and we can imagine how it could arise almost naturally out of the repeated stories of Jewish rejection of the gospel in Acts:[5] Israel's day is past! Because of their unbelief, they've lost their place in the sun, the gospel has gone out to the world, and we Gentile believers are the ones who now enjoy God's blessing and favour.

This simple 'replacement' theology could be backed up by solid references to Jesus' teaching, not least his prediction of the destruction of the temple, and other passages like the parable of the wicked husbandmen, with its indictment of Jewish unbelief leading to the clear conclusion (in Matthew's version), 'The kingdom of God will be taken away from you [Jews], and given to a nation producing the fruits of it.'[6]

Paul is still addressing this Gentile theology in Romans 11:25, *so that you may not be boastful in yourselves.* Essentially, they were congratulating themselves on

---

3. Acts 2:33. The risen Jesus is the hidden 'actor' in the events of Acts 10:44 – 11:18.

4. Rom. 11:18, in his 'olive-tree' analogy.

5. E.g. Acts 8:1; 13:44–47; 18:5–7.

6. Matt. 21:43.

having the *faith* which Israel had failed to have. But in Paul's book, our faith is never something for which we congratulate ourselves, or indeed for which God will congratulate us one day. True, we stand in faith,[7] but we *depend* upon 'the goodness of God',[8] not upon our power to believe. We are saved by grace and not by works.[9]

But in order truly, and deeply, to refute this 'replacement' theology, Paul has mounted a powerful argument in these three chapters of Romans, with the aim of showing that God's 'word' to Israel – the word of covenant promise, which in a profound way made Israel 'first' among the nations – has not been over-thrown by Gentile 'law-free' inclusion in God's people. Actually Paul has been wrestling with the issue of 'Israel and the Gentiles' throughout the letter, starting in 1:16 where he insists that the gospel is 'God's power for salvation *to the Jew first* and also to the Greek'. In other words (he would say to us, responding to our chapter on Acts), don't think that Peter's 'first' in Acts 3:26 is simply replaced by James' 'first' in Acts 15:14! It's much more subtle – and thrilling – than that. In Romans 9 – 11 he presents his mature arguments about this:[10]

a. Jewish unbelief is not total, and not final

In 11:1 Paul poses the direct question whether God has rejected his people, and answers with a very vigorous 'Perish the thought!' As evidence he then proposes *himself.* Like Elijah in his generation,[11] Paul is the proof that 'God has not rejected his people whom he foreknew'.[12] And also like Elijah, Paul can point to the presence of a 'remnant existing by God's gracious choice at the present

---

7. Rom. 11:20.

8. Rom. 11:22.

9. Rom. 11:6.

10. N. T. Wright has been writing about Romans, and chs. 9 – 11 in particular, for his whole scholarly career, and his new book *Paul and the Faithfulness of God* contains a magnificent 100 pages on Romans 9 – 11 (pp. 1156–1258). The section on Romans 11 (pp. 1195–1258) is truly masterful. I only wish to part company from his exegesis at two points, mentioned below. Those who are familiar with his Pauline scholarship will recognize how much I owe to him in what follows – a meeting of minds that goes right back to long discussions in student days.

11. Paul's comparison of himself with Elijah in 11:2–5 is very telling. Elijah too ministered at a time when even he thought that Israel had become completely apostate. But it wasn't true then (1 Kgs 19:18, quoted in 11:4), and it isn't true in Paul's day, either.

12. Rom. 11:2.

time [*kairos*]'.[13] At this point in God's plan – this *kairos*-moment – a saved 'remnant' carries the covenant promise that Israel is still 'God's people whom he foreknew', even though most Jews have not embraced Jesus as the Christ. Paul developed this 'remnant' theology in Romans 9, first by distinguishing within Israel between two sorts of people, 'children of promise' and 'children of [merely] flesh',[14] and then by applying Isaiah's 'remnant' theology to this distinction.[15] Throughout he insists that this is *God's plan*. The remnant is not self-selecting – it does not exist by historical accident, because only a few happen to have believed. The remnant exists 'by God's gracious choice': i.e., he has decided that, at this *kairos*-moment, only a remnant will believe.

Why? we might well ask! The answer takes us to the point dealt with in section c. below, and onward to the theology of the second coming that Paul develops in Romans 11. But first we must note Paul's conviction that the unbelief of Israel is not *final*. His question in 11:11 engages with the Gentile replacement theology which is in his sights throughout: 'So I ask, Have they [the Jews] stumbled so as to fall completely? Not at all!' In other words, does their unbelief mean that we can write them off? No!! The tragedy of their unbelief cannot be minimized, as his very sobering quotations in 11:8–10 show. But they can still be 'saved'. In fact even his own Gentile-focused ministry looks over its shoulder at Israel:

I am apostle to the Gentiles; but as I press my ministry forward and seek to promote it as much as possible, I am constantly hoping thereby to make my Jewish kinsfolk 'jealous' and thus save some of them.[16]

Constantly Paul is looking, and hoping, for the salvation of Jews through his ministry, even though it focuses on Gentiles. The 'promotion' or 'glorification' of his ministry in 11:13 probably involves enabling Jews to see the fruits of covenant membership enjoyed by Gentile believers in their Christ – maybe made concrete through the collection of money for 'the poor in Jerusalem' from his Gentile churches.[17] He wanted his Gentile converts to see clearly how they have stepped into the blessings which should be Israel's: in the terms of the olive-tree picture, how they 'partake of the rich nourishment that comes from the root

---

13. Rom. 11:5.
14. Rom. 9:6–13.
15. Rom. 9:27–29.
16. Rom. 11:13–14.
17. See Rom. 15:25–28.

of the olive'.[18] This explains why he is so incensed by the 'replacement' theology he is opposing here. How will Jews see their own covenant blessings mirrored among people who oppose them and write off their history?

And indeed Paul was seeing constant conversions of Jewish people through his ministry. Romans was probably written from Corinth during the period of time summarized in Acts 18, when Paul was 'arguing in the synagogue every Sabbath and seeking to persuade both Jews and Greeks', and 'Crispus the synagogue chairman believed in the Lord, with all his house, and many of the Corinthians were responding to his words with faith and baptism'.[19]

b. Gentile faith is not a surprise, but a fulfilment of Scripture

Universal Gentile faith is not a surprise – and it's not 'law-free'. Here we are looking back in particular to his argument in chapter 10 (or rather, 9:30 – 10:21), where – in a very dramatic move – Paul says that the response of faith to the preaching of the gospel, which he has seen so often while out on the job as an evangelist, is precisely the *obedience from the heart* that the law has always looked for. Israel was told that she must respond from the heart to the indwelling word of the Lord, and that inner response is what the law seeks.[20] So *anyone* who responds to the gospel, whether Jew or Gentile, is profoundly fulfilling the law! The details of Paul's use of Deuteronomy 30 need not detain us, but the basic point is that, on this basis, Paul argues that 'Christ is the end of the law for *everyone* who has faith',[21] with an emphasis on the 'everyone' so as to include Gentiles and Jews equally.[22] Whoever *believes* in Jesus fulfils the law, whether Jew or Gentile. 'The word of faith that we proclaim' *is* the heart-based word of commitment and obedience for which the Old Testament law was looking.[23]

Paul rounds this argument off by a series of quotations in 10:16–21 that make the point that (a) Israel's unbelief is no surprise to God, but is factored into his plan, and that (b) Gentile faith has likewise all along been on God's agenda. *Neither* is a sudden departure from the plan as far as God is concerned. We look at one of these quotations in more detail now.

─────────────

18. Rom. 11:17. Undoubtedly (though some doubt it), the root of the tree is Israel.
19. Acts 18:4, 8.
20. Paul quotes from Deut. 30:12–14 to make this point (Rom. 10:6–8), though this is a basic aspect of the message of Deuteronomy and is picked up later by all the prophets.
21. Rom. 10:4.
22. Cf. Rom. 10:11–13.
23. Rom. 10:8–10.

c. Jewish unbelief and Gentile faith are interwoven in God's plan

In fact God has woven the two together – Jewish unbelief and Gentile faith – so that each serves the other in his plan, in an amazing way. This is the vital point which is of particular significance for us in 11:25–32, and is really the masterstroke in Paul's argument. He is inspired by Deuteronomy 32:21, which he quotes in 10:19:

> I will make you jealous of a nation who are not a nation,
>> and with an uncomprehending nation I will provoke you to anger.

The principle of 'jealousy' drawn from this verse then shapes his argument through chapter 11. Deuteronomy 32 is the 'song of Moses', which was meant to bear witness against Israel after Moses' death, when they fall into rebellion and trouble (as Moses foresees they will)[24] – in other words, it was provided 'for just such a time as this'. If at any moment in Israel's history, then surely now, after the rejection of the Christ, the message of Deuteronomy 32 comes into play. And within it, Paul finds a message that applies precisely to the spread of the gospel among the Gentiles while Israel lies in unbelief: the blessing of the Gentiles is *God's* response to Israel's rebellion, *in order to call them back to faithfulness* when they see others enjoying the blessings that should be theirs. As we have seen, this is precisely how Paul explains his own ministry in 11:13–14.[25]

The blessing of the Gentiles is thus, paradoxically, one aspect of God's *judgment on Israel* for her rebellion. But Paul has no doubt, I am sure, that God intended this 'jealousy' principle to work, so that there certainly would be salvation-after-judgment for Israel. Moses' Song ends:

> Indeed the LORD will vindicate his people,
>> have compassion on his servants,
> when he sees that their power is gone . . .
> Praise, O heavens, his people,
>> worship him, all you gods!
> For he will avenge the blood of his children,
>> and take vengeance on his adversaries;

---

24. See Deut. 31:27–30.

25. It is probably not surprising that Deut. 32 is one of the most alluded-to Old Testament passages in the New; there are some six quotations and about twenty-nine further identifiable allusions.

he will repay those who hate him,
   and cleanse the land for his people.[26]

We meet this certainty of final salvation in Romans 11:26. In the middle part of Romans 11[27] Paul uses wonderfully expressive language to unpack this jealousy principle further. For him this is a practical way of understanding his ministry right now, and furnishes him with a warning for his boastful Gentiles, sure of their superiority over unbelieving Israel:

> Don't be proud! – be *afraid*. For if God did not spare the natural branches of the olive, he won't spare you either. So here God's goodness and severity are both on display: his severity towards those who fell, but his goodness towards you – provided you remain in his goodness, since you too may be cut off. And they too, if they don't remain in their unbelief, will be grafted in: for God is certainly able to graft them back in. For if you were cut off from the wild olive where you naturally belonged, and were grafted into a cultivated olive – quite contrary to normal practice – then how much more will the natural branches be re-grafted into their own olive tree![28]

We see here not just Paul's *longing* for Israel's salvation (cf. Rom. 10:1), but his *expectation* of it, as the jealousy principle continues to work. He sees it happening already. It is not just a matter of eschatological expectation. He wants his Gentiles to hope for it, too: to 'remain in God's goodness' means (amongst other things) hoping for the re-instatement of the 'natural branches' into their olive tree.[29]

Now we can turn to our passage directly.

3. The second coming and the salvation of Israel

The vast majority of commentators think that in these verses Paul is making an eschatological prediction of an end-time mass conversion of Jews at, or maybe

---

26. Deut. 32:36, 43. Paul quotes the first phrase of v. 43 later in Romans (15:10). In Rom. 12:19 he quotes Deut. 32:35.

27. Rom. 11:11–24.

28. Rom. 11:20–24.

29. It is worth comparing Rom. 5:18 with Rom. 11:11–12: Israel's 'falling away' means reconciliation and 'riches' for the world, but Adam's 'falling away' (the same Gk word, *paraptōma*) means 'condemnation' for all. God acts differently in Israel's case – because of Deut. 32.

just before, the second coming of the Lord.[30] Some make much of the fact that Paul calls this a *mystery* (v. 25), a word that Paul sometimes uses of eschatological events, and suggest that Paul is here passing on a new revelation, not previously known. On this basis F. F. Bruce is able to explain the apparent contradiction between 11:28–29, which says that Israel will be saved on the basis of her ethnic status and calling, and Romans 4:1–12 which says that they will *not*. The answer, Bruce suggests, is that Paul here reports a new revelation, of something which could not have arisen logically or consistently within his previous argument – all Israel will be saved![31]

I think Bruce is wrong on both accounts. First, 11:28–29 is not about the basis on which Israel will be saved. Rather, it underlines the faithfulness of God to his promises. One of Paul's absolute starting points is his conviction of the inviolability of God's word. And that means that the Holy Spirit's strange action in allowing Gentiles to 'attain righteousness by faith'[32] without coming under the law does *not* reverse or undermine God's commitment to Israel expressed in the basic Abrahamic covenant. It cannot.

And secondly, it seems clear that Paul's conviction about Israel's salvation does indeed arise consistently from within his argument. I've tried to show this, in summarizing Paul's use of Deuteronomy 32 and the jealousy principle in Romans 11:11–24. He expects Israel to be saved, because that is where the Song of Moses lands up, even though, en route, the Lord transfers their blessings to a 'uncomprehending nation' in order to make Israel jealous.[33]

So it seems right to summarize the position like this: in 11:25–26 Paul describes the *completion* of the process currently under way, whereby Israel's faithlessness is the occasion for the Gentiles' faith, and the Gentiles' faith is meant to make Israel 'jealous'. Finally the process will fully work, signalled by the 'fullness' of the Gentiles on the one hand, and the salvation of 'all' Israel

---

30. E.g. John Ziesler: 'Paul holds the belief that at the End the Jews who do not belong to the remnant will be moved to "jealousy", and repent' (*Paul's Letter to the Romans*, TPI New Testament Commentary [London: SCM, 1989], p. 286); C. E. B. Cranfield: 'Paul was thinking of a restoration of the nation of Israel as a whole to God *at the end*, an eschatological event in the strict sense' (*The Epistle to the Romans*, vol. 2, International Critical Commentary [Edinburgh: T&T Clark, 1979], p. 577, his emphasis).

31. F. F. Bruce, *Romans*, Tyndale New Testament Commentary (Leicester: Inter-Varsity Press, 1985), p. 208.

32. Rom. 9:30.

33. Rom. 10:19.

on the other. And that will be the moment when 'the Deliverer will come from Zion', marking the final banishing of sin and ungodliness from Israel.

It seems unlikely, therefore, that Paul is predicting a massive, end-time conversion of Jews here. He is writing out of his current experience of the working of the jealousy process, in fulfilment of Deuteronomy 32, and imagining that this process will continue steadily until it is complete. This is supported by the little phrase translated *and so*[34] at the beginning of verse 26. At the beginning of this chapter I translated it *and in this way*, because this phrase much more naturally describes the *manner*, rather than the *timing*, of Israel's salvation. Paul is *not* saying – I think! – that *the fullness of the Gentiles* will be followed by the salvation of Israel when the Saviour will appear to *banish ungodliness from Jacob*. Rather, the salvation of *all Israel* takes place all bound up with the progressive salvation of the Gentile world, because that is how the jealousy principle works. This is exactly what Paul then says in verses 30–32:

> *For just as you* [Gentiles] *once were disobedient to God but have now received mercy because of their* [the Jews'] *disobedience, so they too are now disobedient because of the mercy shown to you – so that they too may now receive mercy. For God has locked up all in disobedience, so that he may have mercy on all.*[35]

The Deliverer comes at the moment of final *mercy on all*, when these two great 'masses' of humanity, Israel and the Gentiles, complete their extraordinary interaction in God's plan. Israel's *disobedience* has a saving effect on the Gentiles; and reciprocally the Gentiles' experience of God's *mercy* has a saving effect on Israel. God uses even our disobedience to further his purposes of mercy. Paul is not saying that Israel's disobedience was a good thing, and neither is ours. Sin always brings disruption, pain and ultimately death, unless God turns it around and uses it for his purpose of salvation. And that is what he has done, says Paul, in the case of Israel's rebellious sin, even her crucifixion of the Christ.

The second *now* in verse 31 is significant: *so that they too may* now *receive mercy*. Not all manuscripts contain it, but all the basic principles of textual criticism support its presence here. It makes it clear that Paul is not just looking forward to an eschatological *mercy* to be received by Israel when the *Deliverer comes*, but also mercy *now* through the patient spread of the gospel through the Gentile world.

---

34. Gk *kai houtōs*.

35. We will consider Paul's use of the word 'all' here when we look at 1 Cor. 15:20–28 in the next chapter.

At this juncture I need to log the two points where I part from the excellent exposition of these chapters by N. T. Wright.[36] The two points are connected with each other. First, he argues that by 'Israel' here Paul does not mean the nation, but 'the Israel of God',[37] the spiritual 'Israel' composed of Jewish *and Gentile* believers in Christ – in other words, the church.[38] And secondly, he takes *the Deliverer will come from Zion* to refer, not to the second coming of Jesus, but to the going-out of the gospel from Jerusalem to the Gentile world, especially through the ministry of Paul himself.[39] Through this gospel proclamation, the whole church is being gathered, Jews and Gentiles.

In relation to the first point, it is certainly true that Paul argues for a redefinition of 'Israel' in Romans 9 – 11. Following the redefinition of 'Jew' in 2:28–29, the first step of his argument in 9 – 11 is to say that 'not all who are "of" Israel, *are* Israel':[40] in other words, 'Israel' is defined not by physical descent but by spiritual kinship. Paul wants to say that *Gentiles* now join God's people – this is the point of his olive-tree picture in 11:17–24. But even in 9:6, the term 'Israel' still refers to the historic people, the descendants of Abraham, and in none of the other nine references to Israel in Romans 9 – 11 (not counting the two in 11:25–26) does Paul divert from this primary reference. In fact, because his argument is all about the relationship between Israel and the Gentiles, it is vital that this is so. So it seems highly unlikely that Paul would divert from this in 11:25–26, even though it is certainly *theologically* possible for him to use 'Israel' in an inclusive sense, to refer to the new Jew-and-Gentile people of God, and he may actually do so in Galatians 6:16.

The second point – that *the Deliverer will come from Zion* refers not to the second coming but to the gospel going out from Jerusalem – is more important for us. I actually argued for this view myself, in a little book on Romans 9 – 11.[41] It seemed to me to make more sense, particularly in the light of the way in which Paul alters the quotation from Isaiah 59:20, inserting *from Zion* in place of 'to Zion'. This seemed to parallel Paul's language in Romans 15:19, where he describes his own ministry in taking the gospel '*from Jerusalem* and as far round as Illyricum'. He was not averse to seeing Old Testament prophecy fulfilled in

---

36. See above, note 10.

37. Cf. Gal. 6:16.

38. Wright, *Paul and the Faithfulness of God*, pp. 1241–1244.

39. Ibid., pp. 1248–1251.

40. Rom. 9:6.

41. Steve Motyer, *Israel in the Plan of God: Light on Today's Debate* (Leicester: Inter-Varsity Press, 1989), pp. 153–154.

his own preaching of the gospel – he does it right there, in Romans 15:21,[42] and he has already done it in Romans 10:15–16.[43]

But now I've changed my mind![44] It seems to me now that this language is more appropriate as a description of the coming again of Jesus Christ, as Saviour and Judge. Paul is looking ahead to the moment when the jealousy process will have fulfilled its purpose. At that moment, *the Deliverer will come from Zion* – the heavenly Zion, that is – to set his seal on the ingrafting of Israel back into the olive tree; the moment when we all experience the 'How much more?' of Romans 11:12, and the 'life from the dead' of Romans 11:15.[45]

The details of the quotation support this reading. Isaiah 59 was clearly a favourite passage of Paul's. He quotes from it earlier in Romans, within the string of quotations by which he asserts the universal sinfulness of humankind in Romans 3:10–18. There, verses 15–17 quote Isaiah 59:7–8. This is significant, because the early part of the chapter is a lament over Israel's sinfulness, expressed first in the third person (59:2–8; e.g. 'Their works are works of iniquity . . .', v. 6) and then in the first person plural (vv. 9–15):

> We wait for justice, but there is none;
>> for salvation, but it is far from us.
> For our transgressions before you are many,
>> and our sins testify against us.
> Our transgressions indeed are with us,
>> and we know our iniquities:
> transgressing, and denying the LORD,
>> and turning away from following our God,
> talking oppression and revolt,
>> conceiving lying words and uttering them from the heart. [46]

---

42. Quoting Isa. 52:15.

43. Quoting Isa. 52:7 and 53:1. Cf. Acts 13:47 (quoting Isa. 49:6).

44. Having himself written so much on Romans previously, N. T. Wright also finds himself in this position (though not on this particular point!). He writes, 'I trust one is allowed to change one's mind from time to time' (Wright, *Paul and the Faithfulness of God*, p. 1211, n. 586). I do it frequently.

45. 'Life from the dead' (11:15) is much better understood as referring to the final resurrection, rather than to some massive revival (against Murray – see above, note 2).

46. Isa. 59:11–13.

In the Septuagint the last part of this quotation uses the same word which Paul uses in Romans 11:31 to describe Israel: 'we have been disobedient' (Gk *apeithein*). It seems clear that Paul would have read this chapter as a lament uttered by Israel as he sees her: *locked up under disobedience*, powerless to save herself. But then the chapter changes:

> The LORD saw it, and it displeased him
>   that there was no justice.
> He saw that there was no one,
>   and was appalled that there was no one to intervene;
> so his own arm brought him victory,
>   and his righteousness upheld him.
> He put on righteousness like a breastplate,
>   and a helmet of salvation on his head;
> he put on garments of vengeance for clothing,
>   and wrapped himself in fury as in a mantle.
> According to their deeds, so he will repay;
>   wrath to his adversaries, requital to his enemies;
>   to the coastlands he will render requital.
> So those in the west shall fear the name of the LORD,
>   and those in the east, his glory;
> for he will come like a pent-up stream
>   that the wind of the LORD drives on.
> And he will come to Zion as Redeemer,
>   to those in Jacob who turn from transgression, says the LORD.

> And as for me, this is my covenant with them, says the LORD: my spirit that is upon you, and my words that I have put in your mouth, shall not depart out of your mouth, or out of the mouths of your children . . . from now on and for ever.[47]

This is glorious – no wonder it was a favourite passage of Paul's. And it illustrates the vital biblical principle concerning God's wrath on which we touched above when thinking about Psalm 18: his wrath is not his passion to judge or punish sin, existing in tension with his parallel, or even conflicting, desire to save sinners. *His wrath is his passion for justice which impels him to rescue his helpless people, even though they are helpless because of their sin.* To look into this would take us beyond our precise focus on the second coming, but it is worth

---

47. Isa. 59:15–21.

remembering that, for Paul, 'the day of wrath and revelation of the righteous judgment of God'[48] is the last act in the drama of *redemption* that holds together all his action in and for his labouring and much-loved human creatures.

The vital point is that Isaiah 59:15–21 contains a string of themes which Paul would have connected with the second coming of the Lord, rather than the first – especially vengeance,[49] repayment according to deeds,[50] wrath,[51] judgment[52] and the universal revelation and acknowledgement of his glory.[53] Even though (of course) Jesus is already the Redeemer[54] for Paul, redemption so far has not been about wrath and vengeance but about mercy and forgiveness; and the final winding-up – the 'life from the dead' to which he looks forward in 11:15 – is yet to be. So it is highly likely that *the Deliverer will come from Zion* in 11:26 refers, in Paul's mind, to the glorious appearance of the Lord which will mark the completion of the jealousy process, the 'fullness' of the Gentiles matching the salvation of 'all Israel', and the moment when God's plan to *be merciful to all* (v. 32) reaches its fulfilment.

Two further points confirm this. First, it is really interesting to wonder – as Wright does also[55] – why Paul does not continue his quotation from Isaiah 59. He breaks off after *this is my covenant with them* and inserts words drawn from Isaiah 27:9, *when I take away their sins*. This is especially odd when we consider how suitable the following words in Isaiah 59:21 are: 'This is my covenant with them . . . my spirit that is upon you, and my words that I have put in your mouth, shall not depart out of your mouth.' This would chime in with all that Paul writes earlier about the gift of the Spirit, and especially about the renewal of

---

48. Rom. 2:5.

49. Cf. Rom 12:19.

50. Cf. Rom 2:6; 1 Cor. 3:13–15; 2 Cor. 5:10.

51. 'Wrath' is always eschatological (end-time) in Paul, except *perhaps* in Rom. 1:18 and 1 Thess. 2:16. See e.g. Rom 2:5; 5:9; 1 Thess. 1:10; 5:9.

52. Cf. Rom. 2:5–10, 16; 14:10; 1 Cor. 4:5; 11:32; Gal. 5:10; 2 Thess. 1:7–9, etc.

53. See e.g. Phil 2:10–11; 2 Thess. 1:10.

54. I have preferred 'Deliverer' as the translation of Paul's Greek here, but Isaiah uses the great Hebrew word *gô'ēl*, usually translated 'redeemer'. I'm partly motivated by the fact that Paul uses the same verb (*rhyesthai*) in his great cry of frustration and longing in Rom. 7:24, 'Who will *deliver* me from this body of death?' He too shares with Israel the frustration of indwelling sin (Rom 7:14–23), and feels the same longing for deliverance as that expressed in Isa. 59. He looks forward to 'the redemption of our bodies' (Rom. 8:23 – a different word).

55. Wright, *Paul and the Faithfulness of God*, pp. 1248–1249.

the heart and the gift of the saving words of confession that fulfil the law in Romans 10:8–10.

Wright's answer to this is to say that Paul 'is taking Isaiah 59 for granted' – i.e., assuming what it says, and adding the extra notion of the forgiveness of those currently 'hardened'.[56] But this hardly convinces. We still need a reason why Paul apparently doesn't want to point to the fulfilment of Isaiah's prophecy about the gift of the Spirit and of the saving 'words' *in this context*. And we have a perfect reason, if Paul wants us to apply *the Deliverer will come from Zion* to the second coming of the Lord, rather than the first. The words that follow in Isaiah 59 would confuse the issue, by reminding us of the *current* blessings enjoyed by those who believe in him. Instead, Paul keeps our attention on the future blessing when sins are forgiven at the final judgment.

Secondly, we must look more closely at the other – even more dramatic – change which Paul has made to his quotation of Isaiah 59. The Hebrew says 'the Deliverer will come *to* Zion'. The Septuagint has, 'The Deliverer will come *for the sake of* Zion'. Paul writes, *As it is written, The Deliverer will come* from *Zion . . .* I can imagine the seminar in the new creation (will there be such? I hope so) where Paul is on the receiving end of indignant objections like, 'But Paul, how could you say "as it is written" when you then change what is written?'

It's fascinating to imagine what he might say. My imagination is this:

Don't worry, guys. I love to combine passages to keep you on your exegetical toes! Do you remember Psalm 14, the one from which I quoted in Romans 3 when I was compiling the list of sins that used to plague us all before the Deliverer came? Along with Isaiah 59, Psalm 14 was my main source for that list of quotations.[57] *Well, that Psalm ends with a glorious prayer for deliverance: 'Who will bring the salvation of Israel from Zion? When the Lord turns round the captivity of his people, Jacob will rejoice and Israel will be glad.'*[58] *I was writing about the 'captivity' of Israel in Romans 11 – her hardening in disobedience. When the Lord Jesus finally came from Zion – from the heavenly dwelling of God himself, to which he returned when he ascended – he brought the 'salvation' for which the psalmist was longing (and me too*[59]*). I don't know if Isaiah had the heavenly Zion in mind. I suspect he didn't, in fact. You'll have to pop across to his seminar and ask. But that's what I was thinking of, inspired by Psalm 14. Israel was finally delivered from all her sins by the Redeemer who brought salvation from Zion, in fulfilment of his covenant promise!*

---

56. Ibid., p. 1249.

57. He quotes Ps. 14:1–3 in Rom. 3:10–12.

58. Ps. 14:7 (my translation of LXX, Ps. 13:7).

59. See Rom. 10:1.

We might press Paul a little on a further misquotation here – or rather, a quotation of a mistranslation. He quotes the Septuagint, *he will turn ungodliness from Jacob*. But this is a mistranslation of the Hebrew, '[he will come] to those in Jacob who turn from transgression'. I think we can imagine Paul's reply. For him, what matters is the substance of the quotation understood within the wider setting of scriptural expectation and theology. He doesn't seem to mind too much about the details.

4. The theology of the second coming in Romans 11

What can we add to our biblical theology of the second coming of Jesus as we read this glorious piece of Romans? We will pick up some further exegetical points as we think about this.

a. Paul prods us to give our biblical theology an 'Israel', as well as a 'worldwide' focus

Remarkably, in resolving the theological question with which Acts leaves us, Paul has taken us back in the direction of Peter's theology in Acts 3. He opposes the simple 'replacement' view which we might take, if we read Acts in a superficial way. The focus on Israel in God's plan has not been replaced by a focus on the Gentile world instead. Paul's olive-tree picture in 11:17–24 has prepared us for this, anyway. The root, I am sure, is the Abrahamic covenant which is the source of the 'rich nourishment' (v. 17) by which Paul's Gentile believers – whether they accept it or not! – are now sustained. And the 'natural branches', therefore, are those who feel a 'natural' connection to Abraham. Gentile believers are 'grafts contrary to nature' (v. 24).

The Deliverer comes *from Zion*, the heavenly dwelling of Israel's God, to renew the covenant with Israel through the forgiveness of Israel's sin. Though the words *this will be my covenant with them* are drawn from Isaiah 59:21, this language would certainly remind Paul's Jewish readers of the 'new covenant' promise in Jeremiah:

> This is the covenant I will make *with the house of Israel* after those days, says the Lord:
> I will put my laws in their mind and will write them on their hearts . . . they will all
> know me, from the least of them to the greatest, because I will be merciful towards
> their injustices, and I will remember their sins no longer.[60]

---

60. Jer. 31:33–34. This is my translation of the LXX, Jer. 38:33–34.

Of course Paul has also – boldly – applied this promise to Gentile believers.[61] But he was very keen for his Gentile converts to know their indebtedness to Israel. 'The Gentiles are in debt to the Jews!' he writes, urging support for his collection project for the poor in Jerusalem: 'For if the Gentiles have shared in Israel's spiritual wealth, they owe it to them to serve them in material things.'[62]

However Paul's emphasis falls on the unity of Jews and Gentiles in Christ. He does not agree with the whole of Peter's early theology, which wanted Gentile converts to become Jewish proselytes. Paul spearheads the 'law-free' gospel, and precipitates the Apostolic Council in Acts 15. And so, though we notice his Israel-focus in Romans 11, we also notice what he does *not* say. A very common feature of premillennial schemes is that Jesus returns *to Jerusalem*, and sets up his kingdom there, in literal fulfilment of the promise that the Messiah will sit on the throne of David. Paul could have said that here, but in fact, as we've seen, he deliberately changes 'to Zion' to *from Zion*, which has the effect of changing the reference of 'Zion'. Whereas Isaiah meant the earthly Jerusalem, Paul makes it refer to the *heavenly* Zion, as in Psalm 14:7. This is all of a piece with the way in which Paul takes Israel-specific features of Old Testament history, religion and theology and applies them broadly to a bigger people of God, now including Gentiles. His treatment of Abraham in Romans 4 is an excellent example of this.

b. The second coming will bring salvation-history to its point of fulfilment

Paul's remarkably positive picture of the second coming here illustrates the possibility of picturing it entirely in terms of salvation and deliverance, without reference to judgment, condemnation or death. These negatives are all left behind. It is not that they are absent – far from it:

> As far as the gospel is concerned, they are enemies of God because of you . . . as you were once disobedient to God . . . they too are now disobedient . . . God has locked up all in disobedience . . . (vv. 28–32).

Vast tracts of human misery lurk within these simple words. But Paul's concern is to hold against all these negatives the overwhelming positive of the grace and mercy of God:

---

61. See 2 Cor. 3:2–3 and Rom. 2:15, where it is explicitly *Gentiles* who are experiencing the fulfilment of Jer. 31:33.
62. Rom. 15:27.

But as far as election is concerned, they are beloved by God because of the patriarchs. For God does
not regret his gifts and his call!... you have now received mercy... so that they may now receive
mercy... so that he may have mercy on all... (vv. 28–32).

'Salvation-history' is the technical expression given by theologians to the 'story
of salvation' told through the Bible. Paul has been wrestling to tell this story in a
different way, opposing the simplistic Gentile version that draws a heavy black
line across the page after the book of Malachi and proclaims a new start, making
the Gentile church now centre stage in God's plan. Paul cannot write off the story
of Israel in this way: it rests on the *irrevocable gifts and call of God*.[63] But he *also* wants
to tell the story in a way which makes sense of his call to be apostle to the Gentiles,
offering to them the relationship with God that Abraham had, without legal strings
attached – not requiring circumcision and observance of the Jewish food laws
and festivals. *And* he wants to make sense of the absolute tragedy of Israel's
rejection of the Christ, *while also* believing that the crucifixion of the Messiah was
not a tragic mistake but actually the vital centre of God's plan.

A tall order! Paul really is dealing in big-picture stuff here. The result is this
amazing vision of interwoven *disobedience* and *mercy*, all orchestrated by God
himself. The crucial verse is the last one, expressing the end of the story: *For*
God has locked up all in disobedience, so that he may have mercy on all.[64]

In the end, it's all mercy, for Paul. We will think about Paul's use of 'all' when
we look at 1 Corinthians 15:20–28 in the next chapter. But we ought to catch
the flavour of it here. Paul's 'alls' are like the spices that bring the curry to life;
without them, the food would be flat and lifeless, but with them, we wonder
whether it's too hot and whether we should have chosen the chicken korma.
But it's worth the risk, his 'alls' say to us: should we imagine anything less than
a saved world? This is Paul's version of Daniel's vision of the kingdom of God
that expands to fill the whole earth.[65] Can we live without that vision? Paul
inspires us with it here.

Paul leaves on one side how the Deliverer might *banish ungodliness from Jacob*
if Jacob would prefer to hold onto it. The whole notion of final judgment
becomes unsustainable, if God sweeps *all* into salvation whether they want it
or not – and Paul clearly believed in the real possibility of final condemnation.
He imputes huge significance to our choice and responsibility.[66] Daniel's terrible

------

63. Rom. 11:29.
64. Rom. 11:32.
65. Dan. 2:44.
66. See Rom. 1:28 – 2:11.

fourth 'beast', persecuting God's people, has here become here the *ungodliness* that infects God's people themselves. God will destroy both! Paul leaves the 'how' within the *unsearchable judgments* and *unmappable ways* of God (v. 33). God is such that he plans our continued rebellion against him as a stepping-stone to mercy.

How different a vision of the second coming this is from that in Luke 17 – and indeed from that in John 14! Whereas Luke's picture of the coming of the Son of Man is dark and fearsome, as we saw, and John's is personal and relational (around the metaphor of 'home'), Paul presents it surrounded by these cosmic 'alls', and sees it ushering in the grand fulfilment of the whole biblical story. These varied passages challenge us to hold several different stories of the future in our minds: different futures-as-present that can inspire and lift us with hope, and with adoration of the God who orchestrates it all. This leads us to the third contribution from Romans 11 to our biblical theology.

c. We need to embrace a 'mystery' which calls us to worship

Paul's use of the word *mystery* in verse 25 is balanced by the little hymn in verses 33–36, which gives us the right approach to understanding what he means by this word. A 'mystery' is not a new revelation that adds some new insight previously unknown – though it might be connected with a new revelation – but it is *something about the ways and purposes of God which transcends our current capacity either to experience, or to understand*. Paul's use of the word thus tends to appear at moments of high spiritual exaltation. So, for instance, Romans ends with another little hymn of praise containing the only other use of the word in Romans:

> Now to him who is able to strengthen you according to my gospel and the preaching of Jesus Christ, according to the revelation of the *mystery* kept secret as the ages of time [*chronos*] crept by, but now revealed and through prophetic writings and by the command of the God of the ages made known, so that all the nations might embrace the obedience of faith: to the only wise God, through Jesus Christ, be glory unto all ages! Amen.[67]

Here the *mystery* is nothing other than 'my gospel and the preaching of Jesus Christ', which of course contains the huge surprise (never suspected by any of Paul's fellow-Jews, including himself before he met Jesus), that God intends

---

67. Rom. 16:25–27.

'the obedience of faith' for *all*, on equal terms. This is called a 'mystery' here partly because it was kept secret, and partly because it is still so surprising and hard to grasp in the light of the covenant with Israel.[68]

And so Paul introduces his final explanation of the way in which God will achieve the salvation of Jews and Gentiles together by calling it a *mystery*, because it partakes of the amazing and inexplicable wisdom of God. It is wholly fitting, therefore, that this passage ends with a 'doxology' (to give it its technical literary description). Chapter 11:33–36 is not a random heart-raising add-on, but a vital piece of the theological jigsaw, underlining the *mystery* of which we must always be conscious when thinking about the second coming. These verses have a lovely chiastic structure, in which the three questions in 11:34–35[69] pick up, in reverse order, the three qualities of God which Paul praises in verses 33a:

A   *Oh, the depth*
   B   *of the riches*
      C   *and wisdom*
         D   *and knowledge*
           E   *of God! How unsearchable are his judgments,*
             and how unmappable his ways!
         D'   *'For who has known the mind of the Lord?*
      C'   *Or who has been his counsellor?'*
   B'   *'Or who has put him in debt with a gift, so that he is bound to repay?'*
A'   *For from him, and through him, and to him are all things. To him be glory*
   to all ages, Amen!

This is such beautiful little hymn. It seems to have just bubbled up from within Paul as he dictated Romans and Tertius scribbled hard to keep up.[70] Contemplating the vastness, and audacity, and inexplicability of God's plan, Paul is overwhelmed – but not so overwhelmed as to be silenced. From somewhere he finds these words, once again inspired by Scripture. The best commentary is found in Ephesians 1, another passage where theology spills over into doxology:

---

68. For other significant uses of the term in Paul, which illustrate its flavour as something transcending either our experience or our understanding, see e.g. 1 Cor. 2:7–9; 13:2; 14:2; 15:51–52; Eph. 3:9–10; Col. 1:26–27.
69. They are all quotations, drawn from Isa. 40:13 and Job 41:11a.
70. See Rom. 16:22.

> ... he has made known to us the mystery of his will, according to his plan which he
> purposed in Christ as a way of bringing all times [*kairos*] to completion: his plan to
> sum up all things in Christ, things both in heaven and on earth ...[71]

'To sum up all things in Christ.' The metaphor that Paul uses here is drawn from literature: the 'summing up' was the synopsis that preceded a play or a chapter in a book, giving readers the essence of the whole. When the whole story is told, Paul says, Jesus Christ will turn out to have been the heart of the plot.

This can only be so (as Eph. 1 makes clear) because the cross makes it possible. *For from him, and through him, and to him, are all things* (v. 36). Were it not for the cross, these three prepositions would make God a monster who initiates (*from*), imposes (*through*) and rejoices over (*to*) all the evil and suffering that his human creatures endure. But – praise him – that is not how he makes the world's evil part of his story. On the cross he receives it into himself, endures it in his own body, embraces it so that it passes *through* him. Israel's disobedience – that rebellious hatred which nailed the Son of God to the cross, representing all the sin of the world – passes *through* him there into nothingness, so that finally there may be mercy for *all* (v. 32), even for those whose hands drove the nails through his. This is how *all things* can be from, through and to the God we worship. In the deepest mystery of all, the world's disobedience and death is therefore also *from* him, included within the *all things* which pass *through* him to the glorious redemption planned for all.[72]

This is not how the world appears at present. But Paul looks forward and sees reality for this vision at the moment when Jesus appears, and the great fullnesses of Israel and the Gentiles come in. This is the future-as-present which holds and inspires him as he brings the argument of these chapters to its great climax.

We must not overlook the starting point of it all in Paul's concern for his Gentile readers, *so that you may not be boastful in yourselves* (v. 25). Those who are convinced (like these Gentiles) that they have provided something that God was looking for, are not going to be too fixed on the idea of *mercy*. But that is Paul's focus here: the *mercy* of God, whereby he brings the completely undeserving into the circle of his salvation. His boastful Gentiles are no more

---

71. Eph. 1:9–10.

72. Paul has several passages where prepositions like these express the relation of God to the world, and it is significant that he makes similar statements both about God (as here) and about Jesus. See in particular 1 Cor. 8:6 and Col. 1:16, where the prepositions 'in ... through ... and to' are used of the Son who is 'the image of the invisible God'.

deserving of God's mercy than any others, and the same mercy will be extended to all.

Paul still has his Gentile boasters in mind, I think, when he quotes Job 41:11a in 11:35: *'Or who has put God in debt with a gift, so that God is bound to repay?'*[73] The quotation of Job is not by chance: Job too wrestled with an inexplicable will of God that tore him apart, but ended up overwhelmed by God's generosity and goodness – and Paul's quotation comes from the final section of Job where he expresses this. Job receives no answers to his complaints; at the end of the book neither he, nor we, are any wiser about why God organizes his world as he does. It is simply the vision of the *mysteries* of creation in chapters 38 to 41 – within which his own inexplicable suffering sits, rooted in the transcendent wisdom and power of God – which brings Job, too, into a place of simple worship at the end of his terrible history.

Looking at the balance of the doxology in this light, it is clear that the Gentile boasters of 11:25 are in particular danger of underestimating the *riches* of God – that is, the richness of his mercy towards the world, both Gentiles and Jews (see the two B elements in the analysis above). They need to widen their vision of God, and catch a glimpse, with Paul, and with Job, of the sheer magnitude of his wisdom and grace.

But it is in the two A elements, embracing the whole paragraph, that its deepest meaning is held. This is not a piece of theology *explaining* the mystery of God, but a piece of worship *extolling* it. Paul worships God for the *depth* of his *riches, wisdom and knowledge*, not *in spite of* the fact that their depth surpasses his understanding, but *because* of this. Paul's boasting Gentiles have erred above all in this, that they think they've got God's plan all explained and tied down, with a bow on the top. And so, while they might *thank* God for his mercy to them, they can never truly *worship* him as Paul does here. This kind of worship proceeds not from understanding, but from glorious, adoring ignorance. We sit, with Job, in a place where our questions fall away and we *love* the God we cannot grasp, because if his judgments were searchable, and if his ways were mappable, he would not be the God we adore.

The chiastic analysis of the hymn could actually be extended a little. The two A elements can themselves be divided. Verse 36a (*for from him and through him and to him are all things*) answers to *the depth* in verse 33, while the final clause, *to him*

---

73. Paul seems to be working from his own translation of Job here: as Dunn comments, 'The quotation from Job ... is markedly different from the LXX [Septuagint], but clearly enough a rendering of the not-altogether-clear Hebrew.' J. D. G. Dunn, *Romans 9-16*, Word Biblical Commentary 38B (Waco: Word, 1988), p. 701.

be glory to all ages, Amen! (v. 36b) answers to the *Oh!* at the beginning of verse 33. Even the smallest word in Scripture has significance. Paul's *Oh!* expresses his glowing heart of worship, giving *glory* to the God who has so amazingly caught up the disobedience of all into his plan.

As we move on to our next port of call in 1 Corinthians 15, it is vital to take with us this theology of the inexplicable wisdom and riches of God which embrace the 'all' of world history under the cross and resurrection of the coming Lord Jesus.

9. 'HE MUST REIGN UNTIL . . . '
(1 CORINTHIANS 15:20–28)

1. Introduction

This is one of the great resurrection texts of the New Testament; a passage at the heart of a whole chapter in which Paul argues for the indispensability of faith in the resurrection – not just the resurrection of Jesus Christ, but that of all who belong to him too. And in this little passage Paul brings the resurrection into direct connection with the second coming, by linking the second coming to the resurrection of *those who belong to Christ* (v. 23).

The angels in Acts 1:11 and Peter in Acts 3:18–21 also make this direct connection between the resurrection and the second coming. But they leave us scratching our heads over the question 'Why?' Why does the risen Christ *disappear* into a cloud? We would expect him to come into his power and rule on it, not vanish into it! Why 'must' heaven receive the risen Christ for a while 'until the times of the restoration of all things'?[1] If the resurrection has already 'raised him to the right hand of God' and made him 'both Lord and Christ, this Jesus whom you crucified',[2] then why is there a delay in him entering into his power and rule?

---

1. Acts 3:21.
2. Acts 2:33, 36.

There are inklings of answers to this in Acts, but in 1 Corinthians Paul tackles this question head-on, as part of the full-orbed theology of resurrection which he develops in this letter, and which reaches a climax in chapter 15, and in this section in particular. It's fine, of course, to long for, and to pray for the second coming of Jesus. The whole Bible ends with that prayer![3] But even more than passion to pray for it, we need wisdom to know why the prayer is needed – and why our prayer is not answered, day after decade after century. Paul helps us with this, gloriously.

2. Background: Corinthian confusion

A little background is vital. Paul has to mount this argument for the resurrection, because there were some in the Corinthian church who were 'saying that there is no resurrection of the dead'.[4] It is important to clarify exactly what they were saying, and what was at stake. The issue was not whether there is life after death: virtually the entire ancient world believed in this, not just Christians. The issue was whether *bodily* resurrection must feature as part of our expectation. They were saying: To be 'made alive in spirit'[5] – is this not the most important thing? And if we have that spiritual life – evidenced by speaking in the tongues of angels, the language of heaven itself[6] – then surely the body does not matter, from a spiritual point of view. Is this not so?

It is highly likely that this pervasive view of the *spiritual irrelevance of the body* underlies what Paul writes about sex and marriage in 1 Corinthians 6 and 7, and about food in 1 Corinthians 8 – 11, and indeed about the 'body of Christ' in 1 Corinthians 12 – 14, as well as this vital section on the resurrection in 1 Cor-inthians 15. In all these places, in different ways, Paul is asserting the *spiritual significance* of the body. 'Don't you know that your body is a temple of the Holy Spirit in you, given to you by God? You don't belong to yourselves, for you were bought at great cost. So go on then – glorify God in your body!'[7] For Paul, we

---

3. Rev. 22:20.

4. 1 Cor. 15:12.

5. Language drawn from 1 Pet. 3:18.

6. See 1 Cor. 13:1.

7. 1 Cor. 6:19–20. 'So go on then' is an attempt to bring out the force of the little Greek particle *dē*, which underlines the dramatic juxtaposition of 'glorifying God' and 'body'. For these Corinthians, that connection was impossible. The body was a place of darkness and shame, because they lived with a sharp Greek dualistic distinction between

know and serve God in our bodies, because that is who we are – bodily creatures called to serve him and empowered by the Holy Spirit in us. 'God raised the Lord, and he will raise us also by his power. Don't you know that your bodies are limbs of Christ?'[8]

This earlier passage in 1 Corinthians 6 makes it clear, that, for Paul, there can be no resurrection of the person without resurrection of the body, because right now, by the Holy Spirit, we are joined in a *bodily* way to Jesus. Hence his insistence that the *eating* practices of the church, particularly at the Lord's Supper,[9] have enormous spiritual significance. Lying behind this, of course, is the theology of atonement. We are saved by the giving of the *body of* Jesus on the cross,[10] and so when we worship, we are bodies-together constituting the body of Christ, joined to the crucified and resurrected Lord by his Spirit who indwells the body and coordinates its gifts and ministries:

> Just as the body is one but has many limbs, and all the limbs of the body together constitute one body, so also Christ! For by one Spirit we were all baptized into one body, whether we are Jews, Greeks, slaves or householders. We were all given the same Spirit to drink![11]

Many have noticed what seem to be several different senses of the word 'body' in 1 Corinthians – to refer to the physical bodies of believers, or of Jesus himself, or to the 'body' that we constitute when we are pulled by the Holy Spirit through baptism, and in worship, into union with the now-risen Christ. But what unites all these meanings is the physical nature of God's work. He made us bodies, he became a body among us in his Son, who gave his body for us on the cross, and now we are called as bodies into physical connection with him and with each other, to be a body animated by his Spirit into works of self-giving service that match his self-giving for us.[12]

And it's vital to see how, for Paul, our *social* identity is part of our physicality, now transformed in Christ. Of course the Corinthians couldn't stop being 'Jews,

---

(*Footnote 7 cont.*) body (bad) and spirit (good). Their response to the shame was either to flaunt the body (hence the sexual excess and gluttony in 1 Cor. 6:12–18) or to suppress and deny it (hence the rejection of sex even within marriage, 1 Cor. 7:1–6).

8. 1 Cor. 6:14–15.

9. See 1 Cor. 11:20–22.

10. 1 Cor. 11:23–26.

11. 1 Cor. 12:12–13.

12. See especially 1 Cor. 12:4–11.

Greeks, slaves or householders'[13] – whichever they were, it was part of the 'given' of their physical identities. But they didn't have to be *divided* by these identities. In Christ, they were called to transcend them, to become 'one', to see their differences rather as *callings* to be used for service within the one body. Hence Paul's stern words about the rich householders who go ahead and feast at the Lord's Supper, forgetting the poor – not 'discerning the body'.[14]

This is why Paul argues as he does about the resurrection in 15:12–19. If there is no *physical* resurrection, 'then Christ has not been raised'[15] – because the risen Christ was not a disembodied spirit but a 'spirited body', to use Nancey Murphy's vivid expression.[16] *He* could not be raised from death, unless *his body* was raised. And, says Paul, the whole gospel is at stake here (v. 14), as is the integrity of the apostolic testimony (v. 15) and the credibility of Christian faith and hope (vv. 17–18). Altogether, 'if our hope in Christ counts for this life only, we are the most pitiable of all people!' (v. 19), because our hope now is rooted in our shared *physical* experience of the risen Christ; but if Christ was not raised then we are deluding ourselves completely.

And so – looking at what follows our passage – if there is no physical resurrection, there is absolutely no point in Paul's rigorous, physically very demanding ministry:

> Why do we put ourselves in danger every hour? Yes, I face death daily – I swear it,
> brothers and sisters, by the size of my boasting over you in Christ Jesus our Lord!
> What was the point of battling with the human beasts I faced in Ephesus? If the
> dead are not raised, then 'let us eat and drink, for tomorrow we die'.[17]

---

13. 1 Cor. 12:13, quoted above.

14. 1 Cor. 11:17–22, 29. The meaning of 'not discerning the body' in 11:29 is a little unclear, but it probably means 'not realizing that *all* those around you – even those most different from you – are the body of Christ, for whom Jesus gave his body, now vividly represented by the bread and the wine shared among you'. It's a subtle and allusive expression!

15. 1 Cor. 15:13.

16. She uses this in the title of her book defending a unified anthropology against a Greek body-soul dualism: Nancey Murphy, *Bodies and Souls, or Spirited Bodies?* (Cambridge: Cambridge University Press, 2006).

17. 1 Cor. 15:30–32. Paul quotes from Isa. 22:13, a passage where the prophet mocks the inhabitants of Jerusalem for their false trust in their own resources, rather than trusting in the Lord for salvation. That seems to be Paul's point about the deniers of the resurrection in Corinth: they don't *know* God (15:34), and instead trust their own ideas.

Paul thus gives absolutely no space to a Greek dualistic anthropology that writes off the body and the realities of our physical existence in this world as of no spiritual significance. He summons the Corinthians, and us, to look forward to possessing a 'resurrection body' – a 'spiritual body' which is not different in *kind* from our present physical bodies but different in *glory*.[18] Our present 'flesh and blood cannot inherit the kingdom of God' because it is subject to 'corruption', i.e., death.[19] How can we enjoy belonging to God's eternal kingdom, which 'shall stand for ever',[20] without being equipped with bodies equal to the job? This means 'bearing the image of the heavenly man'[21] – i.e., being equipped with a body like that of the resurrected Christ, who has already conquered death, the ultimate enemy.

So 1 Corinthians 15:20–28 is surrounded by all this fantastic theology, which we must keep in mind as we turn to it now. We will look at it, of course, with a special eye to discovering how Paul sets the second coming into this theology of body and of resurrection.

3. Structure: An unfolding argument for an unfolding process

Paul never loses his focus on the need to convince the Corinthians of the folly of denying the resurrection. So in this little passage he expounds the significance of believing in it, so as to underline what is at stake. He wants to back up what he has just said about the vital centrality of the resurrection for the whole Christian message. The passage unfolds like this:

Basic statement of resurrection faith (20): *But in fact Christ has been raised from the dead, the 'firstfruits' of those who have fallen asleep.*

This is then unpacked in four stages:

1. The scope of the resurrection (vv. 21–22):

    For since death arose through a man, the resurrection of the dead arises also through a man. For just as in Adam all die, so also in Christ shall all be made alive.

2. The timing of the resurrection (vv. 23–24a):

    But each in his own order: Christ is the resurrection firstfruits; then come all those who belong to Christ, at his parousia; *then comes the end . . .*

---

18. 1 Cor. 15:35–44.
19. 1 Cor. 15:50.
20. Dan. 2:44.
21. 1 Cor. 15:49.

3. The impact of the resurrection (vv. 24b–27a):

> . . . *when he will hand over the kingdom to his God and Father, when he will have nullified every rule, and every authority and power: for he must reign until 'he puts all his enemies under his feet'. The last, the ultimate, enemy to be nullified is death: for 'he subjected all things without exception under his feet'.*[22]

4. The goal of the resurrection (vv. 27b–28):

> *Now when it says that 'all things without exception have been subjected' to him, it is clear that this does not include the one who did the subjecting of all things to him. When this goal is reached, then the Son will subject himself to the One who subjected all things to him, so that God may be all in all.*

In the translation I've brought out the fact that Paul uses the interesting word *parousia* to refer to the second coming (v. 23). This Greek word has almost become an English technical term to refer to the second coming, associated especially with scholarly discussions. It has a significant background, which we will explore when we look at 1 and 2 Thessalonians.[23] It actually means 'presence' more than 'coming', and Paul uses it not infrequently in this sense.[24] However it has the flavour 'presence as opposed to absence', and so can connote 'arrival', a *becoming* present.[25] Ben Witherington suggests that 'Paul may have been the first person to use the term *parousia* to refer to the return of Christ',[26] but this depends (a) on whether the term was already used in whatever version of Jesus' apocalyptic discourse Paul was familiar with,[27] and (b) on the date we give to the letter of James. James too uses this term to refer to the second coming.[28]

---

22. I have added 'without exception' to the translation to reflect the fact that 'all things' is in an emphatic position in the Greek. This seems to be the force of the emphasis! – and it seems to be required by the movement of Paul's thought.

23. Where it appears in both our 'second coming' passages: 1 Thess. 4:15; 2 Thess. 2:1, 8.

24. See for instance 2 Cor. 10:10; Phil. 2:12.

25. See 2 Cor. 7:6–7; Phil. 1:26.

26. Ben Witherington III, *Jesus, Paul and the End of the World: A Comparative Study in New Testament Eschatology* (Downers Grove: IVP Academic, 1992), p. 152.

27. See above, pp. 100–103. Matthew uses the term four times in his version of Jesus' 'apocalyptic discourse': Matt. 24:3, 27, 37, 39.

28. Jas 5:7–8. Personally, I regard James as the earliest piece of writing in the New Testament, and his use of this term is evidence that the word was already used (as reflected by Matthew) in the circulating memories and records of Jesus' apocalyptic teaching – and Paul picks it up from there.

Who first used the word, however, is of minor significance compared to its meaning. As in Philippians 2:12, its implicit opposite is the word *apousia*, absence.[29] The resurrection, paradoxically and amazingly, leads to the *apousia*, the *absence*, of Christ. But why? Why, having risen from the dead, should Jesus immediately become absent, requiring him then later to become present again? This question takes us into the heart of this passage, and actually into the heart of our biblical theology of the second coming. We will look at each of the structural stages of the passage in turn.

4. Scope: *In Christ shall all be made alive* (vv. 20–22)

But in fact Christ has been raised from the dead, the 'firstfruits' of those who have fallen asleep (v. 20). This is Paul's rousing assertion that we do not have to embrace the hopelessness of a world in which there is no resurrection – in which the only 'hope' available is the piffling little bits of meaning that we might manage to create for ourselves, before death closes us down and makes a mockery of all our effort. But we see that Paul makes this claim as an assertion not about *us*, but about *Christ*. There is hope, because *Christ has been raised*. But Christ's resurrection gives hope not in the way that Roger Bannister's four-minute mile gave hope to other athletes, that they could do it too.[30] Christ's resurrection changes the world, because he is the *'firstfruits' of those who have fallen asleep*.

The 'firstfruits' were the first pickings of the harvest, which had to be offered to the Lord before the people were allowed to eat any of the new grain. The harvest was all a gift from the Lord; and its origin with him, and the people's unworthiness to receive it, were marked by the ceremony of the firstfruits right at the beginning of the harvest.[31]

The point of Paul's metaphor seems to be twofold: (a) There is an intimate connection, even an *identity*, between Christ and the *all* who then rise in him

---

29. See also 1 Cor. 16:17, where a different word is used for 'absence' but the same point applies to the meaning of *parousia*.

30. This example comes to mind because at the time of writing (in 2014) we are celebrating the sixtieth anniversary of Bannister's achievement (on 6 May 1954) of running a mile in under 4 minutes. Once Bannister had shown it was possible, numerous athletes were able to do the same. And now, the world record for the mile stands at 3 minutes 43 seconds. Praise God, the resurrection does not work like this!

31. Lev. 23:9–14.

(v. 22). They are one harvest, with the *firstfruits* signalling the arrival of the whole. And therefore (b) there is an *inevitability* about the subsequent resurrection of *those who have fallen asleep*. One with us, he has 'fallen asleep', but he has *been raised from the dead* (v. 20); and so, one with him, we too *shall be made alive* (v. 22).

As we saw in summarizing what lies behind this passage earlier in 1 Corinthians, the theme of our *bodily union* with Christ – a union with him by the Spirit which touches and conditions our whole bodily life now, in every aspect – is the crucial piece of theological background. Our resurrection follows from his, because we are one with him! The 'in' in verse 22 (*in Adam . . . in Christ . . .*) carries this theological freight. We remember the message of 6:15–20, that our bodies are 'limbs' of Christ, because they are temples of the Holy Spirit, God's gift to us, and therefore they must glorify God and not attach themselves to the sinful values and practices of the world (gluttony and casual sex). Paul draws the conclusion from this new belonging already in 6:13–14: 'The body is not for sinful sex, but for the Lord! And the Lord is for the body. And God raised the Lord, and he will raise us also through his power.'

So 'in Adam' we are lost in bad bodily practices that condemn us to share Adam's death. But 'in Christ' there is a whole new life, a life both present and future; lived already, if we have been baptized into the body and are serving him there, and yet to be, when the 'firstfruits' are followed by the harvest.

This background in Paul's earlier argument makes the 'alls' of verse 22 all the more puzzling. *As in Adam all die, so in Christ shall all be made alive.* To be 'in Christ' is dependent on faith and baptism, and on being empowered by the indwelling Spirit into the new life. So, as Gordon Fee puts it, 'Both the context and Paul's theology as a whole make it clear that in saying "in Christ all will be made alive," he means "in Christ all *who are in Christ* will be made alive".'[32]

This is surely right. But we must make due allowance for the fact that this is not actually what Paul says. Paul seems to be thinking of two great collectivities: on the one hand the great bundle of humanity that dies 'in' Adam, and on the other the corresponding great bundle that *shall be made alive* 'in' Christ. As we saw in Romans 11, Paul loves to think, and write, in great overarching masses, pitching the 'all' of the Gentile world over against the 'all' of Israel, and adding up the sum to total 'all humanity'. He simply does not touch, here, on the

---

32. Gordon D. Fee, *The First Epistle to the Corinthians*, New International Commentary on the New Testament (Grand Rapids: Eerdmans, 1987), pp. 749–750, his emphasis.

resurrection of unbelievers to judgment.[33] As in Romans 11, this just does not enter his perspective. He can move, without any sense of inconsistency, from 'all' to 'we': from *as in Adam all die, so in Christ shall all be made alive* to 'as we have borne the image of the man of earth, we shall also bear the image of the man of heaven'.[34]

I think that, if we pressed Paul on the reason for this, he would look surprised and say something like, 'So – do you think it's important to dwell on condemnation and loss, rather than on salvation and victory?' And, if we pressed him about 1 Corinthians 15 in particular, he would say 'Those silly Corinthians just needed to have their noses rubbed in the vast glory and meaning of the resurrection – bless 'em! They didn't need stuff on the resurrection of unbelievers.'

5. Timing: *But each in his own order* . . . (vv. 23–24a)

Paul now moves – uniquely in his letters – to write about the *relative timing* of the events of the End. At least, he appears to do so: *But each in his own order: Christ is the resurrection firstfruits; then come all those who belong to Christ, at his parousia; then comes the End, when* . . .

It is a little artificial to divide the passage after the first phrase of verse 24, as I have done. And indeed, that phrase raises a question for us which we cannot answer without looking at the next section, verses 24–26. The question relates to the meaning of *then* in verse 24: does it imply a separation in time between the *parousia* of Jesus and 'the End'? Opinions are sharply divided here, between scholars like Barrett and Fee who make no distinction between the resurrection and the End,[35] and others like Andrew Perriman who do. In his significant book *The Coming of the Son of Man* Perriman argues that 'there is no indication that *all* of his enemies or the *final* enemy, death, are defeated' at the time of the *parousia*. The *parousia* is just the beginning of a sequence of events. In fact, 'The resurrection at the *parousia* of those who have fallen asleep in Christ would constitute, therefore, a limited event within the eschatological horizon of the

---

33. In fact Paul never explicitly writes about this. When he writes of final judgment, he phrases it as if it is applied just to those who are alive at the time of the *parousia*: see e.g. Rom. 2:8–9; 1 Thess. 5:2–3; 2 Thess. 1:8–9. But cf. John 5:28–29 (building on Dan. 12:2); Rev. 20:11–15 for the general resurrection of the dead.

34. 1 Cor. 15:49.

35. C. K. Barrett, *The First Epistle to the Corinthians*, Black's New Testament Commentary (London: A&C Black, 1971), p. 356; Fee, *1 Corinthians*, pp. 753–754.

church in the Roman world: they are absorbed into the metaphor of Christ as firstfruits.'[36]

Perriman illustrates the problem with this view. The more the timeline is extended beyond the resurrection, the more the resurrection is downplayed as the vital focus of Paul's argument. Perriman makes the final resurrection but another foreshadowing event looking forward to 'the End', which follows further down the track.

Perriman does not argue for a big premillennial scheme, but in this respect he reflects something standard within those depictions of the End. The final resurrection is not final at all – actually it is just the beginning of a whole new era on earth, with Christ ruling from Jerusalem and sharing his rule with the resurrected saints. Responding to such a view (represented by other scholars in his day), C. K. Barrett calls it 'unthinkable' that a whole millennial rule of Christ on earth slips in here between the resurrection and the final 'handing over' of the kingdom to God (the End): 'It seems unthinkable that Paul, if he believed in such a kingdom, should pass it over without a word.'[37]

Yes indeed. But the chief problem with this view is its wrong view of time. It applies *chronos* where Paul is thinking in *kairos* terms. He is not constructing a timeline here, but letting us know the shape of the future in God's plan. And it really seems that Moltmann is right: the future is Christ. We live out the story of the Messiah, or rather *his* story is written onto us, so that the resurrection-rule that he has *already* entered becomes ours, as well.[38]

There is more to be said about how the End relates to the resurrection, as we will see. But before we move on, we notice how sharply verse 23 raises the question with which we began. Why is there a gap, a delay, between the resurrection and the End – a gap which requires the *parousia* of Christ because he goes *absent* (apparently) straight after the resurrection? *Then those who belong to Christ, at his parousia* is a glorious, triumphant vision, akin to the great 'alls' of Romans 11.

From our perspective (and indeed from Paul's), the *absence* of Christ, his *not* finally claiming his kingdom, means the preaching of the gospel and the gathering of the church: the *assembling* of 'those who belong to him'. The longer the delay, the more the assembling. With each passing year on the calendar (the passage of *chronos*), greater grows the crowd of 'those who belong to him'. God

---

36. Andrew Perriman, *The Coming of the Son of Man. New Testament Eschatology for an Emerging Church* (Milton Keynes: Paternoster Press, 2005), p. 171, his emphases.

37. Barrett, *1 Corinthians*, p. 356.

38. On Moltmann's view, see above pp. 151–152.

seems to love making human beings and sweeping them into his kingdom, and he doesn't seem to be giving up just yet!

One of the distinctive perspectives of the contribution of the Mennonite theologian John Howard Yoder was his view that the church does not exist for the sake of the world. Rather, he maintained, the world exists for the sake of the church – because it is the world that gives the church the space in which to live out and proclaim the gospel in obedience to the lordship of Christ.[39] Writes Stanley Hauerwas, summarizing Yoder: 'That the gospel is to be preached to the ends of the world is why time does not stop. What it means for Christ to be King is that he rules over history to give the church time to preach the gospel.'[40]

Yoder is well aware of the time-implications of this: we're talking about the impact of God's time – *kingdom* time – onto the *chronos* of world history, so that the latter is made to serve the former. *Chronos* serves *kairos*, until the ultimate *kairos* moment when the number (or 'fullness', as Paul would say[41]) of *those who belong to him* is complete, and the *parousia* of Christ brings the final resurrection harvest of which he was the firstfruits.

6. Impact: *He must reign until . . .* (vv. 24b–27a)

But does the parousia also mean the End, when he will hand over the kingdom to his God and Father, when he will have nullified every rule, and every authority and power (v. 24)? I think so, in spite of the arguments of those who distinguish the resurrection from the End. In addition to the thoughts already suggested, further arguments support this view – three, in fact.

a. The 'powers' and the beasts
What theological and biblical background should we discern behind Paul's 'power' language in verse 24? As with Acts 1:6–11, Paul's theology here seems to rest on Daniel's vision of the beasts and the Son of Man. In Daniel 7, the Son of Man receives 'the kingdom' from the Ancient of Days and thus destroys

---

39. See the exposition of Yoder by Stanley Hauerwas in *Approaching the End: Eschatological Reflections on Church, Politics and Life* (Grand Rapids: Eerdmans, 2013), especially the second essay, 'The End of Sacrifice: An Apocalyptic Politics' (pp. 22–36).

40. Hauerwas, *Approaching the End*, p. 28. Hauerwas passionately affirms Yoder's view.

41. See Rom. 11:12, 25 – also 'the fullness of the times [*kairos*]' in Eph. 1:10.

the power of the beasts, even though this means that the 'people of the saints of the Most High' are handed over to the power of the fourth beast for 'a time, two times, and half a time'.[42] Here in 1 Corinthians, Paul's ultimate vision is the gift of the kingdom back to God who gave it to Jesus Christ, but we have the same notion of the extension of the life and power of the 'beasts' even though Christ, the Son of Man, is reigning. *He must reign until 'he puts all his enemies under his feet'* (v. 25) implies (a) that Christ is reigning now, (b) that his enemies are still powerful, even though he reigns, but (c) a moment is coming when they will be finally 'nullified' and 'under his feet'. This Daniel 7 background would lead us to infer that, when he reappears as the victorious Son of Man, it will mean the final overthrow of all the beasts who oppress the people of God.

That seems clear. But once again we must ask Paul why it happens like this. What is *gained* for the rule of God, which is the rule of his Christ, that the one who is rightfully 'Lord' departs from his world leaving it under occupation by alien powers? We remember the poor widow in Luke 18:1–8 – crying out for justice day and night in weakness before her oppressors. Jesus assures 'God's chosen ones' that they will receive justice, if the Son of Man finds faith on the earth when he comes[43] – but why the delay?

We can tackle this question further by exploring what exactly Paul means by *every rule, and every authority and power*. He does not specifically cite Daniel 7, so we cannot assume that he has in mind the kind of empires or kings that Daniel was thinking of. Paul not infrequently refers to 'the powers' using language like this,[44] and it seems that he means more than just 'the political rulers' – although these are certainly included. A key passage earlier in 1 Corinthians is 2:6–9:

> We speak wisdom among the mature: but it is not a wisdom of this age nor of the rulers of this age, whose power is being nullified. No: we speak the wisdom of God in a mystery. It was hidden away, but God set it apart before all ages for our glory.

---

42. See Dan. 7:12–14, 21–22, 25–27.'

43. Luke 18:7–8.

44. See especially Rom. 8:38–39; 13:1; Gal. 4:3; Eph. 1:19–23; 6:10–13; Col. 1:15–20. Ephesians particularly stands out for its use of 'power' language of all sorts, and the significance of this has been brilliantly unpacked by Clinton E. Arnold in *Ephesians, Power and Magic: The Concept of Power in Ephesians in Light of its Historical Setting* (Cambridge: Cambridge University Press, 1989). See also his more general study, *Powers of Darkness: A Thoughtful, Biblical Look at an Urgent Challenge Facing the Church* (Leicester: Inter-Varsity Press, 1992).

None of the rulers of this age knew it, for if they had, they would not have crucified the Lord of glory. But as it is written,

> 'What eye has not seen, and ear has not heard,
>   what has not entered human hearts,
>   what God has prepared for those who love him . . .'

Paul expounds this secret wisdom of God in 1 Corinthians 1 – 2; God's salvation plan, regarded as 'foolishness' by Greeks and a 'stumbling-block' by Jews because its centrepiece is 'Christ crucified'.[45] A crucified Messiah! What good is that to man or beast? But this is *God's* hidden wisdom, his 'foolishness' which is 'Christ, the power of God and the wisdom of God: for God's stupidity is wiser than anything we can dream up, and his weakness is stronger than anything we can manage'.[46]

God intends to save the world through the *weakness* of a crucified Messiah,[47] and then through the *weakness* of the feeble crowd of nobodies who embrace his folly,[48] and further through the *weakness* of the simple preaching about 'Jesus Christ, and him crucified'.[49] Hence the irony in 1 Corinthians 2:8, quoted above: the 'rulers of this age' would have spiked God's guns and *refused* to crucify Jesus Christ, if they had known that his death was the centrepiece of God's foolish plan to deprive them of their power. They signed their own warrant of nullification when they condemned him to the cross.

So these 'rulers' are clearly the political powers (the Romans) who actually crucified Christ, but also the Jewish authorities who condemned Jesus on the basis of their interpretation of the law, and beyond that the whole cultural machine, both Jewish and Greek, which rejected and rejects the Christ on the basis of its own wisdom. The wisdom of the world is not about to bow to the foolishness of God. Paul of course also sees spiritual forces behind these worldly powers that oppose God, a feature of his thought that appears particularly in Ephesians.

So in 1 Corinthians 15:24, *every rule, and every authority and power* seems to be as all-embracing as the language suggests: all powers, influences and messages that bolster human wisdom and self-sufficiency apart from the grace of God,

---

45. 1 Cor. 1:23.
46. 1 Cor. 1:25.
47. 1 Cor. 1:18.
48. 1 Cor. 1:27–31.
49. 1 Cor. 2:1–5.

every ideology that does not recognize the heart of God's wisdom in the cross, every regime that exalts the powerful and oppresses the weak, every state that maintains its legitimacy by military strength and by its power to demand 'the final sacrifice' from its citizens, all economic powers and movements that throw their weight around for good and ill, and all the Satanic or demonic entities that underlie and bolster these powers in the world.

Before such powers, the church of Jesus Christ – his body in the world – is as weak as Jesus himself was, when they crucified him. In fact our weakness is not just that they might persecute and oppress us, too, but even more that (horror of horrors!) *we cannot live without them*. In many ways, we need the wisdom of the world – its art, science, medicine, technologies and the economic structures that sustain us in our physical life. We pray 'Give us this day our daily bread' and gratefully receive our food from God, but it comes to us mediated by a production system which is sustained by the international banking industry and rooted in global economic and political forces which – whether we like it or not – serve the wealthy nations of the world at the expense of the poorer. We are trapped within the very systems which 'are being nullified' by the message of the cross.[50]

Like Daniel in ancient Babylon, we cannot help but serve the empire, every time we visit the supermarket. But Daniel served Babylon not reluctantly but willingly, seeking to make it a *better* place[51] – until the day when his loyalty to the king conflicted with his loyalty to God. Then he stood firm. Thus far the beast, and no further![52] And similarly, living inevitably under the powers of the 'beasts' that still rule, we – the body of Christ in the world – can act in ways that limit their power, make its effects better, and testify to the different world coming.

This is why Paul immediately follows this resurrection passage with his reference to 'fighting beasts in Ephesus' because Jesus has been raised.[53] That's the shape that kingdom membership has, for Paul: because Christ has been raised, the powers of the beasts have already been overthrown, and the calling of the church, Christ's physical body in the world, is to live out the message of the cross in weakness and in courage, like Jesus himself.

---

50. This awful paradox is explored by Stanley Hauerwas in his essay 'Bearing Reality', in *Approaching the End*, pp. 139–157.

51. See Dan. 1:18–20.

52. See Dan. 6.

53. 1 Cor. 15:32. I think there are compelling reasons to interpret 'fighting beasts' not literally, but metaphorically. Paul may even have been influenced in his choice of the word by the implicit influence of Dan. 7 in the substructure of his argument.

I think that is what Paul has in mind, when he says in 1 Corinthians 2:6 that the powers 'are being nullified' (present tense). I decided on 'nullify' as the best translation of the interesting Greek verb *katargein*, which Paul uses both in 2:6 and in 15:24,[54] because it can express both the thought that the powers *are being nullified* in the present (2:6), and that they *will be nullified* finally when he comes again (15:24). The risen Christ is already reigning over them, but their power continues under his rule *until* the moment when he comes again and they are finally 'put out of commission', 'made redundant', 'disempowered'.[55] The tense of the verb in 15:24, which is best translated *he will have nullified*, suggests that the 'nullification' has been going on already, so that the *parousia* of Christ marks the end of that process.[56] And the means by which the powers *are being* nullified in the present is – as in Daniel – the *weakness* of the church of Jesus Christ.

This needs unpacking a little more. Paul broadens the 'rulers of this age' to include not just *imperial* power and ideology, but religious, cultural, social, economic and spiritual forces also. *All* the powers, whatever they are! But we noticed above how important it was for Paul to see ethnic, cultural and economic distinctions tumbling into insignificance within the body of Christ: 'For by one Spirit we were all baptized into one body, whether we are Jews, Greeks, slaves or householders. We were all given the same Spirit to drink!'[57] The church lives by the wisdom of God which saves us through the weakness of the cross, and brings us *without* all our cultural, national and economic armour into 'one body' with people very different from ourselves. In this body, our national and ethnic identities fall into 'nullification', and we find our significance instead in the gifts which the Spirit calls forth among us, by which we serve each other and the

---

54. This word is quite a favourite with Paul: he uses it twenty-five times in all, including nine times in 1 Corinthians. 'Destroy' is the usual choice in English versions in 1 Cor. 15:24, so e.g. NRSV, ESV, NIV (1984, 2011), NLT. Other options are 'put an end to' (NKJV) and 'overcome' (GNT). But there are other verbs which more directly convey the notion of destruction, and Paul seems to have looked for one which expresses both a *present process* of disempowerment (2:6, present participle), and a *future moment* of final 'nullification'. Sticking with 'destroy' as the basic meaning of the verb, NRSV has 'who are doomed to perish' in 2:6. But this loses the sense of a process happening right now. NIV is much better: 'who are coming to nothing'. Barrett translates it 'bring to nought' (*1 Corinthians*, p. 354).

55. These are all other possible translations of *katargein*.

56. So also Barrett, *1 Corinthians*, pp. 357–358. 'Christ's reign means his session at the right hand of God, during which one enemy after another is subdued' (p. 358).

57. 1 Cor. 12:13.

world. The powers are already tumbling, when the church lives and worships as it should.

This is the reason why bodily resurrection is so important for Paul. *In the weakness of our flesh* we are one with Jesus, living his life now in the world in ways which already explode the world's values. Together, joined in him by the Spirit, and seeking to live his life in weakness before the world, we 'announce the death of the Lord, until he comes'.[58] For he is already reigning, and we live under his lordship now in the *weakness* by which he is the Saviour.

So – to return to the question with which we began – this is what is gained by the delay, by the *absence* of Christ which then requires his *parousia:* the church, his body in the world, has the space to live out the good news of 'the death of death in the death of Christ',[59] which means the death of all other reigns than his. Slowly, in and through the life of his body on earth, the power of these other rulers are gradually being 'nullified', until he comes again and completes the process. As we saw in Acts 3, God acts to refresh his world and his people in many ways before the final *refreshment* which will be the *restoration of all things* in Christ. And we herald the End through all such moments and experiences of refreshment!

b. The death of death: The ultimate enemy

Another strong argument for identifying the *parousia* with the End emerges from verse 26: *The last, the ultimate, enemy to be nullified is death.* In a deep sense, death has already been defeated by the resurrection of the Son of God as the *firstfruits* of the final harvest. So when that harvest arrives and *in Christ shall all be made alive . . . at his parousia* (vv. 22–23), this surely means the final defeat of death, *the last, the ultimate, enemy.* That enemy is defeated when all are made alive *at his parousia*, not at some later date!

This is confirmed by Paul's description of death as *the last enemy.* I have translated this as *the last, the ultimate* in order to bring out its particular force. Because Paul mentions this after the disempowering of all the other powers, *last* is usually taken in just a temporal sense: after the other powers, then death will be nullified. But once again, this imports a *chronos* time scheme into a *kairos* statement. In his commentary, Gordon Fee draws out the logical progression which he sees in these verses. The defeat of the other powers and the final assertion of God's authority follows from the resurrection:

---

58. 1 Cor. 11:26.

59. This is the famous title of Puritan John Owen's treatise on the meaning of the cross, published in 1648.

It is basic to Paul's view of things that Christ did not rise from the dead, but that God raised him. Therefore, the inevitable chain of events set in motion by Christ's resurrection has ultimately to do with God's own absolute authority over *all things*, especially death.[60]

I'm sure Fee is right. So I think that *last* means not so much 'the last in sequence' as 'the ultimate in significance'. God's ultimate rule over the powers is shown through the resurrection of Jesus, because that heralds the defeat of the ultimate enemy, death. And it's not difficult to see how, out of all the 'powers' Paul names, *death* is the ultimate one. For the other powers all use death as their ultimate resource – the *fear* of it, the *threat* of it, or the *infliction* of it. A frequent theme in Hauerwas' marvellous collection of essays *Approaching the End* is his perception that the nation state ultimately rests its legitimacy on its right to maintain armed forces in order to threaten or kill its enemies, and on its capacity to demand of its citizens that they make 'the ultimate sacrifice' to defend the state. *The state* claims a legitimate power, not only to inflict death on others, but also to ask its own citizens willingly to lay down their lives for its sake.

This is a horrifying appropriation of God's prerogatives – he alone is truly the giver, and the taker, of life. And it is also a horrifying parody of the claim that really only the Son of God can make upon us who are his: only he can ask us to lay down our lives, in weakness, for him. And he will only ask that, because beyond our sacrifice he makes our death the door to eternal life. But the state cannot give life, only death. And the *threat* of death, building on the *fear* of death, underlies most of the ways in which the powers are able to exert influence in the world. Daniel's beasts 'devour' and 'crush' and 'break in pieces' and 'stamp' and horrify even Daniel.[61] But if death is no more?

If death is no more, suddenly the powers lose their power as well. So the destruction of *the last, the ultimate, enemy* (v. 26) means the end of the powers, even of those better ones that gain power over us by seeking to fend off the threat of death as much as possible.[62]

---

60. Fee, *1 Corinthians*, pp. 746–747, his emphasis.

61. Dan. 7:5, 7, 19, 28.

62. I'm thinking of the power of science and technology, which can hold out such promise, especially in the realms of health care and food production, while also enslaving us in an endless circle it calls 'progress'. How many of us both bless and curse the computers that rule our lives? Or think of the Internet, which offers both instant access to limitless information, and terrible opportunity to exploit and degrade the bodies of others. The energy behind it all is the fear of death. See Heb. 2:15.

What a glorious prospect for *all those who belong to Christ* (v. 23)! Truly, in him the ultimate enemy of our race, the death that claims every human life, has been overcome, and at his *parousia* we will rise to eternal life, and the world will be made new.

c. All things under his feet: the Psalm 8 vision

The third argument for identifying the *parousia* with the End follows on from this. Verse 27 – *for 'he subjected all things without exception under his feet'* – follows directly from the statement about the defeat of the last enemy in verse 26. This is actually a quotation of Psalm 8:6, a verse to which Paul alludes elsewhere also.[63] Though death is not mentioned in Psalm 8, Paul takes *all things* to include death and all the 'powers', along with 'all sheep and oxen, and also the beasts of the field, the birds of the air, and the fish of the sea, whatever passes along the paths of the sea'[64] – everything over which God has placed humankind. This is the Psalm 8 vision, reflecting on the Genesis 1 commission to 'fill the earth, and subdue it, and have dominion . . .':[65] human beings are meant to rule! And in Christ the Firstfruits Man – and thus far in him alone – the vision has been fulfilled. But when the final resurrection takes place, then it will be true also of *all* humankind. So the subduing of death, the last enemy, carries with it the subduing of all things, all other powers in all creation, under the feet first of Christ, and then of all who belong to him.

So Paul's use of Psalm 8:6 to give scriptural support to the subjection of *death* under Christ's power shows that, in Paul's mind, the defeat of death entails the ultimate fulfilment of the Genesis 1 vision: a world united under the blessed and benevolent lordship of the *human* rulers placed in charge by the God who made both it and them. At the resurrection – when Jesus comes again – this glorious vision will become a reality.

7. Goal: *so that God may be all in all* (vv. 27b–28)

These last two verses are a reflection on the quotation of Psalm 8:6. Paul understands the Genesis 1 commission as a task given to humankind to fulfil on behalf of God who made the world over which we are called to rule. It is not just a call to a privileged sharing of his rule but, as it turns out, a summons

---

63. See Eph. 1:22; Phil. 3:21; also Heb. 2:8 (a very significant quotation of this psalm).
64. Ps. 8:7–8.
65. Gen. 1:28.

to *bring back* an errant world under his dominion. And only Jesus, the Man at his right hand,[66] has the power to do this, because of the cross and through the resurrection. But having fulfilled this commission, Paul's vision is that all things will then be restored to God who made them, so that *God may be all in all* (v. 28).

He expresses this elsewhere in terms of 'reconciliation'. For instance, in Colossians 1, having first said that

> in Christ all things in the heavens and on earth were created, things visible and things invisible, whether thrones or dominions or rulers or authorities, all things have been created through him, and for him,[67]

he then adds

> and through Christ God [was pleased] to reconcile all things to himself, making peace through the blood of his cross, whether things on earth or things in the heavens.[68]

This is the same vision as in 1 Corinthians 15, including verses 27–28. This final *reconciliation of all things to God* is the restoration of all authority to God by the Christ who has won peace with God for all things 'through the blood of his cross', so that now God is *all in all*. This isn't a pantheistic vision of 'the all' being absorbed back into the deity. Rather, this is about the submission of all things (again) to the one who first called everything into being. It's the final goal of salvation, the final reconciliation when the powers are all *nullified* in their anti-God defiance, and restored to their under-God role as vehicles of redeemed life in his kingdom.

It might be that Paul is particularly addressing something in the Corinthian church here – maybe a view that at his resurrection Christ (rather than God) became the supreme Lord of the universe. Perhaps this was the view of the 'Christ party' in Corinth.[69] Whether this is the background or not, it was clearly vital for Paul – essential for his understanding of the relationship between the Father and the Son – to make it clear that the glorified and resurrected Son of

---

66. Cf. Acts 5:31.

67. Col. 1:16.

68. Col. 1:20. I have clarified 'he' and 'him' in these translations, especially in the second where it is actually a little unclear who is the subject of the verb 'to reconcile'.

69. See 1 Cor. 1:12. Anthony Thiselton takes this view of the underlying purpose in 1 Cor. 15:27–28: Anthony C. Thiselton, *The Last Things: A New Approach* (London: SPCK, 2012), p. 119 – citing others also.

God does not maintain an independent glory in relation to the defeated powers and the resurrected human race, but hands the glory of his victory back to his Father who raised him from the dead in the first place.[70]

This all shows how little *theological* sense it makes, to see the harvest-resurrection as just a preliminary event within an end-time sequence. A typical scenario is that the raptured and resurrected saints rule with Christ through his thousand-year reign, but at the end of this period Satan is released, the nations are again deceived, armies are raised and a final battle takes place (which may or may not be the battle of Armageddon) at which this rebellion is subdued and the final judgment is brought in. This all depends on importing a literal reading of Revelation 19 – 20 into the implied sequence here in 1 Corinthians 15.

We will look at Revelation in due course, but for the moment let us note how Paul's *theology* will not allow that the powers continue under the reign of Christ *after* the final resurrection in this way. They continue under his reign *now*, but when the final enemy is defeated, their power to oppose the rule of God ends and they are 'nullified' – either destroyed, or (as Paul prefers) *reconciled*, to the God 'for whom' they exist anyway.

So we reach the end of our reading of this marvellous passage. What a treat – and what a vision. For us the universe is a *hopeful* place, because even the most distorted manifestations of anti-God power and human corruption will yield to the power of the cross. Even though we are just poor widows campaigning for justice against the indifferent and self-interested Goliaths of corporate greed, political cynicism and ideologically-driven cruelty, we *know* that we 'ought always to pray, and not give up in weariness',[71] because Jesus is *already* the Lord we name,[72] and he will one day complete the work of salvation by bringing to us all the resurrection we long for. At his *parousia!*

We turn now to a passage that brings an even sharper focus to bear on the *parousia* of the Lord.

---

70. 1 Cor. 6:14. As Gordon Fee notes, it is vital for Paul that 'God raised the Lord' – that the Father was the agent of the resurrection of his Son. Cf. 15:15, 'we have testified of God that he raised Christ'. Paul usually uses a passive form of the verb (e.g. 'Christ has been raised from the dead', 15:20; cf. 15:4, 12, etc.), but God is the implied subject. So Fee, *1 Corinthians*, p. 726, n. 64.

71. Luke 18:1.

72. 1 Cor. 12:3.

10. THE COMING OF THE LORD – PART ONE
(1 THESSALONIANS 4:13 – 5:11)

1. Setting the scene

This chapter and the next, on 2 Thessalonians 2:1–12, belong closely together. There is much to connect them with each other, and we have already looked a little at them both in order to develop our understanding of Mark 13.[1] So we will set the scene here for both this chapter and the next – the two passages bear upon each other and we need to interpret them together.

The two letters to the church in Thessaloniki were written quite close in time, the first not long after Paul's visit in Acts 17:1–9, and the second not long after that.[2] In the second letter, Paul is still reminding them of what he said during

---

1. See above, ch. 4.

2. It used to be widely maintained (and still is by some) that 2 Thessalonians was not written by Paul. However the consensus of scholarly opinion now seems to rest on Paul's authorship of both letters. Some scholars argue that the letters were written in the other order – 2 Thessalonians first, followed by 1 Thessalonians (e.g. recently Charles A. Wanamaker, *The Epistles to the Thessalonians*, New International Greek Testament Commentary (Grand Rapids: Eerdmans, 1990), pp. 37–45. However in my view the relationship between the letters – and behind them the relationship between Paul and the church in Thessaloniki – is best explained if they were written in the canonical order.

his visit,[3] and this suggests that not much time has passed. It seems that both letters were written from Corinth after the arrival there of Silas and Timothy, who are associated with Paul in the writing of both.[4]

This raises an interesting question, as to why Paul wrote a second letter so soon after the first. Getting letters around the ancient world was an expensive and time-consuming business. And the answer seems to be that Paul was concerned about their eschatology – which is fortunate for us, because we therefore learn much more about Paul's eschatology than we would have known, had they not developed strange ideas (and practices) which he wanted to correct. It is worth starting, therefore, with Paul's reasons for writing the somewhat urgent second letter.

After an introduction commending them for their growing faith and love, and for their 'endurance' in the face of persecution,[5] Paul reminds them that their suffering is preparing them for the kingdom of God, which will arrive

> with the revelation of the Lord Jesus from heaven with his mighty angels in flaming fire, bringing just judgment to those who do not know God and do not obey the gospel of our Lord Jesus. They will receive the verdict of eternal destruction, banishment from the face of the Lord and from his glorious strength, when he arrives to be glorified by his holy ones, and to be marvelled at by all who believe on that day – all who received our witness to you with faith.[6]

The words here are quite different from those in 1 Corinthians 15:20–28. No mention of the resurrection of those 'in Christ' (though he writes about this in 1 Thess.[7]), and no talk of the destruction of the 'powers' and of death. Instead of the powers, Paul's language is personal here, focusing on the *people* who refuse the gospel and the knowledge of God. Why is this? We are at an earlier point in Paul's ministry here, so it is possible that his ideas move on between this point and the writing of 1 Corinthians. But the time gap is probably only about five years, and it is more likely therefore that factors in the different situations in Corinth and Thessaloniki are leading to these differences of language and emphasis.

---

3. 2 Thess. 2:5.
4. See Acts 17:14–15; 18:5; 1 Thess. 1:1; 2 Thess. 1:1.
5. 2 Thess. 1:3–4.
6. 2 Thess. 1:7–10.
7. 1 Thess. 4:16.

It stays personal throughout the letter. After the fascinating eschatological passage (2:1–12) on which we will focus in the next chapter, Paul exhorts the Thessalonians to 'stand firm, and hold on to the traditions you were taught, either by word or by letter from us'.[8] In particular, they need to stand firm against evil influences,[9] especially the influence of 'every brother who is living in idleness and not according to the traditions which they received from us'.[10] Paul then spends nine verses exhorting the Thessalonians to follow his example of hard work, and not that of these 'loafers'[11] who are 'not busy working but just busybodies'.[12]

Paul addressed this tendency to loaf around also in 1 Thessalonians,[13] but it seems that things have got worse, because his language in 2 Thessalonians is much stronger. What caused this increasing and worrying tendency to sit around with their feet up? The answer, agreed by most scholars and commentators,[14] is supplied in 2 Thessalonians 2:1–2:

> Concerning the *parousia* of our Lord Jesus Christ, and our being gathered to meet him, we ask you, brothers, not to be shaken quickly in mind or to be alarmed, whether by some spiritual 'word' or some other message, or by a letter supposed to be from us, to the effect that the Day of the Lord is right upon us.

I take this last phrase to mean that some members of the Thessalonian church – or maybe the whole church – are agog with excitement that the 'Day of the Lord', so powerfully described by Paul in the preceding verses, is about to occur; and some of them, carried away with the certainty that it's just around the corner, have given up work and are sponging off other members of the church.

Some argue that they were believing that 'the Day of the Lord has already come', which is an equally possible translation of Paul's Greek.[15] But it is hard

---

8. 2 Thess. 2:15.

9. 2 Thess. 3:3.

10. 2 Thess. 3:6.

11. This is Ernest Best's translation: E. Best, *The First and Second Epistles to the Thessalonians*, Black's New Testament Commentary (London: A&C Black, 1972), p. 336.

12. 2 Thess. 3:11. Paul's Greek contains a play on two forms of the verb 'to work'.

13. 1 Thess. 4:11.

14. So e.g. Best, *1 and 2 Thessalonians*, pp. 175, 334; F. F. Bruce, *1 and 2 Thessalonians*, Word Biblical Commentary (Waco: Word, 1982), p. 91.

15. So NIV; there are similar translations reflecting a belief that the day of the Lord is now past in NASB, NKJV, RSV, GNT. NRSV and REB 'is already here' sits on the fence! But ASV has 'is just at hand'.

to make sense of this. It is just possible that some of the Thessalonians had adopted an extreme form of the spirituality that Paul tackles in 1 Corinthians: in Corinth, they believed that, in spirit, they were already exalted, 'reigning'[16] and speaking the languages of heaven, so that the body didn't matter and would simply be shed like an unwanted banana skin when death or the *parousia* came. Maybe in Thessaloniki they had gone even further and were arguing that the 'Day of the Lord' had already happened – so they are now completely exalted and redeemed! But this extension of a 'resurrected already' spirituality is most unlikely, for nobody in the early church believed in a Day of the Lord or a *parousia* of the Christ which could pass unnoticed. The universally shared vision was of something like 2 Thessalonians 1:7–10, or 1 Thessalonians 4:16–17. Belief in an invisible *parousia* is a feature only of the modern period, when failed predictions of the second coming have been justified after the event by readjusting the expectation – he *did* come again, but not visibly![17] Even the loafers would accept that the *parousia* will be very noticeable.

So it is necessary, I think, to understand Paul's verb in 2 Thessalonians 2:2 in the sense in which he uses it in 1 Corinthians 7:26, where he refers to the '*impending* crisis' in the light of which the Corinthians must live faithfully. We don't know to what crisis he was referring there, whether to some political or ecological crisis or the coming *parousia*, but whatever it is, it is 'impending' rather than present. The verb means literally to 'stand over' and thus to 'press in upon',[18] and so can refer either to 'things present'[19] or to something 'imminent', as in 1 Corinthians 7:26 and – I suggest – here in 2 Thessalonians 2:2.[20]

---

16. 1 Cor. 4:8.

17. The most prominent readjustment of this sort in the modern period is Charles Taze Russell's prediction of the second coming in 1914, which after the event was explained as Christ's coming to power in heaven, but not yet on earth. (Russell first taught that Christ would come in 1874, but this was also subsequently interpreted as a coming to *heavenly* authority.)

18. The verb is *enistēmi*, which according to Bauer, Arndt and Gingrich can either mean 'be present, have come' or 'impend, be imminent' (W. Bauer, *Greek-English Lexicon of the New Testament*, transl. William F. Arndt and F. Wilbur Gingrich [Chicago: Chicago University Press, 1957], p. 266).

19. As in Rom. 8:38, in contrast, there, to 'things future'.

20. I am not alone in taking this view: amongst recent commentators, so Gene L. Green, *The Letters to the Thessalonians*, Pillar New Testament Commentary (Grand Rapids: Eerdmans and Leicester: Inter-Varsity Press, 2002), p. 305.

Jesus foresaw just such eschatological overenthusiasm: 'Many will come in my name, saying "I'm the one!" and will deceive many.'[21] And throughout the history of the church (not just in the modern period) there have been countless charismatic figures who have proclaimed themselves as 'the one' to unlock the secrets of eschatology and give people a new excitement about the end times just around the corner. So it fits much better with Paul's desire to calm them down – 'not to be shaken quickly in mind or to be alarmed' – and to protect them from being 'deceived',[22] if the Thessalonians had got themselves into such an eschatological stew that some (maybe those already inclined to be 'loafers') had given up work altogether because they believed that 'the Day of the Lord is right upon us!'.

Paul gave them plenty of eschatological teaching when in Thessaloniki: 'Don't you remember that I was saying all this to you when I was with you?'[23] It looks as though the particular issue which he addresses in 1 Thessalonians 4:13–18 – the issue of the death of believers before the *parousia* – is a new topic, not discussed when he was with them. But immediately after writing about that he continues, *But concerning God's times* [chronos] *and moments* [kairos]*, brothers, you don't need me to write to you, for you yourselves know perfectly well . . .* (5:1–2); and so it seems that he is back to reminding them of what he taught them while with them. How blessed we are, that the Thessalonians were so slow to take it on board and got themselves into such a mess! They needed to be reminded, and so in these letters we get priceless insight into Paul's teaching that otherwise we would not have.

Having said this, however, it is possible that 1 Thessalonians itself may have encouraged these Thessalonian eschato-freaks into their overenthusiasm. 1 Thessalonians 4:13 – 5:11 emphasizes the glorious *suddenness* and *unexpectedness* of the *parousia*, and therefore our need to be constantly prepared, 'awake' and not taken off guard. A superficial hearing of this could have registered *imminence*, rather than suddenness, and they could have heard *let us not sleep, like the rest of humankind, but let's stay awake, and sober!* (5:6) to mean 'Let's not stay entangled with the distractions of mundane life like everyone else – let's give up work and concentrate on looking for the Lord to appear!'[24]

Whether this is true or not, it is certainly interesting to note the two different directions in which Paul's teaching tends in these letters. The emphasis in

---

21. Mark 13:6.

22. 2 Thess. 2:2–3.

23. 2 Thess. 2:5.

24. It's worth bearing in mind the comment in 2 Pet. 3:16 that 'the uneducated and weak' could seriously misunderstand Paul's eschatological teaching!

1 Thessalonians on the suddenness and unexpectedness of the Lord's return – *like a thief in the night* (5:2) – is matched in 2 Thessalonians by an emphasis on the definite events that must precede it, and specifically on the appearance of *the lawless one* whose arrival is closely tied to *the appearance of the parousia* of the Lord Jesus.[25] 'Be prepared, it could happen at any time' (1 Thess.) is followed by 'calm down, there are things that must happen first' (2 Thess.) – a difference which some have even seen as an inconsistency. I don't think it is inconsistent, but we will need to grapple with this as we look at Paul's teaching here.

Before we launch into our exposition of the first of these two inspiring *parousia* passages, one other vital piece of scene setting is to remind ourselves of Paul's relationship to Jesus' eschatological teaching here.[26] Commentators have often overlooked this, but Jesus' teaching provides the vital horizon against which we must read Paul. It is not that he slavishly reproduces what Jesus said, though clearly he wants to remain faithful to Jesus' teaching as he creatively re-expresses it and allows other Scriptures – especially Daniel – to impact his eschatology.

There is much discussion of Paul's reference to *the word of the Lord* here (4:15). He calls on this *word* as the basis of the teaching and encouragement he gives, but what exactly is it? In the scholarly debate I am intrigued to note that the option I argued for above – that Paul is drawing in a general way on Jesus' apocalyptic teaching, as evidenced by his numerous allusions to it, both here and in 2 Thessalonians – is not usually canvassed as an option. The choice, as laid out, for instance, in Ernest Best's long discussion, is that:

- *either* Paul is quoting a specific 'word' of the earthly Jesus (but Jesus did not say anything about the dead in Christ rising first, so it can't be that – unless this is a word not recorded in the Gospels);
- *or* this is a specific word of prophecy communicated from the risen Christ, maybe through another piece of apocalyptic writing, but more likely through another prophet or even direct to Paul (this is Best's view – 'by far the most probable');
- *or* Paul is filling in the gaps in Jesus' teaching, and using his own authority to say what he thinks Jesus would have said, maybe having prayed about the Thessalonians' question first.[27]

---

25. 2 Thess. 2:8.

26. See above, pp. 100–105.

27. Best, *1 and 2 Thessalonians*, pp. 189–193.

It is important to bear in mind the truth contained in this third option: Paul handles all Scripture, including the teaching of the Lord, with the creative freedom that comes with his call to be an apostle. He is the one charged with the task of bringing us to the *spirit* of the word, beyond just its *letter.*[28] So he never just quotes the letter of Jesus' teaching as if it were a new law. But he is deeply imbued with Jesus' teaching, and of course it carries enormous authority for him, alongside the other crucial Scriptures to which – Paul will have recognized – Jesus himself refers. So I am suggesting a fourth option here, different from the three offered by Best: what we meet, in both letters, is a beautiful and creative rereading both of Jesus' teaching and of the vital underlying Scriptures, especially in Daniel.

2. Structure and purpose

This section of 1 Thessalonians falls into two segments, each ending with *therefore encourage one another* . . . (4:18; 5:11) and each beginning with Paul's regular formula for introducing a new topic about which he knows his readers are asking questions: *Now concerning* . . .[29] Paul has heard from Timothy about the church, a message that brought him huge encouragement: 'How can we give enough thanks to God for all the joy that we feel before our God because of you?'[30] But clearly also Timothy has brought various questions from the church, and in the second half of the letter (chs. 4 – 5) Paul tackles these.

His concern is chiefly pastoral, as the emphasis on *encouragement* shows. In answering the first question, his aim is *so that you may not grieve as others do, who have no hope* (4:13). In fact 'encouragement' has been a major theme of the letter so far. Paul uses the word[31] twice to summarize his ministry to them in the past:

> Our encouragement was not based on deception, or on impurity or trickery, but we speak out of the commission that God has given us, in entrusting us with the gospel . . .[32]

---

28. See 2 Cor. 3:4–6.

29. This is clear in 5:1, but in 4:13 it has been combined with another of his regular introductory formulae, 'I don't want you to be ignorant . . .' A more helpful translation of 4:13 would be, 'Now concerning those who have fallen asleep, we don't want you to remain ignorant . . .' For examples elsewhere, see 1 Cor. 7:1, 25; 8:1; 12:1.

30. 1 Thess. 3:9.

31. Gk *parakalein*.

32. 1 Thess. 2:3–4.

Like a father with his children, we encouraged each one of you, urging and testifying so that you might walk worthy of the God who is calling you into his kingdom and glory![33]

He uses it to express what he wanted Timothy to give them:

We sent Timothy, our brother and God's co-worker in the gospel of Christ, to strengthen and encourage you in your faith, so that no-one would be shaken by these persecutions.[34]

He reveals that this is what Timothy gave him, when he learned that the Thessalonians' faith and love were burning bright:

So we were encouraged over you, brothers, in all the pain and affliction we felt over your faith – because we live, if you stand firm in the Lord![35]

He uses the word to introduce the final section of the letter in which he addresses their questions:

Turning to the other matters, brothers, we ask you and encourage you in the Lord Jesus just to do it more and more – you received from us how you ought to live and please God: you're already doing it – keep going![36]

Then follows some vital teaching about God's will for sexual purity.[37] And then finally the word appears again as he encourages them in 'brotherly love' and hard work:

We encourage you, brothers, to do it more and more, to be ambitious for a quiet life, to look after your own affairs and to work with your own hands . . .[38]

So the two commands to *encourage one another* in 4:18 and 5:11 are not throwaway concluding exhortations. This 'encouragement' – which wraps up

---

33. 1 Thess. 2:11–12.
34. 1 Thess. 3:2–3.
35. 1 Thess. 3:7–8.
36. 1 Thess. 4:1. I've tried to bring out the jerkiness and awkwardness of Paul's Greek here.
37. 1 Thess. 4:3–8.
38. 1 Thess. 4:10–11.

in one word the four elements of (a) instruction, (b) fellowship (relational closeness), (c) mutual responsibility in a shared acknowledgement of neediness, and (d) exhortation to grow beyond what we are – is basic to the gospel and vital for the Christian life; and is *the main 'point' of all talk about the parousia.* Paul teaches about the 'Day of the Lord', not in order to make sure that they have God's future timetable clearly in mind (this would be to focus solely on *chronos*), but so that they may be able to *encourage one another and build each other up one-to-one, as indeed you do!* (5:11) This is to prioritize *kairos* in God's plan: both the *parousia* as the ultimate *kairos*-moment, and the *kairos* of the present moment, when I am sitting with a needy brother or sister in the depths of grief or pain, and seeking to find encouragement with them in those depths.

We must not lose this vital Pauline emphasis! He is not interested in giving us end-times instruction so that we can predict the *chronos* of God's timetable. He wants us to have in our hands the tools whereby we can allow the good news to touch our pain and inspire our action in the world.

3. The dead in Christ shall rise first! (4:13–18)

The Thessalonians had asked Paul a question, through Timothy. Reading back through Paul's answer, it seems as though their question may have been,

> *Dear brother Paul: you taught us that the Lord will come again in glory within one generation. Is this not what the Lord himself said? So what about those who die before he comes – where are they, and will they not miss out on the glory of his coming?*

Behind this question lies the deep grief of those who have lost loved ones and who don't know, now, if and how they are still related to them, and how they will relate to the *parousia.* Paul responds to that grief, wanting the Thessalonians to grasp the true hope that is theirs 'in Christ'. What we meet in verses 14–17 is a creative rereading of Jesus' eschatological teaching in the light of their question, inspired by other Scriptures and based also – of course – on Paul's own sense of his apostolic authority and God-given prophetic insight. We can expound these verses around the three main actors involved in the drama here: *them, us* and *him.*

a. Them: The dead in Christ
Where are they, and how will they feature in the *parousia*? Paul digs behind the basic perspective, in all three Synoptic Gospels, that Jesus will come 'with power

and great glory'.[39] For Paul, the glory of Jesus is always the glory of God, and God's glory in Jesus has chiefly been displayed in his resurrection. That's the heart of it, for Paul: the glory of Christ at his *parousia* is the glory of the resurrected one. And, as we saw in 1 Corinthians, Christ's resurrection is the 'firstfruits' of the general resurrection harvest of all who are his. And so he writes (v. 14): *For since[40] we believe that Jesus died and rose again, so it follows that God will bring, with him, those who have fallen asleep in union with Jesus.* Paul imagines the dead in Jesus accompanying him as he returns in glory – brought *with him* by the God who 'raised the Lord and will raise us also by his power'.[41] He rephrases this perspective in verse 16: *The Lord himself will descend from heaven . . . and the dead in Christ shall rise first.*

These two perspectives just sit side by side for Paul. On the one hand, they are already 'with' him and so come with him, when he comes. On the other, because they are 'in' him they rise gloriously to meet him. It seems that it is the combination of these two perspectives which leads Paul to say that the dead in Christ rise *first*. These two great prepositions, 'with' and 'in' Christ, are Paul's answer to the question, 'Where are they now?' It is gloriously true for us, to be able to say that our dead loved ones are *no less* 'in' Christ, and *even more* 'with' Christ, than they were when alive. The 'in' remains the same, the 'with' gets multiplied![42]

However, these two perspectives make us pause and think. How can they both be true, especially in the light of the unified anthropology we meet in 1 Corinthians? If Paul believed that we have 'souls' that can be separated from our bodies, then he could easily say that the 'souls' of the departed are with Christ and return with him at his *parousia*, while their bodies await resurrection on earth. At the *parousia*, body and soul are reunited. But it doesn't seem as though he accepts this Greek dualistic view of the human person – at least, not in 1 Corinthians. Did he change his mind and develop a much stronger view of the body after writing 1 Thessalonians?

This seems unlikely. He doesn't use the language of 'soul' and 'body' here. The expressions he uses – *those who have fallen asleep in union with Jesus* (v. 14) and *the dead in Christ* (v. 16) seem to describe the *people*, not just bits of them. How can these people apparently be in two places simultaneously – returning *with*

---

39. Matt. 24:30; Mark 13:26; Luke 21:27.
40. The Greek says literally '*If* we believe . . .', but 'if' need not express any doubt in Greek, and this is a good instance where 'since' is a better translation.
41. 1 Cor. 6:14.
42. Compare Rom. 14:8 with Phil. 1:23.

Christ while also dead *in* Christ awaiting his return? There is no answer to this here in 1 Thessalonians, but we will return to this issue when we look at Hebrews 9. Watch this space![43]

b. Us: We, the living who are left

Paul uses this expression twice, in verses 15 and 17:

> *For I tell you this by the word of the Lord, that we, the living who are left until the* parousia *of the Lord will certainly not go ahead of those who have fallen asleep . . .*

> *Then we, the living who are left, will be caught up with them in the clouds to greet the Lord in the air. And so we will always be with the Lord!*

Paul's focus is to show that *we, the living who are left* are not privileged at the *parousia*, just because we happen to be still alive when Christ comes. In fact – as we've seen – because they are already *with him*, the dead in Christ meet him first. Paul imagines a grand reunion, with the still-living *caught up with them to greet the Lord.* It is clear that is not a separate 'rapture' ahead of the *parousia*, but a reunion with the already-dead in Christ, at the same moment as we *greet the Lord* on his return.

Two important words need to be unpacked here. First, the word *caught up* is a vigorous word, and possibly needs a more vigorous translation.[44] It's the word used, for instance, of the thief 'seizing' the strong man's property[45] and of a wolf 'seizing' defenceless sheep[46] – or of the Roman squaddies 'snatching' Paul out of the middle of the lynch-mob in Jerusalem.[47] Paul's choice of this vivid word is explained by his later description (in 1 Cor. 15) of what happens to *us, the living who are left*, at the second coming:

> What I mean, brothers, is that flesh and blood cannot inherit the kingdom of God, nor can corruption inherit incorruption. Look, I'm telling you a mystery here: we shall not all sleep, but we shall all be changed, in a moment, in the blink of an eye, at the last trumpet call. For the trumpet will sound, and the dead will be raised incorruptible, and we shall be changed![48]

---

43. Ch. 12 below.
44. Gk *harpazein*, usually translated 'snatch', 'seize', or 'carry off'.
45. Matt. 12:29.
46. John 10:12.
47. Acts 23:10.
48. 1 Cor. 15:50–52.

Here too Paul seems to be distinguishing, as in 1 Thessalonians, between 'the dead' and 'we'. 'We' are 'we the living who are left'. But it is clear that, whether dead or still living at the moment when the *parousia*-trumpet sounds, that moment will mean a massive transformation for all of us. 'Corruption cannot inherit incorruption': there is *dimensional* difference between our present, bodily life and the life of the kingdom of God. Just as dogs can't take PhDs in physics, and fish can't train as airline pilots, so we cannot enter upon our glorious inheritance – the kingdom of God – without a body to match. I know that I shall never strut down a catwalk parading the latest fashions while cameras pop, because I don't have the required body! Similarly I know that I cannot *greet the Lord in the air* without a fundamental rebuild – an ultimate makeover that will turn this frail, unglorious, weak, all-too-human and earthy[49] body into something glorious and – literally – *fit for a king*; for I must be able to stand before him and greet him as he comes, and then *always be with the Lord* thereafter (v. 17). I need vigorous treatment to turn this body around – and the treatment will be applied in that 'snatching' moment, when we are *caught up to greet him* with all the dead in Christ.[50]

Secondly, the word that I have translated 'to greet' implies transformation for more than just those who meet him. It is actually a noun meaning 'encounter',[51] which, as Gene Green comments, 'was almost a technical term that described the custom of sending a delegation outside the city to receive a dignitary who was on the way to town'.[52] Green then quotes Josephus'

---

49. These are the words Paul uses to describe the body in 1 Cor. 15:42–44, 47.

50. Many commentators have argued that Paul's use of 'we' both in 1 Thess. 4:15, 17 and in 1 Cor. 15:51 indicates that he expected to be among *the living* himself, at the *parousia* (so e.g. Best, *1 and 2 Thessalonians*, p. 195; F. F. Bruce, *1 and 2 Thessalonians*, p. 99). But in 1 Thess. 5:10 the matter is open – *he died for us so that, whether we wake or sleep, we may spring to life together with him*. Paul's use of 'we' is quite free, often meaning simply 'we Christians', and of course he had already faced the real possibility of death through persecution on several occasions. On this occasion, Paul's 'we' just expresses his solidarity and fellowship with the anxious Thessalonians concerned about their dead loved ones. So it is better not to draw firm conclusions about his expectation of the time of the *parousia* from his use of 'we' here. So A. L. Moore, *1 and 2 Thessalonians*, New Century Bible (London, etc.: Nelson, 1969), pp. 69–70; Anthony C. Thiselton, *The Last Things: A New Approach* (London: SPCK, 2012), pp. 95–98.

51. Gk *apantēsis*.

52. Green, *Thessalonians*, p. 226.

description of the reception given in AD 70 by the population of Rome to their victorious new emperor Vespasian, returning flushed with victory from his campaign in Judea: the dignitaries met him first, and then the general populace lined the roads as he approached the city, cheering and calling out 'benefactor', and 'saviour', and 'alone worthy to be emperor of Rome!' As Vespasian entered Rome, says Josephus, 'the whole city was full of wreaths and incense, like a temple'. The new emperor pushed his way through the crowds who began to offer sacrifices and to party in streets and neighbourhoods.[53] We meet the expression in Acts 28:15 of the members of the church in Rome coming out to greet Paul – doubtless not with as much noise as for Vespasian, but maybe with even greater eagerness. And – perhaps most significantly of all – it is used in Matthew 25:6 of the bridal party (the ten sleepy bridesmaids) going out to 'to greet' the bridegroom as he arrives at the bride's house.[54]

The point to be drawn from Paul's use of this term is simple, but with huge implications: we rise to greet Jesus when he comes, not so that we can then travel further 'up' and *always be with the Lord* in heaven, but because *he is returning victoriously to the earth which is now entirely his, with all other powers nullified, including death, the last enemy.* He comes to take up his reign on the earth that he died to save. As we rise to greet him, we welcome him back, and like Rome transformed by the arrival of Vespasian, so the earth will be transformed by the arrival of the Lord. It's not just we who need to be reclothed for the occasion. The cosmos needs to dress up, too. And what a makeover!

> Right now the creation is standing on tip-toe, waiting for the revelation of the children of God . . . for the creation itself will be set free from its bondage to decay and released into the freedom of the glory of the children of God.[55]

What that will look like, we can scarcely imagine. The creation itself will rise to greet its king in a whole new blooming of its life, matching the 'freedom' of God's children.

---

53. Green, *Thessalonians*, p. 227; Josephus, *Jewish War*, 7:68–74; http://www.ccel.org/j/josephus/works/war-7.htm. Contrary to Green's assertion, however, Josephus does not in fact use the word *apantēsis*! But he well illustrates the kind of public reception which Paul has in mind.

54. It crops up frequently in the Old Testament, for instance used of Samuel coming out of the town to greet Saul (1 Sam. 9:14), or Abigail coming out to meet David in order to stop him from murdering her husband (1 Sam. 25:32, 34).

55. Rom. 8:19, 21.

c. Him: The Lord himself will descend . . .

For I tell you this by the word of the Lord, that we, the living who are left until the parousia *of the Lord will certainly not go ahead of those who have fallen asleep* (v. 15).

This is the third time in 1 Thessalonians that Paul has used the word *parousia* to refer to the second coming.[56] As N. T. Wright points out, this is not a word with a biblical pedigree. Its background is entirely secular, with two really significant areas of usage (beyond its basic meaning, 'presence') that must have influenced its use in the New Testament: 'The royal arrival of a monarch or similar official, and the manifestation or powerful presence of a divinity.'[57] People would have been familiar with the use of the word to express both these ideas, and both come together beautifully as Paul uses it of the mighty return of Jesus Christ. So we must not miss its political flavour: because it was 'the official term for a visit of a person of high rank, especially of kings and emperors visiting a province',[58] its use with reference to *Jesus*' arrival means very clearly 'Jesus is Lord, and Caesar is not'.[59] He comes to *displace* and *nullify* all other powers – and this is implied even by the simple word used to describe his arrival.

Paul's language takes on a strongly apocalyptic flavour as he continues to describe the *parousia* of the Lord:

For with a cry of command, with the voice of the archangel and with the trumpet of God, the Lord himself will descend from heaven, and the dead in Christ will rise first. Then we, the living who are left, will be caught up with them in the clouds to greet the Lord in the air. And so we will always be with the Lord! (vv. 16–17)

We know well by now that apocalyptic language needs to be heard as *visionary* and *inspirational*, rather than as *literal* and *descriptive*. But to say 'rather than' implies that it might have some 'literal' and 'descriptive' import! We have already thought about the 'literal' import of the notion of *greeting* the Lord at his *parousia* (v. 17): it means that he is arriving as Earth's lord to take up his reign, as in 1 Corinthians 15:24–25. But we should certainly not press this further with questions like, 'Where will this happen?' or 'Will we really hear a trumpet?' or 'How will the archangel's voice be heard worldwide?' Such questions take us in nonsense

---

56. Also 2:19; 3:13.

57. N. T. Wright, *Paul and the Faithfulness of God* (London: SPCK, 2013), p. 1083.

58. Quoting from the article on *parousia* in Bauer, Arndt and Gingrich, *Lexicon*, p. 635.

59. Wright, *Paul and the Faithfulness of God*, p. 1085.

directions, and need to be greeted with the quizzical eyebrow that David would certainly have raised, if anyone had said to him, 'It must have been amazing, to see Yahweh riding on a cherub! – and wow, those arrows he fired must have been sharp. What were they made of?'[60]

So those who maintain that the Lord will descend from heaven *over Jerusalem*, and take up residence there, are surely overliteralizing, and defusing the power of the *vision*. The vision is of a return that impacts the whole earth – it is to *earth* that he 'descends', to take up his kingship, having nullified all other powers. To ask about the mechanics of this – 'How can he be present to the whole earth simultaneously?' – is to turn from the vision and its inspiration of our faith, into a curious and unexciting literalism. I don't know the answer to that question: and, to be frank, I don't care! The *vision* is of a whole earth touched and transformed by the return of its lord, greeted by dead and by living alike who rise to welcome him back. That vision is worth holding onto – and celebrating! For it is this vision which will enable us to *encourage one another with these words* (v. 18).

Similarly, the *cry of command*, the *voice of the archangel*, and the *trumpet of God* all point to the *impact* and *significance* of his coming, rather than to its literal accompaniments. The word translated *cry of command*[61] is not used elsewhere in an apocalyptic or eschatological context, although the book of Revelation is full of angels (and others) uttering a 'loud cry'.[62] On one occasion in Revelation the 'loud cry' is described as 'like a trumpet' – and this turns out to be the voice of the risen Christ himself.[63] In an interesting parallel, the first-century Jewish philosopher Philo uses the word in imagining the great 'cry of command' with which God could gather his exiled people back home.[64]

So the *cry of command*, like the 'loud cries' in Revelation, is that mighty assertion of divine sovereignty whereby all other powers are banished and God's people are raised from death to meet him. 'Truly, truly I say to you: the hour is coming

---

60. See Ps. 18:10, 14.

61. Gk *keleusma*.

62. The phrase 'loud cry' occurs on twenty-one occasions in Revelation. Often these statistics are significant, as multiples of the crucial numbers – in this case, 3x7. The verb *krazein*, which signifies a great, prophetic shout, occurs with seven of the twenty-one, and seven of them concern a mighty announcement made by a single, great angel (Rev. 5:2; 7:2; 10:3; 14:7, 9; 18:2; 19:17).

63. Rev. 1:10.

64. Philo, *De Praemiis et Poenis*, 117, Loeb Classical Library, vol. 8, transl. F. H. Colson (Harvard University Press: Cambridge, MA, 1939), p. 382. This parallel is pointed out by Bruce, *1 and 2 Thessalonians*, p. 100.

– and now is – when the dead will hear the voice of the Son of God, and those who hear will live!'[65]

Probably this gives us the right angle on understanding *the voice of the archangel*, too. Just as mighty angels announce God's decrees in Revelation, so now an *archangel* announces the death of death and the arrival of the kingdom. Maybe Daniel 12 gives us a special handle on the associations in Paul's mind:

> At that time Michael, the great prince, the protector of your people, shall arise. There shall be a time of anguish, such as has never occurred since nations first came into existence. But at that time your people shall be delivered, everyone who is found written in the book. Many of those who sleep in the dust of the earth shall awake, some to everlasting life, and some to shame and everlasting contempt . . .[66]

This is one of the very few resurrection texts of the Old Testament, and here we find the archangel Michael playing a starring role as the 'protector' of God's people.[67] If that was part of the association of the idea for Paul's readers too, they could be confident that their dead loved ones were safe. There is mighty power shielding them.

The *trumpet of God* is likewise a symbol of summons, and of gathering, and maybe Isaiah 27:13 is especially in mind:

> On that day a great trumpet will be blown, and those who were lost in the land of Assyria and those who were driven out to the land of Egypt will come and worship the LORD on the holy mountain at Jerusalem.

God's trumpet summons his people to himself. As in 1 Corinthians 15:52, it summons them out of the grave so that they may live with him. And as in Revelation 11:15, it signals the end of all earthly power:

> The seventh angel sounded his trumpet. And there were loud cries in heaven saying, 'The kingdom of this world has become the kingdom of our Lord and of his Christ, and he shall reign for ever and ever!'

---

65. John 5:25.

66. Dan. 12:1–2.

67. There were seven archangels in Jewish tradition: their names are all listed in 1 Enoch 20:1–7. There Michael is the fourth, the middle one of the seven, and is described as 'obedient in his benevolence over the people and the nations'.

With the trumpet ringing in our ears, we will meet him *in the clouds* (v. 17). This too is first and foremost a symbol, rather than a literal prediction – but all the more meaningful for that. We have already met these clouds in Daniel 7:13, in Mark 13:26 and in Acts 1:9; but before any of these appearances, this cloud pops up leading Israel through the wilderness,[68] and filling the tabernacle[69] and the temple.[70] Isaiah sees it surrounding the Lord,[71] and it descends on the mount of transfiguration.[72] It seems to swirl around, wherever God's *glory* and *presence* are specially revealed. It is not surprising, therefore, that 'the clouds of heaven' where the Son of Man first received the kingdom then form the stage at the End where all the redeemed stand before him, and the beasts of this age are banished once and for all.

The *parousia* of Jesus takes us from this world to the new world, from old earthly bodies to new glorious ones,[73] from relentless grime to relentless grace, from the indifference and mercilessness of systems that can only exploit, to the gracious call and mercy of a loving King who makes all things new, and who will wipe away every tear from our eyes.[74] Only apocalyptic language is up to the task of communicating this vision to us – so that we may truly *encourage one another with these words* (v. 18)!

4. Be ready! Don't sleep! (5:1–11)

The second half of our passage falls into two closely connected sections.

a. Unpredictable – and unexpected? (vv. 1–6)

But concerning God's times [chronos] *and moments* [kairos], *brothers, you don't need me to write to you, for you yourselves know exactly that the day of the Lord will come just like a thief in the night. When people say 'Peace! Security!' then sudden destruction will come upon them like birth-pains in pregnancy – and there's no escape! But you, brothers, are not stuck in darkness so that the day will surprise you like a thief. No, you are all children of light, and children of day. We don't*

---

68. Exod. 13:21.
69. Exod. 40:34–38.
70. 1 Kgs 8:10–11.
71. Isa. 6:4.
72. Mark 9:7.
73. Phil. 3:21.
74. Rev. 21:1–5.

belong to night, nor to darkness. So then – let us not sleep, like the rest of humankind, but let's stay awake, and sober!

The first two verses here are intriguing. Clearly the Thessalonians have asked Paul (through Timothy) about the eschatological *times and moments*. It would be great to know exactly what their question was. We can only speculate – but it must have been something along the lines of the disciples' question in Acts 1:6,[75] which prompted Jesus' response 'It is not for you to know the times or moments which the Father has determined by his own authority' – the only other place in the New Testament where the two words *chronos* and *kairos* appear together.

They must have been asking questions about the eschatological timetable, and like Jesus, Paul bats their question back, but with an intriguing twist in his rather odd use of the word *exactly*. This is just the word that they might have used in their question: Tell us 'exactly', Paul – when will the End come, the kingdom be restored, the Son of Man appear, how 'exactly' will it all take place? The Greek word *akribōs* is typically used in connection with finding out, or communicating, exact as distinct from general information.[76] So Paul's use of it in his reply has a lovely touch of irony about it: only one thing can be known *exactly*, and they already know what that is – that we can't know the exact time of 'the Day of the Lord'!

This passage is a wonderful antidote to speculation about the end-timings: whether about the absolute date, or (much more likely) about the *relative* timings of the various features of the End. It would be so nice to know 'exactly' what to expect! But Jesus' image of *the thief in the night*, which Paul picks up here, underlines the *suddenness* and *unpredictability* of the *parousia*. It's like the timing of the incarnation: why was the Son of God born among us at that precise moment? Paul's answer, in Galatians 4:4, is that he was born 'when the fullness of the time [*chronos*] came' – i.e., when the moment of fulfilment arrived. In other words, he was born at 'exactly' the moment when God decided to fulfil his promise of the gift of a Saviour. The decision rested 'in his own authority',[77] and so the Son was born when he was born. In just the same way, he will come again when he comes again!

These verses hinge around two images, both of which Paul draws from Jesus (but with his own creative twist), and both of which unpack the idea of *predictability* in fascinating ways.

---

75. 'Will you at this time [*chronos*] restore the kingdom to Israel?'
76. See e.g. Matt. 2:8; Luke 1:3; Acts 23:15.
77. Acts 1:7.

(i) Birth pains (v. 3)

Here Paul is addressing those who do not expect the *parousia*, because they are
confident in their own capacity to provide salvation for themselves: *'Peace and
security!'* they say. Paul is echoing Jeremiah and Ezekiel, who both denounced
false prophets in their day for giving Israel false assurance – 'saying, "Peace,
peace", when there is no peace'.[78] For sure, also, he is echoing Jesus' teaching
in Luke 17 about 'the days of Noah' and 'the days of Lot' when the sudden
destruction of God's judgment burst upon people living ordinary, peaceful
lives.[79]

But it is worth asking who, in particular, might be the *people who are saying
'Peace! Security!'* – and undoubtedly N. T. Wright is right when he connects this
to 'the standard boast of the Roman empire'.[80] The so-called *pax Romana*,
celebrated even on Roman coinage, brought a kind of 'peace and security' to
all Rome's subject peoples, and in fact meant that Roman rule was actually very
popular in the Greek world in the first century. Paul doesn't attack this Roman
ideology explicitly, but the Thessalonians would have had no doubt, especially
if they have already heard the political overtones of the words *parousia* and
apantēsis ('greeting') in 4:15, 17. There is a true king, the *real* emperor, whose
parousia we will greet one day, and whose 'revelation' will mean the overthrow
of all boastful earthly powers. Summarizing the message of this whole section,
Wright expresses it powerfully:

> The proud tyrants of this world, with their global protection rackets ('do what we say
> and you'll be nice and safe'), are part of the old order of things, the night-time world
> which will be swept away when the new day, which has already dawned in Jesus, bursts
> at last upon the drunk and sleepy citizens of darkness.[81]

The metaphor of birth pains is a really interesting one to use of this *sudden
destruction*. Birth pains are about new life, not about sudden death! Of course
Paul is influenced here too by Jesus' use of this image to describe the international conflicts, earthquakes and famines which are 'the beginning of the
birth pains', when 'the end is not yet'.[82] In Mark 13 the implication of calling
these things 'the *beginning* of the birth pains' is that the events then directly

---

78. Jer. 6:14; cf. Ezek. 13:10.
79. Luke 17:26–29. See above, pp. 136–138.
80. Wright, *Paul and the Faithfulness of God*, p. 1291.
81. Ibid.
82. Mark 13:7–8.

associated with the coming of the Son of Man (the 'abomination of desolation' and the terrible suffering associated with that, and the appearance of false Christs and prophets bringing deception[83]) really are the birth pains, the full labour which leads to the birth of the new world, when the sun and moon are darkened, the stars fall, the heavenly powers are shaken and the Son of Man appears.[84]

So here in 1 Thessalonians there is again irony; the awfulness of just experiencing the pain, and not the new life! There is no escape from birth pains. They are unavoidable, in fact thoroughly *predictable*, absolutely certain, though the precise date is always unknown. All Paul will give here by way of date is *When people say 'Peace! Security!'* . . . – because the timing rests wholly in God's determination of the *kairos*-moment when this false confidence will be overthrown and the world's true emperor will be revealed. Until then, the whole creation, afflicted by war, turmoil and suffering under alien powers, will continue to 'groan in labour pain' as it longs for its (re-)birth.[85]

(ii) Children of light (v. 5)

This is a beautiful image, but what a powerful paradox it presents. Paul tells the Thessalonians that, though unpredictable, the day cannot take them by surprise like a *thief in the night*, because they *don't belong to night, nor to darkness*. They are *children of day*. In other words – to let the imagery speak – they already partake of the day within themselves, they *belong to* it, they *manifest* it, and they *live by* it. Within them, dawn has already broken. Night surrounds them still, but they are not asleep. They are awake, and watchful, already holding the reality of the day within them as the key animating principle of their lives. Behind this lies not only Jesus' claim to be 'the light of the world', linked to his call to his followers to 'walk in the light',[86] but also Paul's understanding of the Holy Spirit as a downpayment of the new age,[87] part of the *reality* of the new age already given

---

83. Mark 13:14–23.

84. Mark 13:24–26.

85. See Paul's other glorious use of this image in Rom. 8:22: 'For we know that the whole creation is groaning right up to the present moment, labouring with the pain of birth.' See also Conrad Gempf, 'The Imagery of Birth Pangs in the New Testament', *Tyndale Bulletin* 45 (1994), pp. 119–136.

86. John 8:12; 9:5; 11:9–10; 12:35–36. In John 11:36 Jesus uses exactly the same expression as Paul in 1 Thess. 5:5, *children of light* (lit. 'sons of light', Gk *huioi phōtos*).

87. See 2 Cor. 1:22; 5:5; Eph. 1:14. The down-payment metaphor used of the Holy Spirit connects with the Holy Spirit as firstfruits in Rom. 8:23.

within the old. We already glow with the light of the new dawn, before ever it breaks on the world![88]

So the simple question, 'When will it come?' evokes the radical answer, 'It's already here!' We met this in Jesus' words about the kingdom of God in Luke 17:21,[89] and then again profoundly in John 14, where John uses the metaphor of 'home' to express exactly this idea. The home we *expect* is also the home we *experience*, as both Father and Son make their 'dwelling' with us.[90] The Lord who comes at the End also comes now!

This paradox is possible because *the Day of the Lord* they expect (v. 2) is the Day of the Lord *Jesus*. Jesus is the Lord whose day has already dawned in them. We developed some thoughts about this in the introduction above.[91] It is truly amazing that the Old Testament expectation of the coming Day of the Lord, which would involve Yahweh's own 'coming' to his people,[92] has been applied without hesitation to the Lord *Jesus* in the New Testament. When we confess 'Jesus is Lord',[93] we are saying much more than just 'Jesus is in charge'. We are giving to him the great name 'Lord' used of Yahweh in the Old Testament – and therefore all the Old Testament traditions of the 'coming' and of the 'day' of the Lord are applied to Jesus, and fulfilled in him.[94] And because he is with us *now*, the light of that great Day is already 'shining in our hearts'.[95]

This whole passage reaches a climax with this idea. Jesus Christ *died for us so that, whether we wake or sleep, we may live together with him* (v. 10). Paul uses both *wake* and *sleep* here in a different sense from verse 6; here they mean simply 'whether we live or die'. The Lord Jesus shares his life with us, on both sides of the grave. That's the message that will bring comfort to the grieving Thessalonians. But it also makes us ask, what does the life of Jesus in us *look like*, this side of the grave? That's what Paul tackles in the second half of the passage.

b. Expected – and expectant? (5:7–11)
Paul unpacks further the nature of Christian expectation in these verses,

---

88. Cf. Rom. 13:12–14.

89. 'The kingdom of God is in your midst' (or 'within your grasp').

90. John 14:2–3, 23. See above, pp. 159–160.

91. Pp. 15–16.

92. See e.g. Joel 2:31 – 3:2; Mal. 4:4–5. In both texts the 'Day of the LORD' is linked to the coming of Yahweh himself to his people and his world. Cf. also Isa. 52:6–10.

93. See 1 Cor. 12:3.

94. We touched on this also in ch. 4 on Mark 13 (see above, p. 122).

95. 2 Cor. 4:6.

developing his exhortation in verse 6, *So then – let us not sleep, like the rest of humankind, but let's stay awake, and sober!*

> *For those who sleep, sleep at night; and those who get drunk, get drunk at night. But we, who belong to day, stay sober – dressed up in the breastplate of faith and love, and wearing the helmet of the hope of salvation. For God's plan for us is not wrath, but the possession of salvation, through our Lord Jesus Christ who died for us so that, whether we wake or sleep, we may live together with him. Therefore encourage one another, and build each other up one-to-one, as indeed you do!*

Verses 7–8 contain four images: two negative, picturing *lack of* expectation and readiness (sleep and drunkenness); and two positive, picturing the opposite, sobriety and getting dressed up in the armour of faith, hope and love.[96] For Paul, awareness of the coming *parousia* must have a huge impact on life in the here-and-now. Sleep and drunkenness are both images touching *awareness* – in the one case totally lost (*sleep*), and in the other severely impaired (drunkenness). In both cases, because awareness is lacking, no preparations are made for the vital future about to burst in, when dawn breaks.

But those who *stay awake* (v. 6) and *stay sober* (v. 7), watching for the arrival of day, make sure that they are dressed appropriately in *the breastplate of faith and love*, and *the helmet of the hope of salvation*. The other four images (sleep, drunkenness, sobriety and watchfulness) are all drawn from Jesus' teaching,[97] but this armour image is Paul's creation. Later he will develop it into a whole-person and whole-gospel portrait of the Christian life,[98] and he is generally quite fond of using military imagery.[99] The atmosphere of battle has already been evoked by the *cry of command* and the *trumpet of God* in 4:16, and we've already seen how the overthrow of the powers is central to Paul's eschatology.[100] But it is fascinating that he does not develop this language into a 'massive final battle' scenario. This would have been so easy to do – and is much beloved, of course, by the pre-millennial schemes that turn the battles of Revelation into literal expectations:[101]

---

96. Paul began 1 Thessalonians with this triplet (see 1:3). He comes back to these three key Christian 'virtues' here at the end. They often form a trio: see also Eph. 1:15–18; Col. 1:4–5; 1 Cor. 13:13; Heb. 10:22–24.

97. See pp. 101–102.

98. Eph. 6:13–17.

99. See e.g. 1 Cor. 9:7; 2 Cor. 6:7; 10:3–4; Rom. 6:13; 7:23; 13:12.

100. 1 Cor. 15:24–26.

101. Armageddon in Rev. 16:14–16; the battle of the rider on the white horse in 19:19–21; and the final battle against the dragon and his forces in Rev. 20:7–10.

a massive final showdown (or a series of them), the powers of evil ranged across the Middle East, slaughtered by the armies of God so that his kingdom prevails ...

Paul uses the language of battle and destruction in 2 Thessalonians 1, as we've already seen.[102] But he never develops a full final-battle expectation. In 1 Corinthians 15, as we've seen, he uses the word 'nullify' rather than the more powerful 'destroy'; I am sure that the reason for this is that he believes finally in the *reconciliation* of the powers, and not just in their final destruction.[103] They will be 'nullified' in their anti-God stance, as the Lord Jesus finally brings *everything* back to his Father's just and gentle rule.

So it is also fascinating to see how Paul in fact *defuses* this military imagery. He turns it on its head. The church of Jesus Christ does not – *must* not – fight as the world does, by manipulation and power play:

> The weapons of our warfare are not fleshly, but powerful in God to break down fortresses! We tear down bad arguments, and resist everything exalted against the knowledge of God, and capture every thought for the obedience of Christ, and stand ready to subject every kind of disobedience to right judgment, as your obedience becomes more complete.[104]

The enemies of the gospel are to be captured, not bludgeoned. And we meet just this creative, upside-down use of the imagery here in verse 8. The breastplate is *of faith and love*, and the helmet is *of the hope of salvation:* faith and love are precisely the opposite of the suspicion, fear and hatred that take men to war. And the helmet of salvation, i.e., of *safety?*[105] Soldiering is the most dangerous profession in the world. Every modern soldier longs for safety but knows the very real danger of injury and death, as he or she buckles on the high-tech equipment which is meant to protect them. But we have an absolute guarantee of safety – our *hope* is not an illusory, self-deceptive hope-against-hope that God might save us. It is *confidence in the Saviour* who has already borne the worst possible injuries of battle on our behalf, so that we might be sure of survival, with him (v. 10).[106] God's *plan* for us is not *wrath* but *salvation* (v. 9)!

---

102. See also 2 Thess. 2:8.

103. Col. 1:20.

104. 2 Cor. 10:4–6. The translation of v. 6 here is controversial.

105. This double meaning (salvation, safety) is significant both here and in Eph. 6:17.

106. We will find exactly the same upside-down treatment of the battle imagery in Revelation, when we get there.

So the church of Jesus Christ is called to a strategy in the world that responds with *faith, love and hope* to everything we face, because that is how we live in the light of the new day dawning. These are the actions, the *behaviours*, by which we show that we are expecting *the Day of the Lord*. For our expectation is shown, not by what we feel, or say that we believe, but by what we *do*.

Anthony Thiselton draws on the philosopher Wittgenstein in making this point.[107] Wittgenstein asked what 'expectation' is, and discovered that it is not a mental state. If we are expecting someone to visit, our expectation does not rest in our mental activity of 'expecting' the visitor to arrive. In advance of the visit, we might actually be concentrating on other things – maybe trying hard to finish a piece of work before we give our time to our friend. In this case, our expectation will be shown by *not* thinking about what we're expecting. But we'll also have made up the bed, bought in the food, planned what to do during the visit: these are all *activities*, by which we show that we are expecting the front door bell to ring.

Wittgenstein maintained that expectation points backward, compelling us to ask what *lies behind* our expectation – and here too it will be events and activities, rather than mental states, which prompt the expectation. We've been on the phone to our old friend, and arranged the stay! In Paul's case, his expectation of the *parousia* was based on his encounter with the risen Christ, and on the faith he shared with the first Christians, that the resurrection heralds the fulfilment of the story of Jesus embracing the whole cosmos. Similarly our *past* experience of Jesus shapes our *future* expectation of his coming, and that future shapes our present behaviour: it is a *future-as-present*, influencing the way we live right now (and not just the way we 'expect').

Faith, love and hope are the *behaviours* by which the church of Jesus Christ expects the Day of the Lord. We need to be conscious about this, and intentional. To *stay awake*, and to *stay sober*, means exercising the *faith* which sees beyond the present darkness to the light of day, and endures whatever suffering or persecution the darkness flings at us; it means exercising the *love* which prays for our enemies, reaches out with peace in response to hostility and with mercy in response to need, and binds us to our fellow-pilgrims through the night; and it means exercising the *hope* which ridiculously laughs in the face of disaster and never gives up confidence in the new day because it knows that the death of Jesus has won it all. We will find this theme developed further when we look at 2 Peter 3.

Paul's final exhortation (v. 11) makes us responsible for *each other's* growth in this *faith, love and hope: Therefore encourage one another, and build each other up one-to-one,*

---

107. Thiselton, *The Last Things*, pp. 58–61.

as indeed you do! This is concrete encouragement for concrete action and being-in-the-world, resting on sharing the challenge and bearing the heat together. 'Together We Can!' was Barack Obama's campaign slogan ahead of his election as US president in 2008, and the electorate embraced the hope this offered. The world proclaims the hope which it adopts, in fact, from the Christian good news – but which at the same time it distorts by putting *our* action centre stage. We are not the agents of our salvation. Our hope is in the Saviour who alone is the one able to deliver us from the last enemy, death. But ahead of the dawn when all powers, including death, will yield to his rule, *Together We Can* encourage each other to live out the faith, love and hope which will show the reality of his glorious kingdom *now*, even in the darkness of this present age.

11. THE COMING OF THE LORD – PART TWO (2 THESSALONIANS 2:1–12)

1. Introduction

We have already glanced at the glorious depiction of the second coming in 2 Thessalonians 1:7–10, in the introduction to the last chapter. We also discussed the issue that seems to have prompted Paul to write again to the Thessalonians about eschatology, namely the passionate belief of some in the church that the *Day of the Lord is right upon us* (v. 2) – i.e., so imminent that we might as well give up ordinary daily life and work. We mentioned the possibility that they may have been prompted in this, in part at least, by a mishearing of 1 Thessalonians. In fact this may be what Paul is referring to, in his own introductory comments in verses 1–2:

> *Concerning the* parousia *of our Lord Jesus Christ, and our being gathered to meet him, we ask you, brothers, not to be shaken quickly in mind or to be alarmed, whether by some spiritual 'word' or some other message, or by a letter supposed to be from us, to the effect that the Day of the Lord is right upon us.*

The *letter supposed to be from us* may be his own ironic way of referring to 1 Thessalonians. Or it may actually be evidence of the existence of pseudepigraphies even at this early date – letters purporting to be by Paul, but not actually written by him. Paul's addition of his own personal signature in 2 Thessalonians

3:17 may indicate that he wants to prove the authenticity of this letter. Or it might simply reveal his awareness that, in this letter, he is saying something with a distinctly different emphasis compared to his teaching in 1 Thessalonians. Either way, he needs to underline that it really is him, the real Paul, writing this letter.[1]

The Thessalonians have been *shaken* and *alarmed* by this feverish eschatological excitement. Their settled living-out of faith, love and hope, shining the light of the new day into the darkness of the old,[2] has been disturbed by this false teaching – whatever its source – that emphasizes the *chronos-imminence* of the Lord's coming. Martin Luther famously remarked that, if he knew the End was coming tomorrow, he would plant a tree today. He's got Paul right: belief in the imminence of the Day gives *extra* value to the 'ordinary' life we live now, because the Lord calls us to glow with the light of faith, love and hope in the *kairos*-moment of the present, regardless of the exact *chronos*-moment of his appearance.

Once again we bump into the vital significance of the difference between *chronos* and *kairos*, and into the helpfulness of Augustine's distinction between the three sorts of time. Faith, love and hope are the lens through which I receive the present moment, this exact spot in my living awareness of my body-in-the-world, inhabited right now by the Spirit of Christ, and touched by the people who surround me in his body and my wider relationships. I receive this moment with *faith* in his eternal existence, beyond time and space, and in the reality of his grace towards his world in Christ; angled towards the future, I receive the present moment with *hope* because of what I believe about his plans for his world and the certainty of his coming; and angled towards the past, I receive the present moment with a deep sense of the *love* which has shaped both my own story, and the cosmic story told by the gospel. I receive every 'present moment' determined (if possible!) to live it with that same faith, hope and love.

Every present moment can be a *kairos* when I press deeper into God – or I may miss the opportunity and sink into unawareness of him. And similarly every present *kairos*-moment might be the moment when the Day finally dawns! In this relationship with the Lord we live by *kairos*, not *chronos*. From a different perspective, this is exactly what Psalms 89 and 90 taught us: faced with the huge mystery of eternity, viewed from our tiny, bewildering spot within time, we hang

---

1. In fact the phrase *supposed to be from us* could refer not just to the *letter*, but also to the *spiritual 'word' or some other message*. The Thessalonians know precisely what he is referring to, and we don't need to! This is an important interpretative principle for the whole passage.

2. 1 Thess. 5:8; see above, pp. 247–250.

onto the Lord whose 'loving-kindness' calls us into relationship with himself right now, at this very moment. We make him our 'dwelling place', in all his mystery and unpredictability.

But Psalm 90 is a scary place to live. It feels so much more secure to have a definite timetable of God's plan. The Thessalonians have fallen into this trap, and Paul needs to reiterate what he said when he was with them – *don't you remember that I was saying all this to you, when I was with you?* (v. 5). In particular, they have forgotten what he said about the things that must happen first, before the Day can come. It cannot be *right upon us*, because these necessary preliminaries have not happened yet.

Why did Paul not mention these necessary preliminaries in 1 Thessalonians? Some suggest that the difference between the two letters is so sharp that 2 Thessalonians must be by a different author.[3] But Paul is addressing different issues in the two letters: in 1 Thessalonians, the problem of the death of some before the Day, and of how to prepare for it; in 2 Thessalonians, the problem caused by muddling *imminence* with *immediacy*. We met both perspectives already in Mark 13: both the expectation of the Son of Man coming without warning 'like a thief'[4] or a returning slave-owner,[5] and the description of the things that must happen first, before he comes.[6] Doubtless Paul developed both perspectives in his initial teaching in Thessaloniki, but the Thessalonians forgot the latter!

2. Structure and overview

Our passage has a carefully thought-out structure:

A. Don't get too excited about the arrival of the Day of the Lord (vv. 1–2)
B. Because so much has to happen first! (vv. 3–10)
This section has a 'chiastic' structure, which vitally helps us to frame our interpretation of it:

---

3. So e.g. Earl J. Richard, *First and Second Thessalonians*, Sacra Pagina (Collegeville: Liturgical Press, 2007), pp. 19–20. The issue of the authorship of 2 Thessalonians is discussed at length – defending Pauline authorship – by Abraham J. Malherbe, *The Letters to the Thessalonians*, Anchor Bible vol. 32B (New York: Doubleday, 2000), pp. 349–375.
4. Mark 13:32–33; also Matt. 24:43; Luke 12:39–40.
5. Mark 13:34–37; cf. Matt. 24:45–51.
6. Mark 13:7–12, 28–30, etc.

A   Don't be deceived! (v. 3a)
   B   The rebellion and the man of lawlessness must come (v. 3b)
     C   His self-exaltation in the temple (v. 4)

[Interjection – Don't you remember ? (v. 5)]

       D   The restrainer is holding it all back! (vv. 6–7)
     C' The destruction of the man of lawlessness by the Lord
       Jesus at his *parousia* (v. 8)
   B' Satanic signs and wonders performed by the man of
     lawlessness (v. 9)
A' The deception of the perishing (v. 10)

C. God's role in the appearance of the man of lawlessness (vv. 11–12)

Chiastic structures help to reveal otherwise less obvious aspects of meaning. For instance, the parallel between verses 3a and 10 (A–A') helps us see how much is at stake for Paul in *let no-one deceive you in any way* (v. 3). This is not just a throwaway introductory comment. Deception, as verse 10 reveals, is precisely the work of the man of lawlessness who deceives by satanic signs and wonders (v. 9), and is the hallmark of *those who did not receive the love of the truth* (v. 10) – who are also *those who have not believed the truth but have taken pleasure in wickedness* (v. 12). Not being deceived is crucial! *The mystery of lawlessness is already at work* (v. 7), even ahead of the appearance of the *man* of lawlessness. This comment, at the centre of the chiasm, links with the references to deception at the beginning and the end. This is why Paul is so keen to set them straight in their eschatological expectations.

This makes it all the more intriguing, that there are such big exegetical uncertainties for us in this passage. They are: (1) What is *the rebellion* (v. 3)? (2) Who is *the man of lawlessness* (v. 3)? (3) In what temple does he exalt himself (v. 4)? (4) What is *the restrainer* (vv. 6–7)? And (5) how is the appearance of the man of lawlessness related to the *parousia* of the Lord Jesus (v. 8)? – and these are just the big ones!

The reason for this is obvious. Paul is reminding the Thessalonians of the teaching he gave orally to them, so he does not need to spell it all out in the detail which presumably he gave when he was with them. But where does this leave us, hearing the same exhortation not to be *deceived* but to *love the truth?* For instance, I have counted twelve different candidates, supported by various scholars, for the identity of 'the restrainer' in verses 6–7! These multiple suggestions make it necessary to ask, How vital is it for our grasp of *the truth*, to know the right answer? Why has God not provided the means for us to know for sure what Paul was talking about?

One response would be to struggle as hard as we can to peel away the uncertainty, and to dig out the truth shyly hiding under the surface of the text. That is, effectively, the approach adopted by most biblical commentators, who regard problems like these as challenges to their scholarly virility. However, personally I believe that, when there is genuine exegetical uncertainty, the *uncertainty* is part of the meaning, i.e., of the *truth* that God intends for us. Maybe this is because the *search* for meaning is the vital thing, holding meaning in itself; or maybe we need to learn to hold plural perspectives on the same thing, and not try to resolve the uncertainly too much. Or maybe both! *Truth* is bigger than a particular conviction about any of these exegetically uncertain points – and this will be confirmed, I think, as we dig away at this passage.

However, the awareness that Paul interacts with Jesus' eschatological teaching is a great help in bringing some light into the exegetical murk. This is a forgotten perspective in the exegesis of these verses, which we need to recover. As we trace the dialogue between Paul and Jesus, we can see more of what Paul has in mind. He draws on Jesus' teaching, and expands it with reference to other Scriptures, and adds a good dollop of his own prophetic awareness, expanded maybe in conversation with other apostles and prophets.

Significantly – as we saw above[7] – Paul engages with Jesus' teaching in his two introductory verses (1–2): (a) in his summary of their question to him (*concerning the* parousia *of our Lord Jesus Christ, and our being gathered to meet him*) and (b) in his basic encouragement not to *be alarmed*. The word I've translated 'gathered' is the same word which is used in Matthew 24:31 and Mark 13:27 (in verbal form) to describe the 'gathering' of the elect from the four points of the compass when the Son of Man comes, and the unusual word translated *be alarmed* only appears in the New Testament in these two places – here and in Jesus' eschatological discourse.[8]

So both in his framing of their question, and (perhaps more importantly) in his initial response to them (*don't be alarmed*), Paul draws on the language of Jesus' eschatological teaching. So we might expect that, in the substance of his response, he will draw on Jesus' teaching also. And if we use Jesus' teaching as a lens through which to view 2 Thessalonians 2:3–10, much helpful insight emerges, as we will see.

---

7. P. 101.

8. Gk *throeisthai:* Matt. 24:6; Mark 13:7. The connection made by the use of the word 'gather' is not particularly strong, because it is not infrequently used in the Old Testament of the 'gathering' of the exiles back to the land. But in combination with the concentration of other, clearer references to Jesus' teaching, it adds its weight. The same word 'gather' is also used in Jesus' enigmatic saying about eagles, Luke 17:37.

The best way into the exposition of these verses is to focus on the key exegetical questions, in the light of our analysis above.

3. The 'rebellion' and the man of lawlessness (vv. 3–4a, 9)

Paul tells the Thessalonians that the *parousia* of the Lord cannot take place

> *unless the rebellion comes first, and the man of lawlessness is revealed, the son of destruction, who opposes and exalts himself over every so-called god or object of worship . . . (vv. 3–4).*

The *parousia* of this figure[9]

> *will be marked by the activity of Satan in performing all kinds of powerful signs and deceptive wonders, seeking by all means wickedly to deceive the perishing . . . (vv. 9–10).*

And (Paul's argument runs), because this has not yet happened, the *parousia* of the Lord Jesus cannot be *right upon us*.

As we saw, Jesus prophesied the appearance of a 'desolating sacrilege' or 'abomination that makes desolate'.[10] As we also saw, this draws on Daniel, where the phrase appears three times.[11] In Daniel 11, the appearance of this sacrilege in the temple is the result of the activity of a figure who first appears in Daniel 11:21 and launches himself on a career of deception and conquest. 'At the time appointed'[12] this powerful figure 'shall be enraged and take action against the holy covenant', and his forces 'shall occupy and profane the temple and the fortress. They shall abolish the regular burnt offering and set up the abomination that makes desolate'.[13]

So, responding to the wider picture in Daniel, Paul has personalized the expectation of a 'desolating sacrilege' in the temple in Jerusalem. His use of the description 'man of lawlessness' to describe this figure may have been prompted by Daniel 11:32, 'He shall seduce with intrigue those who violate the

---

9. Yes – Paul remarkably uses the word *parousia* of the appearance of the man of lawlessness in v. 9, immediately after using it of Jesus in v. 8; maybe underlining the way the man of lawlessness counterfeits divine status and actions.

10. Mark 13:14; Matt. 24:15.

11. Dan. 9:27; 11:31; 12:11.

12. Dan. 11:29, Gk *kairos*.

13. Dan. 11:30–31.

covenant', for here one of the Greek versions of Daniel speaks of 'those who act lawlessly toward the covenant'.

The self-exaltation of this figure to divine status also comes from Daniel 11:

> He shall exalt himself and consider himself greater than any god, and shall speak horrendous things against the God of gods. He shall prosper until the period of wrath is completed, for what is determined shall be done.[14]

This clearly draws upon the earlier description of the fourth beast, which also speaks blasphemies against God and is allowed to exercise this power for a limited, determined period, until the kingdom is given to 'the holy ones of the Most High'.[15]

On the other hand the expectation of deceptive 'signs and wonders' comes just from Jesus' teaching:

> And then if someone says to you, 'Look, here's the Christ!' or 'Look, there he is!' don't believe it. For false Christs and false prophets shall arise and shall perform signs and wonders in order to deceive, if possible, the elect. So watch out for yourselves! I have told you it all in advance.[16]

Paul shares Jesus' passionate warning against deception in relation to precisely the same problem – overenthusiastic shouting about the immediacy of the Day. The Thessalonians need to hear Jesus' warning! Paul has associated these deceptive 'signs and wonders' with the single figure of the man of lawlessness rather than with multiple false Christs and prophets, but this is not a contradiction: Paul is expanding and reflecting on the Daniel 11 background to Jesus' teaching. He takes his cue from Jesus that the Daniel 11 prophecy was not completely fulfilled by Antiochus Epiphanes' desecration of the temple in 167 BC, and is yet to be fulfilled in a further desecration of the temple.

Mark 13 therefore helps us to understand *the rebellion* (v. 3). The Greek word here (*apostasia*) can be translated *apostasy* (i.e., a religious defection from faith), and so some have understood Paul to mean either that there will be an apostasy within the church before the Day of the Lord,[17] or some kind of mass defection

---

14. Dan. 11:36.

15. Dan. 7:19–22.

16. Mark 13:22–23.

17. See e.g. J. B. Lightfoot, *Notes on the Epistles of St Paul* (Grand Rapids: Zondervan, 1957), p. 111; Leon Morris, *The First and Second Epistles to the Thessalonians* (Grand Rapids: Eerdmans, 1959), pp. 218–219.

from faith amongst Jews,[18] or maybe both.[19] However the word can also signify political revolt, and perhaps Josephus is especially helpful here. He uses it to describe the revolt against Rome that led to the Jewish war of AD 67–73, during which Jerusalem and the temple were destroyed.[20] Josephus regarded that rebellion as both political and religious, and it is that event to which Jesus is primarily referring in Mark 13 – the time of terrible suffering when 'those in Judea must flee to the mountains'.[21]

It seems very possible, therefore, that *the rebellion* is the awful events surrounding and heralding the appearance of the man of lawlessness, and that Paul is using this word to summarize Jesus' horrifying prediction of this period in Mark 13:14–20. There is dreadful suffering to come for the people of Judea.[22]

4. The temple as the scene of both the rebellion and the judgment (vv. 4, 8)

It seems certain, therefore, that – against this background in Jesus' teaching and in Daniel 11 – Paul's reference to *the temple of God* in verse 4 is to the Jerusalem temple to which both Jesus and Daniel were referring. It is remarkable how reluctant commentators have been to draw this conclusion, preferring to interpret it metaphorically of the heavenly temple,[23] or even of some other 'material building' in which the man of lawlessness will set himself up against God.[24]

But in spite of their different conclusions, all commentators seem to agree that Paul's language 'immediately suggests the Jerusalem temple', as Ernest Best

---

18. So e.g. E. Best, *The First and Second Epistles to the Thessalonians*, Black's New Testament Commentary (London: A&C Black, 1972), pp. 281–283; Charles A. Wanamaker, *The Epistles to the Thessalonians*, New International Greek Testament Commentary (Grand Rapids: Eerdmans, 1990), p. 244.
19. So e.g. Malherbe, *1 and 2 Thessalonians*, p. 418.
20. Josephus, *Life*, 43 (also *Life*, 17, 25, using the closely related word *apostasis*). http://www.ccel.org/j/josephus/works/autobiog.htm
21. Mark 13:14.
22. Paul alludes to this, too, in 1 Thess. 2:16. He was living with the expectation of particular judgment upon the Jews of Judea (see 1 Thess. 2:14). Where would he get this expectation from, if not from Jesus?
23. So e.g. Best, *1 and 2 Thessalonians*, pp. 286–287.
24. So Morris, *1 and 2 Thessalonians*, p. 224.

puts it.[25] And as N. T. Wright (and others) point out, Paul may have been influenced by his own memory of what the Roman Emperor Gaius Caligula attempted to do in AD 40, when he gave orders that a statue of himself should be erected in the Jerusalem temple, in pursuance of his own claim to deity.[26] The problem with this interpretation is hermeneutical, rather than exegetical: what are we to make of the fact that Paul is apparently looking forward to the man of lawlessness setting himself up in the Jerusalem temple *as the immediate prelude to the* parousia *of the Lord Jesus? And then the lawless one will be unmasked, whom the Lord Jesus will destroy by the spirit of his mouth, and nullify by the manifestation of his parousia* (v. 8).

If the lawless one is revealed in the temple, then the temple must also be the scene of his destruction. This does not imply that, suddenly, Paul has started to believe in a localized *parousia* of the Lord: 1 Thessalonians 4:13–17 makes clear to us that he believed in a *parousia* in which the Lord will be present to the whole earth. But one of the focuses of that *parousia* will clearly be the destruction of this rebellion in the Jerusalem temple, which was of course also what Jesus himself taught.

The hermeneutical problem arises from the fact that, from our perspective after the event, we can see that Paul's expectation of a close connection between the *parousia* of the man of lawlessness, and the *parousia* of the Lord Jesus, was not matched by the events! The rebellion did indeed take place, as Jesus predicted, and the temple was desecrated (although in fact no one tried to set themselves up as 'god' like Antiochus Epiphanes in 167 BC). There was very terrible suffering and the temple was destroyed, as Jesus said, but *the* parousia *of the Son of Man did not take place at that moment.* Responding to this, Charles Wanamaker boldly asserts, 'The passage [i.e., 2 Thess. 2:3–4] can no longer be understood as valid, since the temple was destroyed in AD 70 without the manifestation of the person of lawlessness or the return of Christ occurring.'[27]

I think that this difficulty is what motivates many commentators to resist a literal interpretation of *the temple of God* in verse 4. For instance, though he recognizes the allusion to the temple, Wright then pictures Paul 'peering into the foggy future with the aid of apocalyptic imagery, and using Gaius and his megalomaniac plan as an image, a template, for what would surely come one day'.[28] But (a) Paul only knew that this 'would surely come one day' because

---

25. Best, *1 and 2 Thessalonians*, p. 286.

26. N. T. Wright, *Paul and the Faithfulness of God* (London: SPCK, 2013), p. 1290. Josephus, *Antiquities*, 18:261–301. http://www.ccel.org/j/josephus/works/ant-18.htm.

27. Wanamaker, *1 and 2 Thessalonians*, p. 248.

28. Wright, *Paul and the Faithfulness of God*, p. 1290.

Jesus had predicted it; and so (b) this is not about a 'foggy future' but about some literal events which Jesus said would take place within one generation – God's great *kairos* moments, imminent on the stream of *chronos;* and therefore (c) Paul must be referring to something that he expected to happen soon, in the temple in Jerusalem.

In wrestling with this teasingly glorious challenge, it is helpful to try to imagine what Paul would himself have said, had he lived for another ten years or so, and had thus been compelled by events to revisit his understanding of Jesus' teaching.[29] Can we imagine him facing that question, which is precisely the question we face as we seek to interpret both Paul and Jesus today? An answer lies to hand! Once again, it might be helpful to imagine the heavenly seminar at which we present our puzzles to Paul:

Paul, dear brother: you know now that Jesus did not come again at the time of 'the rebellion' and the destruction of the temple. Was something wrong with your expectation at the time of writing 2 Thessalonians? If you had lived ten years longer, what do you think you might have written instead?

> *I lived my whole ministry under Jesus' word that the End would not come, until the gospel had been proclaimed to all the nations. Do you remember in Matthew's Gospel?*
>
> > *He who endures to the end will be saved; and this gospel of the kingdom will be proclaimed in the whole world as a witness to all nations, and then the End will come.*[30]
>
> *I was thinking of that when I used the word 'witness' in writing to the Thessalonians:*
>
> > *. . . when he arrives to be glorified by his holy ones, and to be marvelled at by all who believe on that Day – all who received our witness to you with faith!*
>
> *Notice my assumption there, that 'all who believe on that Day' are the same as 'all who received our witness'! I knew that I was part of that great push, to witness to all the nations within the one generation*[31] *before the rebellion and the coming of the Lord. As you could see, in 2 Thessalonians 2 I believed it would all happen in close connection – the appearance of the lawless one in Jerusalem,*

---

29. The traditional date for Paul's death is AD 64, the Neronic persecution in Rome. Let's imagine Paul living to experience the fulfilment of Jesus' prophecy in AD 70, and give him a little time to reflect on the non-appearance of the Son of Man when the temple was destroyed.

30. Matt. 24:13–14.

31. Mark 13:30.

and then the glorious appearance of the Lord to destroy him and to bring in his universal kingdom. How hard I worked, to achieve that universal proclamation that would pave the way for his universal kingdom! By the time of writing Romans I could say that I had 'fully preached the gospel of Christ in a circle from Jerusalem as far as Illyricum',[32] and I was making plans to press on to Spain via Rome, pursuing my ambition 'to preach the gospel where Christ has not been named'.[33] I thought of myself as fulfilling the Lord's commission to be 'a light to the nations'![34]

But I didn't complete the task. I spent four years in prison, you know – two in Caesarea, then two in Rome[35] – and I began to suspect that something bigger was going on. On my deathbed I urged Timothy to continue:

> *Preach the word! Keep on doing that, whether the* kairos *is right or not. Convince, rebuke, exhort, never let your patience or teaching flag. For a time is coming when people . . . will heap up teachers to tickle their fancy, and will turn their attention away from the truth . . .[36]*

I was still expecting the great apostasia, *you see. But at that point I wasn't expecting to live to see it. But I was already suspecting that the Lord would not come immediately, at the* apostasia *– because we had not completed the task of universal proclamation! The End could not be, until that end was achieved.*

But I would never have believed that the chronos *could extend so long. If you had time-travelled back from 2015 and told me and Timothy that the Lord still had not come, I would have collapsed in praise before our God – who so loves making human beings and sweeping them into his kingdom through the good news.*

This is surely the point: Jesus will not come, until the gospel has been fully preached to all nations. According to the website Worldometers,[37] which is based on United Nations' statistics, there are approximately five births per second in the world, offset by two deaths per second. God is simply passionate about making human beings, and there is no sign of his passion abating. Every prayer for Jesus to come again is *also* (of necessity) a prayer that those yet unborn will lose their place in the plan and their home in the new creation. But every new birth is not just a new mouth to feed but also a new mind and heart to be captured for the gospel.

---

32. Modern Croatia.

33. Rom. 15:19–20, 24.

34. Acts 13:47; Isa. 49:6. Cf. Rom. 15:21.

35. Acts 24:27; 28:30.

36. 2 Tim. 4:2–4.

37. See http://www.worldometers.info/world-population.

What constitutes preaching the gospel 'to all the nations'? Only God truly knows the answer to this. It looks as though Paul took a 'representative' approach: his 'full preaching' of the gospel from Jerusalem to Illyricum was based not just on indefatigable travelling but also on preaching intensively in the crucial population centres (Antioch, Athens, Corinth, Ephesus), from which the gospel could spread outward. Would God be happy with that, as a method for reaching the world today?[38] Or is it essential – for instance – for every individual to have access to the Scriptures in their own dialect, in an atmosphere in which Scripture is not culturally despised but culturally recommended? When will we reach that *kairos*-moment?

We have to leave that question unanswered. And here's another one, also very teasing: if Paul had lived that extra ten years, would he have reckoned that his prophecy of the rebellion and the man of lawlessness was exhausted by the events of AD 70? Or would he believe that – granted the extension of the whole timetable for the sake of the gospel – there is more shelf life yet in that expectation? Having (like Jesus) reapplied Daniel 11 to the expectation of the destruction of the temple, would he encourage us to look for further reapplications? I think this question is more answerable, and takes us into the next section.

5. The 'restrainer' and 'the mystery of lawlessness' (vv. 6–7)

These verses, at the heart of the passage's chiastic structure, are the most puzzling here:

> *And now you know what is holding him back, so that he may be revealed when his right time* [kairos] *comes. For the mystery of lawlessness is already at work; but there is one who is holding it back, and who will continue to do so until he leaves the scene. And then the lawless one will be unmasked . . .*

My translation of the second half of verse 7 is something of a paraphrase. A literal translation will illustrate how difficult this verse is: 'For the mystery of lawlessness is already working; only the restrainer now, until he gets out of the middle.'

Here above all Paul is summarizing something the Thessalonians already know. They know the identity of 'the restrainer', which is both a *thing* (v. 6) and a *person* (v. 7). Though we don't know what Paul had in mind, the idea of a restrainer

---

38. All this received classic discussion in Roland Allen, *Missionary Methods: St Paul's or Ours?* (Grand Rapids: Eerdmans, 1962).

holding back both lawlessness and the *parousia* of Jesus gains extra significance in the light of our hermeneutical question about the non-appearance of the *parousia* when Paul expected it. Something is holding it all back! We are reminded of 1 Corinthians 15:20–28, where we also faced the question why there is a gap between the resurrection of Christ and his *parousia*. And there the answer that emerged is that the powers *are being nullified* now, while the resurrected Christ reigns already, 'until' the moment when all his enemies are subjected to him at his *parousia*.[39] As the church lives out the gospel in weakness, and in the power of the Spirit, the grip of the powers is loosened and the light of the Day begins to shine in the darkness of the old world.

So that would be a not-bad candidate for the restrainer: the present reign of Christ (v. 6), or Christ himself (v. 7), linked to the purpose of God to bring in the End at his chosen moment and not before. He is the already-Lord – his power active through the church – as well as the yet-to-be Lord. But this doesn't quite fit with the language of verse 7b, 'until he gets out of the way / is removed from the scene'. Christ's reign is not 'removed' at his *parousia* – far from it! It seems as though the restrainer is more likely to be something already fully present, to be removed from the centre of the stage when *the lawless one*, and the Lord himself, are revealed (v. 8).

Paul seems to imagine *lawlessness* in two ways here: a *mystery of lawlessness* already at work, and then a particular *lawless one* who incorporates and manifests *lawlessness* in a specially focused way, including making claims to supplant God.[40] And this certainly chimes with experience, as we look at lawlessness in the world – i.e., the capacity of us humans to deal terribly with each other, and to break norms of behaviour which just about everyone, of all cultures, regards as basic to community life. Every day we face the awful reality that we humans are only too ready to do things to other people's mothers and children which we would never dream of doing to our own mothers and children. Or we are driven by inner demons to perform actions which we ourselves find abhorrent in the light of day. What a *mystery*!

But occasionally such evil becomes institutionalized, embedded in a *system* which binds people into horrific behaviour and happenings, whether they like it or not. And sometimes such systems raise up leaders who even look god-like in the powers they claim to exercise over the lives of others. We can all think of

---

39. 1 Cor. 2:6; 15:24–25; see above, pp. 220–221.

40. We are reminded of 1 John 4:1–3, where we meet a similar distinction between 'the antichrist' and 'the spirit of antichrist' – the antichrist is coming, but the spirit is here already, manifested especially in false prophecy.

instances, and so – whether he intended it or not – Paul's prophecy here certainly lives on as a description of how the powers operate in the world. What was true for Daniel in sixth-century-BC Babylon, and for the Maccabees facing Antiochus Epiphanes in the second century BC, and for first-century Jerusalem in the hands first of the Zealots and then of Rome, has been true in many further times and places and continues to be so. Prophecy lives on, and every time the church of Jesus Christ finds itself assaulted again by the powers of evil, we can ask – is this the moment? Is this the point when, finally, the *lawless one* will be overthrown by the mighty and wonderful presence of our Lord Jesus Christ?

There will be a final point when the powers are overthrown, and the power of lawlessness in all its manifestations – including whatever manifestation will immediately precede the glorious coming of the Lord Jesus – will reach its end in him. There may be some very dark times ahead before he comes; we remember the awfulness of the picture of the coming of the Son of Man in Luke 17 – 18, preceded by God's elect crying out to him for justice in the face of rampant corruption and evil.[41] But in spite of the darkness, there is a restrainer! However bad it gets, we can know that evil is constantly *restrained* from its worst possible excesses until the moment when Jesus comes; and then it will be not just restrained, but gloriously overthrown.

So what could this restrainer be? What holds evil back, in the world? As we noted above, 'the restrainer' is a *thing* in verse 6 and a *person* in verse 7. For my money, many different things restrain evil in the world, and therefore many different identifications have been proposed here, and possibly there is truth in several.[42] None of the suggestions are without difficulty. But if we follow

---

41. Luke 18:1–8.

42. The discussion is complicated by the fact that the Greek verb *katechein*, usually translated 'restrain', can also mean 'delay', 'hold fast', 'prevail' or 'possess', with either a good or a bad sense. A good discussion of the options is provided by Wanamaker, *1 and 2 Thessalonians*, pp. 295–302. The sheer variety of suggestions illustrates how difficult the issue is, but the chief candidates are: God himself; the Holy Spirit; secular power and the rule of law, perhaps specifically the Roman Empire and emperor (the most popular option – e.g. Lightfoot, *Notes*, p. 114; Morris, *1 and 2 Thessalonians*, p. 226; F. F. Bruce, *1 and 2 Thessalonians*, Word Biblical Commentary [Waco: Word, 1982], p. 172; John Stott, *The Message of Thessalonians*, The Bible Speaks Today [Leicester: Inter-Varsity Press, 1991], p. 170); the Jewish state and its rulers (B. B. Warfield, cited in Morris, *1 and 2 Thessalonians*, pp. 225–226); some evil spiritual force possessing the world (so Best, *1 and 2 Thessalonians*, p. 301), or the 'mystery of lawlessness' itself and the Roman emperor (so Wanamaker, *1 and 2 Thessalonians*,

through our approach of reading this passage in concert with Mark 13 and Jesus' eschatological teaching, the most obvious candidate for *that which* holds up the arrival of the End, and restrains lawlessness,[43] is the preaching of the gospel, which must take place first. Therefore the most obvious candidate for *the one who* delays the End is the Holy Spirit, who according to Mark 13:11 equips and empowers the church for testimony: 'It is not you who speak, but the Holy Spirit!'[44] Some have objected that 'it is difficult to see in what sense the Holy Spirit would be taken out of the way';[45] but that specific role of the Holy Spirit – to sustain the witness of the church in the face of the persecuting powers – will no longer be needed when lawlessness and all its embodiments in human life and society are finally swept away by the returning Son of Man.

But it doesn't matter! The vital thing is not to feel that we must decide the 'right' answer, but to receive from God (through Paul) the assurance that lawlessness *is restrained*, however dreadful it may seem. And to be encouraged, therefore, to live out the faith, love and hope at the heart of the gospel – to 'stand firm, and hold onto the traditions you were taught', as Paul tells the Thessalonians later in this chapter.[46]

6. The revelation of the Lord Jesus (v. 8)

And then the lawless one will be unmasked, whom the Lord Jesus will destroy by the spirit of his mouth, and nullify by the revelation of his parousia.

---

pp. 253–257); the preaching of the gospel and Paul himself (so Oscar Cullmann, *Christ and Time. The Primitive Christian Conception of Time and History* [London: SCM, 1951], pp. 164–166); the preaching of the gospel and an angelic 'restrainer' (so I. H. Marshall, *1 and 2 Thessalonians*, New Century Bible Commentary [London: Marshall, Morgan & Scott, 1983], pp. 199–200); a couple of prophets misleading the Thessalonian church (so Charles Giblin, cited e.g. by Wanamaker, *1 and 2 Thessalonians*, p. 252); and the persecuted but 'anointed' and faithful church of Jesus Christ (so Andrew Perriman, *The Coming of the Son of Man: New Testament Eschatology for an Emerging Church* [Milton Keynes: Paternoster Press, 2005], pp. 142–150).

43. 'Restraining' has both these aspects to it, I think.

44. Oscar Cullmann and Howard Marshall come closest to this view (see above), but I have not found anyone who specifically makes this double suggestion.

45. David J. Williams, *1 and 2 Thessalonians*, New International Biblical Commentary (Peabody: Hendrickson, 1992), p. 126.

46. 2 Thess. 2:15.

This is the climax of the passage – the 'unmasking' of the lawless one who is at the heart of the *rebellion*, by the glorious *revelation* of the Lord Jesus. I have chosen *unmasked* as the translation here, partly so that the word 'revelation' is available later in the verse to describe the *parousia* of Jesus, but chiefly because it is important to bring out the difference between the two 'revelation' words Paul uses here, and 'unmasking'[47] is definitely what Paul has in mind for the lawless one, I believe. The Lord Jesus will be 'revealed',[48] and in 1 Thessalonians 4:13–18 and 2 Thessalonians 1:7–10 Paul has described what he had in mind for that great event. But the *lawless one* will be unmasked, and in this case the difference between the two words is important.

There is overlap in their meaning, of course, and in 2 Thessalonians 1:7 Paul uses *apokalypsis* ('unmasking') of the Lord Jesus at his second coming. This word means 'unveiling', and of course is used as the Greek title of the book of Revelation, which is a glorious unveiling of the reality of the rule of God through his Christ over the world. But part of that unveiling is a very powerful unmasking of the powers, especially the power of Rome and its empire, which the readers of Revelation are taught to see in a very different light. They lived in a part of the world – Asia Minor – where the power and beneficence of Rome was universally applauded, and the imperial cult (the worship either of the goddess Roma or of one of the emperors in temples dedicated to them) had been introduced by popular demand.[49] But in Revelation this wonderful power, which has brought security, trade and prosperity to the seven cities, is unmasked as *bestial* (drawing upon the imagery of Daniel), and as derived from the power of the dragon, from Satan himself.

We will see more of this in chapter 14 below. The point here is that the *unmasking* we meet in Revelation is *the showing of the true story*, the revelation of the true nature of something which previously looked very different. People thought that Rome was great, so great that they asked for permission to worship it as a goddess – a request readily granted by the Roman senate and emperor. Rome certainly occupied the place of a god (see v. 3) for the cities of Asia Minor. Similarly, the *unmasking* of the lawless one at the *revelation* of the Lord Jesus is a showing of the true nature of this lawless figure, which hitherto looked anything but lawless. This is what the judgment of God is all about – telling the *truth* about the peoples and powers of earth, so that their true nature is revealed.

---

47. Gk *apokalypsis*.

48. Gk *epiphaneia*.

49. On all this, see L. L. Thompson, *The Book of Revelation: Apocalypse and Empire* (Oxford: Oxford University Press, 1990).

So 'the lawless one' was not 'the lawless one' before the *parousia* of the Lord Jesus, except for those with eyes to see. The powers of earth do not parade their lawlessness before their subjects, but their beneficence, greatness and adorability. They perform *miracles* (v. 9), or claim to.[50] They demand loyalty unto death from their subjects, and claim a divine right to inflict death on all enemies of the state; but they dress up the former as willing self-sacrifice by grateful citizens, and the latter as necessary self-defence. This is always how power covers itself with propaganda. But on the dark side the poor are oppressed and God's people persecuted – especially if God's people deny the national ideology by reaching across boundaries to care for those labelled 'the enemy', 'the other', 'the alien'. When Jesus is revealed, this *lawlessness* – this flagrant breach of the first commandment, and of many others besides – will be revealed for what it truly is.[51]

I think this is why Paul describes the action of the Lord Jesus as he does: he *will destroy him by the spirit of his mouth.* Paul draws here on the language of Isaiah 11:4, a passage in which the coming Messiah, the prince of the house of David, is pictured rescuing God's people from the clutches of the surrounding powers who have oppressed them or taken them captive. It is important to set the quotation in its context:

> Therefore thus says the LORD GOD of hosts: O my people, who live in Zion, do not be afraid of the Assyrians when they beat you with a rod and lift up their staff against you as the Egyptians did. For in a very little while . . . my anger will be directed to their destruction . . . A shoot will come up from the stump of Jesse . . . He will strike the earth with the rod of his mouth; with the breath of his lips he will slay the wicked . . . On that day the LORD will extend his hand a second time to recover the remnant that is left of his people, from Assyria, from Egypt, from Pathros, from Ethiopia, from Elam, from Shinar, from Hamath, and from the coastlands of the sea.[52]

Isaiah's picture of the Messiah striking the earth with the spirit of his lips is thoroughly political. This is about the judgment of the named powers that have opposed and oppressed God's people, and gathering them again to himself. The judgment means exposing them for what they are – unmasking their violence

---

50. See Rev. 13:13 – the same is said of the bestial empire pictured there.

51. These reflections are inspired by the perspectives developed by Stanley Hauerwas in *Approaching the End: Eschatological Reflections on Church, Politics and Life* (Grand Rapids: Eerdmans, 2013).

52. Isa. 10:24–25; 11:1, 4, 11.

and injustice.[53] The unmasking of *the lawless one* takes place, says Paul, when Jesus *nullifies him by the revelation of his* parousia. Here he uses the same verb as in 1 Corinthians 15:24, 26, and that connection helps us to see the *lawless one* as an instance illustrating 'every rule, and every authority and power'[54] nullified by Jesus when he comes. As the Son of Man of Daniel 7, he comes to take the kingdom from these usurping beasts, and to rule in their stead.

The word *revelation* underlines this. Jesus is not 'unmasked' when he comes, but 'revealed'. Witherington helps us here, pointing out that this word (*epiphaneia*) is 'another cultic word . . . that was also used of divinized emperors or the visible appearing of a god'. For instance, it is used on coinage minted to celebrate the 'appearing' (i.e., the visit) of the emperor Hadrian.[55] Jesus appears as a royal figure, wielding royal power by which all other powers are nullified – including, Paul will say in 1 Corinthians, the power of death itself.

7. Conclusions

1 and 2 Thessalonians have yielded much for our biblical theology of the second coming of Jesus Christ. He will not come until the glorious task of preaching the gospel to all the nations has been fulfilled. When will that be? We cannot know. So he might come at any moment. But in the meantime he *is already* the Lord who calls us to watch for his coming with the faith, love and hope appropriate for those who live his life and embody his rule in the world. His coming will be visible, and obvious, and will be the moment when he is welcomed back to the earth of which he is already King. And it will mean the overthrow of every manifestation of lawlessness, especially the most flagrant and awful expropriations of divine prerogative, whatever they may be when he comes. And looking ahead to that Day, we must *encourage one another*, and certainly not seek to undermine each other because we disagree over eschatological timetables!

---

53. Ben Witherington III emphasizes this political significance of the *parousia:* 'Jesus . . . is presented as a counter political force of greater power who will come as the Prince of David and destroy the man of lawlessness' (*Jesus, Paul and the End of the World: A Comparative Study in New Testament Eschatology* [Downers Grove: IVP Academic, 1992], pp. 161–162). He thinks that Paul may have been influenced by Caligula's attempt to install his own statue in the Jerusalem temple, and this simply underlines the political flavour of Paul's expectation.

54. 1 Cor. 15:24.

55. Witherington, *Jesus, Paul and the End of the World*, pp. 161 and 280, n. 35.

Now we turn to a passage with a completely unique take on the second coming, found nowhere else in Scripture (though possibly hinted at in Acts 3). Another fascinating journey beckons.

12. THE HIGH PRIEST REAPPEARS (HEBREWS 9:23–28)

1. Introduction

Our next passage consists of one short paragraph from Hebrews 9, which contains both the only reference to the second coming of Jesus in Hebrews, and also the only reference to the 'second' coming in the New Testament:

> ... *so also Christ, sacrificed once to bear the sins of many, will appear for a second time, without sin, for those who are waiting for him to save them* (v. 28).

So ends this short and deep little paragraph, which claims a place in this book because it presents a unique view of the second coming, and thus adds something special to our overall biblical theology. The specialness of it relates to Hebrews' unique view of Jesus, which grows out of the unique way in which the letter[1] uses the Old Testament as a lens through which to view him. Here in this paragraph we are at the climax and conclusion of the central section of the letter (8:1 – 9:28), where the author[2] has presented the heart of his argument

---

1. Yes, it's a letter: see the ending in 13:18–25. Somehow or other, the opening greetings have been lost. What a letter!
2. We don't know who the author of Hebrews was. For many years it was ascribed to Paul, but the writing is very different from his, and Paul would never have included

about the 'high-priestly' ministry of Jesus Christ. Hebrews is unique in the New Testament in developing a *priestly* Christology – that is, an understanding of the person and ministry of Jesus based upon the ideas and symbols of the Old Testament cult, with its priesthood, festivals, sacrifices and physical institutions (in particular, the tabernacle[3]). There are just little hints of this approach elsewhere in the New Testament,[4] but nothing to compare to the brilliant development of this theology in Hebrews.

As we saw also in Acts, the fact that there is only one reference to the second coming in Hebrews does not imply lack of interest in eschatology – far from it. The whole letter is motivated by an intense awareness of the reality of final judgment and of the need for 'eternal' salvation[5] – that is, salvation that lasts beyond death and right through to the age to come. The theology of the letter is deeply eschatological, and develops a powerful sense of what it means to expect and long for God's future by faith: the 'city with real foundations, whose builder and architect is God',[6] the 'greater homeland, that is, the heavenly one',[7] the 'kingdom that cannot be shaken',[8] 'the city that is yet to be'.[9] It is slightly

---

himself among second-generation believers as the author of Hebrews does, in 2:3. The best candidates for authorship, to my mind, are either Apollos or Barnabas – but we will never know, this side of the new creation seminar.

3. It is a really interesting question, why Hebrews never refers to the temple, but only to the tabernacle, the portable worship-shrine which Israel took with them in the wilderness before settling in the land. I try to understand this in Steve Motyer, 'The Temple in Hebrews: Is it There?', in T. Desmond Alexander and Simon Gathercole (eds.), *Heaven on Earth: The Temple in Biblical Theology* (Carlisle: Paternoster, 2004), pp. 177–189.

4. We have already noticed one such hint: the quotation of Lev. 23:29 in Acts 3:23. Other, clearer, hints appear in John 6:52–58; Acts 7:37–50; 1 Cor. 5:7–8; Eph. 5:2; Rev. 5:6; and in Rom. 3:25–26, which is the only other place in the New Testament where, specifically, ideas associated with the Day of Atonement are applied to Jesus and his death. Paul may well be quoting from some kind of earlier creedal statement in those verses, so this kind of theology may well go back to the very earliest years, but it is only in Hebrews that we meet it in developed form! Paul does, however, use sacrificial language in relation to our (or his) discipleship: e.g. Rom. 6:13, 19; 12:1; 15:16; Phil. 2:17; 4:18; Col. 1:22; 2 Tim. 4:6.

5. Heb. 5:9.

6. Heb. 11:10.

7. Heb. 11:16.

8. Heb. 12:28.

9. Heb. 13:14.

puzzling that there is only one reference to the second coming within such an eschatologically-oriented letter, but it comes at a structurally very important point, and is by no means an add-on; it arises beautifully from within the Old Testament symbolism of the letter, as we will see.

2. Structure and message

A little map will give us a sense of where we're about to go, as we explore this glorious passage. It falls into three pairs of verses, each presenting a different feature of the sacrifice made by Jesus, and each ending with an 'appearance' of Jesus: the first in the present, the second in the past, and the third – his 'second' coming – in the future. Three different verbs for 'appearing' are used, each with a slightly different meaning:

a. The object of the sacrifice (vv. 23–24)

> So it was necessary that the earthly copies of the heavenly realities should be cleansed by these means [the blood sacrifices and rituals just described]; but the heavenly realities themselves need to be cleansed by greater sacrifices than these. For Christ has not entered a sanctuary built by human hands as a model of the true sanctuary, but he has entered heaven itself, to appear there now before God, on our behalf.

The first appearance is thus before God, in heaven, here described as a *sanctuary*, and amazingly the object of Jesus' sacrifice is to *cleanse* this heavenly temple. We will look into the meaning of this below. The word *appear* here[10] has the flavour of 'making an entrance' – a dramatic arrival on the heavenly stage, radically affecting the action.

b. The time of the sacrifice (vv. 25–26)

> The point of this is not so that Christ may offer himself frequently, like the High Priest who entered the sanctuary annually, bearing blood not his own; for then Christ would have to have suffered many times since creation. No – he appeared once only, at the end of the ages, in order to do away with sin by the sacrifice of himself.

Because of the parallel with the high priest and his annual Day-of-Atonement entrance into the inner sanctuary, it is a little unclear whether this second

---

10. Gk *emphanizein*.

'appearance' is also in heaven, the heavenly sanctuary, or whether the author is thinking of the incarnation, Christ's appearance in the flesh. On balance the latter seems correct, because in Hebrews Jesus' sacrifice definitely takes place on earth. Just as the high priest, on the Day of Atonement, first offered the sacrifice outside the sanctuary and then entered it bearing the blood of the offering, so Jesus sacrifices himself on earth and then enters heaven.

The word *appear* here[11] carries the nuance to 'reveal' or 'make plain'. Here it refers not just to Jesus' appearance on earth in the flesh, but also implies that the significance of his death has been 'made plain'; his was no ordinary death, but a sacrifice to deal with sin.

c. The climax of the sacrifice (vv. 27–28)

And just as it is our human destiny to die once, and then to face judgment, so also Christ, sacrificed once to bear the sins of many, will appear for a second time, without sin, for those who are waiting for him, expecting salvation.

As we will see, the Day of Atonement is still providing the author of Hebrews with the picture for describing the second coming here. At the end of the day's rituals the high priest appears out of the inner sanctuary, to prove that atonement has truly been made. The word translated *appear* here[12] emphasizes *being seen:* as soon as the waiting crowd claps eyes on the high priest emerging from the sanctuary, they know that the sacrifice has been accepted, atonement has been made, and they (and he) are safe. Salvation is secured!

There are some very complex ideas here, and we will need to dig further, both in the Old Testament and in the rest of Hebrews, in order to pin down clearly what the author is saying about the second coming. In fact we need to unpack three interlinked features of Hebrews' priestly Christology: (1) Jesus as high priest, (2) his death as a sacrifice, and (3) the Day of Atonement as providing a helpful setting for understanding the other two. All three vitally shape what's going on in our passage.

These three ideas – priesthood, sacrifice, and atonement – all have strong resonance in contemporary Western culture. One of them – sacrifice – has a solidly positive flavour and feel, while the other two are strongly negative. As in Britain and Europe we mark the one hundredth anniversary of the First World War, we are frequently reminded of the sacrifice made by the more than

---

11. Gk *phanerousthai.*

12. Gk *horasthai.*

two and a half million young men who volunteered in Britain for military service during the war.[13] They knew that they were laying their lives on the line, motivated according to Peter Simkins by 'patriotism and a widespread collective sense of duty to King and Empire'.[14] In the UK still, the public narrative around their sacrifice is summed up by John Maxwell Edmonds' famous epitaph, used also on many Second World War memorials: 'When you go home, tell them of us, and say, "For your tomorrows these gave their today."'

Still today, 'service' and 'sacrifice' are the dominant metaphors associated with employment in the armed forces in the UK. But 'sacrifice' is also widely associated, for instance, with carers who give up career or leisure or money or other relationships to care for other family members or friends,[15] or with medical personnel who volunteer to work in war zones or disaster areas. We admire and want to support people who make such sacrifices for others. Sacrifice is a good thing, our culture accepts, because it definitely blesses those who receive it. And within this popular affirmation of sacrifice lies a recognition that it works by *substitution*. At personal cost, carers take on themselves the tasks and needs that the cared-for cannot fulfil. Soldiers give their lives so that those back home may continue to live in peace. As we will see, this has its roots in biblical theology.

On the other hand, 'priesthood' and 'atonement' have strongly negative overtones in our culture. Priests are now objects of suspicion or even hatred because of the association with child abuse, and atonement is impossible. The two are connected, in the feelings of those who have suffered abuse by priests or other church ministers: what can possibly atone for their suffering and its lasting consequences? The irony is that, in the past, priests were trusted as the mediators of atonement between God and sinners. But is atonement *ever* possible? asks our culture. Beyond the abuse of children, what can possibly atone for the terrible catalogue of crimes, both in war and not, that left so many lives shattered during the twentieth century?

---

13. In fact, 2,675,149 men volunteered for military service in Britain during the First World War, according to Dr Alex Watson (Alexander Watson, 'Recruitment: conscripts and volunteers during World War One', an article published on the British Library website, www.bl.uk/world-war-one/articles/recruitment-conscripts-and-volunteers, August 2015).

14. Peter Simkins, 'Voluntary Recruiting in Britain, 1914-1915', www.bl.uk/world-war-one/articles/voluntary-recruiting (August 2015).

15. Just over 6.5 million of them in the UK, according to the 2011 census (figures cited on the website of CarersUK: www.carersuk.org/for-professionals/policy/policy-library/facts-about-carers-2014).

Published in 2001, Ian McEwan's novel *Atonement* (turned into an award-winning film in 2007[16]) looks back with horror over the history of the preceding century, and leaves us with one very clear and awful message: *atonement cannot be made*. There is no way back, once deliberate wrong has been done. The story starts with a false accusation of rape, and traces the impact of this betrayal and injustice through the following decades. Its message is hopeless. Following such an act, all you are left with is the awful consequences, and the desperate task of finding a way to cope – which, for the guilty person in the story, means creating a fictional world in which atonement is imagined, although in reality it cannot happen.

Popularly, 'being made to atone' means being *punished*, usually by imprisonment. But punishment does not atone. It can never 'fit the crime'; it leaves victims with their loss, and it simply underlines the reality of a fractured world in which there is finally no answer to injustice, betrayal, exploitation and murder. All we can do is expunge or lock away the perpetrators, and put our trust in politicians and the processes of law and order to protect us as much as possible from future horrors. But we need so much more than the feeble processes of human government and justice!

Our culture has thus lost hope of atonement – of 'putting things right again'. But this is what priesthood is about, in the Bible; about providing a way in which wrong can truly be 'put right', or 'healed', to use a great biblical picture. Healing doesn't change history: the wrong has still occurred, and the scars will stay. But true healing – God's healing – takes us beyond the wrong and the pain to a place where we've gained more, through the experience of loss and restoration, than we would ever have gained if the wrong and the pain had never occurred. That's true *atonement!* And that's what God works for his whole world, in and through Jesus Christ, the great High Priest[17] of the new covenant.

This priestly Christology adds something wonderful to the view of Jesus we have chiefly met thus far, which – drawing on Daniel – is a 'victor' Christology: the central picture is of Jesus' victory over all the opposing powers and forces that hold God's world captive. Glorious! But victory *alone* leaves the victims with their wounds. Are our wounds just the necessary collateral damage gathered on the way to victory? Paul's approach to this – as we saw – is to develop the

---

16. Ian McEwan, *Atonement* (London: Jonathan Cape, 2001). The film, directed by Joe Wright and starring Keira Knightley, James McAvoy and Saoirse Ronan, was released in September 2007 and won the Golden Globe award for Best Motion Picture the following year.

17. Heb. 4:14.

paradoxical theology of the cross: the powers are being overthrown through Jesus' *defeat*, and through the *weakness* of his church, and at his second coming this defeat will be gloriously clear.[18] This is the wonderful, upside-down wisdom of God, who achieves salvation through the cross. It's a powerful vision – but how does it actually work? *How* do Jesus' wounds, and ours, work within God's purpose to bring salvation to the world?

This is where the priestly Christology of Hebrews comes in. It addresses the what, and the how – and the whither – of *sacrifice:* What difference does it make, to interpret Jesus' ministry as a high-priestly sacrifice? How does his sacrifice achieve salvation, in God's plan? And where does sacrifice lead, if that becomes the key theme in our world view (as it does, in Hebrews)? *The glorious message of Hebrews is that atonement for all sins – even the most awful acts of betrayal and murder – has been wonderfully achieved, through Jesus Christ, our great High Priest.* Even more specifically, *Jesus' sacrifice of himself to death for us saves us from the enslavement to death which underlies all our woes.* In order to hear this message clearly, we need to trace the amazing view of priesthood, sacrifice and atonement which Hebrews develops, against the background of these three themes in the Old Testament. We will look briefly at each of them, with an eye to their significance for Hebrews' presentation of the second coming in 9:28.

3. Our great High Priest

Jesus is not called a high priest in 9:23–28, but his high-priestly ministry is at the heart of the way in which the second coming is presented in these verses. Jesus is in fact called a high priest for the first time in 2:17–18:

> For this reason he had to be like his brothers in every respect, so that he might be a *merciful* and *faithful* high priest before God, to make atonement for the sins of the people. For he himself was tested through suffering, and so he is able to help all who are being tested.

This great statement not only introduces this theme, which will be so significant for the whole letter, but it also specifically leads into the next two sections, which in turn pick up Jesus' *faithfulness* as High Priest (3:1 – 4:13), and his *mercy* (4:14 – 5:10). In addition, 2:18 highlights in advance the very significant way in which

---

18. I'm summarizing here what we saw especially in ch. 9; key texts are 1 Cor. 1:26 – 2:8; 2 Cor. 4:5–12; 1 Cor. 15:24–26.

Jesus' high priesthood differs from that of his Old Testament predecessors: *their own suffering* was not part of their ministry in making atonement, but *his* suffering is vital. This is not explained at this early point in the letter. But by the time we get to chapter 9, the reason is clear: he *does away with sin by the sacrifice of himself* (v. 26).

Before we look specifically at his sacrifice, we must notice another vital aspect of his priestly ministry developed in Hebrews: that of mediator, representing both God to us, and us to God – offering *our* sacrifices to God, and communicating *God's* forgiveness, instruction and blessings to us. In the Old Testament priests were essentially mediators in this way, belonging both to God – in special, close relationship to him – and to the people, as one of the tribes (Levi) set apart for this task.[19] The word 'mediator' is used of Jesus three times in Hebrews, on each occasion describing him as the 'mediator of a new (or greater) covenant'.[20]

In a very particular way (as we'll see) this is what Jesus is doing in 9:28, representing both partners to the covenant, both God and us. But he does it in a far greater way than was possible for the priests of the old covenant, for two reasons. On the one hand, he can uniquely represent God because he uniquely partakes of the nature of God himself. This is the message of the glorious opening section of the letter[21] – he is God's own Son, 'the outshining of God's glory, and the imprint of his substance'.[22] On the other hand, he can uniquely represent us to God, not just because he is fully human, sharing our 'blood and flesh',[23] but also because he is a man 'tested in every respect just as we are',[24] in particular tested by sharing our *death*: 'By the grace of God, he tastes death on behalf of everyone.'[25] And yet, in spite of this complete sharing of our humanity, he was 'without sin',[26] and thus 'separated from sinners',[27] so that

---

19. See the summary in Heb. 5:1, echoing Exod. 18:19.

20. Heb. 8:6; 9:15; 12:24. A most helpful study on priesthood in Hebrews, emphasizing this aspect of it, is provided by Albert Vanhoye, *Structure and Message of the Epistle to the Hebrews*, Subsidia Biblica 12 (Rome: Editrice Pontificio Istituto Biblico, 1989).

21. Heb. 1:1 – 2:4.

22. Heb. 1:2–3.

23. Heb. 2:14.

24. Heb. 4:15.

25. Heb. 2:9.

26. Heb. 4:15.

27. Heb. 7:26.

'he does not have a daily necessity, like the chief priests, to offer sacrifices first for his own sins, and then for the sins of the people'.[28]

Though fully entering human life and experience, Jesus remains in that unbroken union with God which belongs to him as God's Son. He can therefore wholly represent both God and us in the sacrifices he offers, bridging the gap between sinners and their Creator, between earth and heaven. This cosmological 'bridging of the gap' is important in Hebrews, and underlies the three 'appearings' in 9:23–28: in each case, the 'appearing' is on the other side of the gap (the first in heaven from earth, the second and third on earth from heaven).

Now let's focus on the sacrifice he offers, summarized in 9:28: *sacrificed once to bear the sins of many*.

4. He offered up . . .

We meet some huge surprises here. The first pops up when we ask, 'What does Jesus sacrifice?' We have already noted the basic answer to this – he offers *his own life* up to death for us. That is surprising enough, in comparison with the high priesthood of Aaron in the Old Testament. But when the author develops this theme further in chapter 5, this offering of his life takes on a unique and amazing shape:

> In the days of his flesh, he offered up prayers and supplications to the one with the power to save him from death, with strong cries and tears: and he was heard because of his fearful reverence. Though the Son of God, he learned obedience from what he suffered, and being made perfect, he became the cause of eternal salvation for all who obey him – having been designated by God a high priest, in the order of Melchizedek (5:7–10).

The author looks at the cross from a unique viewpoint through the special lens provided by Jesus' agony in the Garden of Gethsemane, where he 'offered up' – the regular word for sacrifice – prayers, cries and tears to his heavenly Father. 'Yet not my will, but yours be done', he said,[29] submitting himself to God, ready to give his body to torture and death in obedience to the Father's will. Thus he 'learned obedience', says Hebrews – not because he was previously less than obedient, but because every new and bigger opportunity to do God's will is a new and greater 'learning', and even God's Son could learn in that way.

---

28. Heb. 7:27; cf. Lev. 9:7; 16:6.

29. Luke 22:42.

The Son of God had never before given his body over to death, embracing the suffering that belongs to our flesh and blood. Only so could he truly be like us 'in just the same way'.[30]

Hebrews thus develops a unique perspective on the *life* that Jesus offered for us. He sacrificed not just the physical life of his body on that terrible day when the soldiers whipped him and nailed his arms and feet to the cross. In fact to focus on his wounds and physical pain is to miss the true dimensions of his sacrifice – it is to treat his sacrifice as just like one of the animal sacrifices of the Old Testament, where it is just about the blood and nothing more. No – as one of us, he offers up something even more truly human than just the physical life of his body: his fear and reverence, his submission to God's will, his passionate prayer, his tears and his trust in the God who alone could save him. While the language of Hebrews 5:7 is specially applicable to Jesus' prayer in Gethsemane, Hebrews does not make that connection explicit; these 'prayers and supplications . . . with strong cries and tears' were offered 'in the days of his flesh' – i.e., they were typical of his whole life of faith and obedience. It was a lifelong sacrifice of Jesus' will, mind and heart to his Father, capped by the sacrifice of his body on the cross.

Later in the letter, this is exactly how faith is defined and illustrated, in chapter 11. It turns out that the great 'heroes of faith', as they are sometimes called, were offering exactly the same sacrifice of will, heart and body to God, holding on to him for deliverance and for fulfilment of his promise, and learning obedience and perfection in exactly the same way. There is much to explore here that would take us beyond our focus on the second coming, for this takes us deep into Hebrews' theology. What does it mean to 'obey' Christ – remembering that, according to 5:9, he is 'the cause of eternal salvation for all who obey him'? Those who obey him are not just those who *trust* him to save them, but are also those who *follow* and *imitate* him by living the same life of sacrifice. They are the ones who *wait for him* in 9:28 – no one else is interested! We will pick up a little more on this theology of sacrifice when we look at 9:28 below.

This sacrifice actually *qualifies* Jesus to be a high priest for us: it was not that he was already High Priest, and then offered this sacrifice in fulfilment of his office. No. Verse 5:10 *follows from* 5:9: his sacrifice leads to his 'perfection',[31]

---

30. Heb. 2:14.

31. 'Learning obedience' is linked here to 'being made perfect' – another very surprising thing to say about the Son of God. There is much discussion about the meaning of this, on which we need not pause: see David Peterson, *Hebrews and Perfection: An Examination of the Concept of Perfection in the Epistle to the Hebrews* (Cambridge: Cambridge University Press, 2005 [1982]).

which means that he becomes 'the cause of eternal salvation' for all who obey him, which means in turn that he is 'designated by God a high priest in the order of Melchizedek'.[32] His high priesthood follows from his sacrifice, rather than the other way round. This is another respect in which Jesus' high priesthood is not like that of Aaron and his sons, who went through a lengthy ordination ceremony before they were let loose in the tabernacle.[33]

Of all the Old Testament sacrifices and festivals, the author of Hebrews finds in the Day of Atonement a particularly clear model[34] for the ministry of Jesus:

5. Only the high priest, just once a year . . .

The Day of Atonement was celebrated annually, and was the only occasion on which anyone entered the inner sanctuary, the Most Holy Place, of the temple (or before that, of the tabernacle): 'Into the second tent only the high priest enters, once a year, and always with blood which he offers for himself and for the sins of the people committed in ignorance.'[35]

It was the annual festival at which *all* the sins of Israel were confessed and atoned for by ritual transfer to a scapegoat, which was then driven out into the wilderness. A special focus rested on the 'sins of ignorance', those sins which Israelites might have committed without awareness (and of which there-fore they could not specifically repent). After the sacrifice of the first of two goats:

> Aaron shall lay both his hands on the head of the live goat, and confess over it all
> the iniquities of the people of Israel, and all their transgressions, all their sins, putting
> them on the head of the goat, and sending it away into the wilderness by means of

---

32. This is another great feature of Hebrews' argument on which we need not pause specifically – the use of Melchizedek (Gen. 14:18–20; Ps. 110:4) as a 'way in' to understanding Jesus. Heb. 7 is devoted to this.

33. Lev. 8. This is one reason why the author of Hebrews finds and develops Melchizedek as providing a model for Jesus' priesthood. Melchizedek was not *ordained* – he just *was*.

34. The words he actually uses are 'example, illustration' (Gk *hypodeigma*, Heb. 8:5; 9:23), 'shadow' (Gk *skia*, Heb. 8:5; 10:1) and 'copy, preliminary design' (Gk *antitypon*, Heb. 9:24).

35. Heb. 9:7. The rituals are described in Lev. 16.

someone designated for the task. The goat shall bear on itself all their iniquities to a
barren region; and the goat shall be set free in the wilderness.[36]

So all Israel's sins were symbolically banished, especially all the sins for which
no specific sacrifice had been offered, and maybe even rebellious, 'high-handed'
sins for which no sacrifice could be offered.[37] All such sins would cling to the
people like a foul smell or a filthy stain before God, until symbolically removed
once a year in this way. This helps us to understand why the chief activity of
the Day of Atonement was actually directed at the tabernacle (or temple) itself.
When the high priest entered the inner sanctuary, the Most Holy Place, he was
commanded to sprinkle the blood of the first goat on the covering of the ark:

> Thus he shall make atonement for the sanctuary, because of the uncleannesses of the
> people of Israel, and because of their transgressions, all their sins; and so shall he do
> for the tent of meeting, which remains with them in the midst of their uncleannesses.[38]

The 'tent of meeting' (the tabernacle) was so called because it was the point
at which God and his people met – a symbol of his presence in their midst. But
how can a Most Holy Place exist in the midst of uncleanness? We can best
understand this 'cleansing' of the sanctuary if we imagine sin as a foul-smelling
slime that sticks to the walls and floors and threatens to make the sanctuary
uninhabitable (by God). I remember once being part of a group of young people
tasked with cleaning out a London dosshouse which had become so filthy that
it was no longer possible even for the dossers to sleep there! So I don't find it
hard to imagine sin as filthiness, and the blood of the sacrifice as the glorious
cleanser that makes the sanctuary habitable again by God.[39]

But for the author of Hebrews this is all symbolic, pointing to a reality much
greater and very different. This terrible *restriction* of access to the presence of God
– only one person, only once a year – shows that 'the way of access into the sanctuary had not yet been revealed, while the first tabernacle was still standing'.[40]

For him the Most Holy Place is not really the inner room of the tabernacle
or temple, but heaven itself, the sanctuary where God truly dwells. The

---

36. Lev. 16:21–22.
37. See Num. 15:30–31.
38. Lev. 16:16.
39. This view of the sacrifices is developed by Jacob Milgrom, 'Israel's Sanctuary:
    The Priestly "Picture of Dorian Grey"', *Revue Biblique* 83 (1976), pp. 390–399.
40. Heb. 9:8.

tabernacle of old, and the Day of Atonement played out annually, offered the vision of truly meeting with God, but also said 'not yet! and not like this'. It pictured both access, and inaccessibility; meeting, but also terrible distance. And the repetition of the sacrifices carried a similar message:

> The law can never, by the same sacrifices offered repeatedly, year after year, make the worshippers perfect. For if they were effective, would not the sacrifices have ceased, since the worshippers – now purified! – would no longer have a consciousness of sins? Actually, in those repeated sacrifices there was simply a yearly reminder of sin. For it is impossible for the blood of bulls and of goats to take away sins.[41]

The old sacrifices were like scrubbing the London dosshouse but never actually managing to clean it at all and make it habitable again. But – though ineffective – the sacrifices at least pictured the possibility of cleansing, of true atonement. And that possibility is now a reality! Jesus our great High Priest has 'passed through the heavens',[42] 'passed behind the veil',[43] like the high priest on the Day of Atonement, but this time truly entering *the Most Holy Place*, the very presence of God himself – into intimate 'for ever' relationship with God, as our 'forerunner':

> Because he remains 'for ever', he has a priesthood that does not pass away: and so he is able to offer total, final salvation to all who approach God through him, since he always lives to encounter God on their behalf.[44]

He is one of us, and also the Son of God: and because he has become one with us so completely, sharing entirely our flesh and blood and bearing our death, offering up to God his sinless suffering and his perfect obedience to his Father's will, he has now entered his Father's presence to represent us there, and to encounter God on our behalf.

David deSilva suggests that the first readers of Hebrews would have known exactly what the author meant, because of their experience of clients and patrons in ancient Greek and Roman culture. Social life was highly stratified, by birth and by wealth, and people would seek to improve their position by

---

41. Heb. 10:1b–4.

42. Heb. 4:14.

43. Heb. 6:19. The phrase 'behind the veil' refers to the curtain hanging in front of the Most Holy Place. Hebrews uses exactly the same phrase as in Lev. 16:15.

44. Heb. 7:24–25.

rising up the ladder of society, seeking public honour (and, of course, fearing public shame). One of the key ways of doing this was to seek the acquaintance, and support, of powerful patrons who could exercise their influence on your behalf. And the best way to get an introduction to a patron would be through a mediator – a well-disposed secretary or old friend who could open the door for you and speak nice words about you into the great man's ear.[45]

This kind of thing has been happening since the world began, and still does. But in Graeco-Roman culture it had become an art-form. It could well be that the Hebrews to whom the letter was addressed, had experienced great public shame because of their faith, having lost of all their worldly goods and being 'publicly exposed to insult' and imprisonment (which in that culture was itself deeply shaming).[46] What a message, therefore, that they have a High Priest who can open up the greatest of all doors to them – the door into the Most Holy Place, where they can be received into the presence of the Lord God himself, no less!

deSilva's proposal of this social background is helpful, but it falls down in one significant respect, as we will see now as we turn to look at our passage more closely, using the analysis given above.

6. The object of the sacrifice: Cleansing the heavenly sanctuary (vv. 23–24)

It is worth repeating the text:

> So it was necessary that the earthly copies of the heavenly realities should be cleansed by these means [the blood sacrifices and rituals just described]; but the heavenly realities themselves need to be cleansed by greater sacrifices than these. For Christ has not entered a sanctuary built by human hands as a model of the true sanctuary, but he has entered heaven itself, to appear there now before God, on our behalf.

As we saw above, the point of the sacrificial cleansing of the sanctuary by the high priest on the Day of Atonement was to enable the continued presence of God among his people. The author of Hebrews has already pointed out that the law itself undermines the effectiveness of this ritual. God was indeed present in the

---

45. See David deSilva, *Perseverance in Gratitude: A Socio-Rhetorical Commentary on the Epistle "to the Hebrews"* (Grand Rapids: Eerdmans, 2000).

46. Heb. 10:33–34; 13:3.

Most Holy Place at the heart of the tent of meeting, but he dwelt there in splendid isolation. There was no real meeting between God and his people. The true cleansing needed is that of the place where God truly dwells – not an earthly symbolic holy place, *a model of the true sanctuary*, but *heaven itself*. But the purpose of the cleansing is the same – to enable God's presence among his people, and thus our meeting with him.

So Jesus' *appearance before God* is the vital thing. He appears there of course as God's Son, but also crucially as our High Priest, an office which he bears because, though the Son of God, he is also *one of us*. As we saw, he cannot qualify for that job simply by being divine. Being *human* is the vital qualification. So his appearance – his dramatic entrance onto the stage of heaven – is *on our behalf*.

And that's all that matters! We could misunderstand *on our behalf* to mean that, having been admitted to the heavenly sanctuary, he now sets about persuading God to let us in, too.[47] That would be a grave misunderstanding. This is the point where the analogy with the patron-mediator-client relationships in Graeco-Roman culture breaks down. No, *by his very arrival* as our High Priest in the Most Holy Place of God's intimate presence, the deal is done, the deed is signed,[48] and our entrance is secure. Full, face-to-face fellowship between God and his sinful creation is now totally possible. Jesus by his sacrifice, has made complete *atonement* for us; that is, nothing that we have *done*, nothing that has *been done to us*, and nothing that we *are*, any longer has power to keep us out of God's presence. We storm the walls, in the wake of Christ.

Well, do we? How, and when, does our entrance take place? A widely-sung popular worship song associates it with our worship now, 'within the veil'.[49] This song picks up the imagery not just from Hebrews 9 but also, more particularly, from Hebrews 10:19–25, where the author starts to unpack the practical implications of the theology he has developed:

---

47. We might draw this implication from Heb. 7:24, where many translations say that he 'intercedes' for us in heaven: e.g. NIV, 'he is able to save completely those who come to God through him, because he always lives to intercede for them'. 'Intercession' usually implies asking God for something which might not be given. For this reason I translated this verb 'encounter' above, because it is simply his *meeting* with God which ensures our admittance too. 'Meet' or 'encounter' is a more basic meaning of the Greek verb *entynchanein*.

48. Or – to use Hebrews' own language – 'the covenant is ratified' (see 9:15–17).

49. By Ruth Dryden: copyright 1978 Genesis Music, Auburn, Australia. Published in the UK in *Mission Praise* (London: Marshall, Morgan & Scott, 1983).

So, my brothers, since we have freedom to enter the sanctuary by the blood of Jesus, which forms a brand new, living pathway for us through the veil, that is, through his flesh, and since we have a Great Priest over God's house, let us draw near with a true heart, in confidence and faith, with our hearts sprinkled clean from evil conscience and our bodies washed with pure water; let us not waver as we confess our hope, for the one who has promised is faithful! And let us take thought how to sharpen each other up for love and good works, not neglecting to meet together (the habit of some), but encouraging one another, and all the more as you see the Day drawing near.

Because of Jesus we have complete freedom to enter where he has gone before (v. 19). But that freedom to enter is still a hope we confess (v. 23), not a reality we practice. The great 'sinces' in verses 19 and 21 are not followed by 'let us, too, enter that Most Holy Place'. We are certainly gathering for worship (v. 25), but chiefly we are *making sure that we live the life of 'love and good works'* (v. 24) *appropriate for those who are looking forward to the 'Day' of entry.* The entry is timed, and we are standing in the queue clutching our tickets and waiting for the moment of admission to come. We are called now to 'draw near' (v. 22), not actually to enter – yet.[50]

The imagery in 10:22 adds a truly wonderful dimension to this drawing near. The symbolism of sprinkling and washing would certainly remind the readers of their baptism, but the language is actually drawn from Leviticus 8, so that discerning readers would be reminded of the ordination ceremonies prescribed for Aaron and his sons.[51] Following his ordination, Aaron supremely was equipped to 'draw near'.[52] So here's a remarkable development! Following the entry of our great High Priest into the Most Holy Place of God's presence, we are all now ordained as priests and called to draw near like Aaron and his sons – not to offer literal sacrifices, but 'the sacrifice of constant praise to God, the fruit of lips that confess the name of Jesus'.[53]

Priesthood was very busy in the Old Testament, with a constant round of sacrifices and ceremonies to perform. And so it is for us, too. We are not just

---

50. This verb ('draw near', Gk *proserchesthai*) has a strong association with worship, not only in Hebrews (used seven times: 4:16; 7:25; 10:1, 22; 11:6; 12:18, 22), but also in the Old Testament (e.g. Exod. 16:9; Lev. 9:5, 8; 21:17–18; Num. 16:40). It reminds us strongly that worship is *relational*; it's not about doing the right rituals or saying the right prayers, but about *coming close* to God.

51. See especially Lev. 8:6, 11–12.

52. See Lev. 9:7–8 where the same verb is used.

53. Heb. 13:15.

hanging around, as we wait for the Day of entry: 'Don't forget to do good and to practice fellowship, for with such sacrifices God is pleased.'[54] As we worship, and practice what pleases him – making the sacrifices of faith, like the heroes of Hebrews 11 – we are on holy ground, standing on the threshold of heaven itself, and ready to enter.

So when do we enter? That question is picked up in verses 27–28. But first:

7. The time of the sacrifice: The end of the ages (vv. 25–26)

The point of this is not so that Christ may offer himself frequently, like the high priest who entered the sanctuary annually, bearing blood not his own; for then Christ would have to have suffered many times since creation. No – he appeared once only, at the end of the ages, in order to do away with sin by the sacrifice of himself.

Suffered in verse 26 clearly means 'died', and this is basic to the argument here. It makes no sense to suggest that Christ could have died many times over: the very enormity of the sacrifice means that it has to be a one-off. He can only die once![55] As we saw above, the sacrifice Jesus makes includes his whole life of sacrificial discipleship and devotion to his Father, culminating in the gift of his body on the cross. This sacrifice is sufficient *to do away with sin* – literally to 'cancel' or 'annul' sin, in the same way as the new priesthood of Jesus 'annuls the pre-existing commandments, because they were weak and useless (for the law could make nothing perfect!), and brings in a greater hope by which we draw close to God'.[56]

As the author argues in 10:3, the old repeated sacrifices simply reminded people of their sin. No deliverance there! So with the cancellation of sin, that old sacrificial regime is cancelled also. A whole new priesthood founds for us a greater hope, because *sin* is truly dealt with.

Sin is whatever separates us from God who made us – whatever stops us from 'drawing close' to him. For the author of Hebrews, the essence of sin is *lack of faith*, illustrated by the wilderness generation who 'hardened their hearts'[57]

---

54. Heb. 13:16.

55. Luke Timothy Johnson makes this point: *Hebrews. A Commentary* (Louisville and London: Westminster John Knox Press, 2006), p. 244.

56. Heb. 7:18–19. The word translated 'cancel' or 'annul' (Gk *athetēsis*) is used only in these two places in Hebrews and nowhere else in the New Testament.

57. Heb. 3:8.

and refused to trust God to provide for them on their journey towards the promised 'rest'. 'They were not able to enter, because of their unbelief.'[58] Now, because Jesus has been accepted into the Most Holy Place *as one of us*, all that distance caused by sin has been abolished, and we can enter too – provided we persevere in the *faith* which is the opposite of sin.[59]

When the author says that Jesus offered himself *at the end of the ages* (v. 26), he has in mind the whole span of history reviewed earlier in the letter – essentially the whole span covered by the Old Testament, from creation[60] through the election of Abraham,[61] the appointment of Moses,[62] the wilderness wanderings,[63] the entry into the promised land under the leadership of Joshua,[64] the establishment of the cult,[65] and the prophetic promise of renewal.[66] The author has covered it all, viewing it through an interpretative lens alert to the ways in which it is a 'fragmentary and varied'[67] revelation of God, needing the further revelation in the Son to bring fulfilment and completion. So he has a strong sense in which Jesus brings in *the end of the ages* – the fulfilment of the promises, and the completion of the story. The Greek word for *end* is *synteleia*, which we have met before in Matthew 24:3, in the disciples' question to Jesus that prompted his eschatological discourse: 'Tell us, when will these things be, and what will be the sign of your *parousia* and of the end of the age?'

Matthew uses *synteleia* on four further occasions, always in the phrase 'the end of the age'.[68] Hebrews 9:26 gives us the only other New Testament occurrence of the word, also with 'age' attached but this time in the plural. The plural underlines the clear difference between Matthew and Hebrews. The

---

58. Heb. 3:19.

59. This is all beautifully illustrated and unpacked in Heb. 11:1 – 12:11.

60. Heb. 1:2.

61. Heb. 2:16; 6:13 – 7:10.

62. Heb. 3:1–6.

63. Heb. 3:7–19.

64. Heb. 4:1–11.

65. Heb. 5:1–10; 7:11–28.

66. Heb. 8:1–13.

67. Heb. 1:1. These first words of the letter (Gk *polymerōs kai polytropōs*) summarize the *dividedness* (many different parts across a huge time span) and *variedness* (many different genres and styles) of the old revelation, in contrast to the single new 'speaking' by God's Son.

68. Matt. 13:39, 40, 49; 28:20.

disciples were looking forward to 'the end of the age' as something ahead of them – the point at which (in line with usual Jewish expectation) God's kingdom would be fully ushered in and the world transformed by final judgment and salvation. Their question could be paraphrased, 'What will signal the end of *this* age?' But by using the plural, Hebrews locates the end of all 'ages' in Jesus Christ. All phases, processes and periods of human history reached their *telos*[69] when he *appeared once . . . to do away with sin* by the sacrifice of his body.

But time is still going. History was not obviously caught up into the story of Christ when he appeared. Why is this? There is something profound here that touches into our biblical theology of time. The future is held already in the past. The story that unfolds is the story already told, because it is the story of the Christ who has *already* entered the kingdom that is yet to be – or, in Hebrews' terms, of the Christ who has already fully cancelled all our sin, even though we still struggle against it[70] and must yet 'pursue holiness, without which no one will see the Lord'.[71] Yet the author can write, 'by his will we *have been* sanctified, once for all, through the offering of the body of Jesus Christ'.[72]

This fits perfectly with Augustine's view of both past and future as aspects of the present. But Hebrews makes the same point so much more beautifully and powerfully. Around the once-for-all sacrifice of Jesus, our merciful and faithful High Priest, gather the faith-filled sacrifices of all his people: both the great saints of the old covenant who, before he appeared, lived 'by faith' out of the promises not yet 'obtained';[73] and the saints of the present who make the same sacrifices of faith as they struggle to follow his example, 'looking to Jesus, the champion and perfecter of our faith'.[74] His once-for-all sacrifice makes all other sacrifices, both before and after, valid and meaningful and effective within the vast story of salvation.

And that brings us to the last two verses.

---

69. This is the root noun at the heart of the noun *synteleia*. It is the word used in Rom. 10:4, 'Christ is the end (*telos*) of the law . . .'. Both *telos* and *synteleia* combine the temporal with the purposive; both senses of 'end' in English.

70. Heb. 12:4.

71. Heb. 12:14.

72. Heb. 10:10.

73. See Heb. 11:39.

74. Heb. 12:2.

8. The climax of the sacrifice: The high priest appears for a second time (vv. 27–28)

And just as it is our human destiny to die once, and then to face judgment, so also Christ, sacrificed once to bear the sins of many, will appear for a second time, without sin, for those who are waiting for him, expecting salvation.

As noted briefly above, the author is alluding to the way in which the high priest on the Day of Atonement, having performed the ritual blood-sprinkling in the Most Holy Place of the tabernacle or temple, emerged to show the waiting crowds that the sacrifice had worked: he was still alive. And with the acceptance of the high priest, the whole people was assured of 'salvation'. This is the powerful image applied to the second coming of Jesus here.

We have a vivid and moving picture of what this reappearance meant for Israel, in Ben Sirach (Ecclesiasticus), which describes a Day of Atonement ceremony conducted by Simon son of Onias, high priest 220–195 BC. The description focuses on the last acts of the day:

> How gloriously he emerged from the house where the veil hung, to be applauded
> by the people standing outside! Like the morning star gleaming amongst the clouds,
> like the moon at its fullest, like the sun shining on the sanctuary of the Most High,
> and like the rainbow glowing among the clouds of God's glory . . .[75]

– and a further seven similes follow, giving a powerful impression of the beauty and power of the high priest as he emerges from the sanctuary to conduct the final sacrifice of the day. He makes the last drink offering, the priests shout, the trumpets sound, the choir sings, the people fall on their faces, and finally the high priest pronounces the blessing, actually speaking the divine name on this occasion only in the year.[76]

The author of Hebrews will certainly have known this description, although he does not obviously allude to it here. It helps us, however, recapture the feeling behind picturing the second coming in this way. We are in the crowd who are waiting for him. The whole of the rest of Hebrews helps us know what it means to wait for him in this way; it is not a passive hanging around, but a vigorous faith-filled striving to model our lives on his sacrifice, 'looking to Jesus'. We are not idle as we wait, but the real action is taking place out of our sight, in the

---

75. Ecclesiasticus 50:5–7.
76. Ecclesiasticus 50:8–21.

sanctuary, and is due to reach its climax when the door is flung wide and the high priest strides out, his sacrifice accepted.

This helps us understand why the author of Hebrews locates *the end of the ages* in the past, with Jesus' self-sacrifice when he appeared for the first time, at the beginning of this cosmic Day of Atonement (v. 26). *This is all one sacrificial work, taking place on one 'Day'!* It involves two 'appearings', one either side of the presentation of the sacrifice in the Most Holy Place. But it is one event, and we are actors in this single drama. Actually, we are fellow-priests (our author will say in 10:19–22, as we saw), standing on the very threshold of the sanctuary, and looking for the second appearance of our High Priest *as the signal that we too may enter*. This is a huge difference, of course: no-one but Simon could enter behind the veil when Ben Sirach described the scene. But now all that distance between God and his people has been overcome, and we 'have freedom' to follow Jesus 'our forerunner'[77] into that holy place.

This single-event insight helps us understand the main point that the author is making in these two verses, I think. He is drawing a fascinating comparison between human death and the death of Christ. Each of us dies but once, like Jesus. And then the immediate passage of each of us to judgment, after death, parallels the immediate movement of Christ from his sacrifice to his second appearance. *The parallel makes no sense unless the author thinks that both are essentially one event.* We die, and then are immediately at the judgment. Similarly Christ offers himself, and *within the same action* reappears, bringing salvation to the waiting crowd.

Within this Day of Atonement symbolism, the gap between the ascension and the second coming of Jesus has been collapsed. His *absence* is simply that required by the liturgy. His reappearance is certain, following the acceptance of his sacrifice in the Most Holy Place. And the analogy which the author of Hebrews uses shows that, for him, *the gap between our death and the final judgment is collapsed also.*

This is the clearest scriptural support for the view that, viewed from within the experience of the dying, there is no gap between death and judgment. We die, and are transported straight to the moment when Jesus comes again and the whole creation is renewed. Paul uses the metaphor of 'sleep' to describe the state of 'the dead in Christ', as we saw,[78] and if we interpret that image literally it might point in the same direction: sleep is a living unconsciousness, with no sense of the passage of time. Here in Hebrews, the author has undermined the

---

77. Heb. 10:19; 6:20.

78. 1 Thess. 4:13, 15.

significance of time altogether as a framework for evaluating the question, 'Where are the dead in Christ?' Time has been overthrown by the death and ascension of Jesus Christ, so that now the 'one-act' salvation he effects (one cosmic Day of Atonement) is paralleled by our 'one-act' movement through death to the final judgment and the renewal of all things.

We wondered whether this might be the case, when thinking about the 'home' in John 14:3 and whether it was appropriate to read that passage at funerals.[79] Here in Hebrews the author hints at something like this when he says of the heroes of faith that they all, 'even though so distinguished because of their faith, did not receive the promise, because God was looking forward to something greater, involving us – so that they might not reach perfection without us'.[80]

God's plan, he seems to say, is that we should all – the people of both old covenant and new – 'reach perfection' together. What a day that will be! I think that this is what Jesus offers to the dying thief beside him when, with one of his own last breaths, he says, 'Truly, I tell you, today you will be with me in Paradise.'[81] 'Paradise' is the Greek word used to describe the Garden of Eden,[82] also referred to as 'the Garden of God',[83] but nowhere else in Scripture is the word used as Jesus uses it in this wonderful offer from the cross.[84] Within our biblical theology, I think that we can interpret Jesus' offer in this way: he invites the dying thief not into some limbo state awaiting the final judgment, but into the glorious paradise of the new creation, the Eden of God's remade universe, immediately open to those who die 'with Christ'. Effectively, therefore, we are hearing that the moment of our death is the moment at which each of us experiences the *parousia* of the Lord Jesus, as he flings wide the door of the sanctuary and invites us in. At death we pass beyond time to that glorious moment when the powers are overthrown, judgment is executed and all is made new by the powerful word of the returning Son of Man.

This helps us understand the strangeness we met in 1 Thessalonians 4, where the 'dead in Christ' both come with him, and rise to meet him.[85] From our perspective, they are still part of our world, their bodies laid to rest in the ground.

---

79. Above, p. 164.

80. Heb. 11:39–40.

81. Luke 23:43.

82. E.g. Gen. 2:8–10.

83. E.g. Ezek. 31:8–9.

84. The closest parallel is in 2 Cor. 12:4, where Paul mentions a vision which involved being 'caught up' to paradise, also described there as 'the third heaven'. Cf. also Rev. 2:7.

85. 1 Thess. 4:14, 16.

From *their* perspective, they are already part of the victorious remade universe under Christ the Lord. The 'coming' is the moment of intersection between the two, when the *kairos* of the new intersects with the *chronos* of the old.

This means that those who die in Christ do not experience separation from their loved ones, because they are immediately one with them and with Christ in the new creation. There is no waiting. The waiting is for us, who remain, who stay within *chronos* and are not whipped away to the *kairos* of the New Jerusalem. It seems strange to think that my mother, who died in 2010, already (at this moment) experiences me in my resurrected and glorified state. But then expressions like 'already' or 'at this moment' are completely meaningless in this statement, because no kind of time embraces her experience and mine within one framework. Her *kairos* is no longer part of my *chronos*.[86]

We inevitably imagine the End (the second coming) as an event in time: the next thing, after the thing that immediately precedes it, whatever that might be. But it is not. The second coming is the moment when *chronos* finally yields to the glorious *kairos* of God's new creation, and *the judgment* occurs. We've seen enough to know what this is – the transformation of the world under the word of the Judge, and the true telling of the story of every life, leading either to life with Christ or to death apart from him. The statement in Hebrews 9:27 (*it is our human destiny to die once, and then to face judgment*) applies to all human beings.

But for now, we wait outside the sanctuary. For us, Jesus' movement from entry to exit feels anything but instantaneous. Every further moment of delay reinforces the question: Is he really coming out again? Just like the worshippers of old. Is this the year when Simon messes up the sacrifice, fails to cover his own sin and Israel's adequately, and meets his end in there? 'Our God is a consuming fire . . .'[87] – we cannot mess with him! The waiting crowd faced the challenge of *waiting well* – trusting their high priest to perform the sacrifice correctly. And so also do we: the challenge of living well in the meantime, until he appears; not allowing the passage of time to undermine the vigour of our expectation, and keeping alive the sacrificial faithfulness that connects his priestly story, and ours.

And that takes us very nicely on to our next port of call, 2 Peter 3, where the emphasis falls on *how to prepare*.

----

86. Interestingly, Paul Davies explains how, because of relativity, it is also impossible to speak of events happening 'at the same time' across a huge spatial divide (e.g. *About Time: Einstein's Unfinished Revolution* [London, etc.: Viking, 1995], pp. 70–72: 'simultaneity, like motion, is relative').

87. Heb. 12:29, quoting Deut. 4:24; a basic biblical principle in the relationship of God with sin.

13. BE PREPARED! (2 PETER 3:1–18)

1. Introduction

Our self-imposed brief was to avoid general biblical eschatology and focus on passages touching on the second coming. This passage just scrapes in because of the reference to the *parousia* in the sceptics' mocking question in verse 4: *Where is the promise of his* parousia? In context, this must be the *parousia* of Jesus. Apart from this, 2 Peter 3 is about *the day of judgment* (v. 7), *the Day of the Lord* (v. 10), and *the Day of God* (v. 12), and without the *parousia* reference we would have to leave the passage regretfully aside. How great that we can include it! Here we see the *cosmic scope* of the second coming more clearly than anywhere else (apart from Rev. 19).

There are many interesting questions surrounding this passage: most notably its authorship (is it really by Peter?), its relationship to 1 Peter, and its relationship to Jude (for there are many overlaps in language between 2 Peter and Jude). Fortunately, we do not need to address any of these questions in order to hear clearly what the author (I'm going to call him Peter) says about the *parousia*. In 2 Peter 3 the overlaps with Jude are only slight.

Peter's main concern in the letter has been to prepare and strengthen the readers to cope with the false teaching which he knows they will face.[1] The long

---

1. See e.g. 2 Pet. 2:1.

central section (2:1–22) is an extended denunciation of these false teachers. Chapter 1 prepares for this by emphasizing two themes: (1) the vital necessity of godly character as a protection against corruption (1:3–11) and (2) 'the prophetic word' as the vital means of being 'established in the truth' (1:12–21). These themes both continue into chapter 3, as we will see. For Peter, 'the prophetic word' has both Old Testament and New Testament versions, and we will see this also in chapter 3.

In many ways this passage is unique, but we also see many connections with our overall biblical theology of the second coming. Here too we meet a theology of time, and of expectation, and of hope; the connection between the second coming and judgment, and the restoration and recreation of the whole *cosmos*; the suddenness and unexpectedness of it, and our need therefore to be ready, living lives of repentance and holiness. So 2 Peter 3 serves to begin to pull our biblical theology together, before our final excursion into Revelation.

There are many interesting points of detail in the exegesis of this passage, which I pass over in what follows, in order to concentrate on the main thrust of Peter's message.[2]

2. Structure

The passage has an interesting and quite complex structure. It begins and ends (vv. 1–2 // vv. 15b–16) with reference to the prophetic word which is the foundation for our lives now. In verse 2 Peter urges his readers *to remember the words spoken beforehand by the holy prophets, and the command of our Lord and Saviour given by your apostles*. Here the *prophets* are almost certainly the Old Testament prophets (as in 1:19–21); throughout this passage, Peter alludes to Old Testament prophecies, as we will see.

This emphasis on 'living by the word' is then picked up by a balancing reference at the end of the passage to *Paul*. Paul exemplifies the apostles who pass on the teaching of Jesus (v. 2). His writings may be tough to understand in places, says Peter, and can be *twisted* by the *ignorant and unstable* (v. 16), but he wants his readers to hear what Paul writes about *the patience of the Lord* and about *these things* generally – i.e., about the last things. *He talks about these things in all his letters* (v. 16) is an interesting comment on the significance of eschatology in Paul's writings.

---

2. Decisions about some of these details have affected my translation at several points. The best guide to all the detail is undoubtedly the Word commentary by Richard Bauckham, *Jude, 2 Peter*, Word Biblical Commentary 50 (Waco: Word, 1983).

These references to the prophetic and apostolic teaching bracket the whole passage:

A   Really think about the prophetic and apostolic teaching! (vv. 1–2)
    B   What not to be: sceptical and scoffing about the *parousia* (vv. 3–4)
        C   What the scoffers willingly forget: God's judgment (vv. 5–7)
            D   What we mustn't forget: God's patience (vv. 8–10)
        C' What we must willingly prepare for: God's promise
            (vv. 11–13)
    B' What to be (rather than scoffing): spotless, relying on God's
        patience (vv. 14–15a)
A' Really think about Paul! (vv. 15b–16)
E   Armed with foreknowledge, watch out for yourselves and grow in
    grace vv. 17–18

The three C–D–C' paragraphs all contain a powerful statement about *the Day*, in the second half of each paragraph (vv. 7, 10, 12b–13), bolstering the particular focus in each case. The D paragraph gives the key focus, introduced by the emphatic *Don't you forget this one thing*. The final paragraph (E) signs off the whole letter, but looks back in particular over this final chapter.

We will take each of the paragraphs in turn, starting with *the scoffers*.

3. What not to be: Sceptical and scoffing about the *parousia* (vv. 3–4)

First of all you must know this: in the last days scoffers will come, scoffing, impelled by their own desires, and saying 'Where is the promise of his coming? From the day the fathers fell asleep, everything has stayed just as it is now, from the beginning of creation!'

There is deep irony here: the *scoffers* deny the reality of the *parousia*, but their coming has been predicted as evidence that we are now *in the last days*. Far from undermining faith in the *parousia*, they strengthen it for those who listen to the prophets and the apostles of Jesus!

What prophecies or sayings does Peter have in mind? There are similar references to scoffers in Jeremiah and Ezekiel, in both cases expressing scepticism about the fulfilment of prophetic predictions.[3] But Peter is probably thinking of specific prophecies like that predicting the 'false prophets' who will 'seek to

---

3. See Jer. 17:15; Ezek. 12:22.

deceive, if possible, the elect'.[4] This may underlie his whole concern with false teaching – in 2:1 he uses the same expression ('false prophets') as in Mark 13:22. As we saw, this prophecy lies behind Paul's concern for the Thessalonians, who might also be 'deceived'.[5] These are the scoffers whose scepticism might infect believers.

Peter's concern is so up to date! We live in an age when faith in the second coming of Jesus puts you straight into the lunatic fringe, along with exponents of extraterrestrial walk-ins, Heaven's Gate devotees, Star Trek groupies and New Age magic crystals. The dominant secular humanist culture in Western societies groups all such 'faiths' together and regards them as incompatible with a 'scientific' world view. In his swingeing attack on all religious faith, Richard Dawkins reserves special criticism for 'American "rapture" Christians' who would welcome a nuclear Armageddon because it will hasten the second coming.[6] For him, evolutionary humanism dispenses with all gods in favour of a world view which says something very similar to Peter's sceptics: from the moment of the Big Bang, *everything has stayed just as it is now*, and will continue to do so as the evolutionary process unfolds.

The problem is, everything has *not* continued *just as it is now*. The evolutionary story actually tells a tale of constant upset and disaster afflicting planet Earth. Bill McGuire's powerful book *Apocalypse*[7] not only attests the way in which the Greek title of the book of Revelation has become a cipher for world-shattering disasters, but also explodes all confidence that this old world will continue *just as it is now*. Volcanos, tsumani and extreme weather events have constantly made us human beings feel insecure on our planet. In particular, a massive asteroid strike, which could seriously degrade the planet or even make it uninhabitable, is not just possible but *inevitable*, given enough time. The Chicxulub impact wiped out the dinosaurs 65 million years ago. If the Hale-Bopp comet, which passed the sun in 1997, had collided with earth, the explosion on impact would have been much, much greater.[8] All of these extreme planetary events serve

---

4. Mark 13:22.

5. 2 Thess. 2:3, 9–10.

6. Richard Dawkins, *The God Delusion* (London: Transworld Publishers, 2006), p. 341.

7. Bill McGuire, *Apocalypse: A Natural History of Global Disasters* (London: Cassell, 1999).

8. Forty-four times greater, according to the estimate by Paul Weissmann cited in the Wikipedia article on the Hale-Bopp comet (Paul R. Weissman, 'The Cometary Impactor Flux at the Earth', *Proceedings of the International Astronomical Union* 2 [2007], pp. 441–450).

in the Bible as *symbols* of the ultimate extreme event which will impact life on earth, the *parousia* of Jesus Christ.

4. What the scoffers willingly forget: God's judgment (vv. 5–7)

For they willingly forget this, that of old there were heavens, and an earth, formed from water and through water, by the word of God; and by water and God's word the then world was destroyed by a flood. The present heavens and earth are being stored up by the same word for fire, kept for the day of judgment and destruction of the ungodly.

The Bible recognizes what a contemporary evolutionary perspective has confirmed – this world is an insecure place. There has been a massive flood that wiped out all life on earth,[9] heralding (says Peter) another massive destruction by fire. But the evolutionary picture sees us as random victims of random cataclysms. Peter's picture is that it all happens *by the word of God*. God's word is mentioned in all three verses here – as the agent of creation (v. 5), of the destruction by flood when only Noah was saved (v. 6), and of the final judgment by fire (v. 7). The word by which Peter wants his readers to live[10] is no mere sacred book or inspired prophetic utterance: this is the powerful word that calls the cosmos into being and then destroys it. To live by *that* word is to be in the ultimate safe place.

Peter uses *fire* as his particular image for *the day of judgment* here. He will unpack this *fire* in more detail in verses 10 and 12. There was an ancient tradition, possibly reflected here, that the world is subjected to 'recurrent destructions by flood and fire alternately',[11] although for Peter there are just two judgments, the Genesis flood, and the fire for which the cosmos has been *kept*. He is probably influenced by prophetic texts like Deuteronomy 32:22:

For a fire has been kindled by my wrath,
    one that burns to the realm of death below.
It will devour the earth and its harvests
    and set afire the foundations of the mountains.[12]

---

9. Gen. 7:20–23.

10. Especially 3:1–2; cf. 1:16–21.

11. See Bauckham, *Jude, 2 Peter,* p. 301, where the evidence is set out.

12. NIV, 1984. Deut. 32, as we've seen, is a passage full of hope of restoration.

Peter uses two unexpected words here for the present position of the cosmos in relation to this coming judgment: it is being *stored up* as if in a treasury,[13] and *kept* as if being protected.[14] Both words are normally used of good things, although Paul uses *thēsaurizein* of 'storing up wrath' for the day of judgment in Romans 2:5. But here it is *the heavens and earth* themselves which are being *stored up* and *protected*. Why these words, when destruction is coming? Maybe Peter is influenced by the underlying thought that *the destruction of the ungodly* is actually good for the planet. Whereas the 'cosmos' is destroyed by the flood in verse 7, it is not the cosmos but *the ungodly* who are destroyed in verse 8.[15]

This keys into a hot topic in the interpretation of this passage. Scholars are divided between those who argue that Peter expects the *destruction* of the present cosmos, and those who believe that Peter expects its *cleansing* and *renewal*.[16] This is especially significant for the next two sections.

5. What we mustn't forget: God's patience (vv. 8–10)

Don't you forget this one thing, dear friends, that one day with the Lord is as a thousand years, and a thousand years as one day. The Lord is not slow in keeping his promise, as some consider slowness, but he is being patient towards you, not wanting any to be destroyed, but all to come to repentance. But the Day of the Lord will come like a thief, and the heavens will pass away with a crackling roar, the heavenly bodies will burn and dissolve, and the earth and all its works will be laid bare to view.

Scholarly interest focuses around verse 10, of course, in order to work out exactly what Peter is saying about the heavens and the earth at the *parousia*. Is this destruction or renewal? But Peter's own interest rests chiefly in verses 8–9, I think, as he pursues his emphasis on the *present impact* on our lives of living by the word of God. God's word makes it clear, he says, that God has a very

---

13. Gk *thēsaurizein*.
14. Gk *tēroun*. Cf. 2:9, where Peter writes about the 'wicked' being 'kept for the day of judgment' (same word).
15. The same Greek root is used in both cases: *apolousthai* / *apōleia*, to destroy / destruction.
16. For a full review of options, see Jonathan Moo, 'Continuity, Discontinuity and Hope: The Contribution of New Testament Eschatology to a Distinctively Christian Environmental Ethos', *Tyndale Bulletin* 61.1 (2010), pp. 21–44, esp. pp. 30–38.

different relationship to time. Peter has Psalm 90 in view here! God is not bound to the slow passage of time, as we are, and in any case his *slowness* is actually *patience*. In all likelihood, Peter also has in mind the passage which we met when looking at Luke 18:7[17] – Ecclesiasticus 35:19. He uses the same verb[18] to make the same point, that God does not delay, but acts with 'patience' towards people. In the last part of verse 9 Peter may even be echoing the teaching of Paul in 1 Timothy 2:4. Paul too is a source of the *word of God* by which we must live, as Peter will say in verse 16.

So although the *day of judgment* is about *the destruction of the ungodly* (v. 7), God does not want anyone to be in that position when the day comes – hence the patience. In the phrase *not wanting* (v. 9), Peter uses a verb which suggests planning and intention, rather than just wish or desire:[19] by being patient God *acts* to achieve his plan that 'all might be saved and come to a knowledge of the truth', as Paul puts it.[20] Interestingly, the Bible will not let us presume that God's plan will succeed in every case, even though it is God who is 'planning'. Peter does not shrink from talking about *the destruction of the ungodly* as though there will still be those who persist in their 'refusal to worship',[21] in spite of God's plan.

However patience is not endless. The Day will come *like a thief*. 'Thief' is a strange image to use for the Day, because nothing will be stolen – far from it. We need the background in Jesus' use of this image to know that the point is the *suddenness and unpredictability* of the thief's arrival.[22] Here too Peter shows how the prophetic teaching underlies what he writes.

There then follow three descriptions of the impact of the Day:

- *the heavens will pass away with a crackling roar,*
- *the heavenly bodies will burn and dissolve,*
- *and the earth and all its works will be laid bare to view.*

Let's deal with some of the details here, and then try to understand exactly what Peter is saying.

---

17. See above, p. 130.

18. Gk *makrothymein*.

19. Gk *boulesthai*.

20. 1 Tim. 2:4.

21. The word translated *ungodly* (Gk *asebēs*) means 'irreligious, not worshipping'.

22. Matt. 24:43–44; also Luke 12:39–40. We saw how Paul uses it in 1 Thess. 5:2, 4. It appears also in Rev. 3:3 and 16:15, as we will see.

The verb *pass away*[23] is the one used in Mark 13:31, 'heaven and earth will pass away, but my words will not pass away'. Adams is probably right: Jesus is not just engaging in rhetoric here, claiming that his teaching is more durable than the most solid and durable thing imaginable (heaven and earth). Jesus is expressing his conviction (shared with all those listening) that one day heaven and earth *will* pass away – but at that point his teaching will endure.[24] Peter is probably reflecting that belief also.

The phrase *the heavenly bodies* is translated 'the elements' in several of the main versions,[25] reflecting the belief that Peter is influenced by Stoic ideas here. This word (Gk *stoicheia*) was used by Stoic philosophers to refer to the four 'elements': earth, air, fire and water. They believed too that the world would eventually be destroyed by fire. Adams argues strongly for the influence of this Stoic background on 2 Peter.[26] But as we have seen, Peter is actually very concerned to root what he writes (and his readers' faith) in the prophetic word. It is unlikely that he would suddenly base his teaching on Stoic cosmology. From the second century onwards, *stoicheia* was regularly used to refer to the heavenly bodies (sun, moon and stars), and most commentators understand it in this sense here, too,[27] not least because it fits so well with the picture in Isaiah 34:4. In one of the Greek versions of Isaiah, this verse is translated 'all the powers of the heavens shall melt', using the same word ('melt') that Peter uses in his second reference to the *stoicheia* in verse 12.

So it seems that Peter is influenced by Isaiah in what he writes here. 'All the host of heaven shall rot away, and the skies roll up like a scroll'[28] – a passage which is actually about the judgment coming upon Edom (and which uses 'fire' as an image for this judgment, as the oracle develops[29]). The *stoicheia* are the heavenly bodies which sit between the *heavens* and the *earth*, so there is a nice sequence through Peter's three descriptions.

---

23. Gk *parerchesthai*.

24. Edward Adams, *The Stars Will Fall from Heaven: Cosmic Catastrophe in the New Testament and its World*, Library of New Testament Studies (London: T&T Clark, 2007), pp. 161–164.

25. E.g. NIV (1984, 2011), NRSV, REB, JB.

26. Adams, *Stars Will Fall*, pp. 216–229.

27. So Bauckham, *Jude, 2 Peter*, pp. 303, 316; Moo, 'Continuity', pp. 33–34; J. N. D. Kelly, *The Epistles of Peter and of Jude*, Black's NT Commentary (London: A&C Black, 1969), p. 364; Charles Bigg, *The Epistles of St Peter and St Jude*, International Critical Commentary (Edinburgh: T&T Clark, 1910), pp. 296–297.

28. Isa. 34:4.

29. Isa. 34:9–10.

So what is Peter saying here? The clue, I think, is in the third description, *the earth and all its works will be laid bare to view.* This line sits in parallel to the last line of the previous section, *kept for the day of judgment and destruction of the ungodly* (v. 7). There, we noted the surprise that Peter doesn't re-emphasize *the destruction of the cosmos* from verse 6, but makes it clear that this judgment is all about destroying *the ungodly.* So also here, the cosmic destruction is suddenly personalized. *All its works* is literally 'all the works in it', i.e., everything *done* on the earth will be exposed. This is about the uncovering of everything before God, being laid bare before his judgment, as Jesus said: 'Nothing is covered that will not be revealed, and hidden that will not be made known.'[30]

The essence of judgment is God's total knowledge of every *work.* Of course, he knows everything already, so the difference in this eschatological 'laying bare' is that it is *public.* Everything is laid bare, not just to God's eyes but to the eyes of all, so that all can see the truth, hear the judgment and know that full justice has been done.

I think that this is sufficiently radical a change in the way things are to make the 'cosmic collapse' language in verse 8–9 appropriate, without any need to take it literally. The whole order of things needs to change, for all *the works done* in the earth to be laid bare for all to see, and for God to judge publicly. There is plenty of scriptural precedent for such language being used of earth-shattering changes like this, as we have seen.[31]

The next paragraph, however, suggests more.

6. What we must willingly prepare for: God's promise (vv. 11–13)

Since everything is to be dissolved in this way, what sort of people should you be? People engaged in holy lifestyles, godly, looking forward to and hastening the coming of the Day of God by which the heavens will be dissolved in fire, and the heavenly bodies [stoicheia] will burn and melt. 'New heavens and a new earth', as he has promised – that's what we expect! – in which righteousness will dwell.

Peter longs for his readers to feel the impact of this expectation *in the present.* This future-as-present will have a transforming effect on our lives, if we truly embrace it. And, as this little paragraph develops, it becomes clear that *since*

---

30. Matt. 10:26; Luke 12:2.

31. We noticed Deut. 32:22 above, which might have influenced Peter's language here – and where a massive conflagration which 'sets on fire the foundations of the mountains' is a picture of God's coming judgment on Israel.

everything is to be dissolved in this way means more than just 'since the world is going
to be turned upside-down and all the secrets are going to come pouring out
into the light of day'. There's a whole new world a-coming, *new heavens and a new
earth*, in line with the prophetic promise in Isaiah[32] – a world *in which righteousness
dwells* and for which therefore we must prepare now by living lives that match
that home-yet-to-be.

This expectation of *new heavens and a new earth* tells us to read the 'destruction'
language in verse 10 more literally. The dissolving of the heavenly bodies, we
now discover, is not just apocalyptic language for something world-changing
afoot. We're talking total makeover here! – the dissolution, 'passing-away', of *the
present heavens and earth* (v. 7), to be replaced by a new creation. The exposure of
all earth's *works* to divine scrutiny and judgment (v. 10) is but the preliminary to
this total renewal. In Isaiah 65:17, to which Peter refers, the special verb *bārā'*,
to create, is used, which is 'used in the Old Testament only of divine action, to
express those acts which by their greatness or newness (or both) require a divine
agent'.[33] God will step in, in creative action parallel to the creation of the first
heavens and earth. As Motyer comments, '*heavens* and *earth* represent the totality
of things, as in Genesis 1:1.'[34]

The Day of God arrives, and *because of this*[35] the present heavens and earth bow
out, to be replaced by the new ones.[36] It is pretty much beside the point to
debate whether or not Peter envisages the total destruction of the present
cosmos or merely its cleansing and renewal. The answer, of course, is both –
because the renewal is so total that nothing less than 'new creation' can properly
describe it. So we can agree with Adams that 'the writer of 2 Peter has expressed
as clearly as he could that the existing cosmos is to be destroyed',[37] and also
(with Moo) that 'though both heaven and earth are "reserved for fire", the
purpose of this fire is expressly stated to be . . . to do away with *human* evil'.[38]

Both perspectives are true, because *we* are the connection between the old
world and the new; we who now *expect* and *hasten* (v. 12) the coming of the Day,

---

32. Isa. 65:17; 66:22.

33. J. A. Motyer, *The Prophecy of Isaiah* (Leicester: Inter-Varsity Press, 1993), p. 66.

34. Ibid., p. 529.

35. Notice 'by which' in the translation above. The Greek preposition *dia* means 'by'
    or 'because of' here.

36. We will come back to this in the next chapter on Revelation, where the final vision
    of the 'new heaven and new earth' draws much on Isa. 65 and 66.

37. Adams, *Stars Will Fall*, p. 254.

38. Moo, 'Continuity', p. 35, his emphasis.

so that the ungodly may be destroyed, and the new cosmos be created *where righteousness dwells* (v. 13). We long for it! *Hasten* does not mean that we can make it come faster by wanting it harder, but points simply to the intensity of the longing that lies behind the prayer 'Come, Lord Jesus! Don't delay!'

7. What to be (rather than scoffing): Spotless, relying on God's patience (vv. 14–18)

> *Therefore, dear friends, as you expect all this, work with passion to appear before him spotless and blameless in peace, and regard our Lord's patience as salvation, as also our dear brother Paul has written to you, out of the wisdom God gave him . . .* (vv. 14–15).

We come back to the underlying point that motivates Peter throughout this chapter. He does not want his readers to be taken in by the *scoffers*, who dispute the prophetic word of promise (v. 4) and whose ungodliness will lead to their destruction on the Day. Rather, he wants them to prepare passionately for the coming of the Lord, regarding the delay not as a problem but as an opportunity. His *patience* is *salvation* – i.e., an opportunity for salvation, both for themselves and for others.[39]

To appear before him (v. 14): Peter uses the same word as used in verse 10 for the 'laying bare' of the works done in the earth. We too – our *works* – will appear before the Lord. Peter wants us to be *spotless and blameless* on that Day, but how can that be achieved? This is where Peter's signing-off at the end of the chapter is so vital. It is not a throwaway final encouragement:

> *So take care of yourselves, dear friends, since you know all this in advance. Take care not to be led astray by the deception of the lawless and lose your own confidence. Grow in the grace and knowledge of our Lord and Saviour Jesus Christ: to him be glory both now and on the day when the new age dawns! Amen* (vv. 17–18).

This is the only explicit mention of Jesus Christ in 2 Peter 3, although he is certainly the *Lord* whose Day will come *like a thief* (v. 10). Only the Lord who is the *Saviour* can keep us safe, by his *grace*, from *the deception of the lawless*.[40] Apart

---

39. Peter probably has Rom. 2:4 in mind in his reference to Paul.

40. 'The lawless' here is a different Greek word from Paul's 'the lawless one' in 2 Thess. 2:8, but it might still draw on the same tradition of the battle between truth and 'lawlessness' which will be decisively won when the Lord's day dawns.

from him we are thrown on the resource of our own capacity to generate *works* of spotlessness and blamelessness. That is no basis for *confidence*! But *the grace and knowledge of our Lord Jesus Christ* will enable our confidence before the day of judgment to be strong, and peaceful. We need not worry.

The final doxology, *to him be glory* . . . picks up the thought that it is the *ungodly* who are destroyed at the End – those who do not *worship*. Worship *now* fore-shadows worship *when the new age dawns* and is basic to that confidence in Jesus the Saviour whose grace will bring us home.

Now for the final treat! We turn to the book of Revelation, which bubbles with this spirit of worship.

14. 'SEE, I AM COMING SOON!' (REVELATION 19:11–16)

We reach the last stage of our journey with the book of Revelation – a wonderfully appropriate place to land up. Not only does Revelation round off Scripture for us, but it ends with a passionate prayer for the second coming: 'Yes indeed, come, Lord Jesus!'[1] As we will see, that prayer is no throwaway last line, but fits beautifully into the structure of the whole book. This glorious book – so powerful and so fought over in the history of interpretation – makes a good claim to be the most 'eschatological' book in the Bible, in the sense that here, possibly more clearly than anywhere else, we bump into the reality of the world's ultimate accountability to God.

This does not mean that it is all 'about' the End. Far from it, in fact. It is 'about' the world and God's lordship over it in and through Jesus Christ, the Lamb of God. And the vital endpoint of that lordship – as we've seen already in Daniel, and in Paul, and could have seen in many other places also – is the renewal of all creation as the world is rescued from the other 'lords' who have tried to grab it from its rightful King.

Interestingly, once again, the second coming of Jesus actually plays a surprisingly minor role in this big vision, though nonetheless vital – as we'll see. Our agenda in this chapter is (a) to have an end-to-end look at the second coming

---

1. Rev. 22:20.

in Revelation, which will lead into (b) some reflections on the overall structure of the book, so that (c) we can then look with understanding at 19:11–16, which is the 'best bet' for a visionary description of the second coming itself.

The fact that 19:11–16 might *not* be a picture of the second coming (we'll think about that when we get there) arises from the amazing apocalyptic language of Revelation. When the veil that separates matter, space and time from God, 'heaven' and eternity is drawn back – and that's what Revelation does[2] – then finally apocalyptic language is the only appropriate medium in which to express the truth that emerges. We can only grasp the amazing reality of God through vivid pictures that break the boundaries of 'normal' perception and touch us at a deep level emotionally and imaginatively, as well as cognitively. As we saw with Psalm 18 and other passages, we have to handle this apocalyptic language with great sensitivity.

1. A quick Revelation overview: 'I am coming soon!'

The starting point for a study of the second coming in Revelation has to be the remarkable description of God in the opening greeting:

> John to the seven churches in Asia: grace to you and peace, from the one who is, and who was, *and who is coming*, and from the seven spirits which are before his throne, and from Jesus Christ, the witness, the faithful one, the firstborn from the dead . . .[3]

God is 'the coming one' – a description which probably looks back to Exodus 3, where God reveals himself to Moses as 'the one who is' (the first element of the description here),[4] tells Moses that he is 'the God of your father, the God of Abraham, and the God of Isaac, and the God of Jacob'[5] (the one who *was*), and says 'I have come down to deliver you from the hand of the Egyptians . . .'[6] (the 'coming one'). So 'coming' here has the flavour of 'coming to save', and at the same time we are reminded that, when the Lord comes to save his people,

---

2. The Greek word for revelation (*apokalypsis*) – the title of the book – means 'uncovering', with the connotation of drawing back a veil that hides a reality not normally seen.

3. Rev. 1:4–5.

4. Exod. 3:14.

5. Exod. 3:6.

6. Exod. 3:8.

he often sends others to spearhead the work, as with Moses in Exodus 3. That thought leads straight into the little doxology that follows the greeting:

> To him who loved us and freed us from our sins by his blood, and made us a kingdom, priests for his God and Father, to him be the glory and the power to all ages. Amen![7]

Jesus is the one who has done the rescuing, on behalf of his Father. Immediately we hear of *his* 'coming':

> Behold, he comes with the clouds, and every eye shall see him, and all who pierced him, and all the tribes of the earth shall mourn because of him. Yes, Amen![8]

We are on familiar territory! Daniel 7:13 lies behind the first words here, pointing (in this case) to Jesus' second coming, rather than his first – an impression confirmed by the other allusions here, to Zechariah 12:10 and to Genesis 12:3.[9] So his work of rescuing and redeeming – through his blood – is summed up in his fulfilment of the Daniel 7 vision of the Son of Man who overthrows all other powers and reigns on behalf of his Father. John hints at the centrality of the cross in this process by referring to Jesus' being 'pierced', and suggests that the whole world will 'mourn' in repentance for rejecting him.

Then the opening description of God is repeated as God himself speaks, adding an absolute divine assurance that the Son of Man will truly come as promised:

> 'I am the Alpha and the Omega', says the Lord God, the one who is and who was and who is coming, the Almighty.[10]

So we notice a very close connection between the 'coming' of the Lord God and the coming of Jesus. In fact, it seems as though God comes *in* the coming

---

7. Rev. 1:5–6.

8. Rev. 1:7.

9. From Zech. 12 comes 'shall see', the 'piercing' and the 'mourning'. From Gen. 12 comes the phrase 'all the tribes of the earth' (also Gen. 28:14). This beautifully illustrates the complexity and subtlety of Revelation's use of the Old Testament, where we often find Old Testament passages being creatively combined within the visions. Here the allusion to Gen. 12 quietly reminds us that God's concern with 'all the tribes of the earth' is first and foremost in order to *bless* them.

10. Rev. 1:8.

of his Son, who redeems us by his blood and then comes on the clouds in glory.
This is confirmed a few verses later where it is the risen Jesus Christ who says
to John,

> Don't be afraid! I am the first and the last, and the living one: and I was dead, and
> behold I am living for ever and ever and ever![11]

'The first and the last' is equivalent to 'the Alpha and the Omega' in verse 7,
the first and last letters of the Greek alphabet – two images suggesting the way
in which both God and the risen Christ bookend the whole of existence. Our
minds jump to the end of the book, where there are two equivalent statements,
also spoken in turn by God and by Jesus. First God says,

> 'It is accomplished! I am the Alpha and the Omega, the beginning and the end. And I,
> yes, I, will give to the thirsty from the spring of the water of life, free of charge!'[12]

And then Jesus says,

> 'Behold I am coming quickly, and my reward is with me, to give to all what their work
> deserves. I am the Alpha and the Omega, the first and the last, the beginning and the
> end!'[13]

The final statement picks up all the forms in which this 'ultimacy' of God and
of Christ is expressed. And we notice how the associated themes also have a
pattern: *coming* (1:8), *life* (1:17–18), *life* (21:6), *coming* (22:12–13). So the coming
of Jesus Christ is tied to the coming of God to give life to his world, and his
coming is double: he comes to die, and he comes in glory.

In fact Revelation 22:12 is the sixth of seven occasions when Jesus says 'I
am coming' in the book:[14]

---

11. Rev. 1:17–18.
12. Rev. 21:6.
13. Rev. 22:12–13.
14. This is not the only instance of something which occurs seven times in Revelation
    (or indeed, a multiple of seven). There are many numbered 'sevens' but also many
    non-numbered as well, including some apparently incidental features in the text. In
    addition to the seven 'I am comings', there are seven four-element descriptions of
    all humanity (e.g. 5:9, 'every tribe and language and people and nation'), differently
    worded each time; seven beatitudes (e.g. 1:3); seven 'Lord God the Almighty'

- 'I am coming to you' (to the church in Ephesus) (2:5).
- 'I am coming to you quickly' (to the church in Pergamum) (2:16).
- 'I am coming quickly' (3:11).
- 'Behold, I am coming like a thief' (16:15).
- 'Behold, I am coming quickly' (22:7).
- 'Behold, I am coming quickly' (22:12).
- 'Yes! I am coming quickly' (22:20).

And the last is then followed by John's own prayer, to round off the book: 'Amen! Come, Lord Jesus!' We notice the pattern here – three in the opening seven letters, one in the main body of the book, and three at the end in the concluding section (22:6–21) after the end of the vision. Actually this reflects the fact that surprisingly, in the main vision account which constitutes the heart of the book,[15] Jesus himself does not speak. He speaks at the beginning, in the seven letters (chs. 2 – 3), and at the end (22:6–16), but not in between – except, of course, for the tiny voice which interposes between the sixth and the seventh 'bowl' visions:

'Behold, I am coming like a thief. Blessed are those who stay awake, and keep their clothes safe, so that they may not be publicly exposed and shamed in front of people!'[16]

So this is a very precious moment – the only point in the main vision where we hear the voice of the risen Jesus. His hiddenness in the vision seems to match what he says here: when he comes, it will be like a thief, with no warning, and so we need to make sure we are ready at all times.[17]

(e.g. 1:8), and seven descriptions of God 'who sits on the throne' (e.g. 4:9); the term 'Messiah' occurs seven times, as do references to the altar in the heavenly temple (e.g. 6:9) – etc. The description of Jesus as 'the Lamb' occurs twenty-eight times – seven times four. This all confirms to me that the seven 'I am comings', and their position in the book, are part of the deliberate *construction* of Revelation, evidence of what Richard Bauckham calls John's 'meticulous literary artistry' in obeying Jesus' command to 'write what you see' (1:19). (Richard Bauckham, *The Climax of Prophecy: Studies on the Book of Revelation* [Edinburgh: T&T Clark, 1993], p. 30. On pp. 29–37 Bauckham surveys these numerical features of the book.)

15. Rev. 4:1 – 22:5.

16. Rev. 16:15.

17. The language is influenced of course by Jesus' own teaching – Matt. 24:42–43, echoed by Paul (1 Thess. 5:2–6).

Coming between the sixth and seventh bowls, this little voice speaks at a point where, in the earlier seven seals and seven trumpets visions, there have been substantial interludes in the action. Between the sixth and seventh seals, we have the interlude concerning the sealing and protection of God's people.[18] Similarly between the sixth and seventh trumpets, we have the interlude concerning the universal preaching of the gospel and the protection of the witnesses who carry the message.[19] In both cases, the interlude is about God's people, their *calling*, their *resourcing* and their *hope* in the midst of the terrible things described by the seals and the trumpets.

This little 'word' from the risen Christ in 16:15 similarly forms an interlude, in an equivalent structural position and with the same purpose. The surrounding visions are truly terrible, visions of dreadful suffering and chaos, drawing on the imagery of the plagues in Egypt and of Daniel's description of the beasts, as well as on Ezekiel's description of the great armies which will march on Israel from the north.[20] What is our supreme resource and calling, in the midst of the worst suffering the world can throw at us? It is to *keep hope alive* by hearing the quiet voice of the risen Christ speaking in the darkness, encouraging us to hold on because day is near, and to stay prepared for day even in the darkest night. It seems to follow on particularly from the preceding 'I am coming', addressed to the church in Philadelphia: 'I am coming quickly! Hold on to what you have, so that no one may take away your crown.'[21]

The first two 'I am comings' are particular warnings to the churches in Ephesus and Pergamum, encouraging them to repent and get their spiritual act together, or else the risen Christ will 'come to you' and sort them out. In the case of Ephesus, it sounds as though he might snuff out the lampstand of the church altogether.[22] In the letter to Pergamum, he threatens to come in judgment against the group who have imported pagan worship practices into the church.[23]

In sum, these 'comings' cover the whole range of the coming of Christ that we have noticed elsewhere: his coming in the flesh to share our death and sin, in the Spirit to teach and correct his church, and in glory to save his whole creation. They are all part of the story of the one Christ.

---

18. Rev. 7:1–17.
19. Rev. 10:1 – 11:4.
20. Ezek. 38 – 39.
21. Rev. 3:11.
22. Rev. 2:5.
23. Rev. 2:14–16.

There are no other direct references to the second coming of Jesus in Revelation, apart from the passage on which we will focus below, 19:11–16. So now it is important to look at the structure of the book, in order to see how the fact of the second coming may be implicit in its message.

2. The structure of Revelation: The missing 'appearance'

The way in which Revelation is structured around series of seven is obvious. The seven letters (chs. 2 – 3), seals (chs. 6 – 8), trumpets (chs. 8 – 11) and bowls (ch. 16) are specifically numbered. Not so obvious, but also clearly true on careful study, is that the central section of the book between the trumpets and the bowls (chs. 12 – 15) also relates a series of seven unnumbered heavenly signs, namely: the woman and the dragon (ch. 12); the beast from the sea (13:1–10); the beast from the land (13:11–18); the Lamb and the 144,000 (14:1–5); the angel with the gospel (14:6–13); the Son of Man on the cloud (14:14–20); and finally the seven angels with the plagues (ch. 15), who become the agents in the next series of seven, the bowls. These heavenly appearances are marked by the introductory phrase in each case – 'And I saw . . .' or 'And I saw, and behold . . .' – with an obvious connection between the first ('A great sign appeared in heaven . . .', 12:1) and the seventh ('And I saw another great and wonderful sign in heaven . . .', 15:1).

In the case of the obvious, numbered sevens, it is clear that each series has a parallel structure. In each case the seventh in the series is the first in the next or introduces it closely.[24] In each case, too, numbers one to four form a distinct series, and numbers five, six and seven are then different, with the action moving up a notch and becoming more severe, or greater, or more final.[25] These observations have produced the so-called 'recapitulation' theory of the structure of Revelation, associated originally with William Hendriksen,[26] who suggested that each series takes us through the whole period between the two comings of Christ, exploring a different feature of the story, and in each case leading up to a vision of the End in the sixth or seventh item. This certainly seems to be the

---

24. With the exception of the first series, the seven letters, which stand outside the main visionary sequence and form an introduction to the whole vision.

25. This is not so true of the seven letters.

26. W. Hendriksen, *More Than Conquerors: An Interpretation of the Book of Revelation* (London: Tyndale Press, 1962).

case when we compare the sixth seal[27] with the seventh trumpet,[28] the sixth sign[29] and the seventh bowl.[30]

When we look at these climactic visions, we meet many themes and images associated with the second coming. For instance, the sixth seal:

> And I saw, when he opened the sixth seal, and there was a great earthquake and the sun became black like sackcloth, and the whole moon became like blood and the stars of heaven fell onto the earth like a fig tree dropping its late fruit when shaken by a storm, and the sky was split off like a scroll being rolled up and every mountain and island was moved from its place. And the kings of the earth and the aristocrats and the generals and the rich and the powerful and every slave and free person hid themselves in the caves and the rocks of the mountains 'and say to the mountains and to the rocks, Fall on us and hide us'[31] from the face of the one who sits upon the throne and from the wrath of the Lamb: for the great day of their wrath has come, and who is able to stand?[32]

This is fantastically vivid, vigorous writing. We have met several of these images before, in Psalm 18 as well as in Daniel 7, Mark 13 and Acts 2. As a symbolic word-picture of the chaos and terror felt by a world being finally called to account, it is completely unbeatable. Here it is 'the great day of their wrath' which comes, rather than Jesus himself, but the references to 'the face' of God and to 'their' wrath make it clear that *this is a visitation*. The rightful rulers arrive to displace the pretenders.

We find the same end-of-it-all flavour in 11:15–19, in 14:14–20 and in 16:17–21, though with different emphases in each case. In 11:15–19 (the seventh trumpet), the focus is on the heavenly praise and delight that greets the trans-formation of the world as it 'becomes the kingdom of our Lord, and of his Christ'.[33] In 14:14–20 (the sixth sign), in contrast, the emphasis is on the rigour

---

27. Rev. 6:12–17.

28. Rev. 11:15–19.

29. Rev. 14:14–20.

30. Rev. 16:17–21. The series lead on from each other, as is especially clear in the case of the seals and the signs: in both cases the seventh in the series *is* the next series which follows (compare 8:1–6 and 15:1–8).

31. These words are a quotation (though not word for word) from Hos. 10:8. In addition there are discernible echoes of at least twelve other Old Testament passages in these few verses, as well as several New Testament passages.

32. Rev. 6:12–17.

33. Rev. 11:15.

and comprehensiveness of the final judgment, pictured as a harvest conducted by the Son of Man. And in 16:17–21 (the seventh bowl), the emphasis is on the horror and destructiveness of God's judgment of the 'powers'.

So what about the last section of the book, chapters 17 – 22? This too flows right out of the end of the bowl series, developing the theme of 'the judgment of the great whore'[34] which is the focus of the seventh bowl, and there is much in these chapters that bears upon the coming of the Lord. It is structured, as many have pointed out, around the contrast between two women who are also cities – the great whore, who is Babylon, the earthly city (chs. 17 – 18), and the bride of the Lamb, who is the new Jerusalem, the heavenly city (chs. 21 – 22).

The appearance of 'the holy city, new Jerusalem, coming down from heaven from God, prepared like a bride adorned for her husband'[35] presents us with one of those moments when Revelation surprises us by reversing what we expect. The symbolism often does this, and we will see some beautiful examples shortly when we look at 19:11–16. What we *expect* is that the Lord Jesus will 'come down' to be with his church, on earth. Jesus himself used marriage imagery of the coming of the Son of Man: we are like the bride and her brides-maids, waiting for the bridegroom to come.[36] But in Revelation 21 it's the other way round – the *bride* comes down to join her husband. The change is a beauti-ful way of signalling that, in the new heaven and the new earth, nothing is as expected. But the result is the same: 'Behold, the dwelling of God is with humans, and he will dwell with them, and they shall be his peoples, and God himself will be with them . . .'[37]

Between the sections devoted to the two women-who-are-also-cities, chapters 19 – 20 are concerned with the judgment of the powers on which the power of the great whore rested – the dragon and the beasts. In fact they are judged in reverse order to the order in which they appeared, giving the whole sweep of chapters 12 – 20 a chiastic shape:

A The dragon appears and attacks earth and God's children (12:1–17)
   B And delegates his authority to the two beasts, who enslave and deceive the world (13:1–18)
      C But all judgment lies in the hands of the Lamb and the 144,000, before whom all the nations are called to account (14:1 – 16:21)

34. Rev. 17:1.
35. Rev. 21:2.
36. Matt. 25:1–13.
37. Rev. 21:3.

D Including the great whore, who rides on the back of the
    beast, ruling over the kings of the earth (17:1–18)
    D' But who is destined to fall magnificently (18:1 – 19:5)
    C' And when the Lamb rides into battle with his army (19:6–16)
  B' The beasts will be overthrown (19:17–21)
A' And so will the dragon, the source of all deception (20:1–15)

This overview analysis shows broadly how our particular passage (19:11–16)
fits into the sweep of the second half of the book. In discussing the meaning
of these great symbols, there is a general scholarly consensus that the first
readers would hear Rome described in chapters 17–18, as the great whore is
depicted. This is not to say that the great whore *is* Rome, but that Rome
embodied the qualities of this terrible, merciless but awesomely attractive and
temptingly rich and beneficent power – and so might other powers, too. This
is how this kind of symbolism works! And so using Rome – both the city and
the empire – as a kind of interpretative key, we can say that

a) The great whore represents the physical manifestations of power: cities,
   ships, armies, the infrastructures of organization, power and control.
b) The second beast represents the ideological substructures of such
   powers: the propaganda, the reasons why people give their loyalty (even
   their worship) – in Rome's case, the ideology surrounding the imperial
   cult.[38]
c) The first beast represents power or empire as such – the raw power
   manifested in (b) and in (a), demanding absolute loyalty.
d) And the dragon shows us where all this non-God power finally rests – in
   Satan the fallen angel who tries to take over God's world and to produce
   a parallel kingdom, warring against God's.

We are very much back in the orbit of Daniel and the powers, although Daniel
never uncovered satanic power underneath the terrible 'beasts' he saw. But the
main point for us is that the rider on the white horse comes from heaven (19:11)
to rid the world of the beasts and the dragon, the powers that have usurped
God's rule by working behind, and through, even apparently benign secular
powers like Rome. At its best Rome secured peace and brought great wealth
for some – brilliantly depicted in chapter 18. But the drawing back of the veil
reveals what really underlies the power of the imperial Roman eagle; ultimately,

---

38. We touched on this in looking at Luke 17, see above, p. 139.

the anti-God power of the dragon, the ancient serpent, the destroyer from the abyss, the deceiver.[39] And the destruction of this ancient power of evil follows finally when the rider and his armies issue forth from heaven with victory to win.

There is another way to analyse the structure of chapters 17 – 22, following the approach we applied earlier in thinking about the structure of chapters 12 – 14. Revelation naturally falls into visionary episodes, usually introduced by 'And I saw . . .' or 'And I heard . . .' or some equivalent marker. And often the precise wording of these introductory markers is important – they are not all equivalent to each other. If we apply this approach to chapters 17 – 22, what emerges?

The result is rather remarkable. It turns out that in these chapters we encounter a series of six heavenly appearances, each revealing something crucial about the world and its judgment or redemption:

1. One of the seven angels reveals the woman on the beast (17:1–18).
2. Another angel announces the fall of Babylon (18:1 – 19:10).
3. The rider on the white horse appears and destroys the beasts (19:11–21).
4. The angel with the key appears, heralding the destruction of the dragon (20:1–10).
5. The great white throne of judgment appears, and the One sitting on it (20:11–15).
6. The heavenly Jerusalem appears, revealed by another of the seven angels (21:1 – 22:9).

These are the great movements in the visionary story in these chapters. There are other 'And I saw . . .' or 'And I heard . . .' introductions here,[40] but they do not carry the same weight, as signalled both by the language used and by what then happens, and how the action moves on (or not) from what precedes it. In this list of six appearances, the first clearly goes with the sixth, because in both cases 'one of the seven angels who had the seven bowls' says 'come, I will show you . . .' to John, and then reveals respectively 'the judgment of the great whore' and 'the bride of the Lamb'.[41] The introductions to the intervening sections also have a pattern:

---

39. Rev. 12:9; 9:11; 20:10.
40. E.g. Rev. 18:4; 19:1, 17, 19; 20:4.
41. Compare 17:1 and 21:9.

- Angel coming down from heaven (18:1);
- Heaven opened (19:11);
- Angel coming down from heaven (20:1);
- Heaven and earth flee away (20:11).

These literary markers are so clear that the obvious question becomes very pressing: why only six heavenly appearances, and not seven? All the other equivalent series in the book have seven elements. And this is indeed a puzzle, until we remember Jesus' threefold 'Behold, I am coming soon!' in the epilogue, followed by that final prayer, 'Yes indeed, come, Lord Jesus!'[42] *By its incomplete last section, Revelation points beyond itself to the actual coming of Jesus, the final heavenly appearance which will bring everything to completion, including its own literary structure!* The seventh heavenly appearance is yet to be.

This is why that final prayer is no throwaway conclusion. It is a prayer for the real completion of the grand story of judgment and redemption just pictured, without which the whole book is – well, just pictures; mere fancies of imagination with no real-world substance. This is why the book ends with such a powerful assurance of its absolute, *complete* truth:

> I bear witness to everyone who hears the words of the prophecy of this book: if anyone adds anything to it, God will add to that person the plagues written about in this book; and if anyone takes away from the words of this written prophecy, God will take away that person's share in the tree of life and in the holy city – all written about in this book.[43]

But its truth is definitely *not* complete if there is no final heavenly appearance to expect or pray for – the *real* arrival of the rider on the white horse, and with him the *real* 'new heaven and new earth'.[44] If this does not really happen, the book is nonsense, not true prophecy at all. So it is absolutely vital, in fact, that Revelation ends in this open-ended way, so beautifully signalled by the literary structure of the last section of the book. 'Even so come, Lord Jesus!'

But this raises a particular question for our section, 19:11–16: if the second coming of Jesus is the seventh, still-expected heavenly appearance, does that imply that the vision of the rider on the white horse must be about something else, and *not* a vision of the *parousia* of Jesus? The best way to tackle that question is to look more closely at the passage itself.

---

42. Rev. 22:7, 12, 20.

43. Rev. 22:18–19.

44. Rev. 21:1.

3. The rider rides forth from heaven (vv. 11–16)

And I saw heaven opened, and behold, a white horse, and one sitting on it, called Faithful and True; and in righteousness he judges and goes to war. His eyes like a flame of fire, and on his head many crowns, having a name written that no one knows but himself, and wrapped round him a cloak dipped in blood, and his name is called The Word of God. And the armies in heaven were following him on white horses, wearing fine linen, white and pure. And out of his mouth comes a sharp sword so that he may strike the nations, and he shepherds them himself with an iron rod, and himself treads the winepress filled with the wine of the furious wrath of God the Almighty. And he has a name written on his cloak, and on his thigh: King of kings, and Lord of lords.

This is a truly amazing passage, full of intense apocalyptic symbolism. George Beasley-Murray writes,

Not even in this book of highly imaginative pictures is there a greater concentration of symbolic representations of a single event than here. When John comes to describe the parousia of the Lord, he is forced like all others to resort to sheer picture-thinking. The coming of the Lord is an event which transcends the thought and imagination of man.[45]

I'm not sure that Beasley-Murray is right about the uniqueness of this passage in Revelation. It certainly has a rival in the opening vision of Jesus Christ in chapter 1, where we meet a similar intense 'concentration of symbolic representations'.[46] In fact, our minds are drawn back to that passage by the repetition of two of the images here: his eyes like a flame of fire,[47] and a sword coming out of his mouth.[48] So Revelation is actually bracketed by these two visionary appearances of the risen Christ in glory: the first introducing the whole vision and the letters to the churches in particular, and the second introducing the final acts of judgment and redemption that bring the whole visionary story to its climax. As we'll see, it also looks back to the description of Jesus in the opening greeting.[49]

But I'm sure that Beasley-Murray is right about the purpose of this apocalyptic picturing: how else can we imagine the second coming, and hear its truth? We can easily imagine Paul's 'cry of command, archangel's voice and trumpet

---

45. G. R. Beasley-Murray, *The Book of Revelation*, New Century Bible (London: Marshall, Morgan & Scott, 1974), p. 278.

46. Rev. 1:12–16.

47. Rev. 1:14; 19:12; see also 2:18.

48. Rev. 1:16; 19:15; see also 2:12, 16; 19:21.

49. Rev. 1:5.

of God' as well,[50] but the fact that we don't find any of those images here indicates to me that we should not take any of them literally. Rather, we should let these glorious pictures tell their own story to us. Like all great symbols, they reach beyond themselves into the ineffable, and invite us to follow.

Commentators generally, like Beasley-Murray, see this passage as a symbolic depiction of the second coming.[51] And our structural analysis of Revelation 18 – 22 does not stand in the way of this. The prayer for the coming of the Lord at the end actually needs this prior description of it: this is how we know what to pray for! Generally, too, commentators agree that this vision introduces all that follows: the second coming of the Lord means the final judgment of all powers of evil[52] and of all humankind,[53] and the re-creation of earth and heaven so that they are no longer two, but one place where 'the home of God is among mortals'.[54]

So what might this picture of the second coming convey to us? The best way to hear it is to let the images simply speak in their own voice as clearly as possible, giving special weight to the ways in which they have pedigree – either elsewhere in Scripture, or (more particularly) elsewhere in Revelation. We observe that the description covers four areas: Jesus' *advance* (heaven opened, horses and the armies of heaven), his *appearance* (face and clothing), his *names* (four of them here), and his *actions* (summarized as 'judging and going to war' in v. 11). We will look at these in turn.

a. His advance (vv. 11, 14)

And I saw heaven opened . . . (v. 11) – a truly dramatic event heralding a truly momentous action. Nothing like it has happened before in the storyline of Revelation. It looks back to the beginning of the vision, 'After this I saw, and behold a door, opened in heaven . . .'[55] But whereas that was an aperture opened

---

50. 1 Thess. 4:16.

51. So also, for instance, Robert Wall, *Revelation*, New International Biblical Commentary (Peabody: Hendrickson and Carlisle: Paternoster, 1995), p. 228; Ben Witherington III, *Revelation* (Cambridge: Cambridge University Press, 2003), p. 242; G. B. Caird, *The Revelation of St John the Divine* (London: A&C Black, 1966), p. 240; R. H. Mounce, *The Book of Revelation*, New International Commentary (Grand Rapids: Eerdmans, 1977), p. 343.

52. Rev. 19:17 – 20:10.

53. Rev. 20:11–15.

54. Rev. 21:1 – 22:6, quoting 21:3, NRSV.

55. Rev. 4:1.

for John to look through and enter, now the whole of heaven is flung wide open for the risen Christ to exit. This Christ is the one 'who opens and none shall shut, and who shuts and none can open',[56] so this opening has a powerful finality and authority to it.

... and behold, a white horse, and one sitting on it ... (v. 11). White horses are symbols of victory and conquest, and we have already met one in 6:2, where the wording is identical. Because the parallel is so close, some commentators argue that the rider in 6:2 is also Christ,[57] but this seems highly unlikely in the context there. The 'four horsemen' together stand for the 'powers' that offer a counterfeit world unity, an awful alternative to the glorious vision of cosmic unity around the throne in chapter 5. It's a satirical picture, because this 'unity' – proclaimed and enforced by Rome, of course – depends on conquest, war, economic exploitation and death.[58] Some gain from it – most notably the ones who get to ride the white horses, like the generals who are then mocked in 6:15 – but there are so many losers in that version of world unity. There still are.

But now! There comes One who will truly secure the unity of earth and heaven in one new glorious creation.

And the armies in heaven were following him on white horses, wearing fine linen, white and pure (v. 14). A whole retinue, all in white, underlines this victorious advance. But there's more going on here. Who are these riders? In 14:4 the 144,000 'follow the Lamb wherever he goes', and the counting of the 144,000 in chapter 7 draws on the numbering of the tribes *for battle* in the book of Numbers.[59] The 144,000 is a *military* image. So that's who they are here in chapter 19 – the 144,000 following the commander-in-chief. But what an army! In chapter 14 they distinguished themselves not by learning to fight but by learning to play harps and sing.[60] And in chapter 19 they are hardly dressed for battle – in fact all this *fine white linen* is the beautiful garb which, just a moment ago, was being draped around 'the bride of the lamb' in preparation for her marriage.[61] This 'force' is dressed for a wedding party, not for a battle!

---

56. Rev. 3:8.

57. E.g. John Sweet, *Revelation*, SCM Pelican Commentary (London: SCM Press, 1979), pp. 137–138.

58. This is what the four horsemen symbolize!

59. See Num. 1:17–46.

60. Rev. 14:2–3. Behind the image lie the singing Levites of 2 Chron. 20:20–23, who marched into battle before the army of King Jehoshaphat.

61. Rev. 19:8.

This is a beautiful example of the way in which Revelation uses symbolism to turn things on their heads and get us thinking. *Paradoxes* abound. Sometimes these involve striking differences between what John *hears* and then *sees*: for instance, in chapter 5 he hears that 'the Lion of the tribe of Judah has conquered', but then sees not a lion but 'a lamb, standing, as if slain'.[62] In chapter 7 he hears the 144,000 being counted from all the tribes of Israel,[63] but then sees 'a vast crowd, which no one could count, from every nation and tribes and peoples and tongues'.[64] Similarly here in chapter 19 John has *heard* the announcement of 'the wedding of the Lamb', and a description of the bride getting dressed;[65] but what he now *sees* is a battle-array, with the troops dressed in the bridal garments.

What does this mean? Clearly, the followers of Jesus Christ do not *fight*, even though they are pictured as an army. The bridal garments are explained as 'the righteous deeds of the saints',[66] and then these 'righteous deeds' are described as 'holding the testimony of Jesus' which is 'the spirit of prophecy'.[67] So Jesus' retinue are those who bear witness to him by their worship, their endurance, their obedience and their faithfulness, even unto death,[68] and who thus speak by 'the spirit of prophecy' into the realm of the beasts and the dragon. In Revelation 12 we hear that 'they have defeated him [i.e., the dragon, the Devil] by the blood of the Lamb and by the word of their testimony – and they did not love their life so as to avoid death'.[69]

Using 'the blood of the Lamb' to defeat the powers of evil does not just mean that they trust in the cross as the means of their deliverance. Clearly, it also means that they take the blood of the Lamb upon themselves by being ready to add their blood to his, and to give up their lives as he has done. *The cross* is the means of the Lamb's victory. So here is an amazing paradox: this victorious army, dressed in white, has won its victory through being defeated.

---

62. Rev. 5:5–6. 'Standing as if slain' involves another paradoxical, 'impossible' symbol, incorporating the glorious paradox of death and resurrection in one vivid picture.

63. Rev. 7:4.

64. Rev. 7:9. The odd (ungrammatical) mixture of singular and plural here reflects the Greek – it underlines the mixed ethnicity of this crowd, in contrast to the single 'race' of the 144,000. The parallel with other 'hearing then seeing' visions convinces me that these are alternative pictures of the same lot – the redeemed people of God.

65. Rev. 19:7–8.

66. Rev. 19:8.

67. Rev. 19:10.

68. See e.g. Rev. 2:10; 13:10; 14:12; 15:2–4.

69. Rev. 12:11.

They are the martyrs and the persecuted who have 'washed their robes and made them white in the blood of the Lamb'[70] – another gloriously paradoxical image that lies in the background. Like the two witnesses in chapter 11, they are both totally invulnerable *and* completely defeated – because the Lamb and his followers win their victory over the powers not by conquest (that's the way of the powers!), but *by (apparent) defeat.*[71]

That is why this army in 19:14 looks so odd. Not a sword in sight. Their victory has already been won, and they are on their way to the celebration – 'the marriage-feast of the Lamb'.[72] I think this is why *himself* is oddly repeated twice in verse 15: the victorious Christ *shepherds them himself with an iron rod, and himself treads the winepress* of God's wrath. *Himself* could be translated *by himself* here – i.e., 'alone': Christ alone undertakes these acts of final victory, on his way to the feast with his invited guests.

b. His appearance (vv. 12, 13, 15a)

The descriptions of Jesus' appearance are interspersed through the passage, as if John (and we) can only actually glance at him, and then must look away. We cannot *inspect* or *study* him. We just get glimpses of him within the wider picture of what he is and does. This is quite unlike the vision in 1:13–16, which is all about the appearance of the risen Jesus: but that direct sight is too much for John, who collapses to the ground 'as if dead'.[73]

His eyes like a flame of fire . . . (v. 12). No wonder we have to look away! This image is part of that earlier vision,[74] and also turns up in the letter to Thyatira,[75] where it seems to be connected to Jesus' description of himself as 'the one who searches the depths of every mind and heart, and I will give you – each of you – according to your works'.[76] So these 'flaming eyes' are about the *absolutely piercing discernment* which enables him to give *precisely measured judgment* to all.

---

70. Rev. 7:14.

71. See Rev. 11:5–6, followed by 11:7–8. In this sequence of invulnerability but then defeat, the witnesses repeat the history of 'their Lord' (11:8). This is always the experience of the church of Jesus Christ when it truly bears his name.

72. Rev. 19:9.

73. Rev. 1:17.

74. Rev. 1:14.

75. Rev. 2:18.

76. Rev. 2:23. This is drawn from the Lord's description of himself in Jer. 17:10: Jesus as Judge steps into the role of God himself. Jesus literally says (as in Jeremiah), 'I am the one who searches kidneys and hearts' – 'kidneys' symbolize the inner depths of feeling and thought.

In thinking about the judgment associated with the second coming, this is a vital principle. His judgment is absolutely just, related precisely to 'the works' of each,[77] and thus involves a perfect understanding of those 'works'. Actions and motivations are often an uncertain mixture of good, less good and bad, and it is very hard, sometimes, to see where 'right' truly lies in the world of greys that we usually inhabit. How wonderful, that there is One with eyes of flame that see the exact truth, and who thus can judge with complete justice. Judgment is finally the Lord's, because he alone can tell our stories with full truth. He can tell the story of our lives with far clearer discernment and far greater truth than we can tell them ourselves.

This is why Paul insists that we should not 'take vengeance' ourselves, and instead 'so far as you can, live at peace with all', surprising our enemies with acts of generosity and grace, because '"Vengeance is mine, I will repay", says the Lord'.[78] The point is, we can live by *grace* OK, the path may be difficult, but at least it's clear. We have to love our enemies,[79] that is, reach out with openness, generosity and forgiveness to all, whether Christian or not, even to those whose views and lifestyles we don't like, and whatever their attitude to us. A tough call, but at least clear. But we cannot live by *judgment*, imposing our judgment on others, because that means truly knowing the depths of the heart, and teasing out motivations which may be unknown even to the owner of the heart concerned. Each of us, in forming and expressing our 'judgment' of others, may be motivated by things in our own hearts of which we are unaware.[80]

So only God can judge truly: in fact, only the risen Christ, whose *eyes like a flame of fire* equip him alone for the task of 'searching the depths of every heart and mind'.[81]

---

77. See also Rom. 2:6–11; 2 Cor. 5:10.

78. Rom. 12:18–20.

79. Matt. 5:44.

80. As Jesus says so clearly in Matt. 7:1–5.

81. This statement in Jer. 17:10 (quoted in Rev. 2:23, as we noted) is preceded by the warning, 'The heart is devious above all else; it is perverse – who can understand it?' (17:9). Here the Septuagint simply says, 'The heart is deep above all else . . . who can know it?' In fact 'deep' is probably a better translation than 'devious', because the Hebrew word (*'āqōb*) simply (and vividly) expresses the way in which our own hearts can gang up on us and spring surprises that leave us gasping to understand ourselves. Similarly the word translated 'perverse' (*'ānuš*) means just 'sick' or 'weak'.

. . . and on his head many crowns (v. 12). A powerful image of power! The dragon wore seven of these,[82] and the beast wore ten,[83] but the Lord Jesus has just 'many'. It's not even a matter of comparing precise numbers of crowns, on the 'my Dad's bigger than your Dad' principle. He simply has 'many' of them – his authority is overwhelming, and final.

. . . and wrapped round him a cloak dipped in blood (v. 13). Commentators disagree about this image: whose blood is this, on the cloak of the risen Christ returning to claim his kingdom? Is it that of his enemies, drawing on the use of a similar image in Isaiah 63:1–3?[84] Is it his own blood, a vivid symbol of the cross by which he is victorious?[85] Or is it the blood of the martyrs who follow him into battle?[86] None are impossible, and perhaps the vital thing is the way the image makes us reflect on all these significances. He is about to tread the Isaiah 63 winepress of God's wrath in verse 15, so maybe the first interpretation has less force: it is a little incongruent that he should already bear the marks of what he is about to do. But nothing is impossible in Revelation.

The second view has more power. According to Revelation 5:6 ('I saw . . . a Lamb, standing, as if slain'), Christ's woundedness – his 'slain-ness' – is not only part and parcel of who he now is, but is also his qualification to rule. He alone is able to open the scroll, because 'he has conquered', and his victory has been won by his death.[87] So it would fit entirely, if this very different image of the victorious Christ should also remind us of the basis on which he rules. He does not rule by the bare exercise of power, winning by overwhelming force. That would be what Walter Wink has called 'the myth of redemptive violence'[88] – the myth that animates Hollywood and indeed much foreign policy in our fallen world: *if you're on the side of right, force employing destructive violence is always justified in order to conquer evil.* Our Lord Jesus does not rule by that principle, even in his final judgment. His badge of office is his own lifeblood shed by his enemies – because he truly does love his enemies, and by the wonderful upside-down magic

---

82. Rev. 12:3.

83. Rev. 13:1.

84. So e.g. Beasley-Murray, *Revelation*, p. 280; G. K. Beale, *The Book of Revelation*, New International Greek Testament Commentary (Grand Rapids: Eerdmans, 1999), pp. 957–960.

85. So e.g. Wall, *Revelation*, p. 231; Sweet, *Revelation*, p. 283.

86. So Caird, *Revelation*, pp. 242–244. This view has not been widely followed by others.

87. Rev. 5:5, 9.

88. Walter Wink, *Engaging the Powers: Discernment and Resistance in a World of Domination* (Minneapolis: Fortress Press, 1992), pp. 13–31.

of heaven their terrible act of rejecting his love by nailing him to the cross turns out to be the means of their own forgiveness, and of the defeat of the evil that animates their hatred.

So what of his sword? *Out of his mouth comes a sharp sword so that he may strike the nations* (v. 15). Is this the destructive violence of overwhelming power? This image comes from Isaiah 49, where the Servant of the Lord talks about his preparation for the worldwide ministry to which the Lord has called him:

> Listen to me, O coastlands,
>> pay attention, you peoples[89] from far away!
> The LORD called me before I was born,
>> while I was in my mother's womb he named me.
> He made my mouth like a sharp sword,
>> in the shadow of his hand he hid me;
> he made me a polished arrow,
>> in his quiver he hid me away.[90]

Here the 'sharp sword' and the 'polished arrow' are weapons of *instruction*, vividly underlining the universal significance and power of his message. This is 'the warfare of the word', as Alec Motyer puts it: the sword speaks of the *effectiveness* of his word and the polished arrow of its *accuracy*.[91] No destructiveness here! But Revelation takes us forward to the End. What happens finally if the invitation to 'listen' and 'pay attention' is rejected, and the truth of the message is denied? Truth is finally truth, and before its sharp edge all lies, and 'the father of lies' in particular,[92] will be cut down – even if the truth is that weakness is the way of strength, and the cross is God's route to salvation.

Ultimately truth overpowers all non-truth, in fact *devours* it. *Eating* something is the ultimate expression of overpowering – and this is why, I believe, this vision is followed by the gruesome invitation to 'all the birds that fly in mid heaven' to gather for 'the great feast of God', and to devour the flesh of all who have lived by the power of the dragon and the beasts.[93] Untruth is swallowed up by the truth of the one who is the Word of God. So the beasts are 'thrown alive into the lake of fire burning with sulphur, and the rest were

---

89. 'Peoples' here is the same word as 'nations' in Rev. 19:15.

90. Isa. 49:1–2.

91. J. A. Motyer, *The Prophecy of Isaiah* (Leicester: Inter-Varsity Press, 1993), p. 386.

92. John 8:44.

93. Rev. 19:17–18.

killed by the sword coming out of the mouth of the one sitting on the horse, and all the birds gorged on their flesh'.[94] Truth *is* finally 'powerful to demolish strongholds', as Paul puts it.[95]

c. His names (vv. 11, 12, 13, 16)

Great emphasis falls here on the names the risen Christ bears:

Faithful and True (v. 11)
A name written that no one knows but himself (v. 12)
The Word of God (v. 13)
A name written on his thigh: King of kings and Lord of lords (v. 16)

The three lines in verses 12b–13 are particularly striking: *bearing a name written that no one knows but himself, and wrapped round him a cloak dipped in blood, and his name is called the Word of God . . .*

Is his name known, or unknown? This is yet another instance of Revelation's gloriously paradoxical symbolism. There is much biblical background here, part of which is the significance of *names* in the Bible. As Greg Beale puts it, 'In the OT to know a name means to have control over the one named', and he adds that it might be appropriate to translate 'know' in verse 12 as 'own'.[96] No one can 'own' the name of Christ – except, of course, those to whom he reveals it. This is not an absolute ban on knowing his name. In fact Christ has already promised the Philadelphians that

the one who conquers, I will make a pillar in the house of my God: and you will never leave again, and I will write on you the name of my God, and the name of the city of my God, the new Jerusalem which comes down from heaven from my God, *and my own new name.*[97]

In line with this, we learn that in the new Jerusalem 'the throne of God and of the Lamb will be there, and his servants will worship him, and they will see his face, and his name is on their foreheads'.[98] His *servants* and followers not

---

94. Rev. 19:20–21.

95. 2 Cor. 10:4.

96. Beale, *Revelation*, p. 955 and n. 366.

97. Rev. 3:12. In Isa. 62 both Jerusalem and the people are given new names to symbolize the salvation God has achieved for them.

98. Rev. 22:3–4.

only know his name, but have it written on them: a wonderful symbol of mutual connection and self-giving. But in Revelation 19, advancing into a hostile world as its Judge, the risen Christ reserves his name for himself. That world can know him as *Faithful and True*, and as *the Word of God*, and as *King of kings and Lord of lords*, but not by the unique and special 'name' that connects him only to his servants, to those who have 'conquered' as he has.

To go further, it would be helpful to unpack the structure of the passage:[99]

[Intro] The Judge, Faithful and True, appears (v. 11)
    And I saw heaven opened, and behold, a white horse, and one sitting on it,
    called Faithful and True: and in righteousness he judges and goes to war.

A   Equipped to judge – the unknown name (v. 12)
    His eyes like a flame of fire, and on his head many crowns, having a name written
    that no one knows but himself . . .

  B   God's Word goes into action (v. 13)
    . . . and wrapped round him a cloak dipped in blood, and his name is called
    the Word of God.

    C   The army of the saved who hold to 'the word of God and the
       testimony of Jesus' (v. 14)[100]
       And the armies in heaven were following him on white horses, wearing fine
       linen, white and pure.

  B' And strikes the nations with the wrath of God (v. 15)
    And out of his mouth comes a sharp sword so that he may strike the nations,
    and he shepherds them himself with an iron rod, and himself treads the
    winepress filled with the wine of the furious wrath of God the Almighty.

A' Equipped to judge – the well-known name (v. 16)
    And he has a name written on his cloak, and on his thigh: King of kings, and
    Lord of lords.

The phrase *he has a name written* appears twice (vv. 12, 16), and this is the basis of this chiasm. Beale argues that, therefore, the names are the same – i.e., the

---

99. Beale, *Revelation*, p. 956 suggests this 'chiastic' structure.

100. See this connection in 1:2, 1:9 and 20:4, the only other places where the phrase 'the word of God' appears in Revelation. It is not surprising that the armies of the Redeemed follow. They are the ones who know deeply what it means to hear and to follow the Word of God, which is Jesus.

name hidden in verse 12 is then revealed in verse 16.[101] Does this follow? The significance of the hidden name (see above) would suggest that it stays hidden throughout – it is known only to Christ himself and to those privileged to receive it from him. *King of kings and Lord of lords* is his public name, emblazoned across his cloak and visible to all.

This name has a biblical background,[102] and a history within Revelation: the Lamb is called this in 17:14, in counterclaim to Babylon 'the great city that holds kingship over the kings of the earth'.[103] That in turn has background in Daniel 2:37, where Nebuchadnezzar king of Babylon is called 'king of kings', but only because 'the God of heaven has given [you] the kingdom, the power, the might, and the glory'. Babylon, Rome – all human 'empire' – claim to rule, but that sort of rule is like rape: self-centred, exploitative, violent and cruel. Revelation 18 describes in amazing detail how 'the kings of the earth' and 'the merchants of the earth' have 'committed fornication' with the empire by engaging in an exploitative trade in luxury goods 'and in human lives'.[104] But in contrast the rule of Jesus Christ, King of kings, is invitatory not compulsory: the invitation goes out to join the feast, and 'the kings of the earth bring their glory' into the new Jerusalem.[105]

So Jesus, bearing this name, occupies the position and authority of God himself, exercising his rule and judgment over the world. He is *the Word of God*, a title which is then explained by the image of the *sharp sword* from his mouth (see B–B' in the structure above). He speaks God's own final word of judgment and truth over his creation, bringing all the tyrants to book, condemning all exploitative powers and all satanic evil to the 'lake of fire'[106] – and with them all who finally cling to their own power, and do not hear his word.

Working backwards through his names, we reach the introductory description of the Lord Jesus: he is *called Faithful and True; and in righteousness he judges and goes to war*. The name *Faithful and True* has already been used of Jesus in Revelation 3:14, and twice in what follows the words of God – written down by John in this book – are called 'faithful and true'.[107] So this first title connects with the second, *the Word of God* – which in turn connects, as we have seen, with the true

---

101. Beale, *Revelation*, p. 956.

102. Deut. 10:17 and Dan. 4:47 (just in the LXX), cf. also Dan. 2:47.

103. Rev. 17:18.

104. See especially Rev. 18:3, 9, 13.

105. Rev. 21:24.

106. The beasts: Rev. 19:20; Satan: 20:10.

107. Rev. 21:5; 22:6.

judgment he exercises in verse 15. So, as *Faithful and True*, he *judges in righteousness*. This leads us to focus finally on his actions.

d. His actions (vv. 11, 15)

His judgment is unfolded for us not just in this passage but more particularly in the succeeding visions: the destruction of the beasts, the final battle and the destruction of the dragon, the opening of the books and the final judgment, and then the arrival of the new heaven and new earth. This is all about the *righteous judgment* of the *King of kings*.

Three great and glorious biblical words are connected here: truth (Heb. *'ĕmet*, righteousness (Heb. *ṣedeq*), and justice or judgment (Heb. *mišpāṭ*). The name *Faithful and True* neatly combines both meanings of the word *'ĕmet*, which is frequently used in the Old Testament to express God's truthfulness and faithfulness towards his people. And not infrequently we find *'ĕmet* combined in different ways not just with *ṣedeq* and *mišpāṭ* but also with the great word *ḥesed*, 'steadfast love'. That word does not appear in this vision (in fact, it may be related to the secret name, the name of covenant love that unites the risen Christ with his followers and is unknown to the world). But *ḥesed* certainly lurks in the final vision of the new heaven and earth, especially in the great covenant language used in 21:3–7.

All four words appear together in a verse we have already met:

> Righteousness and justice are the foundation of your throne;
> steadfast love and faithfulness go before you.[108]

We started here, in Psalm 89, with the psalmist's complaint that God – although bursting with these glorious qualities and promises to match – has failed in his covenant commitment and has not *gone to war* on behalf of his anointed king. But now, in Revelation 19, there is no gap between promise and fulfilment. The one who is *Faithful and True*, and whose throne is built on judgment and righteousness, now *goes to war.* 'There is no more delay!' as the angel cries in 10:6. What the psalmist longed for, but did not see, is now a reality: Christ *strikes the nations, and shepherds them himself with an iron rod, and himself treads the winepress filled with the wine of the furious wrath of God the Almighty* (v. 15).

---

108. Ps. 89:14. All four words also occur together in Isa. 16:5, another closely related passage: 'And a throne shall be established in steadfast love (*ḥesed*), and one from the tent of David shall sit upon it in faithfulness (*'ĕmet*), judging and seeking justice (*mišpāṭ*), and swift in righteousness (*ṣedeq*)' (my translation).

We face the same issue as troubled Ethan the Ezrahite, the psalmist of Psalm 89. Why the delay? Why do God's steadfast love, faithfulness, righteousness and justice not prompt him *now* to 'go to war' against the powers of evil in the world – especially those powers which, now as in Ethan's day, concentrate on persecuting and destroying God's own chosen people, those to whom he says he has committed himself? Why do we have to wait?

The answer, of course, lies precisely in those qualities of righteousness, steadfast love, faithfulness and justice. The Lord tells Abraham that he will not destroy Sodom if there are even just ten 'righteous' people there, in response to Abraham's challenge, 'Shall not the Judge of all the earth do what is just (*mišpāṭ*)?'[109] The Lord will not act in judgment until – as he puts it earlier to Abraham concerning the Amorites – 'iniquity is complete'.[110] Paul sees this process as 'storing up wrath for yourself on the day of wrath'.[111] God's *judgment* against sin is perfectly clear to all, but he does not exercise his judgment so that there may be time for repentance[112] – even for the enemies of God's people.

This is actually because he is *righteous*. Throughout the Bible, God's *righteousness* is not primarily the quality that impels him to *judge* the world. Rather, his righteousness is that which he expresses through showing mercy, and *saving* the world. His righteousness is, precisely, his faithfulness to his covenant promise and the 'steadfast love' which undergirds it. So he cannot be wholly righteous through *going to war* against his enemies, if there still remains a possibility that those enemies may yet repent, and be saved.

Not infrequently we find that 'righteousness' and 'salvation' are the two sides of the same coin. For instance:

My salvation will be for ever, and my righteousness will never end.[113]

Thus says the LORD, 'Keep justice, and do righteousness, for my salvation will soon come, and my righteousness will soon be revealed'.[114]

---

109. Gen. 18:25.

110. Gen. 15:16. Cf. 1 Thess. 2:16.

111. Rom. 2:5.

112. Rom. 2:2–4; 2 Pet. 3:9, 15.

113. Isa. 51:6, my translation. Cf. Isa. 51:8 where the same words are reversed.

114. Isa. 56:1, my translation. The Septuagint here translates 'righteousness' with the Greek word *eleos*, mercy.

> The LORD has made known his salvation, in the sight of the nations he has revealed his righteousness. He remembered his steadfast love and his faithfulness to the house of Israel: all the ends of the earth have seen the salvation of our God![115]

God's righteousness needs to be mirrored in his people by a passion for what is right – and what is right usually means mercy to the poor and sinful, in imitation of God's own passion to save. Ultimately, however, when mercy is no longer possible, the work of salvation will be completed by the justice which will put God's world finally to rights, through the destruction of all remaining evil – in other words, the Saviour will *go to war.*

When he goes to war, he *shepherds* the nations (v. 15). How peculiar! *He shepherds with an iron rod* is a quotation from Psalm 2:9, where the Septuagint mistranslates the Hebrew – it confuses the verb 'to break' with a very similar word meaning 'to shepherd'. John, the author of Revelation, has preserved the mistranslation (though doubtless aware of it), not just here but on the two other occasions where he quotes the verse.[116] The one who wields the ultimate authority in the universe – the King of kings and Lord of lords – prefers to *shepherd* with his iron rod rather than to smash things up. I have no idea what that will look like, when the day of judgment comes!

4. In conclusion . . .

What of us, right now? In Psalms 89 – 90, as we saw, the psalmist's response to the awful non-fulfilment of God's promise – God's apparent *lack* of faithfulness – was to take refuge in the big picture, in God's immensity as Lord of time and eternity. Whatever the little picture might look like, the God who is 'from everlasting to everlasting' is nonetheless 'our dwelling-place', and though now we feel his 'wrath', we can yet trust him for his 'steadfast love'.[117]

And so for us! In our hearts right now, in this future-as-present moment, looking out on the appalling injustices of our world and feeling deeply the pain of the innocent, we find ourselves knowing deeply that one day the God of faithfulness, righteousness and justice will *go to war* and his enemies will be scattered. This hope in God's ultimate justice is absolutely essential for right living now – for this is *God's* justice, not ours; a justice which transcends all

---

115. Ps. 98:2–3, my translation.
116. Rev. 2:27; 12:5.
117. Ps. 90:1–2, 9, 14.

present rivalries and partisan powerplay, and focuses on Jesus Christ the Lord, Saviour and Judge of all. We leave all judgment to him, just as we ascribe all salvation to him.

I have not written about the millennium in chapter 20, because that is not part of the second coming vision of Revelation. Chapter 20 is all about the destruction of the dragon (see the structure of these chapters noted above), and alongside that the vindication of his victims – the faithful martyrs[118] who in chapter 19 ride horses into battle behind their Lord. We have no space to unpack that vision, and it would take us away from a strict focus on the *parousia*. The concluding visions in Revelation 19 – 21 are not meant to be read as if in chronological order, I believe, reflecting the *chronos* of planet Earth. There is a kind of *theological* time here, expressed through the successive destruction of Babylon, the two beasts and the dragon – but this is much more about God's *kairos* than earth's *chronos*!

Yet it is worth asking about the martyrs, the 144,000 who go into battle with Jesus in chapter 19, reign with him in chapter 20, and then reappear as his bride in chapter 21. They are an army in wedding garb in 19:14 – weapons not allowed! – apparently on their way to the wedding feast of the Lamb. But in the final chapters of the book, amazingly, this much-heralded event[119] never appears. A horrible feast takes place in 19:17–21, where the birds are invited to 'gather for the great supper of God'[120] and gorge themselves on the flesh of his fallen enemies. But this ghastly orgy is *not* the wedding feast of the Lamb – it is rather a 'macabre parody' of it,[121] a 'terrible counterpart'[122] in 'grim contrast'[123] to the glorious feast which we *expect* to see described in chapter 21. The bride appears,[124] but no feast takes place – unless it is the offer of the leaves of the tree of life 'for the healing of the nations'.[125] But that hardly seems like a wedding feast.

This may be another indication that the final, seventh vision is yet to be – the real, cosmic return of the Lord Jesus Christ. As in Jesus' parable, the bride awaits

---

118. Rev. 20:4.

119. Rev. 19:7–10.

120. Rev. 19:17.

121. Michael Wilcock, *The Message of Revelation: I Saw Heaven Opened*, The Bible Speaks Today (London: Inter-Varsity Press, 1975), p. 185.

122. Beasley-Murray, *Revelation*, p. 282.

123. Caird, *Revelation*, p. 247.

124. Rev. 21:2, 9.

125. Rev. 22:2.

the appearance of her husband.[126] Is that it? Where do the followers of the Lamb eat with him? The risen Christ is yet to come, but he is also already present, patrolling among the lampstands that represent his church[127] – and issuing an invitation to eat with him *right now:*

> Behold, I stand at the door, and knock. If you – any of you – hear my voice and open the door, I will come in to you and feast with you: and you with me![128]

So we end with the thought which has become quite a feature of our biblical theology of the second coming, and which we already found in the seven 'I am comings' in Revelation: namely that, ahead of his final coming, Jesus comes to us now in ways which anticipate the glorious banquet at which the bride will be joined to him for evermore. The Laodiceans had shut him outside the door of their church, by their pride and self-sufficiency. The risen Jesus, 'the faithful and true witness', told them straight: 'You say, I am rich, I have prospered, I need nothing! – not knowing that you are wretched, pitiful, poor, blind and naked.'[129] We can only truly know him if we renounce the world's values and let the story of Jesus be written into our lives – the story of joy in the midst of weakness, love in the face of rejection and persecution, hope in darkness, peace in the storm, and faith as we live embedded in our lost and perplexed world. That truly is to let the light of his dawn shine already in the darkness of this world's old night – until heaven opens, the trumpet sounds and the whole form of creation is changed by the gladness of his coming.

The feast can begin now, even before that dawn – but what a feast it will be, when morning breaks! Truly, 'blessed are those who are invited to the Lamb's marriage-banquet!'[130]

---

126. Matt. 25:1–13.

127. Rev. 1:20.

128. Rev. 3:20. This verse, 19:9 and 19:17 are the only occasions on which the word 'feast' is used in Revelation.

129. Rev. 3:14, 17.

130. Rev. 19:9.

INDEX OF AUTHORS

INDEX OF SCRIPTURE REFERENCES